Rutgers
since 1945

RIVERGATE REGIONALS

Rivergate Regionals is a collection of books published by Rutgers University Press focusing on New Jersey and the surrounding area. Since its founding in 1936, Rutgers University Press has been devoted to serving the people of New Jersey, and this collection solidifies that tradition. The books in the Rivergate Regionals Collection explore history, politics, nature and the environment, recreation, sports, health and medicine, and the arts. By incorporating the collection within the larger Rutgers University Press editorial program, the Rivergate Regionals Collection enhances our commitment to publishing the best books about our great state and the surrounding region.

Rutgers since 1945

A HISTORY

of the

State University of New Jersey

Paul G. E. Clemens

With an Essay by Carla Yanni

RUTGERS UNIVERSITY PRESS

New Brunswick, New Jersey, and London

Library of Congress Cataloging-in-Publication Data

Clemens, Paul G.E., 1947–
Rutgers since 1945 : a history of the State University of New Jersey / Paul G. E. Clemens ;
contributions by Carla Yanni.
pages cm. — (Rivergate regionals collection)
Includes bibliographical references and index.
ISBN 978–0–8135–6421–0 (hardback) — ISBN 978–0–8135–6422–7 (e-book (web pdf)) —
ISBN 978–0–8135–7384–7 (e-book (epub))
1. Rutgers University—History. 2. Rutgers University—Students—History. I. Title.
LD4753.C54 2015
378.9749'41—dc23
2014040070

A British Cataloging-in-Publication record for this book is available from the British Library.

Visit our website: http://rutgerspress.rutgers.edu

Manufactured in the United States of America

To the memory of my friends and colleagues,
Michael Moffatt and Richard P. McCormick

CONTENTS

PREFACE

This work began with two friendships. I met Michael Moffatt soon after I arrived at Rutgers in the mid-1970s. The faculty was still small enough, and faculty meetings still of enough consequence, that one often encountered colleagues outside one's own discipline. At that time, Michael was a cultural anthropologist working on South Asia, but he soon turned his attention to student life on the Rutgers campus. Two works followed, *The Rutgers Picture Book: An Illustrated History of Student Life in the Changing College and University* (1985) and *Coming of Age in New Jersey: College and American Culture* (1989). I have used both in teaching, and both initiated remarkable discussions among the students about campus life at Rutgers.

The other friendship was actually two. Katheryne L. and Richard P. McCormick were among the senior members of the Rutgers community who made me welcome at the university. They took me to my first Rutgers sports event, a women's basketball game, and invited me to their home. Over the years, Dick recounted stories about the school's past and gave me copies of his books on Rutgers; my marked-up, dog-eared copy of *The Black Student Protest Movement at Rutgers* (1990) is one testimony to his generosity. After his retirement, he passed along his unpublished essays on the university's history. One of those essays, "Going Bigtime, the Rutgers Experience," on the athletic program, alerted me to just how rich the archival material was for documenting the school's history.

When I first approached this project, my idea was to update McCormick's 1966 *Rutgers: A Bicentennial History.* McCormick ended his story in the early 1960s, and while 1966 was a celebratory moment, it provided no particular historical significance *point de départ* for a sequel. McCormick's book had as its central theme the transformation of a private college into a university ever more closely tied to state government. That theme seemed equally relevant to any revisiting of the school's history, but where to begin? In 1864, when the New Jersey legislature selected Rutgers Scientific School rather than Princeton University or the State Normal School at Trenton for the land-grant designation under the federal Morrill Act? In the late nineteenth century, when New Jersey hesitantly and indirectly began funding various aspects of education at Rutgers? Or perhaps at the end of World War I, with the establishment of the state-supported New Jersey College for Women?

Instead, this chronicle begins in 1945. World War II transformed America and its relationship to the world, and one of the themes of the work I planned to write was about the way the larger culture shaped what had been fairly insular colleges. Nineteen forty-five was particularly important for two other reasons. First, New Jersey reorganized public education that year and designated Rutgers the State University of New Jersey. Second, Rutgers merged with the University of Newark in 1945; with legislative approval a year later, the new university acquired a geographical reach that has continued to expand into the twenty-first century. Thus, 1945 is the starting point, rather than the better known date of 1956 (when the legislature explicitly defined Rutgers's relationship to the state and created the Board of Governors, six of whose eleven members were appointed by the governor).

Four themes unify this study. One emphasizes the parallels between postwar Rutgers and the development of many other public universities and links those parallels more generally to the nation's history and, more recently, to the globalization of modern culture. A second theme is that money matters. The school's accomplishments and deficiencies are directly related to funding—from tuition, from state appropriations, from national research grants, and from corporate and alumni support. Third, the book chronicles changes in the student experience at Rutgers, and the emphasis given that aspect of Rutgers history sets this study apart from other studies of modern universities (and follows the lead of Michael Moffatt). Finally, this work highlights the significance of Edward J. Bloustein's presidency in changing the trajectory of Rutgers's history and transforming the school into a major research university (as well as one with aspirations to field big-time athletic teams). Rutgers's move into the ranks of elite research universities is what is most unique about the school's contemporary history. Federal and state support for higher education made it inevitable that many of the flagship state schools of the Midwest and West became research universities. Nothing about Rutgers's past made its future inevitable. For what was essentially a collection of liberal arts colleges, an effort to play catch-up with schools like Washington, Wisconsin, and Maryland was challenging; to the extent that the enterprise succeeded, much of the explanation lies in the Bloustein presidency.

The organization of this book is unusual. The first three chapters trace the history of the university from World War II through the presidency of Richard L. McCormick. They focus on successive presidential administrations and emphasize policies and events that shaped the university. These chapters resemble McCormick's *Bicentennial History* most closely (and retell a little of his story). Subsequent chapters are topical. Three of them, including one contributed by my colleague Carla Yanni, emphasize student life; two chapters cover athletics; one deals with aspects of Rutgers's public recognition; and one explores Rutgers's path to prominence as a research university. Some of these chapters are subdivided into studies that follow a particular program, organization, or activity across a broad swath of time. The goal of these topical chapters is to retell the postwar Rutgers story from different vantage points, giving more emphasis to the undergraduate experience than is customary in university histories.

This is not a comprehensive history. It could never be. Individuals, departments, and schools one might expect to find in the text often go unnamed. Richard P. McCormick realized as he concluded his *Bicentennial History* that the school was already too large in the 1960s to mention all of its many distinguished individuals and programs in a single volume. The goal has been to focus on the contemporary postwar state university through overviews, illustrative examples, and occasional anecdotes. Some of the chapters I had anticipated writing—about the admissions process, the relationship of the state to the university, university governance— dropped out or were incorporated into other sections. Several of the topics that I discuss deserve fuller treatment—the early history of Livingston College, the Board of Governors, the Bloustein presidency, and the reimagining of urban universities in Camden and Newark.

Finally, a modest disclaimer is in order. I have been at Rutgers for forty years, more than half of the period about which I have written. I know and respect many of the individuals whom I discuss, and I have long considered myself a citizen of the university. I teach in the New Brunswick History Department and use it as a case study, but I might equally well have focused on two or three other departments. Over the years, I have attended at least one game, match, or meet for virtually every intercollegiate sport in New Brunswick/Piscataway when a student of mine participated. While my personal experience at Rutgers University has been invaluable in the creation of this book, I hope that it has been tempered by my perspective and training as a historian.

ACKNOWLEDGMENTS

I am particularly grateful for the help I have received from my undergraduate assistants from the Aresty Research Center, Alice Chunn, Caitlin Foley, Christa Hannon, Eric Knecht, Sarah Morrison, Rabeya Rahman, Jennifer Stice, and Erin Weinman, as well as graduate student Christina Chiknas. I profited from the research work of students in the fall 2013 History Seminar (taught with Thomas Frusciano) and the spring 2013 History and Art History Seminar (taught with Carla Yanni). In spring 2013, undergraduates in my Byrne Seminar on Rutgers history and in my lecture course, "Development of the United States to 1877," responded to a draft of the chapter on student life. I have relied on essays by a number of undergraduates, including Lauren Caruana, Yarden Elias, Caitlin Foley, Laura Granett, Chelsie Güner, Chelsea Intrabartola, Owen Kaufman, Daniel Kleinman, Matthew Knoblauch, Rabeya Rahman, Eric Schkrutz, Joseph Seider, Marc Snitzer, Sarah Stuby, and Peter Weinmann. Former students Lee D. Krystek and Carolyn Siegel Stables gave me permission to reproduce their political cartoons; Sauni Symonds gave me permission to reproduce the cartoon done by Ingrid Wilhite. Mariah Eppes, Astrid M. Lesuisse, Justin Lucero, Dean L. Medina, Christopher M. Price, and Alec Wong helped with photographic work.

Three individuals helped me throughout my work in numerous ways, Thomas Frusciano and Erika Gorder in Special Collections and University Archives, as well as Richard L. McCormick. McCormick, Ann Fabian, Lydia A. Edwards, and Rudolph Bell read carefully several chapters of the manuscript and offered insightful criticism. Elisabeth Oliu did invaluable research for me on the history of the Rutgers library and read my treatment of the topic. Other readers to whom I am indebted included Jeremy Ballack, Jesse C. Clemens, Sarah-Elizabeth C. Clemens, Suzanne Delehanty, Thomas Frusciano, Noreen Scott Garrity, Marianne Gaunt, Beth Gianfagna, Nancy Hewitt, Kathleen Jones, Temma Kaplan, Sara Lampert,

Steven Lawson, Paul Leath, Richard Lutz, Michael Oriad, Barry Qualls, Chris Rasmussen, Donald Roden, Marlie Wasserman, Matthew Weismantel, and Carla Yanni.

In Special Collections and University Archives, I received assistance from Ronald Becker, Catherine Carey, Stephen Dalina, Bonita Grant, Albert King, David Kuzma, Nancy Martin, John Mulez, Fernanda Perrone, and Caryn Radick. Other librarians who helped me were Katie Elson Anderson (Camden), Stephanie Bartz, Natalie Borisovets (Newark), Vibiana Bowman Cvetkovic (Camden), Kayo Denda, Mary Fetzer, Thomas Glynn, Barry V. Lipinski, James Niessen, Julie Still (Camden), Jeffrey J. Teichmann, and Krista White (Newark). At the Office of Institutional Research and Academic Planning, I was assisted by James K. Burkley, Robert J. Heffernan, and Philip S. Paladino. Isabel M. Meldrum spent numerous hours helping me locate relevant records. In the Division of Intercollegiate Athletics, I had help from Max Borghard, Laura Brand, Fred Hill, Kevin MacConnell, Janine M. Purcaro, Heidi Rhone, and Betsy Yonkman. At the Zimmerli Museum, I was helped by Kiki Michael, Stacy Smith, Judy Soto, and Julia Tulovsky.

From the outset, staff of the Rutgers Oral History Archives helped me with the project. I especially thank Sandra Stewart Holyoak, Shaun Illingworth, and Nicholas Molnar. Among the many interviews I was able to sit in on were those with Rudolph Bell, Diane Bonanno, Terence Butler, Roger Dennis, Neil Dougherty, Elmer Eaton, Lloyd Gardner, Patrick Gardner, Frederick Gruninger, Daniel Hart, Mary Hartman, Allen Howard, S. Mitra Kalita, Peter Klein, Paul Leath, Clement Price, Norman Samuels, Joseph Seneca, Robert Snyder, Linda Stamato, Rita K. Thomas, and Kenneth Wheeler. I conducted informal interviews with Noemie Benczer-Koller, Todd Clear, Thomas DiValerio, Howard Gillette, Marjorie Myers Howes, Richard Lutz, Ellen Mappen, Roy Maradonna, Margaret Marsh, Sandra Petway, Fred Roberts, John Sherer, and Fred M. Woodward. Among the former undergraduates and graduate students I spoke with were Eleanor Ahsler, Sigfredo Carrion, Nancy Newmark Kaplan, Kathleen R. Kerwin, Ann Kiernan, Susan Ann Laubach, Kyle Madison, Melba Maldonado, Gualberto Medina, Sarah Noddings, Charlene Cato Piscateli, Mary Ann Poggi, Judy Pease Smith, and Deborah Valentine.

In New Brunswick, I thank for assistance on various aspects of my work: Kenneth Able, JoAnn Arnholt, Michael Beals, Dorothea Berkhout, Gregory S. Blimling, Deborah Epting, Carlos Fernandez, Philip Furmanski, Ziva Galili, Judith Grassle, Jane Hart, Jochen Hellbeck, Benjamin Justice, Carol Koncsol, Paul Kuznekoff, Peter Lindenfeld, Marie Logue, Louis Masur, Phyllis Micketti, Carla Ortiz, Stephan Pappas, Ronald Ransome, James Reed, Alla Rosenfeld, Edmund Scheer, Jerry A. Sellwood, Stacy Smith, Judith Soto, Patrick J. Szary, Julie Traxler, Harvey Waterman, Kerri Willson, Nancy Winterbauer, and Yael Zerubavel.

At Camden, I was helped, in addition to people mentioned above, by Mary Falls, Nancy Maguire, Anna P. Piccoli, Michael Sepanic, and Thomas L. Snyder. At Newark, I was assisted by Todd R. Clear, Jan Ellen Lewis, Eleonora Luongo, Helen S. Paxton, Irwin Primer, and Sandy M. Reyes.

Among those who directed me to materials I used in this study were Morris Moses Kafka, Mark Regnerus, Andrea Weiss, Dan Xie, and Tony Ziselberger.

Marlie Wasserman saw this project through from conception to final submission. Others at Rutgers University Press to whom I am indebted are Jennifer Blanc-Tal, Marilyn Campbell, Allyson Fields, Anne Hegeman, Carrie Hudak, Peter Mickulas, and Leslie Mitchner, as well as copyeditor Beth Gianfagna and indexer Sharon Sweeney.

As I worked on the book, I was encouraged and assisted by two department chairs, James Masschaele and Mark Wasserman. Three members of the department staff, Felicia Norott, Dawn Ruskai, and Candace Walcott-Shepherd, helped me obtain materials; several others, including Timothy Alves, Tiffany Berg, Mary Demeo, Matthew Leonaggeo, Melanie Palm, and Matthew Steiner, assisted with numerous practical problems.

The encouragement I received from Jesse and Sarah-Elizabeth went well beyond their willingness to read chapters for me.

Paul G. E. Clemens

I would like to thank my energetic and detail-oriented research assistant, Laura Leichtman, as well as Joe Mugavero of Rutgers Facilities. The staff members at Special Collections and University Archives went out of their way to help me. Greg Blimling shared his scholarly and practical knowledge of residence halls generously. I benefited from student insight and original research in three seminars, one taught with Alison Isenberg in 2005, another in 2009, and a third in spring 2013, which I taught with Paul Clemens. I owe a debt of gratitude to Professor Clemens, who encouraged me to write the essay included in this volume, and who made the exploration of Rutgers's history richly rewarding.

Carla Yanni

Rutgers
since 1945

1

Becoming a State University

The Presidencies of Robert Clothier,
Lewis Webster Jones, and Mason Gross

In 1945, at the end of World War II, "Rutgers" consisted of two small, elite, liberal arts colleges in New Brunswick, both still clinging to their status as private schools, plus some half-developed professional schools. As Rutgers approached its 250th anniversary in 2016, the university had become *the* state university, a research institution, and a member of the prestigious Association of American Universities. The university now had two law schools, two medical schools, and a firm presence in Camden and Newark as well as in New Brunswick–Piscataway. This chapter explores the beginnings of that transformation, as Rutgers and New Jersey's residents came to accept the implications of the school's status as a state university.

The narrative that follows highlights what was local, particular, and unique. Yet for all its unique features, Rutgers University followed a trajectory of development in the post–World War II era that paralleled that of many other state universities. This is not surprising, as its development was shaped by external factors—most crucially the national economy and the university's relationship with the state and federal governments—that affected all of higher education. Thus I begin with, and will return periodically to, the national context.

The immediate postwar period was the golden age of higher education. Never before, and perhaps never again, would higher education lay claim to such prestige, popularity, and prosperity—the "three Ps," as David Thelin calls them, which defined the place of colleges and universities in

American society for a generation of Americans.[1] This commitment to higher education was born of a fortuitous conjunction of factors. Americans believed that education would smooth the transition to a postwar economy, provide tools to win the Cold War, and open career paths for an expanding middle class. But beyond any one belief, or the manifestation of that belief in public policy, was a growing sense in the late 1940s and into the 1960s that higher education was vital to American life and an essential priority for the state. The baby boomers inherited that understanding from their parents, and they would be the chief beneficiaries, in terms of access to colleges and universities, of its practical implications.

In the years between the end of World War II and the 1970s, the intensified commitment to higher education manifested itself in at least four distinct ways. First, enrollments shot up at universities and colleges throughout the United States. In essence, if the state had previously promised most Americans the opportunity to attend a K–12 school system, the children of the (white) middle class now assumed they would attend college as well. And most of them did so. Second, state governments stepped up their financial support of higher education. Educators knew by the early 1950s that enrollments would skyrocket when the first baby boomers came of age, and these school administrators lobbied incessantly and largely successfully for government funding for additional classroom buildings and more professors. Third, the states reinvigorated or established two-year and community colleges in the hopes that they would provide an affordable transition between high school and a four-year university or at least practical job skills that would make attendance at a four-year institution unnecessary. Each of these factors reflected a national consensus on the importance of educating students beyond their high school years. University faculties, however, not only taught undergraduates but also pursued their research interests. In the 1950s, the federal government did for research what state governments were doing for teaching: supported it generously with taxpayer dollars. Collaboration between university-based scientists and the government—the fourth key factor—had helped win World War II, and the partnership continued after the war, stimulated particularly by the challenge of successful Soviet technological development. Most of this money came from competitive grant programs, using a peer-review system to select the most qualified recipients, and most of it went to researchers at elite universities. The National Science Foundation, the National Institutes of Health, and various federal departments poured money into higher education. This money, however, often paid for released time from undergraduate teaching (and thus at times worked at cross-purposes with public policies to improve and expand universities' teaching programs).

Rutgers entered this period still very much a school bound to its past. Essentially a collection of liberal arts colleges, with the little research conducted at the university being carried out at the agricultural and engineering schools, and anxious about its dual identity as both a private and public institution, Rutgers faced a set of political and educational challenges that set it apart from most other state universities. From the outset, school administrators saw the growing demand for admission to college as a positive development. How to meet that demand, however, was problematic. To add classrooms and professors meant getting more state money for operating costs and capital expenditures. Taxpayers had to be convinced that Rutgers really was a public university, *their* state university in fact, and legislators had to be given greater say in the oversight of the institution. Along the way, university officials, faculty, students, and alumni had to accept that growth—educating a larger proportion of the children of the New Jersey's middle class—meant jettisoning some of the traditions of the liberal arts colleges that had once defined Rutgers. Rutgers faculty did research, and their careers and identity were shaped by their scholarly commitments, but in the first decades after the war, Rutgers was not a "research university" in the sense that a select few of the most prestigious schools in the United States were becoming. At Rutgers, national trends played out in meeting the expectations of a growing state population that a state school could offer them an affordable and rewarding college education.

The Administration of Robert Clothier

Robert Clothier came to the presidency of Rutgers in 1932, at a time when it was a collection of private colleges supported by tuition revenue and endowment funds but was also an institution, "the State University of New Jersey," that received state funds dedicated to the Agricultural College, to the New Jersey College for Women (NJCW), and to technical and scientific programs at the men's college. Organizationally, the public/private divide created enormous financial and administrative problems; more fundamentally, it embodied an identity crisis that Clothier would face throughout his long tenure as president.

Clothier was born in Philadelphia in 1885, educated at Haverford School, and then attended college at Princeton (where he became editor of the student newspaper, *The Princetonian*). After graduating, he worked as a reporter for the *Wall Street Journal* and then for the War Department during World War I. After the war, he again served in the private sector before returning to Haverford as headmaster. In 1929, he accepted a position as dean of men at Pittsburgh University, and he remained there until the Board of Trustees elected him president of Rutgers. In Richard P. McCormick's words, Clothier was "distinguished in appearance, gracious in manner, and warmly sensitive to human relationships," qualities that made him "especially effective in sustaining the morale of students, faculty, and alumni during an extremely trying period."[2] He was also committed to maintaining the university's autonomy from state control, even as he accepted the financial imperatives that made some type of educational partnership with the state government a necessity.

Before World War II, during the disastrous years of the Great Depression, Clothier oversaw the establishment of a separate graduate faculty, the acquisition of land in Piscataway (then called River Road campus, later the Heights, and today Busch campus), the building of much of the College of Agriculture, the establishment of University College, the founding of the University Press, and the creation of the Department of Alumni and Public Relations (this last step crucial if Rutgers was going to obtain the financial support necessary to remain a largely "private" university). Partnership with the federal Works Progress Administration brought men and money to campus to help construct much-needed new facilities, including a football stadium "dedicated [in 1938] on the occasion of the football victory over Princeton."[3] During World War II, Clothier committed Rutgers to the war effort, welcoming to its campuses the Army Specialized Training Program, which provided short-term technical training to enlisted personnel, and which helped compensate for a precipitous loss of enrollment at the men's college—but which also meant that "historians, botanists, or classicists struggled with [teaching] classes in mathematics, mechanical engineering, and navigation" made necessary by wartime exigencies.[4] At the women's college, the administration transformed the curriculum to assist the war effort, offering courses that prepared students for everything from language translation and mechanical and engineering work to serving in the Red Cross or USO. Before war's end, nearly six thousand students of the colleges served in the armed forces, and more than two hundred would perish in the fighting.

The postwar world of the late 1940s brought with it enormous challenges for Rutgers: the uncertainties of a conversion to a peacetime economy, the fears of the Cold War and the outbreak of hostilities in Korea, and, closer to home, the ambiguous relationship of the university to the state. Even before the war ended, Clothier took the initiative in helping to define Rutgers's position as the state university. Technically, the status "state university" applied only to some of the divisions of Rutgers College, as well as the New Jersey College for Women and the Agricultural College (definitions extending back to 1917, although state financing dated to well before that). The state responded positively to Clothier's request, and in 1945, the legislature enacted a bill designating Rutgers's multiple units collectively the state university and, even more critically, placing them in a coordinate rather than a subordinate relationship to the New Jersey State Board of Education. The school, now an "instrumentality of the state," gained in status without losing its autonomy.[5] There had been significant opposition. Some came from a taxpayers' association. Other critics questioned the school's religious status (Rutgers had, in fact, ended its ties to the Dutch Reformed Church in 1920) and asked why state funds could not be used for Catholic schools (meaning Seton Hall) as well. Such opposition was ineffective in blocking the legislation; but in the next legislative initiative, a state construction bond issue, this opposition would triumph.

Before the bond referendum, however, the trustees expanded the university in a way that had important long-term consequences. During the Great Depression, the trustees had considered purchasing several colleges in Newark (known as the "Dana group") to add to the presence the university already had in the city, but nothing came of the idea initially. These schools had subsequently become the University of Newark, and despite grumblings from some trustees about acquiring an urban university, Clothier moved decisively in 1946 to merge the schools. Rutgers acquired a law, business, and pharmacy school, and a college of arts and sciences—altogether about two thousand students and a converted brewery that served as a classroom building. In 1950, Rutgers acquired the two-year "College of South Jersey" (later Rutgers-Camden), a much smaller institution than Newark, and incorporated its unaccredited law program under the umbrella of the Newark school.

In 1947, Rutgers began to work for a state bond referendum to finance construction on its three principal campuses. These were years of heady enrollment growth, a result of the passage of the Servicemen's Readjustment Act of 1944 (the G.I. Bill), which helped pay the costs of college for returning veterans, and of growing ambitions to develop the research potential of the school. Perhaps even more important, Clothier and the board had come to realize that the university's capital needs could not be met without substantial state aid. The bond referendum that the state approved and the electorate considered was a $50 million proposal that would aid not only Rutgers but the state colleges and welfare agencies as well. The opposition focused on Rutgers and challenged its legitimacy as a public university. The opposition won. In the November 1948 election, with a turnout of more than a million people casting ballots, the referendum lost by more than eighty thousand votes. The rejection was, again in McCormick's words, "a multiple catastrophe for the University."[6] Defeat signaled a lack of public acceptance of the 1945 effort to gain public support without giving up the autonomy of a private institution. It left the university with mounting deficits from its own borrowing to expand its facilities and without any way to improve its inadequate faculty salaries. Most serious, it undercut efforts to prepare for the baby boomers. Rutgers administrators knew that by the mid-1960s far more young people would want a college education, and the school was now handicapped in building the dormitories and classrooms to accommodate these students.

In January 1951, Robert Clothier retired. He had shepherded Rutgers through the Great Depression and World War II; now he was sixty-six years old and in poor health. He reminded the Board of Trustees that they faced great challenges: the war in Korea, the looming Cold War, fiscal retrenchment occasioned by the defeat of the bond issue, and the misguided efforts to surrender Rutgers's autonomy to the state. He praised the "partnership" that had developed between the university and the state government but cautioned that Rutgers "must never yield its freedom from political control."[7]

The Administration of Lewis Webster Jones

On September 7, 1951, the Board of Governors, at a special meeting presided over by New Jersey governor Alfred Driscoll, appointed Lewis Webster Jones to replace Clothier as university president. Jones had administrative background at a liberal arts college and a state university, which put him in a good position to meet the challenges of Rutgers's rapidly evolving mission. Born in Nebraska in 1899, Jones attended Reed College (noted for its innovative liberal arts curriculum) as an undergraduate, and obtained a Ph.D. in economics from the Robert Brookings Graduate School. He worked as an economist in Europe before joining the faculty at Bennington College, a northeastern liberal arts institution, in 1932. He served as the school's president from 1941 until 1947, when he left to take a similar post at the University of Arkansas. He would be the first Rutgers president to embrace the challenge of defining what it meant to be the state university. This, of course, was what the trustees expected him to do; but no one could have anticipated the way in which the intrusion of Cold War politics into the academic life of the campus would also define his presidency.

Soon after his arrival, Jones laid out his approach to education in a series of speeches, including one in May 1952 at his inauguration to an audience that included New Jersey political leaders. Beginning with the premise that the United States was engaged in "a war of ideas and moral values"—which referenced both the Cold War and the destructive "current mood of fear and distrust" within America—Jones proposed a cooperative task that would link the university to the citizens of the state, to bring "knowledge and reason to bear on the conduct of our daily lives."[8] He pointed to such recent achievements as the construction of the New Jersey Turnpike and the drafting of a new state constitution as evidence of what that meant. Jones worried that modern culture was mass culture, and that subordination of the individual to the will of mass culture was the "essence of barbarism"—a leveling down toward mediocrity rather than up toward excellence of America.[9] Unlike the conservative thinkers he cited, however, Jones believed that higher education could and must reverse this trend. Colleges need not turn out "dangerously skilled barbarians"; they could provide "an education which deliberately sets out to teach students that civilization is their responsibility."[10] As general as these themes were, they forecast how the Cold War and the emergent partnership between the state and the university would shape Jones's administration.

More concretely, Jones warned of the coming crisis that a growing population posed for higher education: "As a nation, we are in the position of parents who, having prepared for one baby, are blessed with triplets. Our joy, like theirs, is not unmixed with consternation."[11] He affirmed the state university's commitment to educating the majority, not merely the elite, and to providing opportunity, with state scholarship support, for women and men, all races and all religions—a point which, however obvious today, did not seem so at the time. He applauded the leadership Rutgers had shown as a land grant school in making New Jersey agriculture as productive as any in the nation; he emphasized that the Newark and Camden campuses would require resources to serve their students; he suggested the role television might play in educating a growing student population; and he asked for better educational opportunities for citizens sixty years of age and older.

Three interrelated issues defined much of Jones's presidency: the effort to obtain from the state adequate resources to support the school's mission as *the* state university; the undertaking of a substantial building program (often without the state aid the university needed) in order to prepare the university for the explosion in enrollments in the next decade; and a decisive move to redefine and strengthen the relationship between the university and the state. As Jones assumed the presidency, four major building projects were already under construction or completed: a new chemistry building financed by the state was dedicated just as Jones took office, while royalties from the drug streptomycin, developed in the laboratory of Selman A. Waksman, underwrote the construction of the Institute of Microbiology, completed in 1953. Both buildings were at the Heights (Busch campus). Demarest Hall, a much-needed new dormitory at the men's college, was dedicated in 1951, and the same year, construction began on a student center at the NJCW. Both buildings were the result of the first serious capital campaign undertaken by the university since the post–World War I era, and the NJCW construction, in particular, was the result of fund-raising efforts of alumnae of the NJCW, working with the New Jersey State Federation of Women's Clubs. The university had also acquired the buildings of the College of South Jersey, and was beginning modest classroom additions to that campus.

Other notable building projects included the construction of three nine-story (six floors of rooms) dormitories, Frelinghuysen, Hardenbergh, and Livingston (later, Campbell), on a narrow strip of land adjacent to the Raritan River canal, each with classrooms in the basements in an effort to integrate living and learning; the beginning of the Neilson Campus complex at Douglass College (which in 1955 had changed its name from the New Jersey College for Women), which would provide housing for almost five hundred women when completed in 1960; and the "Ledge" student center at the College for Men. In each case, the university gambled by borrowing money to construct what it hoped would be self-liquidating projects (the loans to be paid off through student rent payments). A state appropriation of $2 million began the construction of a much-needed new library, and a second appropriation of the same amount allowed for its completion, while additional capital appropriations went toward a library for the College of South Jersey, the law center at Newark, and an agricultural sciences building. As valuable as these additions were, and as creative as the university was in financing new construction, the efforts had to be weighed against the anticipated capital needs of almost $45 million, as detailed in a report for the Board of Trustees in 1954—money that was essential to meet the surge in admissions, which was expected to push undergraduate enrollment from a little under the current five thousand to nineteen thousand by 1970.

Complicating the university's response to the anticipated enrollment surge was the defeat, previously discussed, of the 1948 higher education bond issue, and the subsequent defeat in 1954 of a bond issue to support a state medical and dental college. In the latter instance, the plan for a state medical school had been initiated by Governor Robert Meyner, but when it became apparent that Rutgers would be the home of the new medical college, opposition arose in Essex County. Jersey City had hoped that its financially distressed medical center would become the new state medical school, but when it became clear that this would not happen, it offered the center to Seton Hall University, which then announced the creation of a new state medical school before the bond issue went before the voters, and the measure went down to defeat.

Rough-and-tumble New Jersey politics took their toll on the state university, but they also pointed to a larger problem, exploited adroitly by the university's political opponents. Despite becoming a public institution in 1945, Rutgers was not clearly perceived as *the* New Jersey state university in the mid-1950s. This fact lay behind key institutional changes initiated in 1955. During the early 1950s, the trustees had experimented with several reconfigurations of university governance, all designed to give the school a more efficient organizational structure. In 1955, radical surgery replaced mere tinkering. The trustees, tied legally and historically to Rutgers College, were not abolished, but overall control of the university passed to a new, much smaller body, the Board of Governors, six of whose eleven voting members were to be appointed by New Jersey's governor. The university's budget would now go to the State Board of Education (as well as the legislature). The trustees themselves became a smaller body, with more limited powers, and acted in an advisory capacity on most matters. The last historic links with the Dutch Reformed Church were severed, as was the tie with Rutgers Preparatory School. A court case and a legislative act secured the legitimacy of the arrangements, and in August 1956, the new Board of Governors met for the first time. Put simply, the creation of the Board of Governors gave the state of New Jersey a larger role in the university, and gave the alumni, the link to the past (and still heavily represented on the Board of Trustees), a reduced role.

But for many state residents, the defining moment of Jones's presidency was the university's response to the Cold War. Tensions between the United States and the Soviet Union had existed even while the nations had been military partners during World War II; when Harry S. Truman replaced Franklin D. Roosevelt in 1945, these tensions rapidly escalated, beginning with disagreements over postwar Poland, and continuing almost unabated through the mid-1960s and the Cuban missile crisis. Truman asked the American people to approve the continued funding of military expansion as a protection against Soviet communism. He coupled this in 1947 with an order leading to loyalty investigations of all federal employees. Ultimately, more than three million Americans were investigated, and while many would be fired as "security risks" for alcoholism or homosexuality, very few were found guilty of disloyalty or Communist Party membership. Anticommunism had been a part of American political culture since the end of World War I, drawing strength from deeply committed anticommunist crusaders and the Federal Bureau of Investigation, but in the late 1940s, it became a national obsession, supported by both conservatives and liberals, by Democrats as well as Republicans, and orchestrated not only by federal congressional committees but also by state and local actions to expose and root out communists and destroy the credibility of fellow travelers whose past or present liberal commitments defined them as soft on communism.

The anticommunist crusade came quickly to American campuses. While public universities were supposedly constrained in investigating their employees by constitutional protection for free speech and a tradition of academic freedom, these same institutions were particularly vulnerable to pressure from state legislators, who controlled their purse strings. In late 1948, Norman Ledgin wrote in a *Targum* column titled "Campus Witch Hunts Can't Happen Here," that "Tom Paine and Sam Adams would recoil in horror if they could view" the "great fear" that was sweeping across American colleges.[12] He praised President Robert Clothier for standing against the hysteria. At Rutgers, however, the process of adjusting to Cold War realities actually began in late 1950, under Clothier. A special committee of faculty, trustees, and alumni, headed by Congressman Clifford Case, revised the school's by-laws to include a new statute on academic freedom. The statement upheld the right of the faculty member to express scholarly opinions, however controversial, in the classroom, but noted a professor's special obligations as a citizen and representative of the university when making public statements that could reflect on the school. In short order, this statement would be used against professors who claimed a federal Fifth Amendment right *not* to speak about possible Communist Party involvement.

Among the most prominent investigations of communist influence in public life was the one carried out by Pat McCarren's Senate Internal Security Subcommittee (SISS). McCarren focused initially on the Institute for Pacific Relations (IPR), a think tank that supported much of the best research on the Far East, but which McCarren believed was infiltrated with communists, working to destroy the U.S. relationship with Nationalist China. In the course of the hearings, witnesses named Rutgers-Newark classics professor Moses I. Finley as the organizer in the 1930s of a communist discussion group at Columbia University. Finley's name had previously arisen in a New York State investigation of communism in New York City schools, and it came up again when McCarren turned his attention to communist influence in the schools. Having been identified as a communist by others, Finley now found himself subpoenaed to testify before the SISS. So was a second Rutgers professor, Simon Heimlich, who taught mathematics at the School of Pharmacy, and whose name had come up in an earlier House Committee on Un-American Activities (popularly known as HUAC) hearing.

Rutgers did not respond initially to the news of Finley's appearance. Finley, an untenured but widely respected member of the faculty, discussed the matter with the administration and denied in person and in writing that he had ever been a communist. At the congressional hearing, he stated he was not a communist but pled the Fifth Amendment in response to questions about former party membership. Heimlich interpreted his summoning as an attack on academic freedom and resolutely refused to cooperate with the committee. For the anticommunist investigators and for much of the public, pleading the Fifth Amendment was virtually an admission of guilt, but based on recent events, most notably the Alger Hiss case, witnesses had reason to worry that an assertion that they had never been communists, if contradicted by other witnesses, could form the basis of a perjury indictment.

To the SISS neither case was particularly important, as neither professor had anything to do with IPR, but when the local press latched on to the case and Republican governor Alfred Driscoll called for the university to do something, President Jones acted. He released Heimlich's passionate defense of his position to the public and created a special committee (again, of faculty, trustees, and alumni) to investigate the matter and report to him. Tracy Voorhees, a trustee prominently associated with efforts to block communist expansion in Europe, was appointed chair of the committee, which informed Jones that a refusal to testify about former communist membership fell under the 1950 by-law revisions. Jones then appointed a faculty committee to consider the charges against Finley and Heimlich. The committee, as Ellen Schrecker notes in her study of the case, took its role as a "grand jury" seriously and grounded itself in the history and purpose of the Fifth Amendment, before reporting to Jones that nothing the professors had done constituted "misconduct" and that the special responsibilities which the by-laws imposed on them as professors were matched by their heightened vulnerability to public criticism.

The professors did not win this battle. A little over a week later, the Board of Trustees (with Governor Driscoll in attendance) voted unanimously to dismiss Finley and Heimlich. In a statement issued in January 1952 interpreting the board's action, Jones drew a distinction between the freedom to be silent, as a civil right protected by the government, and academic freedom, which included a responsibility to provide rational explanations to public authorities. Pointing to the ongoing Cold War, Jones continued: "Under all the circumstances of our relations to world communism, a minimum responsibility would seem to be that members of the University state frankly where they stand on matters of such deep public concern, and of such relevance to academic integrity, as membership in the Communist party, even when by a straightforward statement they believe they might incur certain personal risks."[13]

The policy of immediate dismissal for pleading the Fifth Amendment claimed a third victim. In February 1953, Richard Schlatter, a distinguished historian at the New Brunswick campus, and Abraham Glasser, a tenured member of the Newark law faculty, were subpoenaed by HUAC. Schlatter, who had been a communist at Harvard during the 1930s and later left the party, testified willingly (but with considerable personal anguish) and suffered no professional consequences at Rutgers. In 1941, Glasser had resigned "without prejudice" from a position in the Justice Department (and found work in another federal agency) after he had given information about the Spanish Civil War to a man thought to be a Soviet agent. That record, probably leaked to subsequent employers by the Federal Bureau of Investigation, had come up several times, and led to his being subpoenaed. Glasser was combative throughout his appearance, and pled the Fifth Amendment to numerous questions. The law school faculty committee reviewing the case found no reason not to apply the new policy; offered a choice of resigning or being fired, Glasser resigned.

Pressure to revisit all three of the cases mounted over the remainder of Jones's presidency, but neither the Board of Trustees nor the Board of Governors ever voted to reconsider Glasser's forced resignation or the earlier cases of Heimlich and Finley. Rutgers was censured by both the American Association of University Professors (April 1956) and the Association of American Law Schools (December 1957). The university, in turn, questioned the application to its decision of standards that neither association had endorsed at the height of Cold War anticommunism in the early 1950s, but it also revised its regulations on academic freedom and eliminated the "immediate dismissal" provision. Shortly thereafter, the AAUP removed its censure and suggested that the university revisit the cases (which it did not do).

What can one conclude about this controversy, which spanned Jones's years as Rutgers president? In the 1950s, many liberals and humanists—and Jones was both—were as deeply committed, on their own terms, to fighting the Cold War as were the anticommunist crusaders of the Federal Bureau of Investigation, HUAC, and SISS. In his public statements, Jones defended academic freedom, albeit in less than absolute terms, and he would have fought to protect Heimlich, Finley, and Glasser if they had cooperated with federal investigatory bodies. He clearly valued Finley as a member of the Rutgers faculty (as he did Richard Schlatter), and after Finley was dismissed, recommended him for a position at Cambridge University in England. Moreover, Jones, even more than the Board of Trustees, worked to assure "due process" protection to faculty members. At the same time, he believed that membership in the Communist Party was itself

grounds for dismissal, or as he stated in his inaugural address, "We cannot of course tolerate conspirators who claim the university's protection
in order to destroy freedom."[14] If the trustees drew a line in the sand over
the issue of pleading the Fifth Amendment, Jones articulated the defense
of that policy, and then engaged in an effort to assure that politicians, the
press, and educational leaders nationwide would hear his views. Public pressure, from the press and the governor's office, might have forced
Rutgers to respond to the fact that first Finley and then Heimlich pled
the Fifth Amendment in Senate hearings, but the path that Jones and the
board followed, they set themselves.

Jones clearly worked in harmony with the trustees but not with the faculty. Faculty protest over the dismissal of Heimlich and Finley was short-
lived, and not unanimous, but nonetheless substantial; after all, the faculty
committee's unanimous decision had been ignored. The University Assembly—an all-faculty group—met less than a week after the board decision,
and with perhaps 40 percent of the faculty in attendance, heard from Tracy
Voorhees, debated the recent events, and then voted on four resolutions,
three of which supported the initial faculty recommendation. The assembly endorsed, by a vote of 182–104, the initial report of the faculty committee of review, which had recommended that no action be taken against the
two faculty members who pled the Fifth Amendment. Balancing that vote
was a second, passed 205–41, to endorse the board's statement that there
was no place in the faculty for a communist. There was general agreement that the faculty and board needed to revisit the university policy on
academic freedom independently of the current cases. The assembly then
conducted a poll of the entire faculty, in which 583 out of 690 members of
the university community participated. On this ballot, the vote to support
the initial faculty recommendation was closer (312–261, with 10 abstaining), and a vote to ask the trustees to reconsider was closer still, but support for the board's statement that communists were not qualified to teach
at Rutgers was overwhelming (520–52, with 11 abstaining). An emergency
committee of faculty members—which included historian Richard P. Mc-
Cormick, economist Broadus Mitchell, and Willard Heckel of the Newark
Law School—drafted a statement challenging the board's handling of the
firings, and then pled their case at an emotional board meeting in late January 1953. Soon thereafter, attention turned to the much more protracted
case of Abraham Glasser, but the confrontation had defined the parameters of academic commitment both to free speech and to anticommunism,

and left a residue of distrust between the university's administration and its faculty that the next president would work hard to correct.

In mid-August 1958, Jones unexpectedly submitted his resignation to the Board of Governors and accepted a new position as director of the National Conference of Christians and Jews. In his final address, given at the fall convocation, he reported on the "encouraging progress" Rutgers had made during his presidency. The campus was "rejuvenated, handsome, self-confident, instead of down-at-the-heel and apologetic"; and new buildings had been built, or were sprouting up—men's and women's dorms, the horticulture and biology buildings, the Ledge and the study center at Douglass.[15] He also cited the new professional schools for social work and library science, the world renown achieved by the Institute of Microbiology, and the growing recognition of the University Press. His frustrations with gaining adequate state support, however, overshadowed these accomplishments. In states like Michigan and California, Jones argued, public officials understood that great universities were an asset to be nurtured, and the teaching and research at these schools differed in kind from what went on at other institutions. "Don't settle for mediocrity," he warned the students (and through them, the state), "and for Heaven's sake don't plan for it."[16] Jones hardly mentioned Newark or South Jersey, a common oversight in this era, and he did not reflect on the controversy over academic freedom.

The Administration of Mason Gross

When Jones announced his resignation, the Board of Governors turned to Mason Gross, the provost and vice president, as acting president, and in February 1959, the board unanimously voted him the sixteenth president of Rutgers. Born in Connecticut in 1911 and educated at Cambridge University, Gross returned to the United States to pursue a Ph.D. in philosophy under Alfred North Whitehead at Harvard University. He became an instructor at Columbia University, but after America's entry into World War II, he enlisted and served in the Army Intelligence Corps. Returning to Columbia briefly when the war ended, he moved to Rutgers in 1946 as a philosophy professor and assistant to the dean of arts and sciences. Just three years later, he became Rutgers's first provost, appointed to assist President Clothier, and he remained in that position until he became president himself.

1. Mason Gross at Old Queens. This undated photograph was taken while Gross served as provost under President Lewis Webster Jones, about midway through a two-decade-long career at Rutgers. He still has the frame of the student athlete who had rowed crew at Cambridge University in the 1930s, before earning a Ph.D. at Harvard and serving in the Army Intelligence Corps during World War II.

SOURCE: R-Photo, presidential photographs.

Mason Gross came to the presidency with several advantages. As the university was still quite small, Gross knew many of the New Brunswick faculty personally. His teaching, which he continued as president, and his earlier involvement with student affairs, made him sensitive to the concerns of undergraduates in an era when undergraduates would increasingly demand to be heard. He also had more than a decade of experience with the university's complex organizational structure and the benefit of President Jones's efforts to anticipate the coming surge in enrollments and to convince New Jersey to take seriously its responsibility to the state university. Finally, Gross served in an era when the American people and their elected officials regarded higher education as the foundation for America's future—a golden age for public universities, even if budget struggles did not make it seem so at the time.

Gross's inaugural address challenged the university and the state to think more creatively about education. He chose as his theme the need to understand the vitality and significance of the cultures of Africa and the Middle and Far East. Framing the talk implicitly in terms of the Cold War struggle in these regions, he asked why Americans "seem to be completely baffled by the discovery that in many parts of the world, the very notion that something is Western is cause for dislike." Americans throw back at these peoples an "arsenal of clichés" when they would be better served by working to create "fresh intellectual vigor" in their own educational system.[17] In another address, early in his tenure as president, Gross reflected on the notion of "excellence," a term that was to become a keyword in defining higher education in the decades to follow. He found it, he said, in both musical performance and athletic endeavor, both of which were central to higher education; but, more generally, in creative activity, which "evokes in you directly a sense of tremendous excitement and joy."[18] The seriousness of the times—and here he mentioned the "Communist menace," Laos and Berlin, Castro and Trujillo—only made the freedom of the individual even more crucial, and that freedom, Gross said, is a "joyous notion."[19] Both these talks recast the meaning of education in ways that students and faculty members would be debating during the 1960s; but Gross was equally committed, just as Jones had been, to keeping the coming demographic crisis in higher education in the eyes of the state's citizens and officials. What might hit other states by 1970, would hit New Jersey, Gross predicted, by 1965: unprecedented demands for admissions and resources inadequate to meet those demands. He warned that New Jersey had been rendered "educationally impoverished" and "culturally almost bankrupt" by policies that left the welfare of its citizens dependent on the universities, theaters, orchestras, and museums of New York and Pennsylvania.[20]

Gross's tenure saw the university and the state make a massive commitment to educating more students. In 1958–1959, the year Gross became president, Rutgers enrolled almost seven thousand undergraduates and just over two thousand graduate students; the admissions office projected that ten years later the undergraduate population would be more than eighteen thousand students, and the graduate population over five thousand. The challenge of preparing for this wave of students was met in part by new capital construction, funded by three state bond issues. In November 1959, voters passed a $66.8 million bond issue by a comfortable margin (Rutgers's share was $29.8 million), after the university spearheaded a campaign that enlisted numerous faculty speakers and drew broad-based support from labor unions, civic organizations, and religious bodies. In 1964, voters added a $40.1 million education bond issue (Rutgers gained $18.8 million); and in 1968, despite worries about a backlash against campus disruptions nationwide and at the culmination of a tight race for the presidency between Richard Nixon and Hubert Humphrey, the New Jersey electorate overwhelmingly approved $990 million in new bonds, $202.5 million of which went to educational institutions, including $62.8 million for Rutgers. Rutgers's effort to win public approval for the bonds, the spread of the largess across the state to its many colleges, and a general sense that "education mattered" help explain this set of triumphs for the state university.

These bond issues, coupled with federal loans, grants, and gifts, transformed the university. In Newark, where classes and offices were located in twenty-one scattered buildings, none of which had been originally designed for educational use, the university acquired twenty acres of blighted downtown land from the city and began to build, aided by a federal urban renewal grant. A new law center (Ackerson Hall), a library, humanities building (Conklin Hall), science building (Seth Boyden Hall), and student center were followed eventually by the Graduate School of Business Administration, a fine arts building, and a gymnasium. In Camden, at the College of South Jersey, a new student center and a science building were erected, followed by additional instructional buildings, a law school building, and a gymnasium. As dramatic as this building program was, far less bond money was devoted to it than to the New Brunswick–Piscataway campuses. Camden students and faculty protested that they were being shortchanged. Later, when greater efforts to attract more black students to Rutgers began, the Newark faculty petitioned unsuccessfully for a greater share of the 1968 bond money to meet anticipated enrollment increases.

In New Brunswick, a new four-dorm complex on "Bishop campus" (Clothier, Brett, Tinsley, and Mettler) was added to the three recently built "river dorms"—allowing the men's college, limited to eight hundred students in the mid-1950s, to provide rooms for more than twenty-eight hundred students. The gymnasium was enlarged, a new classroom building (Scott Hall) and dining hall (Brower) were constructed, a language lab was situated behind Van Dyck Hall, and the Graduate School of Education building was completed on the opposite side of Voorhees Mall. More modest additions to Douglass added dormitories and a dining hall on the Neilson campus as well as a new library and gymnasium (Loree). The third bond issue underwrote construction of a classroom and office building (Hickman) and a food science building on the adjacent campus of the College of Agriculture. In large measure, the New Brunswick campuses that would welcome students at the beginning of the twenty-first century were now in place.

What happened in Piscataway, across the Raritan River, was even more dramatic. At the Heights (Busch campus), major additions were made to the existing science buildings: the Nelson Biological Laboratories were begun in April 1959, followed by a physics building and an engineering complex. The second bond issue paid for the Library of Science and Medicine, while corporate donations and federal funds helped construct a building for the College of Pharmacy (moved from Newark). The third bond issue provided for a mathematics, statistics, and computer building (Hill Center), additions to the Wright chemistry building, and a psychology building. The new Library of Science and Medicine and the pharmacy building complemented the two-year medical school that the state authorized Rutgers to establish and which graduated its first, small class in spring 1968.

Just to the east of the Heights lay Camp Kilmer, owned by the federal government. Since the end of World War II, much of the 1,500-plus acres were no longer being used, and Rutgers acquired 540 of those acres in the early 1960s to build Livingston College and fulfill a vision of multiple liberal arts colleges within a larger university, what was called a "federated college system." The fourth component of the federated system was the newly (1965) renamed College of Agriculture and Environmental Science, and the fifth was University College (which offered extension courses and served primarily the needs of older, returning students).

In fall 1967, Rutgers submitted to the state a prioritized building list for 1969–1974 that included ninety-five new projects, more than half of them new buildings, the remainder additions or land acquisitions, which had a combined price tag of more than $300 million. In President Gross's last year in office, 1970–1971, Rutgers had six projects under way costing more than $36 million, plus five new ones that cost an additional $16 million, and seven projects on the drawing board that would require about $20 million. Many of these new buildings were to be built on the Camden or Newark campuses.

The other aspect of the story of the university's financial expansion was contained in the operating budget. When Mason Gross became president, Rutgers had a budget of $28.2 million, of which $12.2 came from state appropriations. In 1970–1971, the year in which Gross announced his retirement, the total operating budget was $115 million, and the state contributed $57 million. Yet every year Rutgers had received less than it had requested, and every year Gross had argued that Rutgers had a great deal of catching up to do as a "state university which was grafted on the sturdy but admittedly ill-equipped and relatively small institution which was Rutgers in 1945."[21] The appeals had stressed the need for more faculty, more competitive salaries, and more resources for the libraries. Thanks to Gross's insistence, academic salaries had risen enough by the late 1960s that the American Association of University Professors rating of Rutgers salary scales had changed from "C" to "A." Better salaries, in turn, gave Rutgers the ability to attract and retain a faculty that would enhance the academic reputation of the school under Gross's leadership.

Of all the projects that marked the Gross presidency, two endeavors stand out.

One was the development of a medical school. In June 1961, Gross announced that, after a long period of planning, a $1 million grant had been obtained from the W. K. Kellogg Foundation that would allow Rutgers to establish a two-year program of medical education. Existing biology programs were strengthened, and new departments in anatomy, pathology, and pharmacology were created, with the necessary buildings added to the science complex on the Heights. Within the year, DeWitt Stetten Jr., a biochemist and specialist on arthritis, had been recruited from the National Institutes of Health as the first dean. Provisional accreditation was obtained in 1963. Even before construction began on the $16 million core building at the Heights, the first group of students was admitted in fall 1966; they studied in temporary quarters at the Heights and on Kilmer campus. In 1968, all fifteen graduates of that first class were accepted to four-year schools. Meanwhile, the state approved a plan to make the Rutgers Medical School a four-year institution by 1972, and the university entered into negotiations to purchase Raritan Valley Hospital as the site for the clinical facilities needed for the school.

Then, abruptly, everything fell apart. Following the recommendation of Governor William Cahill, the New Jersey legislature moved to sever the medical school from the university and place it under a stand-alone board that governed the New Jersey College of Medicine and Dentistry (NJCMD). Cahill expressed concerns about the small number of graduates of the Rutgers school and high cost of the planned hospital construction. He complained that leaving the medical school as a part of Rutgers would mean "perpetuating a system which says only academic geniuses can become doctors" and not produce enough graduates who were committed to general practice rather than academic research.[22] There were, however, other factors at play. The move had the backing of political leaders in Essex County, where NJCMD was located, and it also came at a time when the state and the university were squabbling over the school's fiscal autonomy and its handling of student antiwar protests. At least some legislators supported the move as a rebuke to what they perceived as Gross's mismanagement of the university, and Gross's own testimony in Trenton could do nothing to stop the political steamroller Cahill had set in motion. Rutgers's fledgling medical school became part of the NJCMD.

A poignant footnote: in 1970, the new medical school building and the adjacent, recently constructed Library of Science and Medicine, both virtually empty shells, now stood side by side on the Heights campus, their umbilical cord severed. Rutgers designated the door facing away from the medical school as the library's front door, and the tunnel connecting the two structures was sealed off, with each institution retaining a key to its own entrance only. It would take almost a decade to iron out—imperfectly—the formal and informal relationship between the two institutions, and another half century for Rutgers to reclaim the lost opportunity of building a research university around a medical school.

The other major undertaking was the creation of Livingston College. In early 1965, Ernest A. Lynton, who had joined the physics faculty in 1952, was appointed dean of the first (and as it turned out, the only) college to be built on the Kilmer property. Over the next four years, Lynton recruited the nucleus of a new faculty, and he involved students and professors from the men's and women's colleges in planning the new school. The planners wanted to decentralize education, even as Rutgers itself grew into a large state university; they wanted a curriculum that would engage students from the start with the problems of the contemporary world; and they wanted to create physical spaces that would connect learning and living. Moreover, unlike Rutgers and Douglass Colleges, the new school was coeducational. The curriculum emphasized technology (computer science) and an interdisciplinary approach to the urban experience as pathways to making education relevant to modern life, while still including most of the traditional liberal arts disciplines. Livingston College was also distinguished by a successful effort to recruit a cross-section of the New Jersey population (more than a quarter of the entering class of 1969 was classified as nonwhite) and to incorporate students as partners in academic decision making. Over the next decade, the challenge of meeting and redefining these goals made Livingston the center of both internal and external controversy.

In spring 1959, as Gross assumed the presidency, national commentators paused for troubled reflections on the apathy and apolitical currents that they sensed had long washed over college campuses. Yet that same semester, Rutgers College students presented to the Board of Governors a "Declaration of Student Rights," signed by virtually every student leader, and the student council continued its campaign to end the mandatory Reserve Officer Training Corps (ROTC) program. However one might characterize the 1950s, from this point on, activism trumped apathy. During the 1960s, Rutgers students challenged *in loco parentis* rules and traveled to Cuba; they joined the Peace Corps, protested the Vietnam War and campus racism, fought for a greater say in college and university governance, and debated the fraternity system as well as attended the campus appearance of such national figures as black leader Malcolm X, socialist spokesman Norman Thomas, Republican politician Barry Goldwater, and southern conservative Strom Thurmond.

No student concern loomed larger than the Vietnam War. Even before President Lyndon Johnson's March 1965 commitment of American marines to combat operations in Southeast Asia, Rutgers campuses had active left- and right-wing student groups engaged in debate about national issues. In the mid-1960s, both the Young Americans for Freedom (a conservative/libertarian student group that grew out of a 1960 meeting in Sharon, Connecticut, the home of conservative commentator William F. Buckley Jr.) and the Students for a Democratic Society (founded at the University of Michigan in the same year and initially defined by the 1962 "Port Huron Statement" drafted by left-wing activist Tom Hayden) had active chapters on all three campuses, although initially the YAF concerned itself primarily with anticommunism, and SDS with community empowerment and organizing.

Then came the "teach-in." Convoked by the faculty, held in Scott Hall on the New Brunswick campus, and running through the night on Thursday, April 22, 1965, Rutgers's first teach-in, which drew perhaps a thousand students and numerous faculty speakers, probed the historical origins and current political significance of what was, at that time, only a modest American commitment to supporting a pro-Western regime in South Vietnam from attacks by communist insurgents. As the *Targum* reported afterward, some students came for the novelty of the event, some for "a chance to be with girls all-night. Some came to learn. Some needed an excuse to cut classes the next day." The highlight for most was a fiery debate between a Douglass political science professor, William Fitzpatrick, and two Rutgers College history professors, Lloyd Gardner and Warren Susman. Fitzpatrick argued that "we are fighting in Vietnam not to save our 'little brown brother,' but to save ourselves," and Gardner in what the *Targum* described as a scorching retaliation countered that "Western civilization was greatest when isolated to the size of Greek city-states, and failed most miserably when it reached out to take lands it was not entitled to take."[23] As Fitzpatrick spoke in rebuttal, the *Targum* captured what happened next: "At this point, Susman apparently had heard enough, and, as he later said, went blind with rage. He jumped up from his chair, raced over to the podium where Fitzpatrick was speaking, quizzed Fitzpatrick as to 'How would you define it?' referring to 'civilization,' and pounded his fist on the podium four times, smashing his watch in the process. It appeared that either Susman would burst a blood vessel, or the podium would crumble."[24]

One had to turn to page 3 of the *Targum* to find the story that would transform the teach-in into a major political issue in New Jersey and raise once again the question of the faculty's academic freedom. After Susman's heated verbal attack on Fitzpatrick, Professor Eugene Genovese, also of the History Department, "hushed the audience" by stating that "those of you who know me know that I am a Marxist and a Socialist. Therefore, unlike most of my distinguished colleagues here this morning, I do not fear or regret the impending Viet Cong victory in Vietnam. I welcome it."[25] The university had a slightly different version of the statement, but in either form, when the remarks appeared in the commercial press, a furious public debate began.

Letters from both sides flooded the university, the newspapers, and the state legislature, either calling for the school to fire Genovese or in support of free speech and academic freedom. A legislative inquiry in June concluded that Genovese had not violated university regulations, but noted that those regulations imposed on faculty members special obligations to consider when speaking in public their role as citizens, members of a learned profession, representatives of the university, and, in particular, in the quasi-classroom-like setting of the teach-in (the same official obligation invoked in the Cold War cases). The report concluded with a recommendation that the university tighten its procedures and regulations. In July, the Republican candidate for governor, Wayne Dumont, went further. He met with Gross, pressed him to dismiss Genovese, and, when Gross refused on behalf of himself and the board, Dumont made the issue a centerpiece of his campaign. In August, the board responded to the legislature in a report to Governor Richard Hughes. The board noted that Genovese's statement "evidenced a lack of good judgment," but concluded that current university regulations were adequate and that Genovese had not violated them. Appended to the report was a statement from the History Department. The department made clear that Genovese was a gifted teacher and scholar, and was so judged by his professional colleagues at Rutgers and elsewhere, and it cautioned against allowing a "mood of hysteria" to repress faculty members who as a matter of conscience spoke out on a public issue.[26] The November election, in which Hughes, who supported the university's position, defeated Dumont, provides an index of how much things had changed from the time of the Cold War crisis during the previous decade.

The first teach-in was followed by many others. Some were sponsored by SDS, some by other antiwar groups, and many were protested by YAF. In April 1966, on the first anniversary of the New Brunswick teach-in, Dumont and Genovese met for an anticlimactic debate. In a comprehensive poll done by the *Targum* in late 1967, 52 percent of the students polled opposed the war, 41 percent supported it, with the remainder undecided, and the strongest opposition to the war was on the Douglass campus. At the same time, the *Targum* estimated that no more than 5 percent of the students were actively engaged in pro- or antiwar efforts.[27]

In fall 1969, the Student Mobilization Committee—a national group—called for a moratorium on October 15 on college campuses across the country as a protest against the war. Gross wrote to the Rutgers community that "we at Rutgers should go beyond protest to a critical examination of basic issues facing the nation." It would be a day, he hoped, to demonstrate the "role of the university as teacher, as guardian of civilized values, and as the critical and moral intelligence which compels the community to ponder its course of action."[28] Neither he nor the university cancelled classes or took a stand on the war. Nonetheless, most classes were cancelled, and elaborate and well-attended programs scheduled on all three campuses. Hosea Williams, from the Southern Christian Leadership Conference, spoke at Newark; MIT professor Noam Chomsky, journalist and antiwar critic Seymour M. Hersh, and U.S. Senator Eugene McCarthy all spoke at Rutgers College. On the smaller, quieter Camden campus, students showed two antiwar films, and the faculty held a teach-in. At Livingston, which had opened that fall, the student-faculty

Academic Assembly, in preparation for the moratorium, approved a resolution demanding an immediate ceasefire and withdrawal of American troops from Vietnam.

Criticism poured in, but also praise. Gross handled the criticism politely but resolutely. He did nothing about the SDS protesters who marched on his home and symbolically nailed a set of demands to his door ("Martin Luther style") calling for the abolition of ROTC (which had become the symbol of university complicity in the war effort) and better pay for food service workers. When, in December, SDS followed up by purposely disrupting a Board of Governors meeting and refusing to leave until its demands were met, the university had the protesters arrested, and the six Douglass students in the group faced suspension as well.

Later that spring, however, after President Richard Nixon announced the expansion of the Vietnam War to Cambodia, the nation's campuses erupted in protest. At Rutgers, a student strike began Friday, May 1. By Monday, strike committees were active on every campus. On May 4, the *Targum* ran an editorial, "Time to act—Strike now," prepared and approved by its staff, as well as those of student newspapers at seven Ivy League schools, Sarah Lawrence, and Bryn Mawr, which called for an end to "a corrupt and immoral war." That same day, Gross spoke to more than two thousand protesters on the lawn in front of Old Queens and expressed his sympathy for their cause. The next day, more than five thousand protesters demonstrated. By May 6, the faculties at each college had essentially ended "business as usual." The Arts and Science faculty at Newark—in a resolution typical of what happened throughout Rutgers (but also on campuses from College Park, Maryland, to Berkeley, California)—voted to "reorient" the energy of the faculty and students to "intensive education" on U.S. involvement in Southeast Asia. They made final examinations optional, and allowed pass/fail course grading. Students and faculty pressured the Board of Governors to abolish ROTC; the state legislature pressured the board to maintain the program. The board sided with the legislature.

Mason Gross, personally committed to many of the same goals as the protesters (if not always to their methods), did a masterly job of preserving as much calm as possible internally, while he and the Board of Governors defended the university's commitment to free and unfettered speech. There is no question, however, that over his years at Rutgers, Gross had subtly shifted his position: from a spokesperson for the restrictive definition of academic freedom in the 1950s, to cautious and not unqualified support for the teach-ins, to his endorsement of the moratorium coupled with his symbolic appearance on the lawn of Old Queens in May 1970. He had moved to the left, although not as dramatically as the faculty and students—and that may well have been crucial to his success in piloting the university through this turbulent era of protest.[29]

During Gross's tenure, black students also challenged the university. Their protests raised questions about Rutgers's essential purposes and aspirations. The civil rights movement that swept the South in the 1950s and early 1960s inspired many faculty and students, and it led to a general awareness, evident in the first years of Gross's presidency, that more had to be done at Rutgers to increase the enrollment of black students. Good intentions brought very slow progress. "In the fifteen years prior to 1967," Richard P. McCormick noted, "only about two hundred blacks had received baccalaureate degrees, out of twenty-four thousand awarded. There were perhaps one hundred black undergraduates in 1965; by 1968 their number had grown to over four hundred, when they constituted about 3 percent of the undergraduate enrollment."[30] The assassination of Martin Luther King Jr., on April 4, 1968, led to a cancellation of classes at Rutgers, a convocation on racism on the New Brunswick campus, and additional efforts by the administration to fund minority programs and hire minority faculty. But it would fall to the black students themselves, on each of the campuses, to impart a "new urgency" to these efforts.[31]

One of those students was Karen Predow. She had grown up in Trenton; followed the college-preparatory track from seventh grade through graduation in 1966 from Trenton Central High School; and been recruited as part of a Rutgers initiative to bring more African American students from targeted high schools to the university. At Douglass, where she was one of two dozen African American first-year students, and a commuter from Trenton, she fit in slowly, more estranged and an object of curiosity among the white students than a target of hostility. Like many African American students at Rutgers in the mid-1960s, she received no financial aid, and her parents paid most of her college expenses; to make ends meet, she eventually completed her fall semester living in the household of family friends in Piscataway. Predow had not been a high school activist, although her parents were members of the NAACP, but she quickly became part of the first effort to organize black students in New Brunswick. That spring (1967), after Rutgers College black students formed the Student Afro-American Society (SAS), she and several other Douglass women accepted an invitation to join, established their own committee within the organization, and eventually charted an independent course for their committee.[32]

Another of the activists who would so dramatically challenge the university for its lack of commitment to the recruitment and retention of black students and faculty was Vickie Donaldson. Donaldson's mother had moved to Newark from Florida to find work in nursing, but Vickie had stayed with her maternal grandmother as she completed her studies at the local (segregated) school system in Quincy, Florida (near Tallahassee). As a teenager, she had been president of the honor society, sung in the church choir, and joined the Congress of Racial Equality. She applied to both Rutgers–Newark and Douglass College, but decided on the Newark campus when Douglass could not guarantee her housing. That summer, 1967, she commuted across the city, at the time of the Newark civil disturbances, to attend Newark Preparatory School and meet her Rutgers foreign language admissions requirement. By autumn, Donaldson was engulfed in a campus where "all the buildings were white," all the walls were white, and all her classmates were white, and the tinted windows shut off the campus from the city.[33] On campus she met Richard Roper, also a southerner, who had matriculated a year earlier, joined the campus NAACP, and then helped found the Black Organization of Students (BOS). Roper convinced her to join.

Donaldson had grown up in the South, Predow in New Jersey. Donaldson had taken part in the civil rights movement, Predow had not. Both had been good students in high school and met the demanding standards for admission to Rutgers; both largely paid for their own education; both joined black student organizations soon after arriving at Rutgers, and both read widely in black nationalist and Black Power literature. And in a movement whose most visible leaders were men, both were women. Both fought not only to bring black people and black culture into the center of the institution but also to transform Rutgers itself.

Each campus had a black student movement. In spring 1968, personal contacts among members of these groups led to collective action. On each campus, a carefully drawn up set of demands was sent to the administration; the demands were arranged serially, each announced on a different day for maximum impact. Under pressure, the Board of Governors met with SAS representatives on April 11 (the assassination of Martin Luther King Jr. a week earlier had produced a sense that something had to be done to improve conditions on campus), and the board then scheduled a second meeting for a week later in the library in New Brunswick (these two meetings were the first the board had ever held with organized student groups). At that meeting, by prearrangement, individual black students read carefully prepared position statements on each of more than a dozen grievances and demands. When the university response proved to be, as the students saw it, too little, too late, BOS acted.

On February 24, 1969, two dozen black students occupied Conklin Hall on the Newark campus and renamed it "Liberation Hall"—the first such protest in the university's history. (Building takeovers were already a popular protest tactic among student demonstrators on other campuses and over the years would be used for various causes at Rutgers.) The students' demands—which were echoed in protests on all the other campuses—included more hiring of black faculty and staff, improved efforts for admission and retention of black students, and development of a black studies program. Gross neither summoned the police to remove the students nor invoked the university policy on disruption but rather met with them, helped hammer out an agreement that would eventually bring the takeover to an end, and while the negotiations were in progress, went to Camden to meet with black students who were staging their own protest. Gross strongly supported the thrust of the students' demands. He warned, however, that the crucial admissions question could only be solved by a state-wide response involving all the colleges, and that such a solution required state funding. He also cautioned that curricular and admissions reforms had to come from the faculty. On each campus, in fact, hastily called faculty meetings worked out responses, all of which, however, fell short of the call for open admissions for black New Jersey high school graduates.

As disruptive protest in Newark broke out again, the Board of Governors, President Gross, and Chancellor of Higher Education Ralph Dungan met in mid-March 1969 and crafted a "surprising solution" to the contentious admissions question. The board committed itself to establishing the Urban University Program (UUP). That program would admit "educationally and economically disadvantaged graduates of the secondary schools in those communities where Rutgers has its primary location," first to remedial courses, if necessary, and then, as fully matriculated students.[34] The program made its debut in September, but never received the full state support it needed, and was never effectively integrated with the individual college faculties who had the responsibility for educating these students. Ultimately, under state pressure, it gave way to an alternative program, the

Equal Opportunity Fund, established in 1968 in the wake of the 1967 urban disruption in Newark. Yet out of the confusion of overlapping programs came substantial and sustained improvement in the admission of minority students to Rutgers.

The university's efforts to address what Gross, much of the faculty, and the board considered legitimate concerns of the black protesters met with skeptical, and more often, hostile responses beyond the university. Rutgers, critics said, had caved in to black demands, lowered its standards, and committed resources without state approval. Dungan, who as early as 1967 had urged the state to address the educational plight of minority students, nonetheless severely criticized the specific response of the university to the crisis. He singled out Rutgers's dysfunctional system of committees, its failure to invoke its policy on student disruptions, and its attempts to run its Newark and Camden campuses from the distant halls of Old Queens. In early May, the state legislature followed up on widespread criticism of the university by asking Gross to answer twenty-one questions about the school's response to the disruptions, the new admissions policy, the distribution of funding among the campuses, and the governance of the university. The first, and most pressing, question was how the university would handle another such incident. Gross stated that "the administration had made it quite clear to all members of the university community that disruption in any form, whether it be occupation of a building, blocking of a building, or the invasion of classes or offices is a violation of University regulations," but went on to argue that specific responses depended on the circumstances, and that calling in the police "inevitably leads to violence and greatly intensifies the gravity of the situation." He explained that the new admissions policy was experimental and envisioned as part of a statewide effort that could succeed only if other colleges, including two-year schools, also increased admissions of and programs for disadvantaged students. Gross challenged Dungan's harsher criticisms of the university, concluding that "Mr. Dungan . . . seems to have assumed that some rather trivial deficiencies gave a true picture of the whole."[35]

Later in May, Frank McGee of NBC broadcast a news report that featured a discussion with Gross on the university's response to the Conklin Hall takeover. McGee asked Gross if the new programs for "impoverished high school graduates" in Newark, Camden, and New Brunswick had not been "conceived in fear" and "extorted by . . . unspoken threats," to which Gross responded that the university had already been pursuing an aggressive recruitment program for minority students, which the black student protesters had felt was not aggressive enough. They were, he concluded, probably right. When McGee followed up by asking Gross how he would "characterize the charge that you were blackmailed," Gross answered bluntly, "I would ignore it."[36]

That summer, Gross and numerous other university officials were called to testify in Trenton about the handling of the takeover of Conklin Hall, the protests at Douglass, Rutgers, and Camden, and the new Urban University Program. The hearings did not solve the problem of funding new admissions and curricular initiatives, or preclude further protest on campus, but they did curb the political fallout occasioned by the bold actions of minority students frustrated by the slow process of change at their state university.

Gross's concern about "disadvantaged students" carried over into athletics. Gross himself had been a college athlete, rowing while at Cambridge, and at Rutgers he enthusiastically attended football games and supported the crew program. He saw athletics as integral to the mission of a public university and envisioned a participatory sports program quite different from the elite sports culture he had known in England. In the late 1960s, when the National Collegiate Athletic Association (NCAA) imposed a minimum scholastic grade-point average requirement for the recruitment and support of a student athlete, Gross led an unsuccessful effort to create a more flexible rule. He worried that the standard would keep disadvantaged students (which meant, at that time, the few black athletes who played on the Rutgers football team) from attending college, and argued that Rutgers was the best judge of whether anyone who applied for admission could meet its rigorous academic standards—a position taken as well by many of the Ivy League schools. Gross lost the fight with the NCAA, but more generally, he helped define the uneasy partnership between athletics and academics that would shape campus life under the next administration.

In May 1970, Gross announced his retirement, effective September 1971. Like the president before him, and most of the presidents who followed, his frustrations in negotiating with the state for support and autonomy probably influenced his decision, as undoubtedly did his health. Internally, in the final years of his administration, there had been important changes: a Rutgers College faculty committee, chaired by historian Warren Susman, had recommended sweeping reforms of the college's general education requirement, and after impassioned debate, the faculty had adopted a new set of requirements giving students far more responsibility for selecting their own courses; the University Senate, which advised the president and the Board of Governors on university policy, added students (with voting rights) to the membership of faculty and administrators; and the American Association of University Professors became the collective bargaining unit for the Rutgers faculty. Each of these changes shaped the university's future, but for the moment they were only footnotes to the central narrative of Gross's presidency. That narrative centered on two themes: first, the sympathetic if not always harmonious relationship of the state to the state university, which allowed for the massive building projects of the 1960s and early 1970s and the tremendous increase in enrollments; and, second, Gross's (and the board's) leadership in addressing the issues raised by a decade of student protest. Yet no one event or policy can capture the energy and excitement of Gross's presidency in the late 1960s. His legacy was to have guided Rutgers through tumultuous times while retaining the respect and affection of so many. "What will Rutgers be when its gadfly goes?" asked the *Newsletter*, for "from the start, Gross was . . . tall, handsome, gracious, potentially dominating."[37]

2

Rutgers Becomes a Research University

The Presidency of Edward J. Bloustein

The almost two decade span from the presidency of Richard Nixon to that of Ronald Reagan reoriented American politics toward conservative social policies, market-driven solutions to economic problems, and fiscal belt-tightening at every level of government. Watergate, Iran-Contra, and innumerable lesser scandals aroused the electorate's skepticism of public officials and injected a new nastiness into the already rough-and-tumble political order. In this climate, making the case for public recognition of and support for higher education became more difficult. The 1970s and 1980s were troubled times, and the golden age for American colleges and universities was definitely over.

During the seventies and eighties, five crucial developments shaped the higher education landscape. First, the enormous growth of federal support for university-based scientific research leveled off; under political pressure from states that had received little aid in the past, Congress increasingly insisted that the aid be distributed more equitably among the nation's universities and that aid go to applied research to produce publicly useful results rather than to support basic or disinterested research.

Second, even as the federal government slowed the dispersal of research dollars, Congress began to allot more money in direct student aid. Soon after the 1957 Soviet launch of *Sputnik 1*, the federal government provided direct student aid under the National Defense Education Act (1958). That money targeted future high school teachers and, increasingly, graduate

students. More dramatically, a 1972 amendment, sponsored by Rhode Island senator Claiborne Pell, to the 1964 Higher Education Act began a
program of direct federal grants to college students who demonstrated
need. Through the Pell Grants program, the federal government allocated
billions of dollars to assist millions of students. The Guaranteed Student
Loan Act of 1978 extended this commitment, but with more ambiguous
consequences. Both programs provided "portable aid," given to the student
rather than the institution she or he attended, so schools became part of a
consumer economy, competing for students (this would help women and
minorities as well as students from low-income households). Moreover, as
direct state support for public education shrank in the 1970s, the federal
programs created irresistible incentives to raise tuition to capture federal
dollars. For students with loans rather than grants, this meant increasingly that they would leave college encumbered by debt. Consumerism
also pushed schools to market themselves more self-consciously, to build
fancy dorms and state-of-the-art recreational facilities, and to invest in
high-profile athletic programs.

Third, with government money (and public skepticism about how it
was spent) came government regulation. Title IX (1972) pressured schools
to provide equal opportunity for women and men to compete in varsity
athletics, and it became a controversial symbol of federal regulation. The
shrinking autonomy of public higher education was, however, far more
general, and included financial audits, cost-overrun hearings, lawsuits
initiated by disgruntled constituents, and compliance regulations that affected teaching, research, and student life. Lawsuits, investigations, and
new statutory rules forced colleges and universities to create more elaborate bureaucracies to deal with a regulatory environment from which they
had previously been largely immune. Whether they liked it or not, state
universities were becoming multimillion (and then billion)-dollar businesses, which required increased staffing and more systematic approaches
to administration.

Fourth, during the late 1950s and well into the 1960s, most educators
believed that America was woefully short of appropriately trained college
teachers and that this was a serious problem if the nation were to win the
Cold War. Federal and foundation policies encouraged universities to turn
out increasing numbers of Ph.D.s., a process that peaked around 1973, just
as college enrollments dropped for the first time since the end of World
War II. By the mid-1970s, the academic marketplace was clearly saturated,

and the aspirations of many young scholars would be thwarted. Finally, stagflation in the 1970s and rising admission costs led to new types of competition for tuition dollars. The two most significant new competitors were the community college system (where articulation agreements linked their two-year programs to entrance into four-year universities) and the for-profit schools, which established universities tried unsuccessfully to discredit.

How, then, did Rutgers become a major research university in the 1970s and 1980s? The time was anything but auspicious for such a development. When, for instance, the University of Pittsburgh had tried to re-create itself as an elite institution in the mid-1960s, the result had been financial disaster, with the ensuing state bailout resulting in a public takeover of what until then had been a private school.

But the Rutgers story would be different. New Jersey was among the most densely populated states; even as student enrollments were shrinking nationwide, increased college attendance in the Garden State provided funds to underwrite institutional growth. Moreover, the glut of new Ph.D.s seeking employment allowed adept deans and department chairs to choose the best candidates, especially in the humanities and social sciences, without having to offer extravagant salaries. The university also imposed more rigorous standards for the research accomplishments expected for tenure and promotion. In New Brunswick, the university reorganized its academic structure and transformed the educational culture. Its leaders challenged the traditional notion that the institution was primarily a collection of liberal arts colleges devoted to undergraduate education. Rutgers, it was decided, could both provide meaningful undergraduate education and become a research university with outstanding graduate programs. The national economic upturn of the mid-1980s and the commitment of New Jersey political leaders to higher education during this period provided crucial support to Rutgers's success in this venture.

During Mason Gross's last year in office, the university conducted a nationwide search that brought Edward J. Bloustein to Rutgers as its seventeenth president. Bloustein was born in New York City in 1925. He served in World War II and on his return earned an undergraduate degree at New York University. He then received a Fulbright scholarship to study philosophy at Oxford University and later returned to the United States for brief stints at teaching in Brooklyn and as a political analyst in Washington, DC. In 1951, he went to Cornell for a Ph.D. in philosophy (1954) and a law degree (LL.B., 1959). While at law school, he edited the *Cornell Law Quarterly*. From 1959 to 1964, Bloustein worked in New York, first as a law clerk and then as a law professor at NYU, before becoming the president of Bennington College in Vermont in 1965. When called to Rutgers in 1971, he was forty-six years old. As was true of Jones and Gross, Bloustein's educational background had not prepared him to lead a state university. Unlike Gross, he was a complete outsider. Yet Edward Bloustein had the longest presidency of the post–World War II era and was the architect of Rutgers's rise to prominence as a major research university. Like past presidents, Bloustein continued to teach; more uniquely, he remained a scholar of the philosophy of the law.

Charting a New Course

"Administrating a college today," Bloustein wrote, "is like playing chess on the open deck of the sinking *Titanic*—to make matters worse, the chess rules seem to be changing as the game proceeds."[1] Contemporary universities, Bloustein argued in his inaugural address, were beset by "uncertainty of purpose and the failure of nerve." They had to return to first principles and become again institutions where "reason resides."[2] In an age of increasingly specialized knowledge, this meant abandoning the fruitless effort of trying to teach everything or of locking in a fixed curriculum, instead allowing students to master different approaches to knowledge. This also meant not allowing government and corporate subsidies to dictate which research a university supported, but rather for the schools themselves to direct research so as to nurture reason and serve society. And this meant rejecting violence as "antithetical to deliberation, the very essence of the academic life," while giving students and the faculty true authority commensurate with that of the administration and trustees of universities.[3] Each of these themes spoke philosophically to the problems that disrupted campus life so often in the late 1960s and early 1970s.

Addressing a joint session of the New Jersey legislature in November 1971, Bloustein argued that Rutgers must "learn to serve the cities and suburbs of this day as effectively as it served the farms of yesteryear."[4] For the university, this required a mission to educate not merely a privileged elite but a cross-section of New Jersey's population, including black and Puerto Rican minorities, lower-middle-class white children, women, and older students. For the state, this required coming up with a tuition formula to

2. Edward J. Bloustein and his wife, Ruth Ellen Steinman. They met as graduate students at Cornell, where he was working in philosophy and she in medicine. This undated picture of the couple walking was probably taken shortly before Steinman had serious, debilitating medical problems (later corrected) and Bloustein a severe heart attack (1976). In eighteen years at Rutgers, Bloustein led a transformation of the university into a major research institution, supported during the 1980s by Governor Thomas Kean and a robust economy, and crowned by membership in 1989 in the prestigious Association of American Universities.

SOURCE: R-Photo, presidential photographs.

keep college affordable and assuring a revenue flow dependent on something other than the property tax. "Tuition in a state university," he told them bluntly, "is really just another form of taxation."[5]

Several initiatives Bloustein undertook or supported indicated both symbolic and substantive ways in which he helped chart a new course for Rutgers. One of these initiatives concerned religion. In 1920, Rutgers had severed its last ties with the Dutch Reformed Church. In 1926, the trustees created the position of university chaplain but also began a two-decade-long debate, which by 1946 had gradually brought compulsory chapel attendance to an end. When in 1974, Bradford S. Abernethy, the longest-serving university chaplain in the school's history, stepped down, the office was replaced by a coordinator of religious affairs. Bloustein appointed Robert J. Tanksley as coordinator, but less than a decade later, in 1981, partly for budgetary reasons but also after Tanksley had become a critic of some of the administration's policies, the president eliminated the office, and moved the responsibilities to the student life administration. Bloustein concluded that the office was not directly relevant to the "academic mission of the university."[6] Many religious denominations continued to have a presence on or near the campuses, but Bloustein had redefined the university in secular terms.

Another departure from the past concerned the campus police. As New Brunswick's College Avenue had become swamped with students' parked cars after World War II, the university in 1952 instituted a parking policy, backed by modest fines and, in 1961, created a department of parking and transportation, under Robert F. Ochs. Over the next decade, Ochs nurtured the growth of the parking authority into a campus patrol, trained by the state police, but committed to the *in loco parentis* policy of the university. As the campuses grew larger and more crowded, they became more dangerous places. In 1970, as New Jersey passed legislation allowing campus patrols full police powers, Ochs and his officers began lobbying for the right to carry firearms. Without firearms, officers were not "real cops," and that made it harder to recruit them and harder to gain the respect of the municipal police with whom they shared jurisdiction, as well as harder for the officers to protect themselves when investigating crimes of violence. Gross had not been persuaded that "guns were necessary on campus," but in 1972, Bloustein, convinced by the report on campus crime that Ochs presented and with the agreement of the University Senate, supported before the Board of Governors a proposal for limited arming.[7] The board approved it. Student and faculty protest stopped neither the decision nor the subsequent expansion of the policy. More generally, the new policy foreshadowed efforts to develop new bureaucratic structures to deal with safety and security issues and to professionalize the staff who performed these duties.

Bloustein also charted a new course in a third area. In the 1960s, there had been a shrill debate over Department of Defense (DOD) funding of university research. That debate had not cut off the flow of government funding, much of it coming from the military, to research universities for both "pure" and "applied" research. In the more austere 1980s, with a skeptical Congress willing to limit federal support for research lacking immediate application to military problems, the National Association of State Universities and Land Grant Colleges asked Bloustein to testify in Washington on the need for continued military funding of university research. He did so in April 1981, arguing the case that the "university research base is in some considerable disrepair, and that more DOD support for research was needed to maintain the federal-university partnership."[8] Some faculty members responded that Bloustein had reversed a "hard-won victory" of the Vietnam era without seeking approval of the university community.[9] Bloustein disagreed. He deplored the past war and the renewed increase in military spending under President Reagan, but he held, nonetheless, that "no free people, no free universities, can long maintain their freedom if they remain aloof and removed from their government and if distrust and suspicion mark their dealings with one another."[10] At Rutgers, the DOD supported research in engineering, biology, food science, mathematics, computer science, and statistics, but the results of that research were, Bloustein stated, open to the public, and much of it was basic research without connection to military weaponry. The opposing positions having been eloquently stated, the debate itself withered and disappeared from university discourse.

Bloustein also struck a different posture toward student dissent and disruption. The university and the individual colleges all had policies on dissent and disruption during the 1960s, but these had seldom been invoked. Bloustein drew a distinction between political activism and civil disorder on campus. He criticized campus administrators for standing silent as demonstrators were "closing down an unpopular professor's classroom, . . . literally chasing military recruiters off the campus," "hooting down establishment speakers," and seizing campus buildings; he stated that the administration would "no longer condone civil disruption, no matter how noble the cause."[11] From this point forward, he concluded, once those involved in a civil disorder had been warned, they would, if the activity did not end, be arrested, suspended, and turned over to the civil authorities for prosecution. During the remainder of his time as president, Bloustein did, in fact, approve civil prosecution of some disruptive student protesters.

None of these steps fundamentally changed much on the campuses, but together they symbolized a cutting of ties with legacies of the Gross years and a recognition that Rutgers was now a different type of university—larger, less secure, more secular, and more diverse in the ways it defined itself. Ironically, the notion of "community" would be invoked with increasing frequency to describe the school's internal constituencies, even as a sense of the campus as a community slipped into the past.

Carrying Forward from the Gross Presidency

Bloustein's presidency began with a flourish, although not one of his making. In 1968, with Livingston about to open as a coeducational college, the Rutgers College faculty voted to admit women as well. Final say rested with the Board of Governors, and the faculty resolution set off three years of acrimonious debate in New Brunswick. To supporters, the admission of women represented a matter of justice, a recognition that other single-sex institutions had already taken the step, and a practical measure to attract better students, women and men, to the college. Opposition came from Douglass College Dean Margery S. Foster and Douglass faculty and alumnae. Douglass, they argued, offered an environment in which women could gain the skills and knowledge necessary to overcome the barriers that made them less than first-class citizens. Admitting women to Rutgers College would almost inevitably force Douglass to admit men, or, at the very least, make it more difficult to attract the best women students to the college. In October 1970, the board rejected the proposal and recommended more cross-registration among colleges by men and women students, but the next spring, after extensive lobbying by Rutgers College faculty and alumni, and the threat of a lawsuit, the board opened the door to coeducation at Rutgers College, finalizing the decision in September 1971, as the new president took over. In fall 1972, the first women, four hundred first-year and seventy-five transfer students, entered the college.

The acquisition of the Kilmer property in the early 1960s, and the creation of Livingston, also helped shape the long debate, extending into Bloustein's presidency, about the federated college plan in New Brunswick/Piscataway. While there was general agreement that students at Kilmer would live in small cluster colleges that integrated learning and living, ideas about the academic organization of these colleges ranged between two opposite positions. Like Douglass, Kilmer might be the home of one or more autonomous colleges, each with its own departments, faculty, academic responsibilities (admissions, curriculum) and resident life components. Alternatively, Kilmer could simply be home to residential units, with instructors drawn from Douglass and the Colleges for Men to teach at these units. As with coeducation, the deans of Douglass and the College for Men pushed for different plans. In this case, the balance was tipped by the newly appointed dean of what was to be Livingston College, Ernest Lynton, who fought for an autonomous college with a special mission. As plans for the new college emerged, however, the problem of how the faculties of autonomous colleges would be coordinated remained unresolved (as did the more general problem of the duplication of many college functions). The initial solution, approved by the Board of Governors in 1967, was to create a dean of the faculty of liberal arts—a short-lived position because it had little budgetary or personnel responsibility—and to allow

New Brunswick–wide departments to organize themselves, with New Brunswick chairs who reported to the provost, and coordinated hiring and curricular concerns. While some departments did just that, others did not.

The 1968 bond issue had included a modest commitment to develop the second cluster college on the Kilmer campus. Planning had begun in 1967, but the project never went forward; rather, under pressure from the state, the College of Agriculture and Environmental Science became Cook College, with a liberal arts orientation, and a partnership with Douglass College. There were now four residential liberal arts colleges in New Brunswick, each with its own faculty and curricular programs, as well as University College and the various professional schools.

As Bloustein arrived, then, the federated college system, except for the modestly used opportunity for students to take courses at other colleges, was only a shell of a structure. This changed rapidly. In March 1972, the university announced a restructuring of the administration, with provosts appointed for New Brunswick, Camden, and Newark, and the creation of a new position of vice president for student services. The New Brunswick provost, Kenneth Wheeler, would have many of the powers that had been denied the dean of the faculty of liberal arts, and he would move quickly to strengthen the role of the New Brunswick chairs. The new vice president would take responsibility for admissions, financial aid, and scheduling—all functions that had belonged until now to the individual colleges. The logic behind this restructuring reflected the growing complexity of the university more than particular concerns about the federated colleges in New Brunswick, but the result in New Brunswick clearly favored centralization.

The next year, Bloustein initiated one committee and Wheeler another to probe how efficiently and effectively the university was operating, and while they reached quite different conclusions about the problems and set off acrimonious debate in New Brunswick in various college facilities, the process resolved only to allow the current (1974) federated system to continue for at least an additional four-year test period. Bloustein's report to the board acknowledged that, in Richard P. McCormick's words, the "system was unbalanced on the side of college autonomy, with harmful consequences" for graduate education, research, and student services, but suggested nothing more radical at the moment than assuring students easier access to courses at colleges other than their own.[12] Nonetheless, by 1974, the federated plan had clearly shifted the balance between centralized and localized control in New Brunswick; one indication of this was the resignation in 1975 of the deans at both Douglass (Foster) and Cook (Charles E. Hess). When in 1978 McCormick drafted a history of the federated system, as background for a comprehensive review that the university undertook, he concluded that federation "survive[d] more as a consequence of stalemate than of consensus."[13]

In athletics, Bloustein faced another problem with its roots in the Gross administration. At the end of Gross's tenure, board members, led by David "Sonny" Werblin, had pushed for a more robust football program, something to take it beyond its "Ivy League" demeanor. Bloustein convened a committee to study the problem, giving faculty members an unusual degree of responsibility for athletic matters, and even before he had the report in hand (which warned of the pitfalls awaiting expansion of the athletics program), announced a university commitment to bigger-time athletics. He also replaced the athletic director and football coach, and appointed Frederick Gruninger to the former position, which Gruninger held until 1998. Under Bloustein, Rutgers increasingly adopted the sports profile of a big-time state university, eventually abandoned its status as an independent and joined a sports conference, accepted state aid to rebuild its football stadium, began systematic efforts through the Scarlet R Club to raise money for athletics, and embraced enthusiastically (while other schools dragged their feet) the opportunity to provide support for women's athletics. Not incorrectly, Bloustein is remembered by many outside the university as the president who did the most to develop the intercollegiate athletic program at the New Brunswick campus.

The university also committed itself to major new academic endeavors during Bloustein's initial years, highlighted by the establishment of three new schools. In 1974, the State Board of Higher Education (BHE), while considering a competing proposal from the College of Medicine and Dentistry (CMDNJ), gave Rutgers the green light for a new professional school to train psychology students for work in schools, clinics, and community centers. The newly constructed psychology building on Busch campus served as the administrative heart of the Graduate School of Applied and Professional Psychology (GSAPP), but it trained students in clinics around the state and even in New York. Its teachers, who mostly held part-time appointments at the university, worked in those same clinics. At Newark, the School of Criminal Justice opened in 1974 for its first class of graduate students: "seasoned police, parole and probation officers—and one inmate" (on release from Rahway State Prison).[14]

That same year, the BHE also selected Rutgers, along with Montclair
State College and Stockton State College, to become centers of influence
in the arts. The university's initial proposal, for a loose assemblage of arts
programs tied to the fine arts facilities at Douglass and Camden, had to be
substantially modified. The result was the blueprint for a new school for
the creative and performing arts in New Brunswick—what eventually became the Mason Gross School of the Arts—that shared faculty with college
programs (mostly at Douglass and Livingston) and offered both undergraduate and graduate degrees in such fields as studio art, music, theater,
and dance.

Program building, however, occurred against the backdrop of economic
chaos. The 1970s witnessed spiraling inflation, economic stagnation, and
higher education belt-tightening. No matter absorbed more of Bloustein's
time than preparing and explaining the budget and defending the university's request to the state for its annual appropriation. In every fiscal year
between 1971 and 1990, the state appropriation went up, from $57 million
in 1970–1971 to almost five times that figure by 1989–1990; but over that
same period the state's share of the Rutgers budget shrank from about half
to about one-third (primarily because overall revenues were increasing
faster than the state appropriation). The university was growing—in enrollments, physical plant, and the number of faculty and staff—and inflation ratcheted up the costs, so whatever the state appropriated was, as the
university saw it, it was never enough. Bloustein launched a $33 million
capital campaign, the first of its kind at Rutgers and an indication of the
new emphasis on fund-raising, but the state appropriation remained crucial. After the administration had devised a budget for the upcoming fiscal
year, the document went to the state BHE, where the chancellor (Ralph
Dungan in the early Bloustein years) usually reduced the request, merged
it with those from the state colleges, and sent it to the governor. The governor usually cut it again, then sent it on to the legislature. It did not help
that during much of this period Dungan and Bloustein battled quite publicly about the university's autonomy.

During Gross's presidency, administrators, faculty, and students had
generally rallied together to make the case to the legislature in Trenton
that various cuts had to be restored; this partnership continued, but it
became more problematic. State funding was tied to tuition, and increasingly the university turned to tuition revenues to make up anticipated
deficits—the cost of attending Rutgers, which had remained about $400 a

year from the mid-1950s until the early 1970s, went up virtually every year thereafter, becoming a larger share of the budget just as state appropriations became a smaller share. At the same time, the faculty, now represented by the American Association of University Professors (AAUP) in collective bargaining, engaged in protracted disputes with the administration, initially over personnel policy issues but eventually over salaries. Thus, natural alliances could and did collapse periodically.

Bloustein inherited not only budget woes but also a tradition of student protest, and as previously noted, he spoke out more strongly than had Gross about student disruptions of the campus, although he initially followed much the same policy. When students had seized Old Queens shortly after the invasion of Cambodia in May 1970, Gross had called them "my guests" and expressed sympathy with their protest. In May 1972, after Nixon announced the mining of North Vietnamese harbors, demonstrations occurred nationwide on campuses. At Rutgers, perhaps a thousand students surged across campus, occupying various buildings, including the College Avenue student center, Old Queens, and the ROTC building. Students also blocked traffic on College Avenue and disrupted the train line that ran through town (the latter resulting in numerous arrests by local police). Bloustein met with the students in Old Queens, listened to their demands, and negotiated their departure from the administration building. Subsequently, students occupied the ROTC building again, and stayed several days, while at Newark, college and high school students rallied downtown, and the faculty and students at the Law School sought ways to challenge the war legally. Bloustein rejected the demand that the university take a stand against the war, stated that ROTC would not be abolished, and promised disciplinary action if students continued to block access to university buildings; but he left the faculty free to adjust the time of their final exams in light of the disruptions. He initiated a review of university investments in war-related industries and formed a citizens' group to meet, as private individuals, with New Jersey's congressional delegates on a "journey for peace."

The 1970s also witnessed a continuation of African American student protest. Some of this involved unfulfilled promises—for example, protest over the demise of the Urban University Program—but more often anger in the new decade arose from the success in increasing the enrollment of African American students on all campuses, and in response to racial politics on the national level that left African Americans frustrated, angered, and beleaguered. There were new protests in 1971 on all campuses, including one by Puerto Rican students at Camden, and still more disruptive actions in 1973. At various times, black students staged a sit-in at a basketball game, withdrew large numbers of books from campus libraries, spilled food in the dining halls, and occupied campus buildings. Each protest was followed by negotiations, committee reports, and renewed efforts—many of these efforts outlined in Bloustein's letter to the community in May 1974, "Promises to Keep." Yet even as Rutgers became a university whose student body resembled more and more a cross-section of the state's population, African American students legitimately complained that retention and graduation rates for minorities were significantly lower than for other students, racism was prevalent on campus, and the university had not addressed the needs of black students in terms of housing, student life, and academic support. In 1979, and again in 1980, renewed protest occurred over the slow progress in fulfilling the promises of 1969.

From the very outset, Bloustein spoke about the need to end the unequal treatment of women at the university. It is probable, however, that neither he nor many of the higher-level administrators (all men) understood adequately the financial commitment or changes in institutional culture required to create a university in which women were as likely as men to be graduate students, faculty members, deans (or even president) and paid or supported as well as men in those positions. The existence of Douglass College, the creation of Livingston, and the admission of women to Rutgers College all opened doors to new possibilities but assured very little. The initial and most persistence push came from Douglass, where, before Bloustein's arrival, two junior faculty members, Elaine Showalter (English) and Mary Howard (sociology), sent their colleagues a report, *The Future of Douglass College, Women, and Education*, calling not only for ending inequalities at the university but for rethinking how the college, and by extension the university, ought to change to meet the needs of women. In spring 1971, a committee of the University Senate issued its own report calling for an ongoing, comprehensive study of inequalities at the university based on sex and for procedures and funding to correct them. In early 1972, Bloustein endorsed the committee's work and asked his deans to consider ways to meet the "need for women's studies, part-time and continuing education for women, graduate education for women, [and] part-time employment in relation to tenure and promotion."[15] At Newark, the response was lukewarm, as a group of women faculty questioned whether the very administrators who had denied women academic recognition in the past could be trusted to implement meaningful change—this at a time when 90 percent of the full professors at the university were men and half of the instructors (the lowest paid and least secure teaching position) were women.

Change came. It helped that there were a substantial number of women faculty already at the university, often working together at Douglass or in exceptional departments or schools, as did the many women, inspired by the women's movement, who returned to college as graduate students and who played key roles in changing departmental culture, especially in the humanities and social sciences. The introduction of women's studies programs, first at Douglass, but eventually at each college, including Newark and Camden; the development of majors in the disciplines out of what originally were only certificate programs; the creation of the Center for American Women and Politics and the Institute for Research on Women; and even the elaboration of New Brunswick intercollegiate athletic teams for women (something Douglass had had for more than a decade) all spoke to change occurring during the Bloustein years. Rutgers–New Brunswick graduate programs in English and history gained visibility and distinction for their commitment to women scholars and scholarship on women, and women's studies itself eventually acquired a graduate program and national recognition as a leader in the field. Inequality, of course, persisted—in salaries, in the percentage of women who were senior faculty members or top-level administrators, in the space allotted to women's programs, and even in the locker-room facilities for a new generation of women student athletes. Once again, in the mid-1980s, faculty women at Newark drew attention to the fact that Rutgers was not meeting its affirmative action goals successfully.

Undergraduates played a crucial role as well in campus dialogues about gender and sexuality. There were feminist groups at Douglass in the 1960s and a gay student organization at Rutgers College by 1969 (and at Newark and Camden in the early 1970s). In New Brunswick, the Gay Alliance staged its first "coming-out" day in fall 1970. New Brunswick women marched in the mid-1970s for safe streets and soon thereafter began to participate in the national "Take Back the Night" movement by walking between the Douglass and College Avenue campuses (and often confronting hecklers at the university's fraternity houses along Union Street). In the late 1980s, student protest helped initiate the first comprehensive survey of university employees about lesbian and gay concerns, with a subsequent report in 1989, from a committee chaired by James Anderson: "In Every Classroom: The Report of the President's Select Committee for Lesbian and Gay Concerns." Anderson, a professor in the School of Communication, Information, and Library Studies, was a gay activist and adviser to the New Brunswick campus Lesbian and Gay Alliance. His committee's report ranged broadly, as had previous reports on women's issues, from improving student life for gays and lesbians, to employee benefits for same-sex partners, to adding to the curriculum courses of interest to the gay community. In some areas, such as creating a less hostile environment for gay students at the university, there was a vigorous, ongoing effort to improve conditions; other issues would fall to Bloustein's successors.

A Crisis of Confidence

After six years as president, Bloustein faced a faculty revolt in fall 1977. The immediate cause was frustration over an impasse in collective bargaining between the university administration and the AAUP. The no-confidence votes that came from faculty meetings at many of the colleges, however, spoke to a second issue: an administration that had lost touch with its professors and increasingly governed without seeking their advice. These concerns were raised with special poignancy by the Douglass faculty, for whose college the federated system posed the greatest challenge, but they were echoed on each campus. Late in the spring, student governance bodies at the various New Brunswick/Piscataway campuses added their call for the president to resign, echoing faculty complaints but also expressing anger over the failure to take student opinions seriously when dealing with the ongoing problem of inadequate dormitory space for the ever-increasing student population. The administration and the Board of Governors initially responded that votes at faculty meetings were an inappropriate and transparent attempt to use these bodies to support the AAUP in a contract dispute, but Bloustein acknowledged that he had not done as well as his predecessor in listening to the faculty, and that doing so was virtually impossible given the changing role of the university president. The summary of his statement to faculty leaders on December 6, 1977, taken from the minutes of his administrative council, is worth quoting at length, as it captures his sense of the predicament:

Dr. Bloustein spoke of the personality differences between himself and his predecessor, Dr. Gross, which could be factors in the lessening of collegiality and of the change in higher education over the past decade from a climate of affluence to one of recession. In his term as president, Dr. Bloustein said he has had to find ways to continue the growth of the university with limited funds as the large sums of money for new growth were not forthcoming. Also, the attitude of the public toward higher education has changed in recent years, and it has been necessary for him as university president to spend much time outside the university at various public functions to promote public relations. He has also been occupied with bringing together all units of the burgeoning university structure into a whole; especially difficult were Newark and Camden, where problems were both fiscal and political.

Dr. Bloustein said he felt he had been selected by the Board of Governors . . . as one who could respond to the new trend toward accountability, to new requirements being imposed by state and federal Governments and [as] one who could bring to the public the identification of Rutgers as a state university. In discharging these responsibilities, he has been away from campus much of the time.[16]

At the university assembly convened in April 1978 to discuss these issues, Bloustein spoke bluntly, saying that upon his arrival he had faced "'a backlash of antipathy' of the public toward the university and higher education; hostility from the legislature, the executive branch of government [Brendan Byrne] and the chancellor of higher education [Dungan]; a series of crises in state funding, and a totally inadequate attempt at outside fundraising for the university."[17] Against his own inclinations, these problems had made him an "outside" president. Once the grievances had been aired and the contract issues resolved, however, the storm subsided with general agreement that the faculty needed a way, other than through the University Senate, to voice its concerns and advise on policy.

In June 1978, the semester behind him, Bloustein returned to Oxford for a sabbatical. He had survived a heart attack in March 1976 and had watched his wife struggle with an undefined and debilitating illness. In fall 1977, he mourned along with the rest of the Rutgers community the death of Mason Gross. It seems likely that while at Oxford, he pondered whether to continue as president.

Reorganization and the Push
to Become a Major Research University

Bloustein returned to the presidency, doing so as the provost, Kenneth Wheeler, was putting in motion a comprehensive review of the federated college system. Wheeler planned a two-step process: first, a committee would identify strengths and weaknesses in the system, then a second committee would recommend steps to correct the weaknesses. In March 1979, Committee I reported that it recognized "broad and formidable strengths" in undergraduate education under the federated college system but warned that graduate education was "fragmented, and subordinated to undergraduate needs"; professional schools too often ignored; research "handicapped"; and governance too "complicated."[18] Even as the first committee reported, Wheeler had already convened Committee II for what he stated was "probably the most important decision-making process in which the university has been involved in at least a quarter of a century."[19]

Committee II, however, essentially recommended maintaining the status quo, with the establishment of a new dean of the faculty of arts and sciences—a response that did not go far enough for Wheeler or the Rutgers College faculty, but was seen by students and faculty at Livingston, Cook, and Douglass as an attack on college autonomy. In early 1980, notwithstanding the opposition, Wheeler recommended to Bloustein a drastic reorganization of academic life in New Brunswick to bring the campus more in line with other large universities. The plan had two essential features, both of which survived heated debate. First, the individual departments in specific disciplines would be consolidated and located on one campus (thus distinct political science departments on each campus would become, for example, a single department on Douglass campus), and their chairs would report to a common dean of arts and sciences. Second, colleges would continue to set graduation requirements and retain student life functions, but would now have "fellows" drawn from the faculty rather than a resident college faculty. All majors would be open to all students and unified departments would offer courses in a discipline, subject only to the requirement that department offerings be available on each campus. Professional school students would affiliate with one of the five liberal arts colleges, but the schools themselves would remain, retaining their faculty and course offerings.

Bloustein had pointed the university in this direction, but now he stayed in the background, presumably because of the no-confidence crisis, allowing Wheeler to move the report forward. Bloustein endorsed Wheeler's proposal and sent the plan to the University Senate, which after much debate and by a narrow margin supported a modified federated system over Wheeler's reorganization proposal. The Board of Governors did not follow the senate's lead. It voted 7–2 in favor of reorganization, largely along the lines Bloustein and Wheeler had proposed, with implementation targeted for fall 1981. Wheeler charged seven new committees with the responsibility of directing the practical steps of reorganization—from physical consolidation of departments to the nature and responsibilities of college fellows. Implementation, which shaped academic life in New Brunswick/ Piscataway for the next three decades, involved countless small dramas (for example, the turf wars over which departments would be located on which campuses) and one major concession—that Cook would remain an autonomous professional school. The small dramas quickly faded from view. Members of new consolidated departments soon learned to work with each other; these departments now had a critical mass of faculty members to compete more readily for national recognition.

This was an exciting, contentious period for the university. Against the backdrop of the long debate on the federated system and reorganization, the university mounted and lost a campaign in 1979 for a new state bond issue, contributed to and then defended itself from the state's master plan for higher education, undertook reviews of the administrative structure of the university and of faculty governance, and began a systematic effort to upgrade graduate education and research.

The opening salvo in the struggle to improve graduate education came from Kenneth Wolfson, the dean of the graduate school in New Brunswick, in a spring 1976 speech to the graduate faculty. He compared Rutgers and the University of California at San Diego, whose cluster college organization seemed to parallel Rutgers's federated system, and noted that what truly set them apart was that at San Diego, graduate education was taken seriously. That school had been allotted $80 million in federal research grants the previous year, while Rutgers had received only $17 million; that school had forty-six members of the National Academy of Sciences, while Rutgers, with a faculty twice as large, had none. Graduate students, argued Wolfson, must become first-class citizens of the university; graduate directors must have the authority to make decisions about graduate education;

and, most crucially, hiring and promotion should be only of those "with the greatest potential to do original, creative and scholarly work."[20] Wolfson captured the tension between commitment to undergraduate teaching, on the one hand, and graduate teaching and research, on the other, which lay behind many of the debates of the 1970s as Rutgers moved toward becoming a research university. Wolfson's remarks previewed a comprehensive report, "Planning for Excellence, 1976–1981," issued by the executive vice president's office, which targeted the 1978 review of the federated system as the moment to correct the woeful neglect of graduate education.

The results were three interrelated actions that together launched the modern trajectory of graduate education at Rutgers. Under the direction of Daniel Gorenstein, a professor of mathematics, a special task force carried out a comprehensive review of graduate education throughout the university. It published two lengthy reports in 1981 and 1982, which were distributed in booklet form to the entire faculty, and provided the administration with a confidential evaluation and ranking of every graduate program. Those initial evaluations were supplemented in future years with periodic external reviews, and program rankings became a crucial element in the distribution of resources within the university. Put simply, strong programs that made good hires got to hire more faculty members. Second, as the review was proceeding, the university launched a new merit scholarship program for graduate education—the first step toward competing for the best applicants to Ph.D. programs. Third, the Graduate School itself was given more control over financial aid, both fellowships and teaching assistantships, and thus the economic resources to plan for excellence. While the approach tilted the balance toward already well-established disciplines, the fact was that few Rutgers graduate programs, with the exception of mathematics and physics, ranked nationally near the top of their disciplines. The result of these steps was to challenge most programs to improve their hiring and to put more emphasis on research accomplishments in their promotion procedures. The initiatives, however, also put Camden and Newark at a disadvantage, since aside from their law schools, they had few programs that compared favorably with New Brunswick, and these campuses more often supported master's work rather than Ph.D. programs. For the next decade, T. Alexander Pond, a physicist whom Bloustein brought to Rutgers in 1982 as the new executive vice president, spearheaded the drive to acquire and focus the resources Rutgers needed to become a major research university.

Nothing more clearly symbolized the new priorities at the university than the rapid addition of centers, bureaus, and institutes (CBIs). As with so many other trends at Rutgers, this too was a nationwide development, especially at large research universities. Most CBIs were interdisciplinary, located in the natural sciences, and funded in part by grants (or "soft money"). Most were also alphabet organizations, known campuswide by their initials. The participating faculty did little or no undergraduate teaching, and their grant-supported research generally had practical applications. Rutgers had a few centers before the 1970s—the Center for Alcohol Studies, the Institute for Microbiology (later Waksman Institute), and the Bureau for Economic Research, for example, but during Bloustein's presidency, especially in the 1980s, the numbers of CBIs grew enormously, to perhaps four dozen, on every campus but Camden. The impetus for many of the new centers was passage of the 1984 bond issue (see below).

Some illustrative examples provide a better sense of the changes. In 1984, the university established the Center for Advanced Food Technology (CAFT) at Cook to partner with the food industry on questions of food safety and quality. Later, CAFT opened an additional Piscataway center to supply laboratory space for food testing to New Jersey companies. In the field of ceramics, which had been part of the School of Engineering since the end of World War II, Rutgers had a long, distinguished tradition, which included grant-supported laboratories and small-scale centers. This tradition, and the close connection of the department to industrial leaders in the field, led to the department's selection by the National Science Foundation (NSF) in 1982 as the site for the Center for Ceramic Research (later named for Malcolm G. McLaren, who led the department from 1969 to 1994). In 1988, as a direct result of the approval of the 1984 bond issue, the CCR moved into a new building, by which time an associated program, Fiber Optics Materials Research, had been approved and likewise funded by the state. A third example was the establishment in 1989 of the Institute of Marine and Coastal Sciences (IMCS). IMCS drew its faculty from several departments at Cook and its funding from government sources such as the NSF and the National Oceanic and Atmospheric Administration (NOAA). Research work on the protection and sustainability of marine resources had both practical consequences and underwrote a broad ecological outreach program for K–12 education.

The university established a few CBIs in the social sciences and humanities as well. There was a cluster of centers on the Douglass campus focusing on women and politics, the Center for the Critical Analysis of Contemporary Culture (CCACC, founded by the New Brunswick English Department), the Rutgers Center for Historical Analysis (RCHA, founded by the New Brunswick history department), and the Center for Urban Policy Research (CUPR) on the Kilmer campus. Although they were less likely than the science centers to attract major grants and foundation support, these centers shared with the others an interdisciplinary focus and a close association with graduate research. Of particular note, however, was a new center, established under the direction of David Mechanic. The Center for Health, Health Care Policy, and Aging Research bridged the traditional divide between the sciences and the humanities and social sciences, and its attention to some of the nation's most pressing public health problems allowed it to attract major government and foundation support.

In 1985, the Rutgers-Newark administration created from its long-standing Institute of Animal Behavior a new Center for Molecular and Behavioral Neuroscience (CMBN), which strengthened Newark's graduate programs and helped bring in more grant support. Newark's other major center had actually come to the campus years earlier, when historian Marshall Stearns had transferred to Rutgers, with Mason Gross's encouragement, his massive personal collection of recordings, private papers, and memorabilia documenting the history of jazz. Stearns had long advised the Department of State on cultural matters, traveled and lectured worldwide, and, through an extensive network of contacts, developed an unparalleled collection of materials. In 1984, the Institute of Jazz Studies became part of the university library system; in the 1990s, it moved to a new home in a remodeled Dana Library.

Debate over reorganization and the new emphasis on graduate education pushed to the back burner the question of faculty governance that had been one cause of the 1976 no-confidence votes. After those votes, Bloustein had established the Joint Committee on University Governance, chaired by Richard P. McCormick. Its 1979 report suggested that faculty governance had become a problem throughout higher education because of "the rise of student power," reduced faculty leverage in a tight job market, growing federal regulation, legal challenges to university autonomy, and the development of bureaucratic structures. Given the already convulsive reorganization of the New Brunswick campus, the committee's primary recommendation—periodic review and reappointment of central administrators—was modest. Almost a decade later, McCormick's son,

Richard L. McCormick, chaired a new committee on faculty governance in New Brunswick, this time responding to criticism by the recent Middle States accreditation visitors. The committee reported that "[t]he greatest deficiency in departmental governance . . . is the remoteness of depart-ments from power and authority. Recommendations that are formulated by conscientious committees and accepted by a vote of the faculty may leave the department and go into a black hole."[21] The result was the cre-ation of a New Brunswick Faculty Council, which reported to the pro-vost and represented departments across the schools in New Brunswick/ Piscataway. In 1991, a somewhat similar body was established at Newark, and, much later, at Camden as well. Unlike the University Senate, which included students and administrators, these newly formed bodies repre-sented a faculty voice on matters of campuswide concern.

Building a Great University Takes Money

In the 1980s, Rutgers still struggled to balance its budget, but the context of the financial crisis had changed. Less inflation and more economic growth in the mid-1980s made it possible for states to renew investment in higher education, and a number of governors, including New Jersey's Thomas Kean, advocated just that. Budget requests were still sliced (but not as much), argued over, and filled in with tuition money (more than ever), but Kean envisioned a high-technology partnership between the state and Rutgers that would provide long-term benefits to both. Voters had approved a $155 million higher education bond referendum in 1971 and defeated another in 1979. With Kean's support, a $90 million "Jobs, Science, and Technology" bond issue in 1984 and a $350 million higher education bond referendum in 1988 gained voter approval, the latter despite a stock market tumble a year earlier.

The groundwork for this electoral success had begun in 1984 with the establishment of a committee composed of top state business leaders and chaired by Harold W. Sonn, the CEO of Public Service Electric & Gas, to survey the "future financing of Rutgers." That committee argued that additional state funds could launch Rutgers into the ranks of elite pub-lic institutions, and from its recommendations came the establishment of the "Fund for Distinction," which combined university investment and rental income, corporate and individual fund-raising, and the realloca-tion of tuition revenues (used, until now, primarily to close the annual budget deficit). As a result, tuition, which had been going up steadily but modestly for more than half a decade, jumped in fall 1985 by an extraordinary 15 percent. The successful "Campaign for Rutgers" followed, with a $125 million target, strong support from Governor Kean, and leadership from throughout the New Jersey business community. In 1990, the student newspaper summarized, "[s]ix years of unprecedented fund raising culminated . . . with the announcement that the Campaign for Rutgers exceeded its goals by 34 percent and raised more than $166 million" from more than forty-eight thousand donors.[22]

Money mattered. Two tangible benefits of state support and aggressive fund-raising stand out. Improved salaries for the faculty allowed Rutgers to compete for, hire, and retain outstanding scholars and researchers. There had, of course, always been a market for scholars, but most faculty members moved once, or not at all, during the course of their careers. Whatever impetus there was to move came from elite private institutions that hired away what they perceived as the best state university scholars and researchers. In the 1980s, the market became far more competitive, faculty members began moving several times during their careers, and many public research universities began to challenge elite private schools for outstanding faculty members. The growth of research-oriented schools, both private and public, also weakened the institutional ties that had once linked a faculty member to a particular institution. CBIs as well as more generous sabbatical policies meant that public universities could offer reduced teaching responsibilities and more time to do research.

During the 1980s, Rutgers strengthened its faculty just as it did its graduate programs by targeting areas of excellence and paying what the market required to build programs. Not all the faculty members supported this approach to allocating resources (especially if they felt it hurt undergraduate education), and thus the direction given by Bloustein, Pond, Gorenstein, and other academic leaders looms large in Rutgers's ascent in the 1980s to the ranks of the top public research universities.

Money also underwrote the continued expansion of the school's physical plant in its four urban locations. The value of buildings and grounds increased from about $250 million, when Bloustein became president, to over $500 million by 1980–1981, and to more than $1.2 billion in 1989–1990—and at the end of that fiscal year, the university had fifty-one new projects under construction at a projected cost of more than $300 million (including new homes for Marine Sciences on the Cook campus and the Center for Molecular and Behavioral Neuroscience at Newark).

Details make a difference, but here I will limit myself to two. First, students paid more than they had in the 1970s and 1980s, but they also received more. The university built bigger and better dorms (now called residence halls), student centers, and recreational facilities, and much of the future building would be directed to upgrading (and replacing) these buildings in order to continue to compete for students. Second, both Newark and Camden expanded. For example, in 1973, shortly after the dedication of a new $5 million building for the Graduate School of Business Administration at Newark, the board committed itself to a set of projects on the Newark campus at a cost of $15.5 million. A new gymnasium (slowed by yet another back-and-forth between Rutgers and the Board of Higher Education), parking deck, additions to the student center (now named for Paul Robeson) and to Dana Library, and renovations of Bradley Hall were set in motion, and all were completed by 1979. At Camden, the board approved a new fine arts building that encompassed performance spaces as well as offices and classrooms, and it was to be located across the street from the next project, a new gymnasium. Camden and Newark, both of which had been commuter campuses, saw their first residence halls in the 1980s—the Camden Tower in 1986, and graduate student housing at Newark in 1987, followed by Woodward Hall for undergraduates in 1990. Both campuses remained largely commuter schools, but the new residence halls strengthened campus life and helped define the colleges as urban universities.

Just as consequential was a building program undertaken, not by Rutgers itself, but within New Brunswick. By the late 1960s, the city had reached a crossroads. No longer an industrial center, its downtown shopping district undercut by suburban shopping malls, and with congested city streets and too many single-family residences being converted to student apartments, New Brunswick was on the decline. A cash-starved city government (to which Rutgers made only modest contributions in lieu of taxes) had difficulty providing adequate services to its citizens, a fact highlighted by racial protests in 1967. Johnson & Johnson (J&J), the pharmaceutical company and the city's leading private employer, after considering leaving for the suburbs, spearheaded a massive redevelopment program. Bloustein participated in the initial planning discussions, and provost Kenneth Wheeler sat on the board of New Brunswick Tomorrow, the public relations arm of the initiative. Bloustein also gave crucial support for the improvement of Route 18, which aroused serious opposition from Rutgers students because the road now ran directly behind the river dorms, and from historical preservationists, because the extension of the project across the Raritan destroyed a section of the historic canal that ran along the river.

The real muscle behind the project came from Devco, the New Brunswick Development Corporation—a private corporation, but with a quasi-public character, in which J&J but not Rutgers played a major role. With key backing from New Brunswick's mayor, John Lynch Jr. (1979–1991), Devco coupled federal, local, corporate, and private funding to rebuild much of the land along the Raritan River waterfront (and in the process to obliterate the old Hiram Market district). In 1976, J&J committed to establishing in New Brunswick its new world headquarters, designed by renowned architect I. M. Pei and completed in 1982; further along the Raritan, it sponsored the building of the Hyatt Regency Hotel. The John Lynch Bridge across the Raritan opened in 1980 (the pillars had been standing in the river since 1970); new retail shops, restaurants, and office buildings followed. Further afield, the relocation of George Street Playhouse, begun by a Rutgers graduate student in 1969, to Livingston Avenue helped seed a theater-restaurant district, which also became the home of the Mason Gross School of the Arts (and later the Bloustein School). Much of this was financed through Devco, or with subsidies from J&J. Student apartments were built south of the main campus, an ambitious development of luxury apartments were constructed along the Raritan in the late 1990s, and the older, high-rise, public-housing Memorial Homes were eventually demolished in 2001. Building continued apace into the second decade of the twenty-first century. Some long-term residents of the city felt bulldozed, literally and politically, by urban renewal projects that fundamentally altered the landscape adjoining the oldest New Brunswick campus of the state university.[23]

The protest that most marked the post-Vietnam years of Bloustein's presidency, however, was not over New Brunswick redevelopment but rather over the question of whether the university should withdraw its investments from companies doing business in South Africa. "Divestiture" was part of a larger strategy to put economic pressure on the South African government to end apartheid. At Rutgers, faculty members, students, and Robert Tanksley, coordinator of religious affairs, first raised the issue in fall

1977. A University Senate committee brought in two reports on divestiture. The majority report, authored by economics professor Sidney Simon, argued that the university could best effect change in South Africa by using its corporate voting rights to pressure these companies and cautioned that corporate withdrawal from South Africa could have devastating consequences for the very South African people whom protesters wished to help. The minority report, from Leila Sadat, a student senator from Douglass College, called for divestiture and questioned proxy voting as an ineffective strategy. Little would change in the terms of the debate over the next decade.

The University Senate sent the majority report back to committee for reconsideration, and passed a motion, introduced by Bloustein, condemning the repressive measures of the South African government as "beyond the pale of the behavior of civilized nations."[24] The resolution also called for a "Day of Concern for South Africa," which was held in early spring. After additional hearings, the senate recommended partial divestiture, a company-by-company investigation of operating practice in South Africa, and decisions about whether to divest based on that investigation. The Board of Governors accepted and strengthened the senate recommendation, and the university proceeded to review investments totaling perhaps $10 million in two dozen or more companies. While at least two board members shared the views of student and faculty protesters that total divestiture was morally necessary, Bloustein argued that entanglement with money connected to South Africa was more pervasive than people realized, and that the board had taken the most constructive approach to the problem. In the fall, the Board of Trustees gave its approval as well.

But the debate did not end. Forums and protests about divestiture continued into the early 1980s, increasingly sparked by a national campus movement and a sense that the new Republican administration in Washington had eased up pressure on South Africa. The 1984–1985 school year signaled the high-water mark. A number of student groups, some representing black and Hispanic students separately, others cross-ethnic coalitions, protested. Angry students blocked traffic on College Avenue, marched on meetings of the Board of Trustees and the Board of Governors, and staged a hunger strike. Assemblyman Alan Karcher, who had sponsored a bill to divest New Jersey pension funds, appeared on campus, as did the Reverend Jesse Jackson, who in the spring drew a crowd estimated

at more than five thousand people. The board remained committed to partial divestiture—the yardstick was now whether or not a company abided
by principles formulated by Reverend Leon Sullivan for socially responsible employment practices—and Bloustein supported its position. The
president also participated as a private citizen in a demonstration at the
South African Consulate in New York City and was arrested for disorderly
conduct. Finally, that summer, prodded by a senate recommendation for
total divestment, both boards heard from their own investment committee
that the university should divest. With final votes that fall, Rutgers joined
a growing list of universities that ended investments in companies doing
business with South Africa.

By Way of Conclusion: AAU Membership

The capstone of President Bloustein's leadership came in February 1989
with an invitation to Rutgers for membership in the Association of
American Universities (AAU). An exceptionally selective body, the AAU
consisted of only fifty-six member schools, split fairly evenly between
elite private schools, such as Harvard and Stanford, and public research
universities such as North Carolina and Wisconsin. In the academic
climate of late-twentieth-century America, when university prestige
and access to federal research dollars were mutually reinforcing factors,
Rutgers had climbed a significant hurdle. In doing so, it took a giant
step forward that many other schools failed to make—and was achieved
by even fewer that had essentially been liberal arts colleges in the post–
World War II era. Behind that step lay several factors. New Brunswick
academic reorganization created consolidated departments that compared
favorably in many disciplines with the best in the country. Bond money
built new research facilities, state money funded graduate fellowships,
and external grants underwrote the expansion of CBIs. Without strong
leadership, much of this might not have happened. That leadership came
from Bloustein himself; from those like Pond, Gorenstein, Wolfson, and
Wheeler, whom Bloustein had wisely appointed; and from many faculty
members, like Richard P. McCormick, who fought for the same goal. In
addition, as Bloustein acknowledged in his public statement about AAU
membership, the propitious relationship with the state during Thomas
Kean's terms as governor had helped make Rutgers a state university of
which New Jersey's citizens could be proud.

3

Negotiating Excellence

The Presidencies of Francis L. Lawrence
and Richard L. McCormick

In 1989, in Beijing's Tiananmen Square, China's military crushed protesters demanding greater democracy. That same year, pro-democracy protests swept across Soviet-controlled eastern Europe; when Mikhail Gorbachev rejected a military response, the breakup of the Soviet empire began. A year later, Iraq's invasion of Kuwait, and the threat it posed to Western interests in Middle Eastern oil, led to multinational intervention in the Persian Gulf War. For the students of the 1990s and the early twenty-first century, the Cold War was history, China was now the world's second-most dominant power, and armed conflict was a daily reality in the Middle East, Pakistan, and Afghanistan. The attacks of September 11, 2001, on the World Trade Center and the Pentagon became for these students what Pearl Harbor and the Kennedy assassination had been for earlier generations of Americans—a tragedy that was equally a moment of redefinition. Here, however, the outcome was the "War on Terror," played out alongside a volatile global economy, climate change, and the politics of oil and water.

American campuses were not immune to these events, but this time the college response had none of the potency of Vietnam-era protests. Students moved out of the humanities and into professional programs. They worried about finding jobs and paying tuition debt, or served in the military. Because of taxpayers' anger, state governments, which in the past had provided much of the financial support for the expansion of public higher education, could not continue to fund public universities as they had in the past. Political leaders campaigned on the promise to slash budgets; while they generally kept on spending, the money went, not to education, but to transportation, medical programs, or assistance to senior citizens. Educational leaders pointed out the benefits to the economy from university-based research, but the message was not always heard by politicians. State governments continued to fund public education, but far less generously; even more so than in the 1980s, public spending was in the form of loans and grants for students rather than money that went directly to universities.

Now, as Rutgers negotiated the path to continued excellence, lobbying for state support while concurrently finding new revenue sources became crucial. Public universities increasingly couched their appeals to state legislatures in terms of "restricted/committed" and "unrestricted/uncommitted" budgetary categories, pointing out that even small cuts in state support had a devastating impact on their schools because so much of a budget was earmarked inflexibly to salaries and fixed operating costs. Somewhat paradoxically, flagship state research universities, strapped as they were for operating revenues, registered billion-dollar budgets and mounted billion-dollar capital campaigns. Inflation concealed a slower economic growth rate, but the sheer size of university operations required attention to issues of organization, management, and efficiency (often to the disdain of traditional liberal arts faculties). Athletics became ever more important to administrators trying to market their schools to students and donors, just as medical schools were essential to universities that wanted a larger share of federal research support. As one commentator saw it, the old "A&M" (agricultural and mechanical) attached to many of the historical federal land-grant colleges might as well have come to mean "athletic & medical."[1] Private, for-profit schools created serious competition for traditional colleges, just as distance-learning programs did for traditional classroom teaching. M.A. programs proliferated, both because students equated professional degrees with job opportunities, and because the M.A. students brought in additional revenue. To many of the better students, an M.A. in the twenty-first century seemed the equivalent of what a B.A. or B.S. from a liberal arts college had signified a half-century before.

Most large schools, especially research-oriented state universities, re-committed themselves to undergraduate education and rewrote mission statements to explain the connection between research and undergraduate teaching. This era also witnessed, however, a troubling, contentious insertion of the nation's political conflicts—the culture wars—into academe. Debates in the public schools about the teaching of creation science and pitched school-board fights over the content of history textbooks affected the educational preparation students received before moving on to college. Critics of higher education attacked "area studies programs"—an inclusive category that might mean anything from women's to Middle Eastern studies—both for undermining the traditional college curriculum and for imposing a politically correct orthodoxy on students. University faculties faced new political obstacles in obtaining government dollars for embryonic stem cell research and investigations of climate change.

Within this context—the struggle for adequate state funding, a renewed commitment to undergraduates, and campaigns to reconnect universities to their several constituencies—the administrations of Francis L. Lawrence and Richard L. McCormick unfolded. President Bloustein had led Rutgers into the Association of American Universities (the elite public and private schools in America and Canada) after a sustained pursuit of "excellence." For Lawrence and McCormick, the challenge was to improve on the progress Rutgers had made. They faced the same problems that beset the world of higher education more generally but also some challenges particular to Rutgers. The university had no medical school, and it had a costly but poorly performing football program. In almost every index, Rutgers ranked near the bottom in state funding. Its satellite campuses at Newark and Camden were starved for resources. Undergraduate education in New Brunswick had not been ignored, but it had been put on the back burner as Rutgers worked to improve its standing as a research university. These were some of the challenges of negotiating excellence over the coming two and a half decades.

Francis L. Lawrence

Rhode Island–born Francis L. Lawrence, Rutgers's eighteenth president, was educated at St. Louis University, and earned a Ph.D. from Tulane in 1962 in French literature. He remained at Tulane thereafter as a professor and administrator. He chaired the French Department and served as academic vice president, provost, and dean of the graduate school before coming to Rutgers. As a senior administrator, he led efforts to end sex discrimination in pay scales at Tulane and to increase the enrollment of minority students at the university. In fall 1990, *Rutgers Magazine*, the alumni publication, introduced him at his new school as "a relatively unknown professional educator who has spent more than three decades quietly helping Tulane University earn a reputation as 'the Harvard of the South.'"[2] He faced unprecedented challenges as president, as the financial climate for higher education darkened nationally, and the growth of the university budget required ever more attention to planning and administration. Internally, he had to deal with student complaints about what they perceived as the imbalance of research over teaching and with their anger over annual tuition hikes. Continuing agitation about an inadequate commitment to minority issues and mounting concern about issues affecting gay and lesbian members of the community would also define his presidency.

In the late 1980s, President Bloustein had asked each of the campus provosts to undertake a review of undergraduate education in the context of a research university. The New Brunswick faculty had already begun the task through a series of academic forums, and the campus report, written by Barry Qualls, an English professor, spoke to the need for major curricular reform. Similar reports were forthcoming from Newark and Camden. In "Undergraduate Education at Rutgers: An Agenda for the Nineties," Lawrence reviewed these reports as well as numerous national studies that reached similar conclusions. What they all noted, he said, was a decided shift in faculty responsibilities "away from undergraduate instruction to graduate instruction or no instruction at all."[3] Teaching was seldom rewarded (especially in awarding tenure) and undergraduate class size had increased. Lawrence praised undergraduate instruction at Rutgers, but said the university had to provide help to the faculty in enhancing their teaching skills; Rutgers also needed better classrooms and methods of teaching evaluation, shorter class periods (most were eighty minutes, not the fifty-minute standard at other schools), and more awards for distinguished teaching. In addition, Lawrence reported, the university had to reevaluate the curriculum, especially in math and the sciences. The goal, the president stated, was to create a "university-wide environment for students, faculty, and staff that is open, civil, supportive, disciplined, caring, and just."[4]

Lawrence recognized that what many faculty members wanted was reassurance that the traditional college emphasis on teaching undergraduates had not atrophied as the university had grown and become more centralized. Lawrence did just that. The first step, taken in response to student concerns, was to provide a new building for the Math and Science Learning Center on Busch campus. A year later, in 1991, the university established Learning Resource Centers at Camden, Newark, and various campuses in New Brunswick/Piscataway. The new centers were modeled on the Educational Resource Center at Tulane, and the first director, Karen Smith, came to Rutgers from Lawrence's former school. The centers taught study skills and provided peer tutoring, as well as some supplemental instruction in basic introductory courses, to complement the already-established programs in New Brunswick/Piscataway.

Both the University Senate and a faculty academic forum had urged the creation of teaching centers. By fall 1992, the university had Teaching Excellence Centers on all three campuses. As Gary Gigliotti, a professor of economics and director of the New Brunswick center, explained: "Most teaching techniques have remained the same for hundreds of years and I don't think in the modern world they're very effective. Going into a lecture hall with just chalk and a blackboard to face 400 kids who are used to MTV doesn't work very well."[5] The centers focused on using technology in newly equipped "smart" classrooms, providing individual assistance to professors on teaching techniques and computer skills, and overseeing the distribution and analysis of mandatory student teaching evaluations (a program begun, in fact, by the students themselves in the early 1970s but subsequently made a university procedure and linked to the promotion process).

Other changes were less dramatic. The university had recognized distinguished teaching with the creation in 1986 of the Warren I. Susman Award, named for the recently deceased historian who had written the first post–World War II plan for reforming the undergraduate curriculum at Rutgers College. Under Lawrence, numerous academic units created their own teaching awards, and the university awards more often took into account Camden and Newark professors. But promotion, the ultimate faculty reward, was governed by standards set during the Bloustein years. Teaching was important, but never to the extent that it could offset less than distinguished research accomplishments. Nor did the Lawrence years see major curricular changes. The curriculum itself was in the hands of individual college faculties or fellows, and thus change occurred piecemeal. Nor did the proposal for shorter class periods get support from the faculty, who preferred teaching twice a week for eighty minutes to three times a week for fifty.

Along with concerns about undergraduate education, Lawrence also inherited virtually catastrophic budget problems. In the late 1980s, the nationwide recession and its ripple effects in New Jersey had undercut even Governor Thomas Kean's strong support for public higher education. In response to the state's underfunding of Rutgers's 1989–1990 (FY90) budget request, Bloustein had convened a Budget Advisory Group; in spring 1990, T. Alexander Pond, who had become interim president after Bloustein's death in December 1989, reconvened this group to deal with what were clearly the dire consequences for Rutgers of Governor James Florio's FY91 state budget. Florio, a Democrat, shared with his Republican counterpart Kean a commitment to higher education, and he had the backing of the state's most powerful Democratic politician, John Lynch Jr.; but with shrinking tax revenues and taxpayer anger, fiscal belt-tightening was inevitable. Florio announced a university budget cut that was more than the cost of running the entire Camden campus. Projects planned with funds from the 1988 bond issue had to be delayed or shelved, enrollments and tuition increased, reserved funds tapped, and hiring frozen. Lawrence faced these problems from the moment he arrived in fall 1990. Between FY89 and FY93, the cumulative cuts to the Rutgers budget totaled almost $100 million (that is, a little less than a third of the total state appropriation for Rutgers in any given year).

The Budget Advisory Group attempted to spread the cuts among the various constituencies within the university, while minimizing the damage to instruction. Tuition increases continued, as did efforts to ensure that all faculty members were teaching full-time (to meet enrollment demands). The university even considered, but did not implement, a proposal to stop paying negotiated faculty salary increases out of its reserves (when state money was not forthcoming). These measures were announced by the university's new vice president for academic affairs, Joseph J. Seneca, an economist and former chair of the state's Economic Policy Committee. Lawrence also led an effort to convince the state to improve Rutgers funding. Both through testimony in Trenton, and with the publication of "The Joint Future of New Jersey and Rutgers, The State University of New Jersey," he made the case that an investment in Rutgers helped both the state and the university.

As state appropriations shrank (or, in some years, failed to keep up with the rising costs of running the school), the university relentlessly, albeit reluctantly, raised tuition each year. The state's Tuition Assistance Grants usually kept up with the increases in tuition, but they helped only those need-based students who were eligible. In spring 1992, when Florio announced his FY93 state budget (recommending no new cuts to Rutgers's budget, but making the previous years' cuts permanent), he introduced a new program, called the Tuition Stabilization Incentive Program (TSIP). In return for a tuition increase of no more than 4.5 percent, the state would add $8.8 million to the Rutgers budget. After Rutgers committed itself to the bargain, the budget process unraveled in Trenton into a furious partisan fight, which ended with a final appropriations bill, passed over the governor's veto, slashing additional funds from Rutgers.

Tuition policy occasioned student protest. Students disrupted meetings of the Board of Governors and occupied various campus buildings. A new student group, CARE (Campaign for an Affordable Education), emerged and for several years staged disruptive protests, underscoring the anger of students. Arrests, civil prosecution, convictions, fines, and community service became commonplace. At most, these protests may have held off even larger tuition increases (see chapter 6).

Budget problems also affected the faculty. Contract negotiations led not only to particular salary settlements but also to three significant changes in personnel policy. Since the 1970s, many universities had fought to prevent the unionization of teaching assistants (TAs). Universities claimed that the pay TAs received was a stipend to support their research (not a salary), and that their teaching was training for their career (not a job). At Rutgers, however, the problem never arose, as teaching assistants had been included in the faculty union, the American Association of University Professors (AAUP), since the beginning of collective bargaining in the early 1970s. Union representation made a difference in their careers. The AAUP stopped the practice of fractionalizing TA lines. A line included state health care benefits, and if a line was split among two or more students (a common practice), all lost their medical benefits. The union also negotiated workload standards to keep teaching assistants from being assigned too many discussion sections or laboratory classes. Part-time lecturers (PTLs), however, did not have union protection. Throughout higher education, schools used PTLs to address budget problems—such lecturers provided low-paid but often highly skilled classroom instruction, and their employment allowed enrollments to increase without the hiring of new full-time faculty. The academic marketplace abounded with stories of PTLs who traveled from school to school each semester, teaching four or even five different courses, and who were paid a very modest amount per course, while unable to find tenure-track employment. In 1988, after a year-long organizing effort at Rutgers by the AAUP, part-time lecturers at Rutgers approved AAUP representation. In summer 1991, with Lawrence's arrival and Richard Norman taking over as chief university negotiator, the AAUP and the university signed the first contract for part-time lecturers.

The third negotiated change in personnel policy came over the issue of merit pay for faculty. Through the 1980s, faculty raises had traditionally been "across the board"—essentially, a percentage increase applied to each professor's current salary. In 1989, the university proposed awarding raises instead on the basis of merit. Merit rewards, the administration contended, reflected the goals of a research university. The AAUP believed strongly in the equity of the existing relationship, and distrusted, equally strongly, the top-down mechanisms that might be used to determine who was (and was not) meritorious. In the end, the university and the AAUP compromised. The 1990 contract (for 1989–1992) included a provision for enhanced merit pay, in addition to across-the-board raises, and the contract finalized in 1993 (for 1992–1995), after bitter dispute about merit pay, again included money set aside for merit-based salary increments. In future contracts, faculty members would receive their raises half in merit pay and half in across-the-board increases, with departments having the initial and primary say in defining and rewarding merit. A proposal raised during the last year of the Bloustein administration thus became established policy under Lawrence.

The budget situation improved modestly in the mid-1990s, and tuition increases stabilized at around 5 percent. Taking a longer view, there was a basic continuity between the Bloustein and Lawrence years. The overall Rutgers budget went up annually (even when state revenues shrank), as it was driven by government grants and contracts brought in by the university's research orientation, as well as by enrollments and separately funded instructional programs. Revenue, which had been at about $735 million when Lawrence arrived, topped $1 billion dollars in FY95, and was around $1.3 billion when he resigned in early 2002. As during the Bloustein years, the state's portion of that revenue decreased a little each year, and the tuition component generally went up each year. The most encouraging aspect of this picture was the steady growth of state and federally funded research money, from some $92 million in FY90 to $242 million in FY02, when Lawrence left office. Very little of this was unique to Rutgers. The same pattern prevailed at other state-funded AAU research universities, as they, too, struggled to maintain excellence.

Under Governor Christine Todd Whitman, the budgeting process changed in one particularly dramatic way. In April 1994, Whitman named some of the state's most prominent educational leaders, including Lawrence, Harold Shapiro (president of Princeton University), and Mary Hartman (dean of Douglass College) to a committee charged with considering how to abolish the New Jersey Department of Higher Education. Hartman chaired the committee. (It is worth noting that the first major policy initiative of New Jersey's first female governor was led by a woman. Hartman, after leaving the position of dean, helped create university programs to develop women's leadership.) The committee's recommendations informed the Higher Education Restructuring Act of 1994. The act abolished the DHE and replaced it with a citizens' advisory group, the Commission on Higher Education, and a council of university presidents, which also had advisory responsibilities. The commission could recommend budget priorities, but individual state-school budget requests now went directly to the Department of the Treasury. The measure addressed Whitman's campaign promise to reduce spending and bureaucracy and gave schools greater autonomy. It also, however, removed an official and a cabinet-level agency that more often than not had been an advocate for higher education.

Budget woes had a dramatic impact as well on building projects. Rutgers proceeded with three of the four phases of construction undertaken with 1988 bond funds, moneys that were supplemented by state appropriations, gifts, and federal grants, but as those projects were completed, far fewer new ones were undertaken. In FY92, the university had sixty-five projects under construction, valued at $254 million; by FY95, virtually all the bond issue projects were completed, and new construction amounted to but $37 million. Among the most impressive additions to the New Brunswick campus in the last phase of bond-funded construction was the $21 million building complex, dedicated in 1993, for the Institute of Marine and Coastal Science on the Cook campus. The institute had been established in 1989; in 1992, the federal government designated it as a national underwater research center (one of six in the country). The institute's new complex, which included a three-story office and conference center, and a research facility with a thirty-four-thousand-gallon seawater storage capacity, facilitated programs to protect the state's coastal estuaries and wetlands and help its marine industries. As a national underwater research center, the institute brought in $2 million annually in federal support.

Cook campus was also the location of Foran Hall, a $32 million Agricultural Biotechnology and Plant/Life Science complex, and the accompanying Chang Science Library, with two-thirds of the construction cost picked up by the 1988 bond issue and the remainder funded by the U.S. Department of Agriculture. The building housed faculty researchers working in agricultural molecular biology (AgBiotech)—again bringing grant money to the university—but also included classrooms and the new library. Other projects—additions to Dana Library at Newark, Alexander Library in New Brunswick, and the Camden Library, as well as the expansion of some of the student centers—brought the building program funded by the bond issue to a successful conclusion. Not until 2012, however, would New Jersey voters again support a higher education initiative.

As bond money ran out, Rutgers turned for financing to the New Jersey Higher Education Facilities Trust fund (HEFT) and the Higher Education Equipment Leasing Fund Program, both recently created and administered by the Whitman administration. Construction increased. In 1996, the Board of Governors approved the building of a new Center for Law and Justice at Newark, underwritten by $20 million from the HEFT fund, $25 million in general obligation bonds, and $4 million in gifts. Completed in 2000, and home to both the Law School and the School of Criminal Justice, the building was one of the largest such projects in Rutgers's history and a stunning architectural structure, with a spiral staircase rising from an entry atrium and classrooms designed to assure that interactive education—the tradition of Socratic dialogue—would flourish. At Camden, completion in 2001 of the 5.5-acre Community Park project west of the main campus provided much-needed varsity sport and recreational playing fields as well as a neighborhood playground. Such construction, which might have been dismissed as incidental twenty years earlier, was critical to student life at a campus now committed to attracting a residential student body and building relations with the surrounding city. In Piscataway, ground was broken in 1997 for phase II of the Science and Engineering Resource Center, then called SERC II, which would become the $10 million Allison Road Classroom Building, known widely as ARC, when it opened in 1998. HEFT money financed the project, which included a five hundred–seat lecture hall (one of the largest at Rutgers), more than a dozen classrooms, computer labs, and space for the Mathematics and Science Learning Center. Perhaps the most significant building project undertaken by the Lawrence administration was not fashioned from brick and concrete: a new computer network for the campus. The strategic planning process (described below) that Lawrence undertook emphasized the need for a basic technology infrastructure at the university. Most other AAU schools had upgraded their campus networks before 1994, when Rutgers began planning RUNet 2000. The goal was to provide a reliable, high-speed network in all the university's residence halls, academic buildings, and administrative sites, and, in fact, by the new century, Rutgers had done just that.

From FY96 on, then, Rutgers renewed its building program. By FY00, the school had $247 million in projects under construction or in design—about the same situation when the Lawrence administration began. But the renewed building program hid two facts about the physical development of the campus: the oldest campus, College Avenue, remained much as it had been in the 1960s, with no new classroom space and little renovation. That, in turn, reflected the fact that it was easier to find funds to build new buildings, especially for centers and institutes with links to government and industry, than to maintain older construction, and deferred maintenance became an increasingly worrying presence for the university.

Lawrence also inherited the previous administration's concern for gay and lesbian rights. As noted above, an organized gay rights movement had existed at Rutgers–New Brunswick since the late 1960s (with smaller movements at Camden and Newark since the early 1970s). The Gay Alliance, founded in 1969, became the Rutgers University Lesbian/Gay Alliance (RULGA) in the late 1980s; throughout that period the alliance sponsored events for gay and lesbian students and worked to win greater acceptance of gays and lesbians among the larger Rutgers community. During that same period, however, there were constant reminders—vicious graffiti, verbal abuse, letters to student newspapers, and antigay protest—of homophobia and intolerance.

A typical story, told anonymously in a sexual orientation survey done in 1987, captured what life could be like for gay and lesbian students: "Last April some other members of the RU Lesbian/Gay Alliance were tabling at Brower Commons. A discussion began which led to another man's coming up to the table, saying 'You gays make me sick,' and [he] proceeded to vomit (induced) onto the table, nearly hitting me and another [student]. He jumped the table grabbing another by the face."[6]

RULGA leaders called on Bloustein to address the issue. Their protest, as we have seen, led to a committee report, "In Every Classroom," and

later, under Lawrence in 1992, the establishment of the Office of Diverse
Community Affairs and Lesbian-Gay Concerns. Cheryl Clark became the
first director of the new office. Clark had arrived at Rutgers in 1969 as a
graduate student; she was a respected poet who brought to her work feminist, lesbian, gay, and African American perspectives, and she had been an
adviser for RULGA. The report and the establishment of the new office,
however, left two seemingly intractable problems for the administration
to address.

Since 1972, Rutgers had subscribed to an equal-employment and affirmative action policy; in 1981, that policy was amended to include sexual
orientation. In addition, Governor Florio had issued an executive order
prohibiting discrimination (in state agencies) based on sexual orientation. But Rutgers condoned such discrimination in two areas, one tied to
the federal government and one to the state government. The university's
ROTC program barred gays and lesbians, and thus kept these students
from receiving the scholarship benefits for which other students were eligible. Rutgers, unlike some universities with traditions of student protest,
had retained its ROTC program in the Vietnam era, for reasons that persisted: the program provided substantial tuition benefits to the students
who joined and provided the military services with college-trained officers. In the wake of "In Every Classroom," the incongruity between the
commitment to end discrimination and the continued policy of ROTC was
obvious. T. Alexander Pond, who as acting president had to address the
question, joined other AAU presidents in calling on the Defense Department to change its policy. He also barred ROTC students from receiving
supplemental financial aid awards from the university and directed that
any Rutgers publication that made reference to ROTC was required to note
its policy of discrimination.

The second problem was that Rutgers provided no employment benefits for same-sex partners of gay and lesbian employees. Benefits were
paid by the state through state-run plans, and only the legislature could
change coverage policy. Acting President Pond stated that Rutgers's provision of same-sex partners benefits independent of the state plan might be
an opening wedge for the state to pass on the benefit costs to the university
more generally. Members of the gay community argued otherwise. Initially
the Lawrence administration considered the possibility of independent
university financing but eventually settled for nothing more than a lobbying effort to change state policy. Resolution of both these problems would

not come for almost two decades, through federal and state action rather than directly by Rutgers.

Lawrence's most ambitious undertaking was to launch, soon after his arrival, a systemwide strategic planning process. Working from the faculty up, through departments and other academic units, each campus articulated goals that could contribute to excellence (still the coin of academic prestige) within the constraints of less robust public support for higher education. The New Brunswick plan, for example, argued that the principles of excellence, centrality, need, diversity, and cost-effectiveness should determine the ways in which scarce resources could best be marshaled to protect demonstrated strengths, particularly in the Faculty of Arts and Sciences, but identified as well strengths across the schools, bureaus, and institutes on the campus. The campus plans, complemented by self-studies by specific administrative units, a marketing survey, and the Quality in Communication Improvement project, had the ultimate goal of providing a flexible, five-year strategy of boosting Rutgers's standing in the elite world of public AAU schools.

In fall 1995, Lawrence appointed thirteen implementation committees in academic growth areas. The committees ranged across the curriculum— from arts and sciences generally, to fields such as cognitive science and neuroscience, international studies, creative arts, public policy and the law, gender studies, education, and environmental sciences. Lawrence himself chaired the committee on international studies, a testimony to the time he spent traveling overseas and working to establish academic relationships with foreign schools. The committees sent their recommendations for specific initiatives to the Board of Governors, and those recommendations then served as the basis for reallocation of resources, requests for state money, and fund-raising. The plan charted a trajectory that the administration hoped would put Rutgers in the top quartile of the AAU by 2010.

It is difficult to determine whether the planning process changed the culture of spending within the university. Since the early 1980s, any planning process had begun with external evaluations of university departments and units, followed by recommendations from a small committee of senior professors (the Committee on Standards and Priorities in Academic Development). After 1995, money continued to go to strong departments that could present a good case for unique opportunities to improve or that could wrestle funding from the government. The plan also raised expectations that were not always fulfilled. Strategic planning did, however, involve many faculty members in setting university priorities, reaffirmed the Lawrence administration's commitment to excellence, and highlighted the development of Camden and Newark as well as New Brunswick/Piscataway.

The plan also reaffirmed the Lawrence administration's commitment to undergraduate education. One of the programs targeted for support under the strategic plan was the Douglass Project for Rutgers Women in Math, Science, and Engineering. Established in 1986 with a state grant, and long directed by Ellen Mappen, the Douglass project provided support and encouragement for Rutgers women interested in fields such as mathematics, chemistry, mechanical engineering, and computer science. First-year courses and summer internships gave women research opportunities in the sciences, and the Bunting-Cobb Math Science Residence Hall allowed participating students to live alongside graduate student mentors in their fields and provided them with computers (at a time when they were not yet commonplace on campuses). The project also sent college women into the high schools to make girls aware of the opportunities in the sciences; partnered with other Rutgers programs, such as the Center for Discrete Mathematics and Theoretical Computer Science, to offer outreach programs; and attracted foundation support for its innovative work.

The saddest moment in Lawrence's presidency grew out of a statement he made in November 1994 when addressing the Camden faculty. In response to a question about standardized tests and minority admissions, Lawrence stated that "disadvantaged" students did poorly on these tests because of their "genetic hereditary background."[7] The entire session with the faculty was being taped, and in January 1995, the Newark *Star-Ledger* reported the comments, setting off a firestorm of public criticism and student demonstrations. Lawrence immediately apologized for his "wounding words," acknowledged that the ideas encompassed by his statement were "monstrously perverse," and explained that his statement did not reflect his true thinking.[8] In impassioned testimony before the Board of Governors in February, a Newark student leader called for Lawrence's resignation, while African American history professor Clement Price, who had participated in the "grand struggle" at Conklin Hall in 1969, responded that "Fran Lawrence is a decent man. . . . Our struggle should be about justice, not revenge." The board, along with many African American faculty members, all of whom expressed shock at the comments, rallied behind Lawrence, noting his commitment to Rutgers's goals of improving the admission and retention of minority students; Governor Whitman concurred. During the remainder of his presidency, Lawrence would redouble efforts to improve diversity and civility on campus.

In a largely unrelated move in summer 1995, a group of the most distinguished professors at Rutgers drafted a petition criticizing Lawrence's leadership and his failure to consult the faculty. Those who spoke publically were worried about what they considered a decline since Bloustein's death in Rutgers's status as an elite research university. When word of the petition appeared in the press, the board issued a lengthy statement supporting the president and applauding the strategic planning process he had initiated. The board noted that Lawrence had helped restore balance between teaching and research and that he had done so while struggling with the very difficult financial situation prevailing throughout higher education. Not until December did the professors actually present their petition to the board, shortly after the New Brunswick Faculty Council had defeated an effort to hold a no-confidence vote on the president. The board stood firm, and the controversy died. While much was different in the mid-1990s criticism of Lawrence from that which had been directed at Bloustein twenty years earlier, in both cases the challenge had come from faculty members who felt that their voices were no longer being heard as the university grew in size and complexity.

What to some looked like slippage was, to the administration, prudent belt tightening and tough policy choices to maintain existing strengths or to venture into particularly rewarding new areas. The 1984 bond issue (voters did not approve a 1990s equivalent) had launched new centers in biotechnology and medicine, computer aids for industrial productivity, fiber optics and plastics recycling, as well as an enormous expansion of existing research efforts in ceramics, food technology, and fisheries and aquaculture. All were thriving a decade later, and all had established crucial links to the state's economy.

Although new CBIs were added more slowly, several major academic initiatives of the 1990s were noteworthy in confirming a pattern of solid growth despite tough economic times. Rutgers, in partnership with Princeton University and AT&T Bell Laboratories, established the Center for Discrete Mathematics and Theoretical Computer Science (DIMACS), and it flourished initially under the direction of Daniel Gorenstein, aided by a $22 million, eleven-year grant from the National Science Foundation. When the initial grant expired, DIMACS continued to operate, having made contributions in a wide variety of fields.

Discrete mathematics treats very large numerical data sets, in which each element is a whole number (hence discrete), and analyzes (usually with computer algorithms) how best to arrange or sequence the numbers. Much of the center's early work centered on improving telecommunications networks and understanding biological processes (work undertaken in conjunction with the Waksman Institute of Microbiology). Other projects contributed to such diverse fields as environmental science, agriculture, and epidemiology. In the wake of the September 11 attacks, DIMACS assisted the Department of Homeland Security in developing ways to detect hidden nuclear materials. The center also sponsored an extensive program for New Jersey secondary school teachers. The defining features of the center—applied, collaborative research, federal and state funding, and outreach to the larger community—reflected more generally the role of CBIs in modern research universities.

Another initiative led to the establishment in New Brunswick of the Center for the Study of Jewish Life. The center, first conceived in 1994, combined academic initiatives with outreach to the third-largest Jewish community in the United States, helped to incorporate existing programs into a new department in Jewish studies, and raised more money through the University Foundation than any other center in the humanities. Starting in 2000, the center hosted an annual Jewish film festival, which presented independent films from around the world. It also created a Holocaust resource center that focused broadly on racism, genocide, and discrimination, and designed programs for secondary school teachers.

In 1997, Rutgers attracted neuroscientist Wise Young to the university from NYU, where he had helped to develop a highly effective therapy for spinal cord injuries. Young established a new center in the Nelson Biological Laboratory on Busch campus in order to continue studying the problem. Collaborative, interdisciplinary work was central to research on spinal cord, brain, and genetic disorders of the nervous system, all areas now being explored at the new center. Coupled with the existing Newark Center for Molecular and Behavioral Neurology, whose research focused on "language-based learning disabilities and drug therapies for neurological disorders," Young's center made Rutgers a recognized leader in a crucial and rapidly developing field.[9] A foundation grant in the same year helped establish the Center for Management and Entrepreneurship (CME) in Camden's School of Business. CME specifically targeted south Jersey's small businesses, offering training in developing entrepreneurial

3. Francis L. Lawrence and a student from the Camden LEAP Academy. Rutgers professor Gloria Bonilla-Santiago championed the opening in fall 1997 in Camden of one of New Jersey's first charter schools, LEAP Academy (Leadership, Education, and Partnership). LEAP began with extended school days; an extended school year; a focus on math, science, and technology; and a kindergarten-to-fifth-grade student population that would expand by one grade each year. Rutgers and LEAP partnered in training teachers and providing support services for the students. LEAP reflected the greater emphasis during the Lawrence administration on contributing to the university's host communities.

PHOTOGRAPHER: Nick Romanenko. Source: R-Photo: presidential photographs.

approaches to their management problems. Here the source of funding came not from government, traditional educational foundations, or a company hoping to benefit directly through partnership with the university, but rather from a charitable foundation set up by a local south Jersey business and political leader—a link that had become even more crucial in the cash-starved 1990s.

In the late 1990s, the Lawrence administration established in Newark the Institute on Ethnicity, Culture, and the Modern Experience, under the direction of history professor Clement Price. In the early 1970s, Price had been among the first African Americans to obtain a history Ph.D. at Rutgers; soon thereafter, he joined the Newark faculty. The preeminent authority on the black experience in New Jersey and the history of Newark, Price had established in 1981, with Giles Wright, the Marion Thompson Wright lecture series (named for the African American historian and teacher whose work documented school segregation in New Jersey). The series brought to Newark each year one of the foremost commentators on the black experience. The series was melded into the activities of the new center, which also sponsored postdoctoral scholarship, helped commemorate Newark's African American past, worked with the city's public school teachers, and introduced in 2005 an innovative annual ethnic dance concert. Among its endeavors were programs remembering the 1967 Newark riots and the 1969 takeover by African American students of Conklin Hall on the Newark campus.

In addition to seeking government and foundation support, the university launched an ambitious capital campaign. Targeting areas identified by strategic planning as central to the university's development, and with significant input from the faculty as to specific needs, the administration began in 1998 a six-year drive to raise $500 million—an ambitious sum, given past performance, but considerably less than what many of Rutgers's peer institutions were seeking during the same era. Forty-two months into the campaign, as Lawrence was about to leave office, the "Rutgers Campaign: Creating the Future Today" had brought in $377 million. Overall, fund-raising had risen from approximately $27 million annually at the time of Lawrence's arrival to about $123 million annually when he stepped down.

With fund-raising came more serious attention to marketing the university—an inevitable consequence of the competition for undergraduate enrollments and tuition revenue. Like other state universities, Rutgers had long projected images of itself in terms of academic distinction and its contributions to the state's economy, health, and environment, and the Lawrence administration, as noted above, did so even more energetically in response to the budget crisis. But marketing, or what the next decade would call "branding," carried this process a step further into the world of advertising. The licensing of various university trademarks had begun under Bloustein in the mid-1980s; a decade later, Rutgers had entered into almost two hundred agreements to market its name or logos. Revenue and name recognition went hand in hand. During Lawrence's presidency, the most visible change came with the introduction of new athletic logos, one for each campus: Scarlet Knights (New Brunswick/Piscataway), Scarlet Raiders (Newark), and Scarlet Raptors (Camden)—each destined for countless products. Such marketing differed little from what had long occurred nationwide; as elsewhere, here also it exposed the university to criticism about its increasingly corporate personality.

Other criticism of the university focused on athletics. Lawrence, more so than most of his predecessors, was a sports fan, and he oversaw the university's move to big-time athletics. A member of the Atlantic Ten Conference in all sports except football, Rutgers joined the Big East Conference as a football school in 1991, then joined for all other sports in 1995—moves that increased the visibility of the program (and the university), as well as its potential costs. The university also rebuilt its football stadium in the early 1990s with support of state bond money, and, more generally, upgraded its athletic facilities throughout the decade. In 1998, when long-serving Athletic Director Frederick Gruninger announced his retirement, Lawrence, under pressure from Governor Whitman, appointed Robert E. Mulcahy, the president of the New Jersey Sports and Exposition Authority, to replace him. Mulcahy embarked on a hiring and spending program to accomplish what had eluded Rutgers for two decades: the fielding of truly competitive football and men's basketball teams. In women's sports, after the departure of Theresa Grentz in 1995, Lawrence and Gruninger hired C. Vivian Stringer, one of the most accomplished basketball coaches in the nation, and one of the few African Americans who had coached elite programs. She went on to lead the Rutgers women's team to a title game for the national championship. Lawrence also established committees to assure that athletes were not being short-changed academically and to assure that Rutgers was meeting its commitment under Title IX to women's sports. In the meantime, faculty critics were calling for a fundamental reconsideration of the university's commitment to big-time athletics (see chapter 10).

In early February 2002, Francis Lawrence announced his resignation. He had been the president of Rutgers for twelve years and had served through the terms of three governors. He had seen the university though some of its most troubled fiscal years. The press speculated that political pressures originating in Trenton had forced Lawrence to leave. Perhaps in part to counter these rumors, four former chairs of the Board of Governors joined the current chair in drafting a commentary praising Lawrence's achievements: attention to undergraduate education, increased commitment of resources to the Newark and Camden campuses, strategic planning to make the university more than a collection of its separate parts, and RUNet 2000. They concluded: "Lawrence did not seek the spotlight. Nor did it fall on him at moments of triumph, such as when he successfully negotiated the first smooth transition to a new contract with the AAUP in memory. . . . Or when he chaired the Kellogg Commission study on life-long learning, whose report is now considered a model for public universities around the country. Or when $222.4 million in research grants were awarded to Rutgers faculty for programs ranging from literature to spinal cord injuries."[10] A subsequent offer by Governor James McGreevey to assist in the search for a new president was turned down bluntly by Board of Governors chair Gene O'Hara, who well understood the risks to university autonomy of allowing politicians an even greater say in how and by whom the school was administered. Lawrence stayed on through the spring and summer of 2002, and then Norman Samuels, who as provost had helped guide the Newark campus through its most dynamic period of growth, stepped in as interim president while the university conducted a national search for new leadership.

Richard L. McCormick

No one could have been better prepared to become president of Rutgers than Richard L. McCormick. Born in New Brunswick, he grew up in Piscataway, New Jersey, just across the Raritan River from the oldest of the Rutgers campuses. His father, Richard P., was a professor of history who became historian of the university. His mother, Katheryne, taught mathematics and chemistry at the New Jersey College for Women and later became the New Brunswick scheduling officer. He attended school in Piscataway, went to Amherst (to which Rutgers College was often compared in the 1950s), and then pursued a Ph.D. at Yale University, where he studied under C. Vann Woodward, a distinguished historian of the post–Civil War American South. In 1976, McCormick joined Rutgers as a historian of American political history; with the publication of his first book, which dealt with New York electoral politics in the era of Theodore Roosevelt, he was awarded tenure in 1981 as an associate professor. As a scholar, his efforts to unite newer work on the ethnic and religious determinants of voting behavior with more traditional studies of public policy made him a rising star in the profession; at the same time, he began to take a more active role in department and university affairs. In 1987, he became chair of the history department and, less than two years later, dean of the Faculty of Arts and Sciences. He helped to establish the Rutgers Center for Historical Analysis (one of the few centers in the humanities at a time when such facilities were proliferating in the sciences) and to launch the Faculty Council (a faculty-only body that advised the New Brunswick provost). In 1992, McCormick accepted the position of provost at the University of North Carolina, Chapel Hill. In 1995, he was named president of the University of Washington. Thus, when McCormick returned to Rutgers, he had an insider's knowledge of the university's organization and culture, a national reputation as a scholar, and executive experience at two large state universities that shared many of the same aspirations as New Jersey's state university.

Within a year, however, stories in the *Seattle Times*, retold in the New Jersey press, disrupted his welcome at Rutgers. McCormick had engaged in an extramarital affair at Washington, and he came to Rutgers only after the regents at the University of Washington had lost confidence in the job he was doing. This did little to erode the support McCormick had received initially from the faculty, but it is less clear how it affected his relationship with the Board of Governors and the public's perception of his leadership.

McCormick's presidency began and ended with plans for a merger between the university and the University of Medicine and Dentistry of New Jersey (UMDNJ). In October 2002, with the search for a new president stalled (because McCormick had temporarily withdrawn his name from consideration), the Board of Governors had asked Norman Samuels, then provost at Newark, to step in as interim president. It was Samuels who had to initiate consideration by the Rutgers faculty of a New Jersey health sciences report, brought in by a state committee chaired by Roy Vagelos. Vagelos had enjoyed a distinguished academic career as a biochemistry researcher before moving in 1975 to the Merck Sharp & Dohme Research Laboratories, of which he became the CEO in 1984.

Vagelos's committee proposed to Governor James McGreevey a major restructuring of New Jersey's research universities, and Vagelos, with McGreevey's backing, became a vigorous proponent of its recommendations. Acknowledging the distinguished record of UMDNJ in community health services but documenting the relatively low ranking of the school in various areas of medical research and its top-heavy administrative structure, the report advocated merging various geographical components of the medical school into three distinct universities located at the three existing Rutgers's campuses (and including the New Jersey Institute of Technology at Newark). Each campus would become a stand-alone research university, but remain part of a statewide system, with a chancellor and board of regents for the system as a whole. While the report discussed the benefits of such a restructuring to nonmedical education, the foundation of the recommendation was a belief that local autonomy at Newark, Camden, and New Brunswick/Piscataway would facilitate collaborative medical research and healthy competition for state and federal support. At the time of McCormick's arrival, the implications of the report were a matter of speculation and debate. One possibility was a complete restructuring of public higher education in New Jersey that would have created three autonomous state schools, with a chancellor to whom all three would report.

Discussions about the merger stretched over much of 2003. Coming from two schools whose strengths included major medical centers, McCormick clearly understood the value of adding a medical school to the university, and he felt pressured by the governor to complete the merger. But Vagelos's planning committee, of which McCormick was a member, could not reach a compromise that would answer faculty concerns about the proposal's impact on fields other than the medical and biological sciences, nor did it address concerns of the Board of Governors about governance and finance. As a result, both Rutgers and the governor by December 2003 announced an end to the effort to restructure higher education in the state. Roy Vagelos, whom McGreevey had appointed to the board, cast the lone dissenting vote on the final decision. Shortly thereafter, he resigned.

Most university presidents think of themselves as faculty leaders, although the days in which a president at Rutgers could actually know a significant portion of the faculty had long since passed. The problems posed by the university's size and bureaucratic complexity to a president who needed to be a faculty leader were compounded by the periodic and often bitter disputes with the faculty union over contract terms. Through his annual addresses, e-mail messages, frequent campus appearances, and policy initiatives, McCormick attempted to correct the problem to which Edward Bloustein had first called attention. One of his initiatives was "Garden State 101," a traveling seminar for new faculty. The seminar, like one that McCormick had introduced at the University of Washington, was an annual multiday bus trip around the state for a group of newly hired faculty members and McCormick. The trip was designed to familiarize participants with the diversity of New Jersey's economy and communities, and, reciprocally, to show the state's inhabitants the university's connection to their lives. In the first tour, in late spring 2004, the bus made stops in Trenton, Atlantic City, Camden, and Newark; in Lambertville for a meeting with New Jersey mayors; along the Delaware and Raritan Canal; in Weehawken to survey the redevelopment of the Hudson River waterfront; and at a farm in Alla-muchy, for a discussion about smart growth and agriculture. The program remained popular until late in the decade when budget cutbacks brought it to an end.

The cancellation of "Garden State 101" was symptomatic of a larger problem. One of the greatest challenges faced by the McCormick admin-istration was improving Rutgers as a research and teaching institution de-spite state budget cuts. What had been an up-and-down roller coaster ride for the Lawrence administration became a swift descent during McCor-mick's administration, one cut after another in state funding.

Public institutions of higher education were facing similar problems across the nation, but it is worth recalling the factors that distinguished budgeting at Rutgers. Rutgers had fourteen different employee unions representing four out of five of its employees, and faculty salaries were settled by collective bargaining with the AAUP/AFT. (In 2005, the AAUP affiliated with the American Federation of Teachers.) The state was asked to fund negotiated salary increases at Rutgers, but it was not obligated to do so, and historically had never done so fully. Contracts covered several years, which meant that the economic circumstances at the time a settle-ment was made between Rutgers and its unions could change drastically before it ran out; the arrival of a new governor in Trenton could also negate assumptions about state funding that had informed the initial agreement. Under Bloustein and Lawrence, increases in tuition had been used to offset shortfalls in state appropriations, but as economic conditions deteriorated nationally, the state legislated a cap on tuition increases. Legislative con-tacts and relations with the governor shaped the bargaining that went on; but even the best of relations had to deal with the fact that annual cuts in state spending were likely during the decade, and that higher education was no longer a top priority for New Jersey's political leaders.

Throughout the 1990s and into the twenty-first century, university presi-dents have complained each year about the failure of state governments to fund adequately public higher education. Rutgers was not alone. Com-plaints, so frequently expressed, one astute and generally sympathetic histo-rian of higher education argued, became tiresome, little more than "chronic whining," and not particularly persuasive when schools had billion-dollar budgets, endowments, and capital campaigns.[11] At the same time, massive cuts to the operating budgets of state schools in Wisconsin, Virginia, and California, as well as New Jersey, stand apart from this recurring dialogue of underfunding. At the very least, these cuts have undermined the distinctive research missions of the flagship schools and pushed increasingly heavy burdens of debt onto middle-class, tuition-paying students—with long-term consequences that remain to be seen.

The paradoxical dimensions of Rutgers's predicament are worth discussion. Overall revenues and expenditures at Rutgers have risen virtually every year, passing, as I have noted, $1 billion under Lawrence and then $2 billion under McCormick. How did Rutgers square this growth with the persistent complaints about underfunding? State appropriations actually went up haltingly through FY01 (July 1, 2000–June 30, 2001), fluctuated through FY06, then began a downhill slide. At the same time, measured in real dollars (what a dollar buys today versus what it had bought in a base year in the past), calculated as a percentage of the overall state budget, or considered as a share of Rutgers revenue, the downward trend has been continuous. This pattern has persisted regardless of the administration in Trenton, under Democrats as well as Republicans. Growth, then, has been financed by tuition increases, and, just as important, by the vigorous pursuit of federal and state grants, along with foundation and donor support. Under Lawrence, research awards to Rutgers faculty members had grown from about $93 million (FY90) to approximately $242 million (FY02); under McCormick, awards peaked at $434 million (FY10) and hovered at around $400 million during the two last years of his administration. The success of the administration and faculty in securing external support was perhaps the most important index of Rutgers's growing prominence as a public research university. This same growth has made it increasingly vulnerable to cuts in other sources of funding needed to maintain the infrastructure on which teaching and research depend—everything from basic building maintenance and security to attracting and retaining distinguished faculty.

While state funding was never adequate, as the university saw it, some years were far worse than others. On several occasions, budget cuts made in Trenton occasioned crises in Old Queens and on the university's campuses. McCormick arrived at Rutgers just as Governor James McGreevey was announcing that Rutgers would have to absorb almost $40 million in cuts to its operating budget (14 percent)—after having absorbed unanticipated midyear cuts in the two previous years in what the state had already promised the university. Then, in March 2006, Governor Jon Corzine's first budget message brought the disquieting news that shrinking tax revenues were forcing a 15 percent reduction in state spending and a cut of some $50 million in state appropriation for Rutgers. Later, in spring 2009, in the midst of a global economic crisis and a state recession that affected employment and taxes (as well as university investments and fund-raising), Corzine again called for drastic cuts in state spending, and Rutgers faced a major shortfall in its state appropriation. Chris Christie, elected in fall 2009 on a platform of tax reform and with a promise to cut state spending, not only reduced the FY11 Rutgers state appropriation but also capped state pension contributions and increased employees' contributions to benefit plans—steps that were occurring nationwide for public employees.

For a typical student, all of this meant paying more—to the tune of $600 to $700 a year—for less. Fewer class offerings; larger class sizes. For a typical custodial worker, it meant that Rutgers would no longer offer English language and citizenship instruction. The cuts usually meant staff layoffs and the cancellation of new faculty searches. With each cut, the university did what it could to protect its teaching mission, but in so doing, it had to apportion disproportionate cuts to vital operating units, which, as noted above, created long-term problems in maintaining the basic infrastructure of the campuses. Few of these mundane matters were of interest to the general public or to Trenton legislators, although the need to eliminate six intercollegiate Olympic sports in New Brunswick in response to budget problems did gain media attention and occasion an ultimately unsuccessful campaign to reverse the decision.

In this context of a decade of state budget cuts, the McCormick administration negotiated four faculty union contracts or memoranda of agreement. The negotiations for an agreement to cover 2003–2007 extended almost a year beyond the expiration of the previous contract. McCormick explained the administration's position in numerous e-mails to the faculty. The union threatened a fall job action, staged a sit-in at Old Queens (led by teaching assistants who carried a coffin down College Avenue to the building), stormed McCormick's office after the university tried to declare an impasse in the negotiations, and presented the Board of Governors with a cake under a placard that declared "Let Them Eat Cake." (Everyone helped consume the cake after the board meeting, a better outcome than what ultimately befell Marie Antoinette.) A mediator brought negotiations to conclusion. In the future, McCormick withdrew from a public role in negotiations—a recognition that such discussions tended to proceed better with minimum publicity, but also a testimony to the difficulty a university president had both in being a faculty leader and in negotiating with the faculty about their salaries.

The 2007–2011 contract was reached on schedule. It included innovative provisions for increasing the number of faculty and for family leave; but the FY09 Corzine budget cuts pushed both sides to a memorandum of agreement that deferred contractual raises. Governor Christie's initial budget triggered an outright salary freeze by the university in June 2010, and the freeze became a major impediment to the negotiation of a new contract for 2011. The eventual contract extension did little more than belatedly restore previously frozen salary dollars. A significant minority of the faculty voted against the settlement—a strikingly unusual occurrence in the long history of labor negotiations at the university. The friction created by the triangular discourse among the state, the university, and AAUP/AFT paralleled what was happening elsewhere in the nation. In Wisconsin, the story was more drastic, as public employees lost their collective-bargaining rights altogether, but there and in New Jersey, a decade of sustained budgetary struggles demoralized the faculty and further eroded public appreciation of the state university as a partner of the state.

For what tuition and state appropriations could not cover, and research grants to its faculty did not bring in, the McCormick administration turned to better marketing, improvements in alumni relations, and a new capital campaign—all part of the common coin of fund-raising for higher education. The university adopted the athletic department's block "R" as its most ubiquitous branding symbol, created an unofficial university seal to make recognition simpler and clearer, and posted the school's new motto, "Jersey Roots, Global Reach," on billboards and buses around the state. In 2006, the Board of Governors made all this official policy by approving a uniform visual identity system. A year later the board approved McCormick's plan for a new Rutgers University Alumni Association. When McCormick arrived, Rutgers had perhaps three hundred thousand alumni, half of whom lived in New Jersey, but less than 10 percent of whom gave to the university (far less than at many comparable state universities). There were almost two dozen distinct alumni organizations, including the venerable Rutgers Alumni Association and Associate Alumnae of Douglass College (the latter particularly successful at cementing school loyalty and fund-raising). These organizations were not eliminated, but a new umbrella organization, with no requirement for dues payments, was created. The alumni magazine went to each member several times a year (along with appeals for support), with the university paying the costs. Against the backdrop of a nationwide recession and state budget crises, the step was a gamble to improve a relationship vital to the future of the university.

The third prong in the strategy to make Rutgers more self-supporting was a new capital campaign. Even by the standards of public universities, Rutgers had a small endowment (approximately half a billion dollars). Like Lawrence before him, McCormick launched an ambitious capital campaign; like Lawrence he struggled to secure major gifts from specific donors; and like Lawrence he left office before the goal of the campaign was met. McCormick had inherited Lawrence's half-billion-dollar capital campaign and brought it to completion with some $615 million raised by 2004. "Our Rutgers, Our Future," the administration's new campaign, set its sights on a billion-dollar target, and by 2012 had brought in a little more than $600 million. Given the economy, the result was better than many expected.

McCormick's fund-raising had a critical impact on undergraduate education. In fall 2004, the university announced a gift from Jerome and Lorraine Aresty, money that would go to developing a center, named in their honor, to involve undergraduates in faculty research projects. Students would learn research skills early in their career at Rutgers, pursue their own projects, and, while doing so, assist faculty members with their research. Many of these students would carry such skills into their major field of study and use them in capstone or thesis courses as seniors. A second gift, from John Jr. and Dorothy Byrne, launched in 2007 a seminar program designed for first-year students. The Byrne seminars were nontraditional courses: running for ten weeks rather than fourteen and graded pass/fail; students received one credit upon completion. Faculty members proposed topics for these seminars based on their own research interests. Eventually, the program added seminars for transfer students as well, reaching an important and too-often ne-glected segment of the student population. McCormick himself taught several Byrne seminars, including one on "Rutgers and the Challenges Facing Higher Education in the Twenty-First Century." While the Ar-esty program gave a small group of students a head start in learning research skills, which could lead to honors work, the Byrne program involved thousands of students and made them aware of what it meant to study at a research university.

4. Richard L. McCormick, 2002, off to a meeting. The photo captures the energy that McCormick brought to the presidency. He championed the second major academic reorganization of the New Brunswick/Piscataway campuses, helped devise and raise funds for the Byrne and Aresty programs that introduced undergraduates to the unique academic opportunities at a research university, and lobbied successfully for a state higher education bond referendum. McCormick's term as president ended with Rutgers reacquiring a medical school that it had lost in 1970.

SOURCE: R-Photo: presidential photographs.

A third McCormick initiative was the Rutgers Future Scholars Program. The program paralleled the Urban University Program fashioned during Mason Gross's tenure to encourage disadvantaged students from Rutgers's host communities—Newark, Camden, and New Brunswick/Piscataway— to apply to the university. The number of students involved, however, would be smaller, and the effort put into assisting each student greater. Under the program, begun in 2008, up to fifty disadvantaged students annually from each of the four communities were identified as they were about to enter eighth grade; thereafter they received academic support, participated in summer enrichment programs, and visited the campus for cultural and athletic events. The university helped train them to take standardized tests, and if they met the university's admissions requirements, they would attend tuition-free. The first students from the program entered Rutgers in fall 2013.

During the Lawrence presidency, the administration had begun to place more emphasis on assisting undergraduates in applying for prestigious national scholarships. This commitment continued under McCormick and brought major results. In 2010, eleven recent graduates received Fulbright scholarships for further work in such places as Spain, Bulgaria, Germany,

Sweden, and France. Among the group was Eric Knecht; he traveled to Egypt to teach English, but his stay was disrupted by the tumultuous political events that swept that nation, so he returned to report on Egyptian electoral politics in the Nile Delta. Rutgers students also became Churchill, Goldwater, Truman, and Gates Scholars. The Truman Scholars included Walter Fortson. When in 2012 he won what is perhaps the most prestigious of all undergraduate scholarships, Fortson was a twenty-seven-year-old former correctional facility inmate. He had been brought to Rutgers by Donald Roden, a history professor, who for more than a decade had worked to develop an outreach program at the Mountainview Youth Correctional Facility. Fortson used his Truman Scholarship to pursue graduate work in criminal justice. In 2013, another student from the Mountainview program, Benjamin Chin, also won a Truman Scholarship.

Except for the acquisition of a medical school—which had systemwide consequences—the boldest step taken during McCormick's presidency was to revisit the 1980 academic reorganization of the New Brunswick/Piscataway campuses. In fall 2005, McCormick explained the challenge to alumni/alumnae:

> Two friends applying to Rutgers can be accepted to different liberal arts colleges with separate admissions standards. Once here, they can sign up for the same course and yet have it count differently toward their degree—even within the same major. . . . Why does this happen? It is an unintended consequence of the university's 1980 reorganization, which unified faculty members from our New Brunswick/Piscataway liberal arts colleges but left many academic decisions under the control of the individual colleges. While reorganization improved Rutgers and led to our membership in the prestigious Association of American Universities, it also separated faculty from decisions about admission standards, core educational requirements, honors programs, and graduation requirements. It also reduced their involvement in academic advising. Adding to the inequality, some outstanding programs are available at only one college, but not at another. As a result, many students cannot take full advantage of all Rutgers has to offer.[12]

The work had begun in spring 2004 with McCormick's appointment of a committee chaired by English professor Barry Qualls. Qualls had participated in the reorganization debates of 1979–1980 and had chaired committees a decade later that drafted two comprehensive plans for improving undergraduate education. The new report, completed in summer 2005, called for merging the four liberal arts colleges in New Brunswick and the creation a new School of Arts and Sciences (SAS). The school would have uniform admission standards, a core curriculum, and graduation requirements that applied to students regardless of the campus on which they lived. What had been college campuses became residential areas, connected to the past by their name, and each with a dean, drawn from the faculty, to help shape cocurricular activities. The recommendation also proposed a major restructuring of the general education requirements, which, like many of the specifics of the plan, would be addressed when SAS implemented the "Transforming Undergraduate Education" report. The debate this time was more muted than in 1979–1980, but again the opposition from faculty and alumnae affiliated with Douglass College shaped the outcome. In the early 1980s, Bloustein had stayed in the background and let Kenneth Wheeler lead the effort for academic reorganization, but now McCormick appeared on all the New Brunswick/Piscataway campuses to discuss and defend the proposal.

McCormick's final recommendation to the Board of Governors included the creation of the Mabel Smith Douglass Residential College—a campus for women, which students could select once admitted to the university, and where they would find distinctive programs to facilitate their education. Cook, soon to become the School of Environmental and Biological Sciences (SEBS)—a name change that occasioned its own debate—remained essentially untouched by the reorganization (except for student services, which were consolidated across the New Brunswick/Piscataway campuses). SEBS's distinctive path testified to its unique roots as a federal land-grant school, to the long history of state support for its autonomy, and to the fact it was as much a professional school as a liberal arts college.

After the board approval of the plan in March 2006, the SAS faculty set to work defining the curriculum and graduation requirements. As students at the various schools outside SAS would be taking many of their general education courses through SAS, the process of defining the curriculum occasioned the first truly inclusive discussion of undergraduate education in New Brunswick/Piscataway. The debate produced a set of general education requirements defined by distinctive approaches to learning and required faculty review of whether any particular course met a specific learning approach. For example, in order to graduate in 2005, Rutgers College students were required to take two courses in the same subject in the natural sciences, with similar requirements in the humanities and social sciences. They could select whatever courses best fit their interests or schedule. Under the new procedures, these general distribution rules remained, but the courses approved as meeting the requirements had to fulfill specific educational goals (for example, "identify and critically assess ethical and societal issues in science"). The traditional math/writing requirements were rewritten as "cognitive skills and processes" requirements, with new emphasis placed on information technology, and students now had to take a course that presented "Twenty-First Century Challenges" (a category that extended the notions of diversity and global awareness present in the earlier curriculum). The faculty also added "signature courses" to the curriculum—large lecture courses taught by the university's distinguished scholars in topics of contemporary interest. "Extinction," "Eating Right: The Ethics of Food Choices and Food Policy," "Energy and Climate Change," and "Genetics, Evolution, and Human Health" were among the early offerings. The larger point was that academic reorganization in New Brunswick/Piscataway prompted the faculty to reassert its commitment to undergraduate education.

In 2006, the Board of Governors approved a childhood studies program in Camden. This interdisciplinary program grew out of the Center for Children and Childhood Studies, established in Camden in 2000. It not only offered undergraduate and master's degrees but was Rutgers-Camden's first Ph.D.-granting program and the first childhood studies program nationally to offer the Ph.D. degree. Within a few years, the program had more than 150 undergraduate majors and both M.A. and Ph.D. students, and it had built partnerships with similar programs in Sweden and Brazil. The board subsequently approved Ph.D. programs in computational biology and public policy, and the transformation of the Department of Nursing into the Rutgers School of Nursing–Camden. The new nursing school, like childhood studies, had links to the larger south Jersey community, and its establishment came propitiously at a time when a national shortage of professionals in the field was challenging the U.S. health-care system.

At Newark, the board approved the transformation of a graduate program into a new School of Public Affairs and Administration (SPAA). SPAA programs trained graduates to improve government efficiency and make state agencies more responsive to constituent needs. Like the new programs at Camden, SPAA developed links with the local community and overseas, especially in China.

It was creative campus leadership in Camden that defined the childhood studies program and convinced the executive vice president for academic affairs, Philip Furmanski, to support the initiative. More generally, Furmanski targeted a number of interdisciplinary areas, many capable of bringing in the outside grants and contracts on which university growth depended and which provided substantial benefits to the state. One such area was transportation, of vital import in a corridor state like New Jersey whose roadways linked New York City to Pennsylvania, and whose Atlantic ports were part of a globalized economy. As part of strategic planning in the 1990s, members of the civil engineering department created the Center for Advanced Infrastructure and Transportation and won recognition from the federal Department of Transportation (DOT) as a university transportation center. The designation put CAIT in position for both New Jersey and federally funded research on a broad spectrum of projects, from congestion management, to harbor dredging and the use of waste materials, to maritime freight movement. In 2005, a new $4.3 million CAIT building was completed on Busch campus, and research and teaching/training offices followed. Begun in civil engineering, the center pulled in faculty and professional staff from allied disciplines. In 2008, shortly after the deadly collapse of a Minneapolis bridge over the Mississippi River reminded people of the vulnerability of such structures, the federal government awarded CAIT a $25 million grant to conduct a long-term bridge performance study. In 2013, CAIT was designated one of five national university transportation centers and awarded almost $3 million by the DOT to lead a consortium study of the nation's transportation infrastructure. Across the Raritan, in downtown New Brunswick, the Alan M. Voorhees Transportation Center (VTC), established in 1998 as part of the Edward J. Bloustein School of Planning and Public Policy, carried out assessments on such diverse subjects as bicycle and pedestrian safety, the environmental impact of transportation systems, the benefits of public transit for New Jersey, and the social consequences of transportation choices. Other interdisciplinary areas targeted for emphasis under McCormick and Furmanski included genetics and stem cell research, nanotechnology, and nutrition, but academic excellence funds went to enhance teaching as well as research and service.

Among the more intriguing university ventures were two projects to transform the New Brunswick/Piscataway campuses. In 2005, McCormick announced a "new vision for the College Avenue Campus" that included the construction of a landscaped pedestrian greenway and the closing of the College Avenue to vehicles. Where College Avenue approached the downtown train station, a multistory Gateway Center would house the visitors' center, the Rutgers Bookstore, the University Press, retail outlets, and parking. A block away, on George Street, the three river dorms, a testimony from the 1950s to planning for coordinated living and learning, but long a subject of complaints from faculty for their inadequate classroom facilities, were to be replaced with new student housing. The entire project dovetailed nicely with the ongoing revitalization efforts in downtown New Brunswick, and a design competition moved the project along; but the key component, the greenway, ran both into budgetary problems and into concerns about what the closing of College Avenue would do to the campus bus system and to traffic more generally. By 2012 the Gateway Center had been opened and College Avenue had been spruced up, but the more ambitious aspects of the design had been abandoned.

The second project was designed to make the campus more energy-efficient. In 2008, Rutgers and the New Jersey Board of Public Utilities jointly financed a seven-acre solar energy farm on the northeast corner of Livingston campus that met about 10 percent of the campus's energy requirements. Three years later, the Board of Governors approved two solar-panel canopies over thirty-two acres of parking lots on Livingston, which would produce almost six times as much electrical energy as the first project. The larger of the two parking-lot projects was juxtaposed between the athletic center and a new Livingston resident hall complex. The fans who used the lot for football and basketball games now saw both the modernization of the campus and the university's leadership in energy conservation.

More generally, the Board of Governors during McCormick's administration continued the pattern evident since the Bloustein years of investing in new academic buildings and in student facilities. In a snapshot taken in 2005, the university had several hundred million dollars' worth of projects under way to add more than two million square feet of new space to its campuses: life sciences buildings on the Newark and Busch campuses, a biomedical engineering building at Busch, an expansion of the law school at Camden, and a new home for the business school at Newark. Just as important were the downtown New Brunswick residential building (Alvin

Rockoff Hall), the massive University Square project at Newark (the first new residence hall at Newark in a decade and a half), and graduate student apartments at 330 Cooper Street in Camden.

The building of residence halls in Newark and Camden was part of a more general recommitment of the university to two of its host cities. Various professional schools—education, nursing, and social work, among others—had a history of civic engagement, and Rutgers students had been doing extensive community volunteer work from the 1960s on, but university relations with the cities of Newark and Camden had long focused on practical questions about policing, taxes, building permits, and the like. Starting during the Lawrence administration and broadening during the McCormick administration, campus-based efforts, led by the provosts/ chancellors, began to contribute more directly to the communities that hosted the university.

Margaret Marsh, the interim Rutgers-Camden chancellor in 2008, made the case for a more active outreach program. Camden, she noted, like other old, midsize, industrial cities, had a crumbling infrastructure, schools that were in crisis, a municipal government that could do little to change the situation, few jobs in the community, little public transportation to take residents to suburban employment, and nothing but an illusion of personal security.[13] For some time, under the leadership of Chancellor Roger Daniels, the School of Business's small business development center, legal clinics run by the Law School, and the Center for Strategic Urban and Community Leadership (which operated charter schools) as well as the new childhood studies program had channeled resources and effort into the community. Marsh proposed expanding the university's efforts to improve the lives of Camden's children and a partnering with North Camden community organizations focusing on schools, waterfront development, affordable housing, and the attraction of new businesses.

Rutgers-Newark, during Steven Diner's tenure as chancellor, sponsored a similar mix of community programs for small-business development, child advocacy, domestic violence protection, legal services, and voter assistance; the university also ran extensive programs in and for the public school system and organized various public service days to promote student engagement with the community. These programs, coupled with the building of new residence halls in the two cities and the future scholars initiative to give some city schoolchildren the opportunity to attend Rutgers, would not "solve" the problems of these cities, as solutions had to emerge from the communities themselves, but they indicated that Rutgers-Newark and Rutgers-Camden had now embraced their identities as urban universities.

It was in Piscataway, however, that the most striking change came to the built landscape of the state university. Following the renovation of the Livingston campus student center and the construction of a new dining hall, the university built a $215 million apartment complex with approximately 1,500 beds in units of four single rooms that shared a kitchen and two baths. Up the road from the apartment complex, work began before McCormick left office on an $85 million building for the Rutgers Business School (a joint Newark–New Brunswick program). Designed by Enrique Norten, the building, with its two towers connected by a raised causeway supported by angled pillars, and with extensive glass paneling (parallel to that in the nearby student apartment towers), provided a gateway to the campus. These projects made Livingston campus, for decades the most isolated of the New Brunswick/Piscataway campuses, the most desirable place for students to reside. It represented an investment, increasingly unique in the era of long-distance learning, in bringing students to live on campus. And, by placing students in the heart of a campus dedicated to professional education, it matched trends in student interests with programs that had revenue-generating potential for the university.

In June 2012, the Board of Governors announced an equally ambitious building plan to transform the College Avenue campus. The university, with help from Devco, proposed to buy most of the land on which the New Brunswick Reformed Seminary stood and to build there a new academic building and an honors college, plus a new residence hall on a parking-lot site (where the "grease trucks," beloved by generations of students, were located) down the street, nearer the train station. Turning that concept into reality by the time of the school's 250th anniversary in 2016 belongs in the next chapter of Rutgers history, but with this move, McCormick erased whatever disappointment lingered from the earlier project to green College Avenue.

President McCormick inherited an athletic program highlighted by a football team that played a challenging schedule in one of the more prominent national conferences; a women's basketball program led by one of the most successful coaches in the history of the sport; and an athletic director committed to achieving big time status comparable to that of many other universities. McCormick initially suggested to the Board of Governors a thorough review of the athletic program, but he could not convince them it was necessary. That moment behind him, McCormick announced that his goals for athletics were academic success, integrity, financial self-sufficiency, and, of course, victories on the field. Throughout McCormick's presidency, Rutgers student athletes did well, in fact, quite well, in the various statistical indicators used to measure academic progress; the football program initially vaulted Rutgers to unprecedented national attention and numerous bowl appearances, while the women's basketball team reached the title game of the national championship tournament. The athletic program, however, even in its best years, was not self-supporting financially, which led to the controversial decision to discontinue several intercollegiate Olympic sports, including men's swimming and crew. Just as damaging were cost overruns on an upgrade to the football stadium and a newspaper exposé on hidden (but not illegal) salary payments to the football coach. After an external review of the university's financial oversight of the athletic program, McCormick announced a commitment to "transparency" and "accountability" in athletic policy, and later brought in a new athletic director, Tim Pernetti, to help assure that those principles would prevail. Pernetti, in turn, faced with the breakup of the Big East Conference to which Rutgers belonged, quietly negotiated the school's move to the prestigious Big Ten Conference, composed primarily of midwestern flagship state universities. Rutgers, like most other public state universities, had become more solidly entrenched in big-time sports, with potentially greater risks and rewards (see chapter 10).

The final drama of the McCormick presidency—and it was both an academic triumph and a political drama—centered on medical education. Governor Christie had asked former governor Thomas Kean to head a task force on higher education. The task force issued its report in January 2011, calling in general for more state support and also pointing to the need to end a decade of indecision about medical education. Christie put together an advisory committee on UMDNJ and for its chair turned to Sol J. Barer, a long-time executive at Celgene Corporation, a major biopharmaceutical company active in the field of cancer research and treatment. The Barer committee delivered it report in fall 2011, recommending the merging of the New Brunswick/Piscataway medical units of UMDNJ into Rutgers University—exactly what Rutgers wanted—but left for the final report questions about north and south Jersey. Christie then added the secretary of higher education to the committee in a consultative role, and the committee sat down to draft a final report with a much more sweeping agenda.

The Barer committee's second report called for a fundamental restructuring of higher education in New Jersey. In north Jersey, the committee argued for a revamped health science university (New Jersey Health Science University) essentially built from the local components of UMDNJ, and greater collaboration (but not merging) with NJIT and Rutgers. In south Jersey, the Barer committee recommended "a broader, expanded research university . . . comprised of the assets of Rowan University and Rutgers University in Camden and encompassing, as well, the recently provisionally accredited Cooper Medical School of Rowan," with the new school to have Rowan's name and to include the Rutgers-Camden law school and business schools as well as the various programs in arts and sciences.[14] The committee justified its recommendations both in terms of the efficiency and entrepreneurial energy that decentralized, autonomous medical institutions could generate and as the best way to serve the regional needs of New Jersey's population. The bargain seemed clear: Rutgers could have the medical school in New Brunswick/Piscataway that it had lost in 1970 and had long wanted back, but at the cost of its Camden campus. The Rutgers administration responded cautiously to this plan, which, backed by a popular Republican governor and powerful south Jersey Democratic political leaders, seemed an irresistible force.

Rutgers officials began to bargain, willing to give up only what they had to in order to get what they absolutely wanted. The initial compromise left Rutgers-Camden half in and half out of the Rutgers system, with Rowan and Rutgers-Camden merged for some purposes but not others. From the outset, the Rutgers-Camden faculty had criticized the merger, and that opposition now exploded publicly. In testimony before the Board of Governors and the Board of Trustees, a Camden faculty member stated that the plan was like a family selling "a child to adopt a cousin," a metaphor that captured the moral outrage galvanized by the opposition.[15] The newspapers depicted the plan as a political answer to what was an educational question, and at Rutgers, the Board of Trustees—largely composed of university alumni and with as much authority to say "no" on this question as the Board of Governors—dug in its heels in opposition. With Governor Christie setting a deadline of July 1 for a resolution, and difficult negotiations occurring on an almost daily basis, the final bill gave Rutgers virtually everything it wanted.

In May 2011, well before the university and the state had worked through the merger plans, Richard L. McCormick announced he would resign at the end of the 2011–2012 school year. Ten years in office was now generally recognized as two terms for a senior administrator; the Board of Governors' unexpected and unprecedented 2011 public decision to reduce the administration's request for a tuition increase spoke to tensions that had grown over the course of the presidency. In an interview with the *Star-Ledger*, McCormick said that his father, author of the 1966 history of the university, had told him that every Rutgers president had either died in office or been pushed out behind closed doors, and he did not want to end his term that way. He departed, he said, "on his own terms," and left a university ready for new leadership.[16] At the May 2012 graduation ceremony, the board surprised McCormick with an honorary degree and a lengthy tribute to his accomplishments.

His had been busy years. Not since the 1980s, that is, the later years of Bloustein's administration, had so much been accomplished. Under McCormick's watch and with his encouragement, the New Brunswick faculty had unified liberal arts education under a newly created School of Arts and Sciences and fundamentally redefined the curriculum. In his early days as president, he had helped to block a controversial deal for acquiring a medical school, and that step had paved the way for a better settlement of the medical school issue near the end of his term. Educational initiatives at Newark had added a new School of Nursing, and, at Camden, a School of Public Affairs and Administration. Like Lawrence, McCormick had carried the university's case for more funding to Trenton, but even more so than Lawrence, his relations with the governor's office had been strained, neither personal nor warm (except during Richard J. Codey's brief administration). McCormick continued Lawrence's and the board's commitment to big-time athletics. When the press and outside evaluators concluded that there was inadequate oversight of athletic finances, McCormick accepted much of the blame and worked to assure greater accountability and transparency in athletics. Unparalleled success of the football team in the early twenty-first century did not translate into a self-supporting program, but the move to the Big Ten, negotiated as McCormick left office, held out hope for a better financial future.

McCormick successfully negotiated the university's pursuit of academic excellence. Given the continuing budgetary problems faced by the university, this was a remarkable accomplishment. Some schools had, in fact, dropped out of the AAU. Rutgers did not. During the turbulent fiscal conditions of the 1990s and the early twenty-first century, Rutgers continued to hire distinguished faculty, and if it lost some faculty members to other universities, there was no flight of top researchers to other schools. The rankings (a uncertain index, at best) of traditionally strong programs remained high, and other programs moved into those same ranks. McCormick left office, as Lawrence had, before the capital campaign he launched reached its target, but still with an impressive total of fund-raising. Awards from government, foundations, and corporations grew significantly as well (as they had under Lawrence). McCormick also worked successfully with other state educational leaders to place a higher education bond issue on the 2012 ballot to help fund ambitious construction projects. In November, New Jersey voters approved the bond issue. To a returning Rutgers alumna, approaching her thirties, what might well have impressed her most was the remarkable development of the Newark, Camden, and Piscataway campuses—all testimony to the burst of construction over the past decade.

From World War II to the Twenty-First Century

In seventy years, there had been a remarkable transformation. Two liberal arts colleges, one for men and one for women, an agricultural school, and an engineering school had been built, unit by unit, into a true state university with a massive undergraduate program, and also into a research university that ranks among the best public institutions in the nation. Stepping back from this top-down history to reflect on both the school and its leadership, one can make two general conclusions.

For the school itself, the Bloustein administration, and in particular, the late 1970s and early 1980s, were crucial. The reorganization of the college system, the physical consolidation of individual departments, and the new attention to graduate education and research all occurred simultaneously. The role of Kenneth Wheeler, Daniel Gorenstein, and T. Alexander Pond in shaping Rutgers into a research university with consolidated New Brunswick departments is the critical element of Bloustein's administration and the post–World War II history of Rutgers. Looking back, however, the creation of Livingston College, and with it a recognition that Rutgers would try to meet its responsibility to provide a college education for the rapidly growing New Jersey high school population, was also important. Livingston, which was coeducational, made the admission of women to

Rutgers College virtually inevitable and forced the university to a planning crossroads. The federated plan—Rutgers's unique equivalent to the cluster-college concept in California—might have built on the Livingston model. The university might have grown by adding smaller colleges, some liberal arts and some professional, with more student-faculty contact and special-ized missions. In the 1970s and 1980s, cluster colleges became research universities, especially if they had medical schools that pulled in federal research dollars, and if Rutgers had held on to its medical school, such a future might have been possible. Of course, it did not happen that way. There simply was not the funding to build more colleges, and those who favored stronger graduate programs won the battle over reorganization. The changes occurred without anyone's fully thinking through the impli-cations for student life and undergraduate education; the changes also fa-vored the academically strongest programs in New Brunswick/Piscataway relative not only to other departments at the flagship campus, but relative also to the development of the Newark and Camden campuses. In each of these areas, subsequent administrations worked to rectify the situation.

Second, the role of the central administration, and of the president, had also undergone profound change. Presidents are faculty leaders, adminis-trators, fund-raisers, politicians, and the public face of the university. In 2012, a president is far less a faculty leader, and far more a fund-raiser, than had been the case in 1945. Marketing and branding have made the uni-versity itself more visible than its highest administrator, and much of the back-and-forth between Trenton and New Brunswick is now conducted by professional staff rather than between president and governor. What remains constant and crucial is the president's administrative role, espe-cially his (and perhaps someday, her) appointment power. Starting with Lewis Webster Jones, each presidency has actually been a partnership with a vice president (initially a provost, eventually an executive vice president), usually with a different disciplinary background than the president, and with primary responsibility for academic affairs. Jones (economics) chose Gross (philosophy); Gross worked with Richard Schlatter (history); Blous-tein (philosophy) with Henry Winkler (history) and T. Alexander Pond (physics); Lawrence (French) with Joseph J. Seneca (economics); and Mc-Cormick (history) with Philip Furmanski (life sciences) and Richard Ed-wards (social work). Among the faculty, many remember eras in Rutgers history in terms of the academic leadership of Alex Pond, Joe Seneca, or Phil Furmanski, names generally known outside the university only to the best-informed public constituencies. Presidents, with the advice of vice presidents, hire, and occasionally fire, deans, provosts (now chancellors), and an expanding list of vice presidents. This, too, is crucial, especially in a university that has built its academic reputation primarily through state-funded hiring, one good appointment decision at a time (and one difficult denial of tenure at a time). The appointment of academic vice presidents and of mid-level faculty-administrators—for example, Catharine R. Stimpson as dean of the Graduate School in the 1980s, Richard Foley as dean of the New Brunswick Faculty of Arts and Sciences in the 1990s, Roger Daniels at Camden, and Norman Samuels at Newark as provosts (chancellors)—represent a crucial but largely invisible contribution a president makes to a university.

These first three chapters have thus traced Rutgers's post–World War II history largely from the perspective of the president's office; what went on elsewhere—in the classrooms and residence halls, on the athletic fields, in science laboratories and faculty offices, and at libraries and museums—is the subject of the remainder of this study.

4

Student Life

Philip Roth enrolled in the Newark Colleges of Rutgers. As he recalls in his 1987 essay, "Joe College: Memories of a Fifties Education," the gritty urban campus, where classes were held in a former brewery, was all that his family could afford, but he hoped that it might be a stepping stone to a law career. Roth acted the college man, with a pipe in his pocket and his lunch in a briefcase, and enjoyed what was for a Jewish kid an unfamiliar camaraderie with Irish and Italian students from the Ironbound district of Newark. But he chafed to get away to a real college town—perhaps to New Brunswick—or any liberal arts college that would give him a scholarship. A friend told him about Bucknell University, about 160 miles from Newark; a campus visit convinced his parents that he should attend, even without financial support. Roth remembered an "unoutlandish little college town," with tree-lined streets, eighteenth-century houses, and "unpretentious civility." Bucknell, a Rutgers athletic rival, was home to 1,900 students.[1]

Bucknell in the 1950s was much like Rutgers–New Brunswick. Fraternity life defined college life, and Roth joined a Jewish fraternity, although one gentile fraternity had invited him to rush. At Sigma Alpha Mu, he helped engineer the "sand blast," an indoor, winter beach party with men and women in swim suits (a violation of the dress code), held inside the fraternity house, with sand trucked in and spread on the building's floor. Eventually, he and two of his closest friends tired of fraternity life, moved out, and began a campus literary magazine, *Et Cetera*. Roth launched left-leaning literary barbs at the high school values of other students and their blindness in preferring Dwight Eisenhower to Adlai Stevenson. His sarcastic attack on the college newspaper and its editor got him censured. He drew closer to his English professors, away from the business and finance majors who dominated campus life; he dreamed of becoming a college professor, not a lawyer. He acquired a steady girlfriend, who would rendezvous with him by climbing into his room through a second-floor window. When his landlady discovered the deception, he saw his life (and his girlfriend's) coming apart. Although their world did not end, the romance did, and both went off to separate graduate schools. Bucknell was "a little college town" and Rutgers-Newark an urban enclave. At each, however, high school values, defined by the largely middle-class, white student population, shaped college life in the 1950s.

Three decades later, writer S. Mitra Kalita experienced college quite differently than did Philip Roth. She was born in Brooklyn, the first child born in the United States to a family from Assam, a state in northeastern India. Her father, an engineer, emigrated in 1971 to work in the lower rungs of the corporate world; her mother followed two years later, working at hourly jobs that helped the family to buy their first home, on Long Island. Kalita grew up as two people: "the one at home spoke Assamese" and "ate with her hands"; the one at school, in the States, "spoke with a thick Long Island accent," and "vacillated between the black Cabbage Patch Kid and the white one."[2] Work took the family to Puerto Rico, where Kalita spent part of her childhood, and found herself even more of an outsider. When the family returned to the United States in 1988, they bought a home in West Windsor, and after Kalita graduated from high school in 1994, she enrolled at Rutgers–New Brunswick.

Kalita became absorbed in work with the *Targum*, gaining the nickname "Rough Draft" and bylining stories on such topics as the death penalty and Black History Month. In her junior year, she was elected senior news editor and in 1997 became "*Targum's* first editor-in-chief of color," for what was unquestionably the most diverse editorial board in the newspaper's 128-year history.[3] Work for the Associated Press, graduate school in journalism at Columbia, a job with the *Washington Post*, and a stint in India all followed. Along the way, she published two books that personalized the experiences of South Asians in India and the United States.

Both Roth and Kalita came from upwardly striving families; both were initially outsiders who adjusted quite successfully to college life, and both made their mark in college and after as writers. As a collection of liberal arts colleges and as a large state university, Rutgers has nurtured the aspirations of thousands of students like Roth and Kalita. There, however, the similarities in their situations end. Roth attended two variants of the American college in the 1950s: a bare-bones urban institution without much in the way of college activities, and an idyllic, small liberal arts school that highlighted everything that college life was supposed to offer. At Bucknell, as would have been true in New Brunswick, fraternities dominated the campus and initially attracted Roth. The students he knew were middle class yet not truly privileged, virtually all of European ancestry (although he would not have made that point), and divided primarily by religion and ethnicity. Two generations later, Kalita's school was qualitatively larger—a place in which one could easily become lost academically and socially. It was also more diverse and offered students far more opportunity to define their own involvement in campus life. Strikingly, her work on the student newspaper involved her in one of the few remaining activities to push back against the fragmentation of college life on the campuses of a large, diverse, modern university.

In this chapter, which chronicles the transformation of college life at Rutgers, I pursue two interrelated themes. The first story begins in the immediate post–World War II era when (after a wartime hiatus) fraternities reasserted their role on the New Brunswick campus and when a highly structured set of dances, cultural and athletic activities, and societies and clubs defined an inclusive, distinctive undergraduate culture. The story ends with the diverse, fragmented student culture of the late twentieth and early twenty-first centuries, a culture largely shaped by youth and consumer culture more generally, and with few of the common threads that tied the student community, and even the faculty, together in the postwar period. The second story, more implicit than explicit, is of the university's relationship to student culture. In the nineteenth century, students defined their own lives, often to the annoyance of the faculty and university officials. Colleges, in response, crafted rules, firmly in place by the end of World War II, to regulate and control student behavior. In the late 1960s, these rules, challenged by the students themselves, fell by the wayside. Once college administrators accepted that fact, they worked to create elaborate college life bureaucracies designed to promote harmonious communities within student culture and to offer students a wide range of options for engagement, recreation, and the search for self-identity.

What follows are snapshots of specific school years interspersed with more in-depth portraits of specific campuses, organizations, and activities. The snapshots of 1946–1947, 1955–1956, 1972–1973, and 1998–1999, and the separate sections on fraternities, Douglass College, residence halls, and recreational sports, emphasize the reemergence of campus life after World War II and the erosion of many of its most significant rituals in the wake of the political and cultural upheavals of the late 1960s and early 1970s. These two alternating approaches chronicle the transformation of campus life in New Brunswick and capture some of the changes that have occurred at Camden and Newark as well.

Postwar, 1946–1947

In fall 1946, Rutgers enrolled more students than in any other semester in its 180-year history. Fifteen thousand undergraduates attended the university, and almost nine thousand of them were ex-servicemen, beneficiaries of the G.I. Bill. These numbers put pressure on campus facilities, and men fresh from the military were impatient with features of campus life that seemed a silly waste of time. Servicemen predominated at the College of Agriculture and were an overwhelming presence in the College of Engineering, but they made up half the population of the New Brunswick College of Arts and Sciences as well. College life, as traditionally defined, was less important to these veterans than a practical education that would let them get on with their lives. As one commented, " . . . freshman week was designed to find out whether or not the freshmen can take it. I, myself, as a veteran, took it long enough, while I was in the army."[4]

Housing—and its lack—aggravated the frustrations of the students. Married students, if lucky enough to get housing, were in trailers; barracks at nearby Raritan Arsenal housed some of the overflow, while "doubles" became "triples" in the dormitories. The student cafeteria was a prefabricated structure, additional makeshift units along the Raritan Canal served as classrooms, and a fraternity house was converted to a student center. But if students had to negotiate uninviting spaces, and if hazing as a rite of passage on the main campus subsided, temporarily, many of the prewar rituals of campus life were re-created enthusiastically.

In the late 1940s, the fall semester revolved around weekend football games, and the spring semester around dances. Homecoming weekend in early November 1946 brought more than two thousand alumni to the main

campus; they attended a luncheon in the cafeteria and then a football contest with the Lafayette Leopards. It was the big game: the Middle Three
championship that pitted Rutgers against Lehigh and Lafayette. That evening many returning alums went to fraternity parties, even though quite a
few of the prewar fraternities had not yet been reestablished. Fraternities
competed to create the most elaborate house decorations for the weekend,
the student newspaper sponsored a contest for the best new fight song,
and the student government of the men's colleges invited the New Jersey
College for Women (NJCW) to supply additional cheerleaders for athletic
events. In the spring, the junior prom and the military ball highlighted the
social calendar. A year later there would be a semiformal "soph hop" and a
Sadie Hawkins dance in the fall as well.

The student activities fee, a modest $12 for New Brunswick men (against
an annual tuition of $400), underwrote the student newspaper (*Targum*),
yearbook (*Scarlet Letter*)—which resumed publication in spring 1947—a
student literary magazine (the *Anthologist*), the debating club, the student
assembly (the meeting body for the entire student population), the music
club and band, and a theater group (Queen's Players, or QP). While the
Student Assembly helped to give the student body a collective identity, so
too did the required two-year military science curriculum and the four-
year mandatory physical education program. At NJCW "dues" covered a
newspaper (*Caellian*), the yearbook (*Quair*), a handbook about the college distributed to each student, a lecture series, the student government
association, and organized athletic activities. The handbook outlined the
extensive rules the women were supposed to follow, the college rituals, and
the "college days" that brought the students or particular classes together.
On each campus, the student newspaper was delivered to individual dormitories, and for the men, to fraternity houses, and left in red boxes in
prominent locations for commuters. Issues often failed to keep up with
demand.

Each campus offered a rich variety of concerts and plays that routinely drew overflow crowds to the College Avenue gymnasium, rented
high school venues, and the Little Theater on the women's campus. The
Queen's Players dated back to the World War I era and had long included
students from both the men's and women's colleges. In its second year of
post–World War II production, the QP mounted George Bernard Shaw's
The Devil's Disciple, which, despite good attendance, left the company financially strapped (but did not keep it from producing two plays the next

year). The university concert series, now in its thirteenth year, brought the Cleveland and San Francisco orchestras to campus, but Rutgers had to cancel the Boston Symphony Orchestra because needed gymnasium expansion had not been completed. Paul Robeson, among Rutgers's most illustrious graduates, highlighted the cultural events of 1946 with a return to campus for a concert. At Douglass, Voorhees Chapel was the site for a new series of chamber music concerts. The Glee Club, a venerable nineteenth-century organization, had added classical music to its repertoire of traditional college songs, now toured extensively, and held a gala weekend in Pennsylvania. The men's choir performed at Sunday services in Kirkpatrick Chapel, and the women's choir at Tuesday services in Voorhees Chapel.

Even in the immediate aftermath of World War II, campus activities made Rutgers about something more than just going to class. And the colleges remained small enough that common rituals and events, such as convocation and student assemblies, drew a significant part of the student population (and often the faculty as well), providing a shared identity. College became a more mature, more autonomous version of the high school world these students had left (and, for that reason, a somewhat awkward transition back to the civilian world for many veterans).

Fraternities

In the prewar period, nothing defined student life at the Colleges for Men in New Brunswick more than the fraternity system. On the eve of the World War II, the nineteen fraternities at the colleges had more than 600 members in a student population of about 1,600. In the immediate postwar period, as many as one in every two students belonged to a fraternity. The oldest of these clubs dated to before the Civil War, and the first fraternities overlapped with and complemented student philosophical and literary societies. By the 1880s, many fraternities had acquired property and provided living accommodations for their members. By the 1930s, a typical fraternity among the twenty on campus had thirty or more members. Each controlled its own membership, all the college chapters were associated with national fraternities, and all had a considerable degree of autonomy from university oversight.

Greeks ran slates of candidates for student government, constituted most of the staff of the *Scarlet Letter*, the college yearbook, and dominated the intramural sports program. The Interfraternity Council (IFC) Ball, a formal dance held each spring, was a highlight of the social season on campus. On the weekend of the junior prom—another social highlight for the college—most of the houses along fraternity row (Union Street and its vicinity) held their own parties. "Greek week" each spring was marked by contests (touch football, but in the 1940s also bridge and table tennis), the induction of new pledges, and a banquet. During Greek week, it was not unusual for the president, the football coach, and a noted outside speaker (for example, Governor Robert Meyner) to address fraternity gatherings.

Fraternities also sponsored much of the charitable activity on campus. In 1947, several fraternities, working with various clubs at the Men's College and the NJCW, sponsored the Rutgers Non-Sectarian Palestine Committee, an unusual foray into extracampus politics. Many Greek houses did better academically than the non-Greek student population, and Greeks often won the major academic awards, distributed in late spring each year. Fraternities provided, a 1963 report noted, "one of the few aspects of university life which is designed, financed, and administered . . . by the students themselves, and created a healthy social life in contrast to the dormitories, which while more modern, lacked any real sense of community or culture."[5]

Yet there were troubles in the fraternity system: hazing of pledges (in a campus culture that encouraged modest hazing of all first-year students), drinking (forbidden under university rules), and discrimination (allowed because fraternities were private). As early as 1943, when the university began planning for the postwar period, President Clothier had asked a committee to inquire into the future of the system. He worried that the high ideals of the fraternities—service, character, patriotism—found little reinforcement in the "lives of the boys," and wondered if Rutgers might replace fraternities with new residential and academic units like the houses at Harvard or the colleges at Yale.[6] Little came of the committee inquiry other than the assignment of a staff or faculty member to live in each house as a mentor (this became, in practice, a residential house mother, defined as "a qualified women of mature years").[7]

One problem mentioned in the committee report was hazing and the excessive drinking that often accompanied it. The initiation rituals for all first-year students at the colleges were themselves a form of hazing, but as these fell into disfavor, greater attention was directed to fraternity practices. Fraternity hazing could be exacerbated by intoxication. Before the war, drinking alcohol had been prohibited in dormitories and fraternities, but in 1947, the university changed its policy because of the influx of veterans. Hazing centered on Greek week. The week, a time of general fraternity celebration, was also known as "hell week," and pledges, about to become brothers, were expected to endure physical and emotional humiliation. Traditional fraternity initiation practices such as paddling and requirements that pledges shave their heads or wear women's clothing in public were designed to humiliate the new members. Even after the mid-1960s, by which time the university, campus fraternity leaders, and national fraternity organizations had all condemned hazing, the practice persisted in some fraternities.

Clothier's committee said nothing about the deteriorating physical condition of many fraternity houses. In contrast, the 1963 committee that reported to Mason Gross on the state of the fraternity system made housing a central concern. Two-thirds of the two dozen fraternities were "occupying physical properties which are inconvenient and undesirable, crowded and unattractive."[8] The committee recommended that the Board of Trustees help finance a new fraternity row on the Heights campus—a proposal that would resurface repeatedly for the next two decades. A decade and a half later, yet another committee was stunned by the "extraordinary filth . . . to say nothing of the numerous building and fire safety code violations" in the fraternity houses they visited, and asked if the university could be satisfied with a "row of flop houses on College Avenue."[9]

More troubling than the housing problems was the fact that fraternities discriminated. Discrimination had three connotations. Fraternities were inherently selective—brothers selected others who were like themselves through a "black ball" system (that allowed one or a few brothers to block membership of someone). The university accepted this. There were predominantly Protestant, Catholic, and Jewish fraternities, and students knew which houses to rush.

Race was a second, deeper problem. Rutgers had long admitted African Americans, but before the late 1960s, there were few blacks at the university. In the immediate postwar period, there were no black students in fraternities, and no attention was given to the issue in the university reports on fraternities. In 1949, the student council (which included a number of fraternity members) finally raised the issue.

The students argued that if a national fraternity discriminated, then the local chapter at Rutgers had to work to change national policy; if a local chapter discriminated, the student council stated, then it should be barred from campus. There must be, the council concluded, "a permanent, unimpeachable safeguard."[10] The council sent its recommendations to President Clothier, with a request that the matter go to the Board of Trustees. For good measure, it added that religious organizations as well should end discrimination (without clarifying exactly what that meant). Later, the council crafted a nondiscrimination pledge that it expected all campus organizations to uphold. The trustees, after lengthy study, adopted the council's position. Rutgers fraternity chapters whose parent body barred "Negroes" from membership had to work to change that policy. At that time, fourteen New Brunswick fraternities had no discriminatory membership clauses, three others were in the process of removing such clauses, and seven fraternities were required by national charters to prohibit membership to blacks (and often Jews). In the mid-1950s, the trustees decided that any local fraternity that had failed by 1959 to convince its national organization to end racial discrimination would no longer be allowed on campus. All but one made the deadline, and that one, after working unsuccessfully to change national policy, disbanded. Thus by the 1960s, overt discrimination had ended, but, in fact, until the late 1960s, there were very few African Americans at Rutgers and even fewer in the fraternity system.

A third aspect of the discrimination problem arose at Newark. In 1960, an undergraduate charged that a professional fraternity in the School of Business Administration—essentially a social fraternity without a house and with membership restricted to a particular academic field—barred Jews. The university could find no evidence to support or reject the claim, concluding only that membership was largely "Christian." As connections forged in college affected opportunities later in life, roadblocks to membership in professional organizations had consequences for students beyond the undergraduate years. A different version of this problem surfaced in New Brunswick. Zeta Beta Tau was the first national Jewish fraternity, and for a long time, exclusively Jewish. In 1954, however, the national organization changed its policy on excluding non-Jews, and the Rutgers chapter, in a symbolic gesture, extended affiliated membership to President Jones, a devout Christian.

Despite these efforts, discrimination persisted. In the mid-1960s, the dean of men reported to the Board of Governors that self-segregation rather than discrimination characterized the Rutgers system. Most fraternities, the dean noted, had Protestant, Catholic, and Jewish members. (He also noted that the fraternity brothers felt the university had no right to ask them about their religious preferences.) Approximately one fraternity in six, the dean indicated, had black members (and a slightly higher proportion of nonwhite members), and most had discontinued the "black ball" system (see above). When, in 1971, the university identified a fraternity that purposefully discriminated, the Board of Governors revoked its charter. In 1972, at the time of the last membership report done for the board, there were only five African American brothers (one in each of five fraternities) among the thirteen hundred fraternity members in New Brunswick.

At that point, however, a new era of race relations had come to campus. The changing demographics of the campus as the university responded to the black protest movement in the wake of the Conklin Hall takeover and the establishment of black fraternities pointed toward a different future.

College as a Way of Life, 1955–1956

Our second snapshot of Rutgers college life, taken in the mid-1950s, captures campuses that had put the postwar adjustments behind. The veterans were gone, but enrollments were up. For the 1955–1956 school year, the colleges for men enrolled 865 freshmen, and Douglass enrolled 440 first-year students. Newark expected about eighteen hundred students on campus and the College of South Jersey more than three hundred. The first new dormitory in decades, Demarest, had been opened on College Avenue in 1951, but despite the addition, the university had to cobble together makeshift accommodations in dorm basements for the overflow student population. The year witnessed student government at Douglass protest the compulsory chapel requirement and saw students at both Douglass and Rutgers call for the reopening of the cases of professors fired in 1952 and 1953 for invoking their Fifth Amendment rights before congressional committees. In the supposedly apolitical 1950s, student leaders had previously taken stands against anticommunist hysteria, compulsory ROTC, and racial discrimination. Student government (see chapter 6) was, however, part of a much broader pattern of college life in the 1950s, as the following schedule of events demonstrates:

Activities Calendar, 1955–1956, Men's Colleges and Douglass College
20 September—Fall Convocation
28 September—All-University Boat Ride on the Hudson

30 September—Douglass Campus Night (Alumni Return)

7–8 October—Rally (NJCW), Scarlet Key Dance, Muhlenberg-Rutgers
 Football Game

18 October—Freshmen-Sophomore Tournament

21–22 October—Alumni Weekend, Song Contest, Awarding of Harmon
 Trophy, and Lehigh-Rutgers Football Game

29 October—Ag Barn Hop

4–6 November—Douglass International Weekend

12 November—Soph Hop (Egyptian Theme)

20 December—Douglass Christmas Formal (and Yule Log Ceremony)

January—Glee Club Pocono Weekend

18 February—Douglass Date with Dad Day

9 March—Junior Prom (Les Elgart Band)

13 April—IFC Block Party

28 April—Hillel Foundation Dance

1 May—Military Ball

4 May—Douglass Spring Semi-Formal Dance and Combined Glee Club
 Concert

5 May—Ag Field Day

5 May—Douglass Parents' Day

8 May—Spring Convocation

10 May—Douglass Sacred Path Ceremony

11 May—Military Field Day

The 1955–1956 social year in New Brunswick began with the sixth annual boat ride. On Wednesday, September 28, with classes cancelled, seventeen hundred college men and Douglass women, and their dates, boarded the *Peter Stuyvesant* at Jersey City and sailed along the Hudson River, entertained by the Rhythmettes (a female vocal group) and a five-piece band, and sustained by whatever beer (but not hard liquor) that the students had brought on board. The year ended with a flourish of activity on all the campuses. Two thousand people attended Ag Field Day. They listened to high school marching bands parading with everything from "beautiful majorettes to baby hogs" and alongside floats strewn with flowers and displaying giant chickens.[11] Before the year-end Military Ball, some fourteen hundred army and air force ROTC members paraded and drilled, received awards, and saluted the queen of the ball. The ball itself was held in the red-white-and-blue-decorated gymnasium to the music of both a dance and a jazz band. At

Douglass, the traditional sacred path ceremony (seniors escorting first-year students, symbolizing moving up a class) concluded the year.

More so than immediately after the war, a broad range of cultural and intellectual activity balanced the social events. In the fall, under the auspices of a student lecture series, British-born poet W. H. Auden spoke at Douglass, historian Samuel Flagg Bemis traveled to College Avenue from Yale to lecture on John Quincy Adams, and Pulitzer Prize–winning poet Robert Frost made one of his many trips to Rutgers to read to the students who jammed Kirkpatrick Chapel. That spring, Rutgers held its second annual academic weekend. Students invited speakers to address the "new conservatism." The program included politicians (Tennessee senator Estes Kefauver and New Jersey representative Peter Frelinghuysen), academics (Harvard historian Louis Hartz and Cornell political scientist Clinton Rossiter), and the outspoken conservative editor and commentator William F. Buckley Jr. A week earlier, the student lecture series had brought to campus the six-time Socialist candidate for the presidency, Norman Thomas. At Douglass, the annual international weekend included an interdenominational chapel service, the showing of a film on discrimination, and numerous panels dealing with the "Twentieth Century Complexion."

The Rutgers Philosophean Society, which could trace its origins back to a similar literary and philosophical club of the early nineteenth century, promoted a book of the year. In 1955–1956 it chose Walt Whitman's *Leaves of Grass* and organized discussions of the book at the colleges for men. The group had begun the program in 1948, with Ruth Benedict's *Patterns of Culture*, and had also featured such classics as Voltaire's *Candide* and John Stuart Mill's *On Liberty* (a welcome assignment, the *Targum* noted, against the backdrop of McCarthyism).

On the drama front, the Queen's Theater Guild (the Queen's Players and New Jersey College for Women Little Theatre) mounted three plays, *Bell, Book, and Candle; Playboy of the Western World*; and, for the first time, a musical, *Wonderful Town*. Production of the musical involved four directors and five dozen students and was rewarded with standing-room-only audiences. The student radio station, WRSU, which was launched in 1948 and mixed live broadcasts with a variety of musical offerings, introduced the College Quiz Bowl, which allowed "the men of Rutgers [to] pit their wits against the comely lasses of Douglass."[12] In the first quiz bowl, devoted to American history, Kappa Sigma fraternity men defeated Corwin-J dormitory women, and later the *Targum*'s staff trumped the *Caellian*'s, but the women of Douglass residence houses routinely beat their crosstown fraternity house rivals that first year. The *Anthologist*, which resumed publication immediately after the war, had in 1952 spun off a humorous counterpart, the *Antho*. It sputtered financially and for lack of writers but did manage one widely distributed issue, *Coop Confidential*, and in 1955 put out its first "theme-issue" on science fiction. The proliferation of clubs and honorary societies on all the campuses further underscored the full return of "campus life" to New Brunswick.

Both Newark and South Jersey mirrored, on a reduced scale, this elaboration of college life. Both were commuter campuses, and both (but especially Newark) had an existence before becoming part of the state university. At South Jersey, students began the campus newspaper, the *Gleaner*, in 1951, and in 1955–1956 it was still doing double duty as a literary magazine. A drama club, the Masquetters, was established in 1951, and a glee club a year earlier. The student government association planned dances and pep rallies. In 1950, students organized the first social fraternity, Sigma Upsilon, without a residence house, but with a proudly stated nondiscriminatory policy; by 1956, there were three fraternities, two with houses, and a social organization, Delta Rho, for campus women. A modest varsity sports program (golf, tennis, and baseball being added to a preexisting basketball program) pitted the school against local rivals (for example, Cheyney State Teachers College and Trenton Junior College) as well as its compatriots at the Newark Campus–Rutgers University (NCRU).

NCRU, a much larger and better-established campus, had a fuller range of student activities. Students published a literary magazine, and the campus newspaper, the *Observer*, competed for and won many of the same national student journalism awards that the *Targum* did. In 1955, it introduced a "co-ed of the week" contest to enthusiastic reader response. The school's sorority (Delta Phi Delta) dated back to 1934, and its oldest fraternity (Glove and Stick) to 1935. Its thespians (the Mummers) staged an ambitious program that included original student plays, Henrik Ibsen's *Ghosts*, and a medieval drama. It had more student clubs than South Jersey did, the four largest of which were associated with the School of Business Administration, and it had a student lounge and snack bar (far from a true student union) on Washington Avenue that gave commuters a place to relax between classes. NCRU, like New Brunswick, had an ROTC program, and in 1956, the second class of Newark students graduated from the school's ROTC program and were commissioned in the air force. The school's basketball team, the "Bombers" (later it would be changed to "Raiders"), traveled to New Brunswick and upended the Scarlet Knights in 1955, encouraged by female cheerleaders.

Much had changed from the immediate postwar campus. The rhythms of ritual life had returned; associations had been reorganized; the number of clubs multiplied. Each weekend, at least in New Brunswick, was filled with an undergraduate activity. Yet this elaboration simply preserved a way of life for young people in transition to adulthood, an all-inclusive college culture that was already in place before the 1950s. At times this culture could be petty and juvenile—in response to a March panty raid by college men on a Douglass residence, Dean Boocock intoned, "the girls were not amused and neither am I"—but it was also one that tied social and academic life together into a common whole.[13] The Philosopheans recognized this problem when they acknowledged that reading Whitman competed with "holidays, open book quizzes, and dates at Douglass" (and so they offered a $400 scholarship for the best essay on the poet).[14] Their conception of college community became harder to sustain as the university grew larger and its students more diverse.

New Jersey College for Women/Douglass College

Students, administrators, and faculty embraced the postwar version of college life most fully at Douglass College.

In 1918, the Trustees of Rutgers College, responding to a vigorous campaign led by Mabel Smith Douglass, established the New Jersey College for Women. The post–World War II NJCW informed new students that its "campus, faculty, and institutional life are separate from and independent of the rest of Rutgers University."[15] Geographically, the school was small and self-contained (all other campuses being more fully mixed with their urban environs); and architecturally, it was singularly attractive. Women lived on three smaller campuses: Jameson, with dormitories, and Corwin and Gibbons, with small houses arrayed in a horseshoe pattern. The college provided numerous academic clubs, honorary societies, and cultural and literary organizations—and most graduates had participated in one or more of these—as well as a faculty deeply committed to undergraduate teaching and to the students. The setting thus reinforced the notion of the college as an intimate, friendly community.

Expansion can fragment any community. Approximately twelve hundred students attended the college in the late 1940s—making the NJCW about the size of an urban high school. In the late 1960s, first-year classes at Douglass were about seven hundred students, and the college was soon expected to top three thousand students, about the size of New Jersey's largest high schools. When a "quiet revolution" did overtake Douglass, however, it was not so much because the number of students had grown but because of the attitudes and goals of a new generation of women.[16]

The college reinforced the school's motto, "wisdom and self-control," through a structured set of class responsibilities and collective rituals. In the late 1940s, a "junior sister" welcomed freshmen to campus, and the new student's upperclass sister protected her from "over-zealous sophomores," and acted as the "voice of experience."[17] Freshmen began the semester wearing a required green costume they made themselves, and sophomores expected the freshmen to have a ready supply of matches, pins, and other items that the sophomores might request at any time. In the fall, a tug-of-war between freshmen and sophomores on campus night, with alumnae looking on, abated the hazing, and at the spring sacred path ceremony, the sophomores admitted the freshmen to full membership in the NJCW student community. Seniors, in cap and gown, and juniors in college blazers watched. Each class had parties and dances, and each shared in a number of all-campus events (campus night, Christmas celebration, parents' day, and somewhat later, a "date with dad" day). By the early 1960s, these traditions had been moved from the front to the back of the college handbook (*Red Book*), sophomores had become sisters rather than tormentors of the first-year students, and the "rules" reduced to what one must wear and were one could walk.

NJCW also regulated its students' lives in more direct ways—sometimes with rules, sometimes with recommendations. A *Red Book* paragraph on appropriate dress told women that they could dress casually, meaning Bermuda shorts to class, but not to chapel assemblies, downtown, or while smoking on the streets. It also laid out the correct clothing for a weekend at the nearby men's colleges. The NJCW objective, more generally, was that women live "graciously and courteously," and again the *Red Book* spelled out the specifics.[18] Then there were more direct rules. Before leaving the dorm each morning, a woman had to make her bed and order her belongings. If a student was going to be absent from the dorm after 7 P.M., she had to sign out. The college set a curfew at 11 P.M. on weeknights, midnight on Friday, and 1 A.M. on Saturday. The only males the college allowed in dorm rooms were relatives (and only on Sunday afternoons), and male friends could only be entertained in the dormitory living room and at specified times during the week. Resident students could not have cars on campus, smoking was prohibited in dorm rooms (but not faculty offices), sunbathing was not allowed in front of dorms, and alcoholic beverages were prohibited on the campus.

Finally, NJCW had an elaborate honor system. The system dated back to the founding of the college, but as it existed after World War II, it was meant more to be a part of a "cooperative plan of living which pervades every aspect of college life" than merely a means of punishing infractions.[19] Each student was expected to assume the responsibility for her own conduct, report herself if she violated rules about classroom honesty or dormitory life, and report others if she saw them do so and not report it. NJCW's parietal rules were a stricter version of the *in loco parentis* regulations that applied to men in New Brunswick, and, of course, similar to those at most women's colleges of that era. They reflected a goal of preparing women for the moral responsibilities of being wives, mothers, and teachers. Meanwhile the college itself offered a curriculum that allowed and challenged these same women to define themselves academically in far broader terms than American society could often accommodate. If there was an inherent contradiction in this, it was not one that found voice in student publications or student government.

Then it all changed. Like college students across the country during the 1960s, Douglass women overturned many of the *in loco parentis* policies of their school. They did so before Livingston College had opened and before Rutgers College had admitted women, that is, before there was local peer pressure to change. The key moment came in February 1968, when, as the *Caellian* reported, "Forty-six Douglass girls stayed out past curfew last night in a 'declaration of student, human, and women's rights,' and as a rejection of administrative authority over their personal lives."[20] Most of them insisted on going before the college disciplinary board as a group. The board called their actions "deplorable" but handed out penalties that the *Targum* described as "a slap on [the] wrist."[21] The incident sparked new legislation by the Douglass Government Association to modify and eliminate the rules. Dean Margery Foster formed a committee on residence college living to advise her on the policies. In very short order, the dean approved the consumption of beer on campus, smoking in dorm rooms

5. The Douglass College newspaper, the *Caellian,* celebrates the end of curfew rules in the dorms. "Debby Douglass" was student vernacular for Douglass women, a term most often used derisively by Rutgers College men.

ARTIST: Carolyn Siegel Stables. Source: *Caellian,* December 5, 1969, 4.

and locks on the door, the end of curfews for all but first-semester students, abolition of the dress code, and finally in 1971, liberalized visitation policies and abolition of the honor system. Of all of these, visitation posed the greatest dilemma, a balancing of individual freedom and privacy. As the *Caellian* analyzed it, at stake was "the idea that there is a basic psychological need for a place that you can call your own," and not everyone was willing to give this up.[22]

In the early 1970s, Dean Foster told newly arriving students: "You who are new students entering Douglass have left secondary school life behind you. Federal and state governments have stated that at 18 you reach majority; so it is as adults that we are very glad to welcome you to Douglass College. . . . As women entering Douglass you will become, if you are not already, aware of opportunities open to women in the world. You will find that you can probably do what you really want to do, *whatever* it is."[23]

"After 206 Years—Women," 1972–1973

Change was also occurring across town, as this third chronological snapshot captures. "Rutgers College, the oldest branch of the University and, until this fall, a bastion of male students, began coeducation, with about 620 women students enrolled."[24] A number were transfer and "upperclassmen," as the *Rutgers Newsletter* put it, and on track to become the college's first women graduates that spring. Overall, the New Brunswick/Piscataway colleges, now with the addition of Livingston, admitted about five thousand new students; Newark an additional twelve hundred; and Camden about a thousand. Collectively, the sleepy little college town and its northern and southern counterparts now taught close to forty thousand graduate students and undergraduates. The Rutgers College dean, Arnold Grobman, noted that among public colleges only the University of California at Berkeley had an academically stronger entering class. In large measure, this was because of the outstanding academic profile of the newly admitted women—whose credentials had been so good that the college had needed to admit far more than it had planned to.

The transition went smoothly. Women, along with the men, suffered because of campus overcrowding—some initially had beds in lounges. Some roomed on all-women floors or wings of a dorm, and others on "coed" floors, sex segregated by rooms. Several of the fraternities admitted women as members (and one or two fraternities already had); within a few years, sororities would be established. Bathroom plumbing could not be changed overnight, but women creatively responded in one dorm by planting flowers in the urinals. In 1971, there had been discussion of the need to add dance classes to accommodate women's recreational interests. When women actually arrived, however, the revamping of athletics went forward far more quickly. The intramural program initially added coed or all-women tennis and volleyball competition, and within a short time, there would be coed teams in such contact sports as flag football. Soon, Rutgers College women had varsity opportunities in basketball, softball, and track. A Douglass sophomore broke another barrier when she walked into the WRSU booth and assisted with the broadcast of the September Lehigh football game. The *Targum* quoted Rutgers College women who thought it "interesting" to be the first at a previously all-male school; it quoted many more who simply took the process in stride. A more telling statement came from a woman who had transferred from George Washington: "When I receive applause for being the sole female in a class of 30, I question the accuracy of the term co-ed."[25]

Women had, of course, long been part of the student body at all the Rutgers campuses except the men's colleges in New Brunswick/Piscataway. "Heterogeneity," the term Philip Roth had used, had not meant women and men together, but the mix of students of blue- and white-collar backgrounds; of Protestant, Catholic, and Jewish faiths; and of Irish and Italian ancestry. Invisible in this depiction were the small number of black, Hispanic, and Asian students—often only one or two a year in a graduation class from the 1950s. By the early 1970s, this had changed dramatically, at least for black and Puerto Rican students, a direct result of the black and Puerto Rican student movements on campus and, more generally, the national civil rights movement. At Douglass and Camden in 1973, blacks made up a tenth of the graduating seniors; at Newark and Rutgers College they still constituted a much smaller percentage (not quite fifty black students can be identified, for example, among the approximately nine hundred Rutgers College seniors). On each campus, however, black students shaped a place for themselves in campus life. At Camden, the Black Allied Students Association (BASA), founded in 1970, scheduled cultural programming that appealed to black students, including an all-black fashion show. By 1973, Delta Sigma Theta, a national historically black sorority, and Omega Psi Phi, a historically black fraternity that traced its origins to 1911 at Howard University, had local chapters. At Newark, the Black Organization of Students (BOS) founded in 1969, played a similar role to the BASA, while the Casa Caribe, founded by the Federación de Estudiantes Latino Americano, became a site for outreach work with local school students. In New Brunswick, the fledgling *Black Voice*, a new student newspaper, and one that would survive into the twenty-first century as the *Black Voice/ Carta Latina*, was in its fourth year of production, and students founded black sororities and fraternities to complement black student organizations that had grown out of the struggles of the late 1960s.

As women entered Rutgers College and black students created new cultural organizations, few noticed that by 1972 the rituals and events that once defined collective campus life had vanished. The military ball was dropped as a "major weekend" in the mid-1960s (field day remained as a politicized, contested event), and the Rutgers College dance committee was replaced by a program committee open to funding any event. In 1969, the college held its last junior prom—declining interest and the size of the student body both played a role in its demise. Douglass retained its international weekend, its elaborate Christmas events, and the (updated) sacred path ceremony, but elsewhere in New Brunswick/Piscataway campus events were more ad hoc creations, such as the spring "Spirit '73" concert in the football stadium, and the numerous dorm, fraternity, and sorority parties. Student newspapers, yearbooks, radio stations, and literary publications, as well as the various government associations now provided whatever remained of once more holistic communities, and student unions and athletic grounds (used by students as both spectators and participants) were now the most common meeting centers. Students, of course, invented new traditions—specific to their many different interests and places of residence—but Rutgers had become a far more diverse set of communities than had been true in the 1950s.

Campus Life, 1972–1973, New Brunswick–Piscataway, as Seen through the *Targum*

Fall 1972

"Coeducation" begins at Rutgers College

Arnold Grobman resigns as dean of faculty

Campus police armed for first time; women added to force

Jane Fonda, Stokely Carmichael, Don McLean, Judy Collins, Julian Bond speak or perform on campus

WRSU licensed as FM station, 88.7

Board of Governors allocates money for new field house [the RAC]

President Bloustein and Higher Education Chancellor Ralph Dungan feud over university autonomy

Rutgers defeats Princeton in first intercollegiate Ultimate Frisbee game

Richard Nixon reelected as president

Spring 1973

Nixon announces Vietnam ceasefire

Albert Twitchell replaced by Fred Gruninger as athletic director; Frank Burns replaces John Bateman as football coach; President Bloustein commits to bigger-time football

Benjamin Spock, Curtis Mayfield, Doobie Brothers on campus; Bruce Springsteen cancels

Basketball team goes to NIT; Dick Lloyd resigns as coach, replaced by Tom
   Young
Controversy over lack of response to "Demands against Racism"; protest
   over alleged police brutality toward Puerto Rican students
Campuswide Paul Robeson tribute (finally)
Ernest Lynton resigns as dean of Livingston
Crime on campus a continuing issue
Campus Patrol newsmaker of the year

In fall 1972, Rutgers College students made history and began a new tradition. While an International Frisbee Association already existed, college
teams had never competed in a match. Young enthusiasts at Rutgers and
Princeton changed that. In the parking lot near the gym, once an athletic
field where the first football game was played, Princeton and Rutgers again
squared off, 103 years later to the day. Before more than eight hundred
spectators, Rutgers came away the victor 29–27. Irv Kalb, the Rutgers captain and author of *Official Rules of Ultimate Frisbee*, commented after the
match, "Princeton really surprised me," as he had expected the twenty men
and women on the Rutgers squad to overwhelm the Tigers.[26] The next
year, Rutgers would became the number one–ranked Frisbee team in the
collegiate world, and it hosted the "Frisbee Octad"—a Frisbee Olympics,
which got equal billing with the varsity baseball team's game with Villa-
nova, the club sport rugby team's match with Yale, and the crew team's
contest with Columbia. The team went on to win the first intercollegiate
national Ultimate Frisbee championship, held at Yale, and the sport, once
established at Rutgers, endured as a staple of undergraduate life in New
Brunswick and on campuses throughout the nation.
   In spring 1973, Zeta Beta Tau (ZBT) sponsored the third annual dance
marathon to benefit the American Cancer Society. This was another largely
homegrown tradition that grew directly from student initiative, and as the
1971 organizers saw it, the "only true all-university [student] function of
the year."[27] The first year, ZBT raised almost $18,000 for charity. Like vir-
tually all events at that time, the marathon was held in the gymnasium on
College Avenue. Two dozen couples danced—with time out for sleeping on
the gym floor—over a three-day period, each couple paying ten dollars to
enter and sponsored by an organization that raised money for the charity.
The winning residence hall (often from Douglass) and fraternity couples
won four-day trips to Bermuda (in subsequent years, it was a round-trip

to Europe); runners-up got color televisions, concert tickets, or trips to the Poconos. Local bands, folk singers, and WRSU provided the music. One year the glee club, dressed as "greasers" and "toughs," did renditions of "The Lion Sleeps Tonight" and "Teen Angel." Surprisingly, the *Targum* noted, many of the dancers knew the steps to the Bunny Hop and how to cha-cha. In the marathon's first year, one of the couples was gay and inter-racial, and when the paper did not report this "first" for marathons, a letter to the editor described the show-stealing dance performance of the two. By 1973, fifty couples were involved, and the marathon raised more than $32,000. By the late 1970s, the total approached $70,000. On several occasions, President Bloustein dropped in to encourage the dancers.

The dance marathon floundered in the early 1980s. After student leaders questioned how the American Cancer Society allocated money received from the dance and some residence halls threatened to withdraw, ZBT switched to Project Hope (and subsequently to other charities). Marathon XVII in spring 1987 raised less than half the money that had been possible ten years earlier, and the event disappeared only to return a decade later, now organized independently, and focused on charities that specialized in childhood illnesses. Less competitive, more a weekend-long party, and more broadly participatory, the new marathon was phenomenally successful. The eleventh annual dance marathon in spring 2009 brought in more than $324,000 "for the kids."[28] In 2014, the students raised $623,000.

At Newark and Camden, organized campus life was more difficult to sustain, especially as many students had come to question the relevance of fraternities and sororities. "Consider the average Rutgers-Newark student," one of them commented. "He comes from a middle-class home. If his parents had been able to, they would have sent him to a good school—maybe Rutgers–New Brunswick or Ohio State—but, because of financial considerations involved, they had to send him to Newark. In most cases he has to work part time after class just to buy gas and pay for parking (and parking tickets)."[29] The student was referring to the difficulty of sustaining varsity athletics at Newark, but his concerns were echoed in every aspect of student life. Newark students had a plaza that served as a meeting place if the weather allowed, and a student center, "several times too small for the number of students who [were] supposed to utilize its facilities," with a grill clogged by "interminable" lines.[30] Students could not really root for most of the athletics teams, as they played off campus, in local high school facilities. For too many, com-

6. In 1967, the Rutgers Married Students Association established a cooperative food store, Heights Hut, on what is now the Busch campus. Initially it sold mostly diary products from the College of Agriculture and Environmental Science farms, but by the early 1970s, the Hut had expanded to a robust grocery store. Here a graduate student, with her two children, makes a purchase. In the postwar era, one of the many challenges for the university was providing support for the increasing population of married graduate students.
SOURCE: R-Photo, buildings and grounds.

muting from home, finding parking, rushing to class, and rushing home defined a school day. Yet, both schools offered multiple cultural activities and hosted clubs, both had active student government associations, and at both, the student newspapers, Camden's *Gleaner* and Newark's *Observer*, alerted students to opportunities for involvement in campus life. Camden's fraternities staged a Greek week in the spring that featured a chariot race and Olympic sports competition, and the campus had a black cultural festival and a Puerto Rican day, while at Newark there was a Christmas ball, a Ukrainian festival, and a black fashion show. These were significant accomplishments despite adversity. This pattern would not change until resident life facilities were built in the late 1980s in both Newark and Camden and the university began to invest more heavily in an infrastructure that would convince student commuters to consider living in Newark and Camden.

Residence Halls and Fraternities Revisited

For Rutgers anthropologist Michael Moffatt, residence halls were at the center of student culture. In 1977, he began his study of student life in the residence halls, *Coming of Age in New Jersey: College and American Culture*, on a whim. "I decided to try passing as an average, out-of-state freshman," Moffatt later wrote, "for the first few days of the fall semester at Rutgers College. I had been on the Rutgers faculty for four years at the time. My serious anthropological interests then lay in south India, but it would be some years before I could get back into the field."[31] When he moved into a dorm (with approval from the college dean) on the quad of Bishop campus of College Avenue, New Brunswick, he looked a little like a holdover from the counterculture of the 1960s. The students realized he was older, but it took his roommates a few days to uncover his identity as a college professor. Moffatt had not mastered the vernacular of popular culture or concealed the copy he bought each day of the *New York Times*. The students did not protest the trick but played their own on Moffatt (shaving cream in his shoes, a sign of his acceptance).

Moffatt's initial foray into late adolescent college culture was followed by two extended stays. These, in turn, were the basis for *Coming of Age*, which he began writing in the mid-1980s. By that time, residence halls had become the center of campus life, especially for first- and second-year students in New Brunswick/Piscataway. Those campuses provided more than eleven thousand beds for college students, and after a construction boom in the late 1980s and early 1990s, Rutgers–New Brunswick had beds for more than thirteen thousand undergraduates and seven hundred graduate students. Newark had seven hundred beds (a third of these were for graduate students) and Camden about five hundred (almost half for graduate students). For both the south and north Jersey campuses the addition of residence halls signaled a new direction in student life. In New Brunswick in the early 1990s, two students in three spent part of their college careers in a residence hall (compared with fewer than one in twenty who lived in a fraternity), and one in four spent their entire four years in university housing.

The dorm residents whom Moffatt came to know thought about their lives in terms of finding a balance between academic work and play, and they thought about play not in terms of the structured opportunities of some bygone age (of which they had no historical memory) but as extensions of their private selves—talking with roommates, partying at fraternities, peer-group pranks on the dorm floor, shooting hoops, and watching television in the lounge with friends. Many belonged to one or more of the numerous student groups, but few participated actively in them. In a typical day, a student studied a maximum of two hours (but crammed before tests and pulled all-nighters to complete papers), attended four hours of class, and slept eight hours (or more). One in eight worked several hours a day. In what had become a large, impersonal university, most students defined themselves not through structured activities provided by the colleges but more informally through peer relationships.

For many students, Moffatt found, music and sex were central to their relationships. Music linked students to each other, connected them more generally to youth culture, and, at the same time, separated them from each other (hip-hop students, for example, from rock-and-roll students). As for sex, Moffatt wrote, "Sexual fun, in fact, could be said to be at the core of college life."[32] In the dorms, however, now generally coed, sexuality was "restrained—if not entirely repressed," and while romances and liaisons developed on dorm floors, what one did sexually with a neighbor one also did as privately as possible.[33] On a dorm floor, women and men could simply become friends, although the price that "a woman had to pay for being treated as near equals . . . was to act like the men."[34] Beyond the dorm, most students sought sexual experience, women more often feeling guilty if sex occurred without genuine caring, while men were anxious if they remained virgins. More generally, in youth culture, gendered conventions about sexuality persisted, even if the traditional double standard (that blamed women for behavior it encouraged in men) had eroded.

Students teased their peers who studied too much and carefully stage-managed their own intellectual ambitions, but there was, nonetheless, in the dorms a general commitment to academic life. Getting good grades mattered to most students more than getting through college with the least amount of work. Most majored in subjects that had a vocational payoff, but they also appreciated good professors and the chance for serious late-night discussions with other students in their dorms. In learning, as in recreational activity, Moffatt emphasized the ability of students to fashion their own culture.

Moffatt believed that student life, broadly defined, and fraternity culture had by the mid-1980s gone in different directions. The 1992 university-wide report on fraternities and sororities listed ten at Camden with 198

members (roughly equal numbers of women and men); two of the fraternities provided housing for their members. At Newark, there were fourteen
fraternities and sororities with 167 members (more sororities and more
women members than fraternities and men); two had houses, but few
members actually lived in them. In New Brunswick, 1,165 men belonged
to one of thirty-three fraternities and 725 women to one of the fifteen sororities—and overall, about one undergraduate in thirteen belonged to a
recognized Greek society. Despite inadequate fraternity housing and the
movement of students into residence halls on all the campuses, the Greek
system, evaluated in numerical terms, was far from irrelevant in campus
life, and university surveys indicated that many nonmembers shared in
some Greek activities.

Moreover, the fraternity system had changed in two crucial ways since
the early 1970s. Camden and Newark had long had sororities, but New
Brunswick had not, until after the admission of women to Rutgers College.
In 1974, women at Rutgers College established the first sorority, which in
1977 affiliated nationally with Gamma Phi Beta. At the time of the 1992
report, the sorority had ninety-eight members (including two dozen Douglass women), making it among the largest Greek organizations on campus, but yet had no housing. By the mid-1990s, the first New Brunswick
sorority acquired a house, on Union Street (the college's fraternity row),
and by the late 1990s, nine sororities had meeting places or houses, many
along Mine Street, just to the west of Union Street.[35]

The other change in Greek life was the addition of chapters of historically black fraternities and sororities. Rutgers College had, in fact, included
a black fraternity, Alpha Phi Alpha, in the 1950s, but it withered (only to
reemerge), and Newark and Camden both had African American sororities and fraternities before New Brunswick. In 1973, black male students
established Omega Psi Phi on the Livingston campus, and several additional African American fraternities and sororities (as well as one Latino
fraternity) were established during the decade. Most were small, and none
had houses. Yet their impact on the black students who participated was
enormous. In a letter to the *Targum* in 1990, Robert Yarbrough, an engineering and finance major and president of Alpha Phi Alpha, described his
initial involvement of "walking on line" with other black pledges as a matter of "confidence and power," and he remembered entering the Livingston
student center with his line of Alpha pledges: "[A]s we entered the front
door, the chatter of mingling students subsided as my line Brothers and I

marched through, chanting an inspiration pledge song."[36] To Yarbrough, pledging rituals were neither foolish nor hazing, but part of a program that built pride through an immersion in fraternity and black culture.

Thus, as Moffatt noted, what had changed was not the relevance of Greek organizations, but the culture that prevailed in fraternities. Nationwide, critics singled out fraternities for sexism, homophobia, excessive drinking, and disorderly behavior. Much of this was new and occasioned by male insecurities with the rise of the women's movement and gay liberation. At Rutgers, such trends were exacerbated by the movement of students into the multiplying residence halls, leaving behind a self-selected group of fraternity men who, those outside the fraternity system argued, became even more likely to engage in antisocial behavior. An assault in 1982 by fraternity brothers on members of another house, numerous hazing incidents, charges of the branding of pledges at one fraternity, the tragic death of a pledge in 1988, and allegations of acquaintance and gang rapes at fraternity parties provided evidence of how serious problems had become. Even if the occurrences were not systemic (and the typical fraternity was not involved in any of these activities), the university had to act.

Throughout the 1970s, university supervision of the fraternities and sororities had been lax. In part, this reflected the retreat from *in loco parentis* that applied to all campus life. It also reflected worries about the school's legal liability if it assumed responsibility for what were private organizations. The faculty reports of 1979 and 1988 both urged a change of direction, and, when the state raised the drinking age for alcoholic beverages from nineteen to twenty-one in 1983, the university acquired an additional responsibility that directly affected its approach to student life. New rules, new administrative positions, new education programs (on such things as drinking and sexism), and closer supervision followed, and by the 1990s, these changes had reshaped Greek life. While Greek leaders resisted some of the changes—especially restrictions on rushing new members—by and large they accepted the new policies, while emphasizing the continuing importance both of the charitable work the sororities and fraternities did and the nurturing of community and leadership within individual houses. In 2004, when there were twenty-one (national) fraternities in New Brunswick, six (national) sororities, and eighteen fraternities or sororities with largely African American, Latino/a, or Asian membership, the university issued yet another report on the Greek system, this time one that took for granted the return of *in loco parentis* (and accordingly, its recommendations were quite detailed). The heart of the report, however, suggested ways to strengthen the system, and while the more controversial of these (concerning housing and support from student fees) were not implemented, they signaled a new acceptance of fraternities and sororities, as a part, albeit a much diminished part, of campus life. While the typical Rutgers student now lived in a residence hall or commuted and had little to do with fraternities or sororities, these organizations nonetheless remained a significant presence on the university campuses because of their parties, intramural participation, attendance at intercollegiate athletic events, and charitable endeavors.

Diversity, 1998–1999

In late August 1998, the *Targum* presented first-year students with a special orientation issue of the paper, *RU101*. Among its imaginative pieces (reminiscent of the definitions the *Red Book* editors created for Douglass students in the 1950s) was the "RU 101 Glossary," which contained dozens of short descriptions of aspects of campus life, including these:

Ag Field Day Toward the end of the spring semester, Cook students show off their well-groomed, well-mannered animals. What used to be a day filled with beer, bands, and barbecues has turned into a day at the local carnival. Why they changed it, we can't say, people liked it better that way. But not the students.

Bishop Beach One of the major places at the University with a stupid name. This grassy area in front of the Bishop House on the College Avenue campus does not have one grain of sand. Bishop Beach is a place where people bring blankets, books, bongos, and bikinis for entertainment. A great place for recreation or relaxing. It's also a great place for people watching.

Cannon War This is a long story. We tried to simplify. Think about *The Simpsons* episode where Homer goes to college and kidnaps Sir Oinks A Lot. We had a cannon a long time ago. Princeton stole it. We stole it back. They stole it from us, and so on. After a joint committee was finally formed to figure out whose cannon it actually is, Princeton obtained the steely relic and now it is on their campus. However, the rivalry still runs strong, and Rutgers folks can still be seen riding down to Princeton to paint the cannon Scarlet Red.

Eden The Internet user's paradise at Rutgers. Eden is a student network and e-mail system.

First-Year Student The good old days of calling people freshmen are long gone. The term first-year student was coined by the University so as to not exclude anyone. From time to time you may hear this dirty "F" word being used around campus.

Grease Trucks Like ice cream trucks with greasy food, the trucks can be found in the parking lot on the corner of College Avenue and Hamilton Street. You will find yourself drawn to the trucks like they were the monolith in *2001*, and find yourself eating a strange variety of bulky sandwiches [Fat Cats] with everything greasy to Middle Eastern delights such as hummus and gyros. The trucks are open pretty late and offer cheap fare, and the slightest breeze will catch your nose and lure you to greaseland.

Passion Puddle The puddle is always surrounded by people studying or pretending to study when they actually just want to look cool. There is a bit of lore that goes along with the puddle. Legend has it that if a Douglass woman drags her unassuming Cook boyfriend around the mud puddle three times they will get married. If they don't, it's just one more Cook guy to dredge out of the lake at the end of the month.

River Dorms With a scenic view over the old Raritan, these residence halls proudly boast the best television reception. There's rumors that someone was able to get NBC, ABC, and FOX all in one room. There are three river dorms: the easy to pronounce and spell Campbell, the easy to pronounce and hard to spell Hardenbergh, and what the hell is a Frelinghuysen? These residence halls also have bland classrooms in the basement, notorious for strange odors.

Rutgersfest A free day of music and festivities held in May on Busch campus. Last year's featured performer was Morphine.

RU Screw The most difficult to describe term used at Rutgers. Basically, you'll know it when it gets you. The RU Screw is the constant action of some higher bureaucratic god that likes to meddle with Rutgers students, whether in their attempts to register for a class or to buy books or to park where they're not supposed to. Think of the RU Screw being like Gargamel's evil spell and Rutgers students are the Smurfs. Sooner or later, the spell may be broken.

Social Black-Out A constant nowadays for Greeks. From some decision passed down by higher powers, social black-out means fraternities cannot have open parties on certain weekends. It seems social black-outs occur weekly at the University.[37]

The *Targum's* list suggested that as diverse as Rutgers had become there were still commonalities in student culture. Author Jon Horowitz mentioned fraternities sparingly, and not particularly favorably. Dorms, now clearly "residence halls," were referenced more frequently. Horowitz included definitions of "TA" and "Recitation," but professors were mentioned only in relationship to the faculty union (always threatening to strike). There were no iconic figures, renowned lectures, or ever-present deans on the list, although the president, as "Fran the Man," was cited. The author noted only one all-campus event *for students*, Rutgersfest (a little more than a decade later it too would be gone) but highlighted several informal meeting places—open, grassy areas that students used as they wished. He lampooned the enforcement of alcohol policy. Traditions were noted, but as memories worth preserving rather than having much to do with the here and now. Only one entry, a teasing description of "PIRG," suggested the history of political activism at Rutgers.

The newspaper also ran a story during the 1990s about what students should do (or have done) at Rutgers. The 1998 version of "101 things to do at RU" included pulling an all-nighter, falling asleep in class, getting written up by your preceptor, listening to WRSU, having your grades held for not having immunization shots, seeing the Rutgers football team win one game, calling home to beg for money, and getting a job. The complete list captured a student world punctuated by small frustrations, tied to popular culture but without many common points of reference, and split between home, work, and the demands of school. Sex was secondary to appearance and drinking to food in these lists, even if sex and drinking loomed large in the public imagination of college life. Academics, although laughed about, figured prominently in the vernacular of student life, again despite perceptions to the contrary.

If most of these students had drifted into a postpolitical age that set them apart from past Rutgers students, what now distinguished campus life was diversity. In fall 1997, to take one example from the Newark campus, a quarter of the female students were white, a quarter African American, slightly less than a quarter of Latina origin, and three in twenty of Asian ancestry or birth. Five female students listed themselves as of Native American ancestry, and 2 percent were at Rutgers on student visas from foreign countries. A larger percentage of the male students at Newark classified themselves as white, but factoring that in, Newark still had become the most diverse college in the nation, an honor it received numerous times in the future. Even on the New Brunswick campus, where students of European ancestry constituted just a little more than half the population, diversity defined campus life. On each campus, women outnumbered men among the undergraduates. At the graduate level, hundreds of students from China, Korea, India, and Taiwan attended Rutgers, and well over a hundred countries were represented among the graduate population (but only few outside Asia—Turkey, Russia, and neighboring Canada—sent truly significant numbers). In another way, however, Rutgers was still a parochial backwater. The typical undergraduate came from New Jersey, while the typical student on each campus came from the county in which her or his campus was located—and to the extent that they had grown up in local school districts that were far less diverse than Rutgers, students, at least initially, did not always embrace diversity as much as ignore it.

Many of the benefits of diversity were intangible, easy to identify but hard to access. Some, though, were quite concrete, most significantly, student activities. The fee paid by students to fund activities, as has been noted, supported about a dozen organizations in the 1950s and early 1960s. By the early 1970s, student government organizations divided funds among a significantly higher number of clubs, activities, and groups—five or six dozen on each campus. A few of these, such as the African Association, Black Women's Association, Chinese Students' Club, Homophile League, Luso-Brazilian Club, and Ukrainian Students' Club at Rutgers College, suggested the growing diversity of the student population. Most of the newly funded organizations, however, were traditional clubs, often associated with particular departments or activities that had carried on in the past without student fee funding. The same was true at Newark and Camden, where only the longstanding Ukrainian Club (at Newark), and the newer organizations for women and African American students reflected diversity.

By the late 1990s, this situation had changed dramatically. There were now more than forty funded organizations that spoke to the ethnic, racial, gender, national, and religious diversity of the New Brunswick/Piscataway campuses. Such groups included the Bengali Students Association, Filipinos in Christ, Korean Catholic Circle, One Hundred Black Men at Rutgers, Sikhs Association, Vietnamese Students, West Indian Student Organization, and Women against Violence, among many others. The lengthy list is a remarkable blueprint of diversity at Rutgers. Particularly striking is the inclusion of so many religious organizations, highlighting one of the less visible but significant changes in campus life in recent years.

Students, then, lived in a world of small communities, rather than in the Rutgers community. Or, they lived outside the university, commuting to class and retreating to home and employment. Those on and around campus shared a residence hall floor or lived in a fraternity or sorority or in overcrowded, off-campus student housing where they had to adjust to living with others, often different from themselves. They also had the opportunity, which many of them took, to join organizations that reinforced or redefined identities they brought with them to campus. If on the international stage, American economic power in the late twentieth century had spread American popular culture globally, on college campuses such as those within Rutgers, back current from world cultures transformed what had once been the domain of white, Protestant, blue- and white-collar suburban America.

Recreational Sports

Of all the activities the university sponsored for a diverse student population none had wider appeal than recreational sports. In the student satisfaction surveys that the university began to conduct in the mid-1980s, student centers, libraries, and student affairs all got high marks; parking did very poorly; touch-tone registration (in the 1990s), intercollegiate athletics, and financial aid fell in the middle. One aspect of college life, recreational services, consistently topped the ranking in New Brunswick, while doing far less well at Newark and Camden. The recreational sports program—swimming pools, gymnasiums, fitness centers, intramurals, club sports, marathon and charity races—central to the consumer culture of campus life today, grew from an older ideal of educating the whole person.

At the men's colleges in the early 1950s, athletics was an educational program that provided all students the opportunity to train themselves physically as well as mentally. It embraced intercollegiate athletics, required physical education, and intramurals. Intramural touch football in 1950 at the men's colleges, for example, drew in 450 students in the fall, basketball more than 700 during the winter, and softball another 700 in the spring (at a time when male enrollment in New Brunswick numbered around 2,500 students). On the Newark campus, first- and second-year students were required to take physical education, and a slightly less ambitious but still extensive program of intramurals existed, but even more so than in New Brunswick, inadequate facilities limited what could be accomplished (a pattern just as evident at the College of South Jersey). Throughout the system, athletics were primarily for young men. At the NJCW, students had gym and modest opportunities to participate in sports through the athletic association, and at Camden and Newark, lack of facilities for women limited athletic endeavor.

Student protest in the 1960s ended required physical education. In the wake of the requirements demise, there remained student demands on all the campuses for opportunities to exercise and to participate in club sports and intramurals. A 1973 faculty report deplored the appalling state of athletic facilities at Newark and Camden and recommended particular emphasis on club sports, intramurals, and the like (rather than intercollegiate athletics).

Slowly, student recreational opportunities improved. In New Brunswick, these activities were detached from the physical education program and transferred to the individual colleges and later to the university division of student affairs. Classes in traditional, competitive team sports—basketball, softball, and the like—disappeared, while recreational classes tailored to students' interests and more often focused on learning individual (or partner) skills proliferated. By the 1990s, these classes included yoga and Pilates, swimming, ballet to Bollywood beats, salsa dancing, golf, outdoor activities such as rock climbing, and martial arts. The traditional intramural program was trimmed back to focus on approximately half a dozen of the more popular sports, in which as many as eight thousand students participated (out of an undergraduate population of more than twenty-seven thousand), but even more so than in the past, these programs appealed to male rather than female students, and while fraternity participation remained strong, far fewer independent teams and resident hall teams competed. The building of the Werblin Center, upgrading of the older campus facilities, and the inclusion of fitness centers in student housing drew in almost two million users a year (many, of course, repeat users) for workouts or swimming. Newark and Camden, with commuter populations, lagged behind, even after the building of gymnasiums. Intramurals, for example, which attracted almost a quarter of the New Brunswick students in the 1990s, involved about 5 percent of the students in Camden and Newark.

The most dramatic change came in club sports. In the first decade of the twenty-first century, Rutgers–New Brunswick sponsored approximately fifty club sports with more than sixteen hundred students (and in some cases, alumni) participating, and men and women joined in relatively equal numbers. Some of these club sports duplicated varsity sports; some were sports with a long tradition at Rutgers or Douglass College, such as rugby, ice hockey, Ultimate Frisbee, and equestrian competition. Still others like cricket, judo, paintball, salsa, and taekwondo reflected the changing interests and diversity of the student population. Most clubs competed against other college teams (and recreational teams more generally) and about a third of them went to national or regional championship events. All required a fee to participate but also received funding through student fees.

In 2006, when the university dropped a number of varsity sports in a cost-saving move, the demoted programs were reborn as club sports. With money from intercollegiate athletics, students formed a swimming club to replace varsity competition. One of its organizers, Kyle Madison, an accomplished high school swimmer and college honors student, helped recruit more than four dozen students, women and men both, for the club. While he was a student, the club practiced and competed (when home) at the Werblin Center (where the women's varsity program did as well) against clubs from Penn State, Vermont, Princeton, Connecticut, and other northeastern universities and traveled at season's end to the East Coast championships at Georgia Tech (swimming in the pool used for the 1996 Olympics). The swimmers had a student coach, paid a $30 fee each semester, and attended daily, but nonmandatory, practices. The program had an appealing casual atmosphere, and the students had fun.[38]

The fencing club got off to a similar propitious start. The club attracted two dozen members, competed under the auspices of a national collegiate fencing association against clubs and varsity teams from Army, Cornell, the University of North Carolina, and other universities, and it participated in the national championships. For swimming and fencing, as with other club sports, there was no recruitment and no scholarship money. Coaching, in sports such as fencing and crew, where students usually lacked high school experience, was crucial and costly.

In the postwar period, with required physical education, and at Rutgers College a vibrant fraternity system, competitive sports had been an integral part of the college experience of most men and women in New Brunswick. The late 1960s and early 1970s had witnessed greater emphasis on allowing students to define their own path through the university (electives replacing requirements), and physical education was restructured to meet student demand—shaped by the growing emphasis in secondary education on participation by both girls and boys in athletics. University students no longer shared a common sports culture (any more than they shared a common, traditional liberal arts education), and more than half of them probably dropped out of recreational activities completely, but those who wanted to couple fitness, health, competition, or recreation with academics now had many more options than they would have had half a century before.

Student Life

College life, historian Helen Lefkowitz Horowitz reminds us, has a long history, and its traditional form has changed, adjusting to broader currents in American culture. The distinctive world of undergraduates was born in the late eighteenth and early nineteenth centuries, a product of struggle between faculties and students. The students of that era, "pleasure-seeking young men" from elite families, representing only a very small fraction of the young adults of the nation, rebelled against the discipline and the classical academics imposed on them by college faculties, and when they lost the open battles, went "underground," forging "a peer consciousness sharply at odds" with that of their professors, a consciousness that found "institutional expression in the fraternity and club system."[39] Throughout the nineteenth century, even as colleges became universities, and schools began to attract more students from the middle class, college life remained a realm where "the young made a world to suit themselves."[40] The trials on the athletics field, rowdiness on campus, drinking bouts in fraternities, prepared them more than the classroom, they thought, for careers in the muscular capitalism of the period.

The early twentieth century saw three significant changes in college life. Women entered what had usually been an all-male preserve. Sexual prowess had always been a part of male campus culture, but now dating, and dating the right girl, helped define the status of male students. Just as important, campus faculties and presidents came to terms with their students. Student life received the blessing of those who ran American colleges, and private student activities of the nineteenth century increasingly received official sanction. College life became more structured, even if it continued to retain its antiauthoritarian rowdiness and anti-intellectualism. Third, as colleges attracted increasing number of students from outside the elite—especially women, Jews, children of immigrant households, and a few African Americans—a growing proportion of the student bodies at many colleges stood apart from what they saw as the essential silliness of college life. College was too important to their aspirations to waste it. Yet other students, especially during the 1930s, turned their backs on the world of clubs and fraternities, becoming deeply engaged in the protest politics of that era. At women's colleges, which increased in number in the early twentieth century, a variation of college life, still pleasure-seeking, but less anti-intellectual and less rowdy than at men's and coeducational institutions, took shape.

College life, as it emerged at Rutgers after World War II, shared much with that at other campuses, especially liberal arts institutions in the Northeast and Midwest, but two distinctive features are worth noting. First, despite the trappings of Ivy League gentility, the men's colleges attracted not the children of the American elite, but the children of immigrants, most often the first in their families to attend college. Campus high jinks were part of their life; anti-intellectualism seldom was. Fraternity brothers proudly boasted that that they did better at academics than their commuting peers. Philip Roth had chosen wisely. Rutgers was more like Bucknell than neighboring Princeton. Second, Rutgers included what were then merely satellite campuses. At both Camden and Newark, some students attempted to create the organizations and activities they associated with college life, and that many had experienced in a different setting in their high school education. For particular students this worked, but campus government, fraternities, and cultural and literary organizations were simply irrelevant to many commuting students, and the university had higher priorities in the 1950s and 1960s than providing the facilities that might have changed this situation. The New Jersey College for Women (Douglass) probably came the closest to replicating college life as it existed at comparable institutions.

At virtually every campus in America in the late 1960s and early 1970s, traditional campus life disintegrated. The collective rituals that made most students part of a common community disappeared. The antiwar and the black student protest movement had something to do with this by mak-

ing the rituals of campus life (especially those associated with fraternities) seem trivial or irrelevant, but a broader sea-change was in motion.
Until this time, campus life had been a privileged, protected enclave for a
small subset of late-adolescent Americans. When, however, the baby boom
generation reached college, and state universities, in particular, accepted
the challenge of mass education, youth culture and campus life became
increasingly synonymous. Students were no longer merely coming of age
in college, they were shaping colleges with values and behaviors they had
acquired from their high school peers, the media, and consumer culture.
Those values might still lead students into traditional activities—student
government, journalism, or clubs—but more often than not, they were
played out in self-selected friendships or through the random acquain-
tances occasioned by a dormitory assignment. The growing diversity of
the student population—Latino/a, African American, and Asian ancestry
students—accelerated the fragmentation of traditional forms of college life
(although it also led to the strengthening of the fraternity system by extending it to African American and Latino/a students, and in New Brunswick, to the creation of sororities).

Again, several features stand out in how this happened at Rutgers. At
Rutgers College, "diversity" initially meant not only the admission of more
African American students but also the admission of women. Just as significantly, the continuation of Douglass as a women's college added to
campus diversity. At a time when many other women's colleges were being
absorbed into coeducational universities, Douglass developed mentoring
programs and mission courses to help women overcome the barriers posed
by society to full equality. New Brunswick/Piscataway, then, had not just
more women, but women more aware of how feminism was changing their
opportunities. The creation of Livingston added a college with a significant minority presence, an urban focus, and, unlike Camden and Newark, a large resident population. The decision in the late 1980s to establish
residence halls on the university's Newark and Camden campuses and to
upgrade the support services (especially athletic fields and student centers) that attracted students to these campuses for more than just classes
signaled a new direction for what still remained largely commuter schools.

Layered on top of these changes, in the past two decades of the university's history, was the increasing enrollment of students of Asian birth and
ancestry, such as S. Mitra Kalita. Occasionally these students shaped activities that brought them together as "Asian"; more commonly, they created

organizations and identified themselves by particular ethnic and national heritages. Overall, Rutgers attracted among the most diverse student populations in the nation. The Newark campus, in fact, often led the nation in the diversity of its student population, and New Brunswick/Piscataway was not far behind.

One is tempted to describe the arc of student life at Rutgers as community to diversity. That shorthand description, however, belies the multiple meanings of community and the contradictory consequences of diversity. The men's colleges were already too large by 1945 for the students to constitute a true face-to-face community. Only the NJCW approached that ideal type, and on both sides of New Brunswick, students were most likely to think in terms of those with whom they lived, in fraternities, residential homes, or dormitories as their immediate community—all of which gave them much in common with students fifty years later. What distinguished the earlier period was the integrative pull of a shared set of activities whose only real counterpart in the early twenty-first century was attendance at football games (an activity that involved, at most, a third of the New Brunswick student population) or walking around campus wearing clothing branded with the Scarlet "R."

Diversity is also a complicated concept. Students, as they understood it, experienced diversity when they left their small, local high schools behind and roomed with new people from different parts of the state—this could be as true in 2015 as 1945. As Rutgers grew and became statistically more ethnically diverse, nothing prevented students from seeking friends among others very much like themselves. Moreover, as students increasingly shared cultural assumptions created by a national youth culture and globalized in the twenty-first century by the Internet, their apparent ethnic differences were perhaps less significant than their personal preferences as individuals. Rutgers–New Brunswick, was, in fact, more diverse, and less a community than its distinct colleges had been at the end of World War II (the latter was not so true of Newark and Camden), but for most students, having fun, making new friends, and charting an academic path that would lead to a career remained constants.

5

Residence Hall Architecture at Rutgers

Quadrangles, High-Rises,
and the Changing Shape of Student Life

CARLA YANNI

Rutgers College students did not always live on campus—from the time of the signing of the charter in 1766 to the opening of the first dormitory, Winants Hall, in 1890, students lived in boarding houses, fraternities, or with their families. Between 1890 and World War II, Rutgers College encouraged students to live in dormitories to conform to the ideal of a closely knit collegiate atmosphere. There was an uptick in enrollment from 1947 to 1949, followed by a period of sustained, permanent growth. In the 1950s, college officials, eager to stave off a severe housing shortage, planned the nine-story dormitory-classroom buildings on the banks of the old Raritan; clean-cut Rutgers College men were housed economically and urbanely in soaring structures that announced the arrival of the forward-looking state university. In the late 1960s and 1970s, college students were members of an activist youth culture, and the planners of Livingston College reacted to the new challenges of higher education by creating small communities within the large and increasingly anonymous university. Today, students have many options for housing, and by the time they are juniors and seniors, they expect to be treated as adult consumers; one of the newest residence halls at Rutgers responds to their needs by affording them access to generously sized comfortable apartments, chain restaurants, and popular entertainment.

This chapter examines three case studies (the River Dorms, the Quads at Livingston, and the Livingston Apartments) to explore key themes in

Rutgers's post–World War II architectural history. The varied designs of these residence halls reflect changes in student life, or, perhaps more accurately, reflect college officials' changing expectations for student life. College dormitories are not mute containers for the temporary storage of bodies and minds. They constitute historical evidence of the educational ideals and aspirations of the people who built them. For the purposes of this chapter, I will look closely at the intentions of the architects and patrons, and concentrate on the buildings at the time they were designed and first occupied.

Before World War II, Rutgers College had only a handful of dormitories, including Winants, Ford, and the Bishop Quad. Fraternity men dwelled in large chapterhouses that lined College Avenue and Union Street, and other students commuted from home or relatives' houses. Some students lived in boarding houses in New Brunswick. The dormitories known collectively as the Bishop Quad dominated campus life from the 1920s until the end of the war. The Bishop Quad was composed of four dormitories, Wessels, Pell, Leupp, and Hegeman. Hegeman, an L-shaped building, opened in 1926. Leupp, completed in 1929, came next. Pell and Wessels, completed in 1929 and 1930, respectively, were sited so that they formed a U along with Leupp. All four structures were arranged to create a traditional collegiate quadrangle. The quadrangle form (a rectangular doughnut) was of long-standing importance, as it harkened back to the colleges of Oxford and Cambridge. This collegiate building shape, along with the closely related U-shaped plan, was a mainstay at Princeton, Yale, and Harvard. The fact that American colleges so skillfully adopted the forms of Oxbridge demonstrates the worldly aspirations of American educators. The quadrangle created an enclosed, or partially enclosed, outdoor space, and turned the college inward, away from the town. Bishop Quad, like many collegiate quadrangles, employed the entryway plan, wherein students entered their bedrooms by staircases that were clustered around landings on each floor. As a result, social groups formed up and down the staircases. The Bishop Quad had common rooms on the ground floors, which aided social interaction, allowing students to mingle. The human scale and courtyards of the Bishop Quad contributed to the small-college atmosphere of the prewar Rutgers.

For the first ten years or so after World War II, Rutgers remained a medium-size liberal arts college. It was primarily a place where New

7. View of the Bishop Quad at Rutgers College. The dormitories are known individually as Wessels, Pell, and Leupp (1929–1930) and Hegeman (1926). This view from inside Bishop Quad's courtyard shows the doors that lead to staircases; students' bedrooms are off the staircases. Hegeman Hall is at the right. Leupp and Pell can be seen at the left. Photograph dated 1936.
SOURCE: R-Photo, buildings and grounds, box 9.

Jerseyans could send their children for an affordable education. Demarest, a residence hall built in 1951, and the first after the war, demonstrated the continuing ambience of a small school. Demarest recalled the colonial period of Rutgers's heritage in its red brick, white trim, and cupola. Even more specifically, the gambrel roof (a roof with an upper slope that is shallow and a steeper slope below, thus giving more ceiling height in the attic) was a signature of the Dutch colonial revival style. Because Rutgers traced its roots back to the Dutch Reformed Church, the choice of this style was appropriate. In 1951, many colleges were constructing modernist buildings, so, to some observers, this choice might have seemed rather nostalgic. Demarest shared a familial relationship with the earlier Wessels, Pell, Leupp, and Hegeman in terms of the style (colonial), color palate (red brick with white trim), and scale (three stories beneath the roof). In plan, however, Demarest employed a hybrid version of the entryway scheme, which included interior corridors: students entered the building from the courtyard, and from there, staircases took them to their rooms.

8. Demarest Hall (1951), exterior in the snow. The gambrel roof is a signature element of the Dutch colonial revival style. Photograph dated 1959.
SOURCE: R-Photo, buildings and grounds, box 9.

Once inside, corridors completely traversed the halls, allowing for students to circulate freely within the structure. Demarest's common rooms soon became a magnet for social activities. (During this time, there was not yet a student center, and the only available space for large social gatherings like dances was the College Avenue Gymnasium, also known as the Barn.) As the yearbook, *The Scarlet Letter*, put it in 1957: "The spacious well decorated lounge [of Demarest] is the scene of freshman mixers with the Douglass frosh, dances, parties, bull sessions, card games, and even studying."[1]

In the 1950s, Rutgers College had a housing shortage. There were many reasons for the upsurge in students. Americans valued state-funded higher education as never before; the economy expanded; Cold War politics led Americans to place their faith in education as a means of defeating communism; and middle-class families expected to send their children to college, as they had once sent children to high school. Rutgers, like many public universities, acted on its obligation to serve the citizens of its state. The school's officials assumed the undergraduate student population would grow from five thousand in 1954 to nineteen thousand by 1970. The residence halls that addressed this urgent need marked a turning point in the history of Rutgers.

The River Dorms, built in 1955–1956, went up only a few years after Demarest and a stone's throw from it—but in terms of architectural style, they came from a different, decidedly modern world.[2] The shift in style and scale did not come easily. Based on university projections, Rutgers had to find space for a thousand men on the College Avenue campus. The dean of men, Cornelius Boocock, did not at first welcome the idea of high-rises. In 1953, he suggested demolishing Bishop House (built in 1852 and now on the National Register of Historic Places) so that Rutgers would have enough space near the Bishop Quad to build a series of low-slung, U-shaped buildings. He also wanted the university to purchase land on the west side of College Avenue for the construction of several more residence halls, again in an attempt to squeeze one thousand students into low-rise buildings. It need hardly be stated that building low requires more land than building tall; thus, owing to the added expense of the purchase of land, Boocock's suggestions about the site were ignored. Boocock stated his preference (which reflected that of his staff) that the new dormitories be sited close to Demarest, that they should be low (three or four stories), that they should have entryways instead of corridors, and that the style be a "traditional type of architecture to harmonize with existing buildings."[3]

In January 1954, at the first meeting between President Lewis Webster Jones and the architectural firm Kelly and Gruzen, the architects rejected every one of Dean Boocock's suggestions. The buildings were not next to Demarest, they were not low, they had internal corridors, and their style was modern, not traditional. The long, thin site along the Delaware and Raritan Canal—land that Rutgers already owned—emerged as the most desirable and least expensive space. The choice to build high-rises was partly generated by the small site and the fact that Rutgers already owned the land, but it was also entirely in keeping with the fashion in dormitory design in the 1950s. From tall buildings in this appealing location, on a clear day, students on the upper floors had spectacular views. The three buildings were angled to allow maximum sunlight and the best views. And with efficient elevators, why build low? Even universities with plenty of land, such as The Ohio State University and Michigan State University, built skyscraper dorms.

The architect, Sumner Gruzen, lobbied for tall buildings when he told the Buildings and Grounds Committee of the Board of Trustees that the new dormitories, taking advantage of modern materials, would be cheaper than Demarest. He estimated Demarest at $2,400 per student and the new

9 (left). The River Dorms, seen from the far side of the Raritan River. Kelly and Gruzen, architects.

SOURCE: R-Photo, buildings and grounds, box 9.

10 (below). River Dorms, site plan.

SOURCE: R-Photo, buildings and grounds, box 9.

11 (bottom). River Dorms under construction. The steel skeletons, reflected in the water's surface, celebrate the modernity of the new residence halls. Photograph dated 1955.

SOURCE: R-Photo, buildings and grounds, box 9.

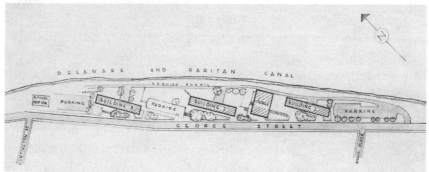

dorms (which also were more spacious) at $2,100 per student. Gruzen said it was any architect's responsibility to insist on "1954 architecture for 1954 students."[4] And Gruzen was supported by Marie Hilson Katzenbach, a member of the Board of Trustees and expert on education in New Jersey, who noted that the buildings at Oxford and Cambridge were diverse in style but always indicative of the period in which they were built. Indeed, construction photos showing the unmistakably steel skeletons dominating the banks of the river, published in the *Rutgers Alumni Monthly*, celebrated the modernity of the structure.

President Jones was present to observe the architects pitch two alternative skyscraper schemes: the first was denser and taller with three thirteen-story buildings. The second was comprised of six seven-story buildings. University officials rejected the three thirteen-story buildings because the scale was far too large. Furthermore, because the footprint of six seven-story buildings was larger than that of three thirteen-story towers, the shorter buildings allowed for more classrooms on the lower levels, which was a desired outcome, as the demolition of many temporary classrooms caused a critical lack of instructional space.

Boocock was not the only one concerned about the new style. Former president Robert C. Clothier (a Princeton graduate) wrote privately to Lansing P. Shield, who chaired the Building Committee of the Board of Trustees, that skyscraper dormitories would lead Rutgers away from the "traditional atmosphere of academic quiet (don't smile) which has prevailed in our dormitory areas heretofore and which is characteristic of Dartmouth, Princeton, and other non-urban universities."[5] Although his parenthetical comment "(don't smile)" suggests that he knew college boys could be boisterous, he was nonetheless perfectly serious about maintaining "a contemplative and reflective experience," which he felt was essential for undergraduate life.[6] He continued, noting that the University of Pennsylvania and Columbia were envious of rural and suburban campuses. Rutgers, in Clothier's opinion, would be mistaken to build what he called "city dormitories."[7] Furthermore, Clothier objected to the fact that the new dorms would block the view from the train—he thought train-riders should be able to see the new library, rather than looming slabs of student housing. Clothier's opinion was not surprising, given that he was president when Demarest was built, which suggests his preference for small-size, historicist dormitories. Clothier's cautions met deaf ears, at least in the 1950s. The turn away from the small-college atmosphere toward the hustle-and-

12. Freshmen standing on a riverside balcony.
SOURCE: R: Photo, buildings and grounds, box 9.

bustle of densely packed dormitories came with a sense of loss. As we will see, however, by the late 1960s, when the Quads were designed for the Kilmer site, small-scale quadrangles had returned to fashion.

Kelly and Gruzen concentrated their efforts for part of 1954 on a plan that included six buildings, each with a complex internal arrangement in which sixty students would be grouped together into a house, and each house would occupy two floors. Skip-stop elevators (elevators that stopped at every other floor) would deliver students to their so-called houses. By August 1954, the architects reduced the number of residences to three. Also around that time, the architects scrapped the complicated double-height units, owing to their anticipated expense, and they instituted a much simpler plan in which the student groups were arranged on single floors. This modification in plan had the benefit of locating the lounges opposite the elevators at the midpoint of the corridors, which would confine the noise (or so they thought) to the center part of the hall.

The architects consulted with Boocock regularly, and in the end, Martin Beck, the project architect for the job, accepted the dean's advice on several important design matters. Boocock argued for an apartment for a married couple who would act in the role of house parents. House-mothers were required by university policy in all residence halls and fraternities, and Boocock explained that the "control of resident students rests on this system."[8] The architects complied, adding an apartment for a resident supervisor (or a married couple). Without uttering the word "suicide," Boocock argued against balconies so high off the ground, saying such a feature in a college dormitory was "not desirable and might even be dangerous."[9] In one set of plans, the balconies were outside of each lounge, and this in itself concerned Boocock, but when another set of plans showed balconies on every room, his memos seethed with frustration. He ticked off many reasons why this multiplicity of terraces was a terrible idea: students would store food and drink (one can speculate that he meant beer) outside, the doors opened inward and would waste valuable floor space in the small rooms, the large plate glass might shatter during "sudden squalls or high winds," and students would dry their clothes on the railings, which would demonstrate their disorderly habits to onlookers.[10] Indeed, the dean implied, the balconies themselves were an invitation to slovenliness and mischief. The balcony design ended in a compromise—the lounges had outdoor terraces, but the individual rooms did not.

As irritated as he was, Boocock wrote to President Jones to say he did sympathize with the architects who were trying to avoid the look of "a low-cost housing project."[11] This loaded comment criticized the whole skyscraper concept (which we know he disliked from the beginning) and builds on the critique mounted by Clothier. Modernism—the style of architecture that rejected the use of applied ornament and historical details—was used extensively for low-income housing. A single slab-shaped building with a repetitive facade made up of rows of identical windows would bring to mind public housing, and three such buildings would summon up images of housing projects even more readily. In that regard, Boocock's remark was apt. On the other hand, as the architects could have reasonably countered, tall modernist housing rose in wealthy urban neighborhoods, such as Miami Beach and Society Hill in Philadelphia. One subtle difference between low-income public housing ("the projects") and middle- and high-income housing was that expensive apartment blocks tended to have balconies, which is probably why the architects included them. The architects made only one gesture toward the academic context, which was that the buildings were clad in red brick.

With the design completed and simplified, the groundbreaking ceremony could be held. The plan of each residential floor of each River Dorm

13. Groundbreaking for the River Dorms, 1955. *Left to right:* Robert H. McBride, president of the student council, RC '55; Lansing P. Shield, RC '17, representing the Board of Trustees; President Jones; and John A. Lynch, mayor of New Brunswick, with shovel. Photo dated March 19, 1955. An architectural rendering of the dormitories forms a backdrop behind the group.

SOURCE: R-Photo, buildings and grounds, box 9.

14. Interior of a hall on a residential floor in Frelinghuysen, one of the River Dorms.

SOURCE: Photo by Laura Leichtman, 2014.

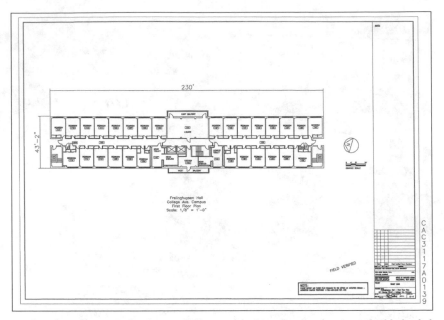

15. Plan of one floor in Frelinghuysen Hall, one of the River Dorms, showing a double-loaded corridor. The lounge is at the midpoint of the hall, opposite the elevators and stairs.

SOURCE: Rutgers University, University Facilities and Capital Planning.

16. Architectural rendering, student bedroom for two.

SOURCE: R-Photo, buildings and grounds, box 9.

was a double-loaded corridor, a long hallway with bedrooms on both sides, doors exactly opposite each other. This basic plan was typical of dormitories, hotels, apartment houses, psychiatric hospitals, and many institutional buildings types. Lounges and elevators were midway down the hall, and the location of this common space was marked on the exterior by projecting balconies. Such corridors were inexpensive to build and allowed for fifty-six people to form one social group per floor. The rooms were doubles. Wardrobes for clothing were placed against the corridor wall to provide storage space and sound-proofing.

The River Dorms included classrooms below the level of George Street. The northernmost had one floor of classrooms, and the other two had two floors of classrooms. These instructional rooms were not exactly underground—they were below grade on the George Street side but above grade on the canal side. Each classroom was square. These were designed for traditional small classes of twenty-five persons. The classrooms looked out at the trees and brush above the Delaware and Raritan Canal. (The proximate portion of Route 18 had not been built yet.) The university boasted that the seating capacity for teaching was fifteen hundred students. Oddly, university officials did not see the sharp increase in student population as a reason to build larger classrooms at this time; either that, or the long, thin shape of the River Dorms did not lend itself to large classrooms, a fact that was lost on later architects who renovated the instructional space by combining square classrooms into nonfunctional rectangular ones.

The individual River Dorms were named Frelinghuysen, Hardenbergh, and Livingston (later Campbell), after early leaders of Rutgers. The names were proposed by a committee that included Richard P. McCormick, then an associate professor, and when the Board of Governors approved the monikers, they gushed: "They have substance as names, roll well on the tongue and possess the dignity proper to the beauty of the buildings they designate."[12]

Located between Frelinghuysen and Hardenbergh was a large recreation center, with a lounge, snack bar, and music room. This building, which was originally known as the Ledge, was designed to include a roof terrace, accessible from a side staircase. The main room was a unified high-ceilinged volume, with a wall of windows that looked out over the Raritan. Gracious and open, the space was a point of pride for the student life staff, who had argued against using that building for a bookstore and post office, which would have cluttered the space. The Bruce Springsteen Band (as it

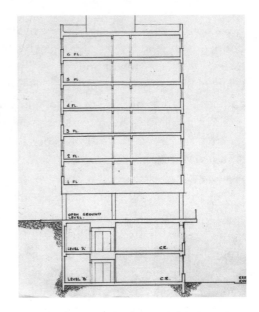

17. River Dorms, cross-section through one building, showing overall height of nine stories: six floors for living space, one level at grade open to the outdoors, two levels of classrooms below grade on the George Street side; classrooms are above grade on the side nearest the canal.
SOURCE: R-Photo, buildings and grounds, box 9.

18. River Dorms. This view, looking south, shows the river, the towpath, and the canal. The Ledge, the glass-enclosed low-rise building, projects outward. The setting for the River Dorms was much more in tune with nature before Route 18 was placed in the location of the canal.
SOURCE: R-Photo, buildings and grounds, box 9.

was once known), among other major musical groups, played there in the 1970s.

The River Dorms soared above everything else at Rutgers College. The three identical slabs were uncompromising in their modernity. The simple, sleek, money-conscious style was a statement of the future-focused goals of state-funded higher education. Additionally, the change in presidential leadership (from Clothier to Jones) may explain the embrace of the modernist style. The River Dorms announced Rutgers's arrival as state university; it was no longer a cozy liberal arts college. While there was a dramatic change in style from Demarest to the River Dorms, there was no equivalent change in the students—there were just more of them.

In contrast, between 1956 and 1969, almost everything about undergraduate education in America was different. Thirteen years after the River

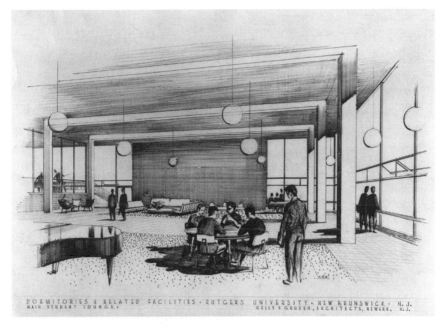

DORMITORIES & RELATED FACILITIES · RUTGERS UNIVERSITY · NEW BRUNSWICK · N.J.
MAIN STUDENT LOUNGE ·   KELLY & GRUZEN, ARCHITECTS, NEWARK, N.J.

19. Interior of the Ledge, later the Student Activities Center.
SOURCE: R-Photo, buildings and grounds, box 9.

Dorms opened, new dormitories on the Camp Kilmer site in Piscataway opened their doors. Long hair and bell bottoms replaced the cardigan sweaters and skinny ties of the 1950s. Sit-ins and protests, the Free Speech Movement, antagonism toward business interests and colluding universities, opposition to the draft, the Vietnam War, and the military—these were all evidence of a forceful youth culture that made college officials rethink the world of higher education from the ground up. As historian Helen Lefkowitz Horowitz wrote: "No one surveying the campus scene in 1959 could have predicted the 1960s."[13] At Rutgers, the response to the 1960s was manifest in the university unit that came to be known as Livingston College.

The founding of Livingston College on the former site of Camp Kilmer, a disused military installation, was marked by a fresh approach to teaching within the ever-growing university, an approach that recognized the difficulties of creating community within a big research university. The program was an almost-utopian scheme for creating small liberal arts colleges (called "unit colleges") on the 540-acre site in Piscataway. Livingston College was one of President Mason W. Gross's greatest achievements, partly because it directed the state's attention to underserviced sectors of society and "announced a major commitment to disadvantaged students, along with a focus on urban problems."[14] Ernest Lynton, a physics professor who became the first dean of Livingston College, recruited faculty, fostered a contemporary curriculum, and promoted diversity. A *New York Times* article emphasized the novelty of this educational experiment, which the reporter said would seek to engage its students with urban problems and social causes. Succinctly put, it would "replace the 'ivory tower.'"[15] The founders of Livingston wanted to transform the culture of higher education: student evaluations replaced traditional grades; students could initiate their own classes; affirmative action was the norm; faculty and students governed together. The intramural football team was called the Black Panthers. In 1965, university officials spoke of three colleges, which together would house nine thousand students and accommodate a few thousand commuters. By 1967, they talked about Livingston College I and II, each for three thousand. (The buildings that current students know as Lucy Stone Hall and the Lynton Towers were originally conceived of as part of Livingston II, and Livingston III was never begun.) The project was finally reduced to one college with a total of three thousand beds, fifteen hundred of which were in the dormitories known as Quads I, II, and III. The values that stood behind Livingston College were such that the architecture had to be innovative and expressive of the challenges of the 1960s.

In November 1965, Dean Lynton and several others from Rutgers went on a tour of UC Santa Cruz, UC Irvine, and the Claremont Colleges. Clark Kerr, then the president of the University of California system, appointed Dean McHenry to serve as chancellor of Santa Cruz in 1961. Kerr cherished the smallness of Swarthmore, his alma mater, while McHenry valued the great library and cultural events at his alma mater, the University of California at Los Angeles. They believed that they could combine Swarthmore and UCLA using the concept of the "cluster college." Lynton kept a copy of an article by Kerr in his files. Published in *Architectural Record* in 1964, "Building Big While Seeming Small," illustrated many buildings at UC Santa Cruz. The article answered Kerr's own widely influential book, *The Uses of the University*, in which he described the large research university as a remarkable invention, but perilously challenged by contemporary forces. He compared the vast offerings of the "multiversity" to an awe-inspiring city; like a metropolis, the multiversity could be overwhelming and dehumanizing. The ambitious plans for UC Santa Cruz impressed

20. Ernest Lynton (*far left*) and members of his staff (Adlerstein, Schaefer, and Miller) examine an elaborate model showing the full build-out of the Kilmer area, reaching to the edge of what is now the Busch Campus. At this stage, planners were imagining three liberal arts colleges in the Kilmer area. North is to the right on this model; the viewer is looking west, from present-day Livingston Campus toward Busch Campus. The golf course is visible on the left side of the model. The warehouses, remainders from Camp Kilmer, are visible at the side of the model closest to the photographer. The extension of Route 18 into Piscataway had not been built yet, so today's sharp divide between Livingston and Busch is not legible. Undated, probably April 1967.

SOURCE: R-Photo, buildings and grounds, box 33.

Lynton, and McHenry of UCSC wrote to Lynton with equivalent enthusiasm after he received Lynton's proposal for Rutgers: "Thank you for sending along the statement for the development of the Raritan Campus. After reading the first paragraph, I was sure you were describing our plans here at Santa Cruz!"[16]

The cluster college combined all the advantages of the research university (library, science laboratories, venues for cultural performances) with the intimate scale of small colleges. At Rutgers, a similar system called the federated college plan held much in common with the cluster college: students would have all the advantages of the large university, but live and study together in smaller social groups with faculty fellows. Another key theme was the integration of academic and nonacademic activities—both in terms of administration and the way the facilities were designed. Most ambitiously, the individual colleges within the cluster college system were intended to be communities of students and faculty like those at Oxford and Cambridge, and like the houses and colleges that were formed at Harvard and Yale in the late 1920s.

In the Livingston *Annual Report* from 1965–1966, the author (probably Lynton) summarized the chief goal as combining the "flexibility and educational advantages of the medium-sized college with the intellectual strength and diversity of a large and growing university. . . . Rutgers is one of the very few major institutions which [is] tackling the problem of size in an intellectually meaningful fashion. . . . Two of these, the California campuses at Santa Cruz and at San Diego, are starting from scratch."[17] But Rutgers did not have to start from scratch. Rutgers–New Brunswick already had individual undergraduate colleges, each with its own identity: Rutgers College (the men's college), Douglass College (the women's college), and the agricultural and engineering schools. By adding even more little colleges, Rutgers would have an organization very similar to that of the highly regarded universities in California, and, at the same time, mend fences with alumni/ae of Rutgers College and Douglass, who feared their private alma maters would be subsumed within a giant new state entity.

The influence from Santa Cruz appeared in two ways—the philosophical level of making the big university seem small, and the more finely grained pattern of the planning of certain dormitories. When Lynton visited California in November 1965, UC Santa Cruz's Cowell College was under construction. Cowell College, designed by Wurster, Bernardi & Emmons, opened in September 1966, well before the Livingston Quads, which opened in September 1969. Cowell recalled the quadrangles of Oxford and Cambridge. Thus in spite of the novelty of the educational philosophy, both UCSC and Rutgers returned to a historic plan, the low-rise quadrangle, and renounced the skyscraper.

In early documents for the residential complexes on the Kilmer site, architects were instructed to think of the dorms as "essentially quadrangles," grouped around the college center, which would include classrooms, a dining commons, and a library. The aim was "to provide spontaneous contact between students and staff without formally organizing this and without destroying individual privacy."[18]

21. Livingston College, view looking south toward Quad III, 1965–1970. Frank Grad & Sons, architects. Photo from 1974.
SOURCE: R-Photo, buildings and grounds, box 33.

The dormitories known as the Quads, therefore, emerged out of very different circumstances from those that gave rise to the River Dorms. The *New York Times* quoted Lynton in June 1969, a few months before the college opened, saying that the new college would have "a very swinging faculty, an exciting student body, a real degree of orientation to everyday problems."[19] The residences at Livingston were planned by the architecture firm Anderson, Beckwith, and Haible. At the same time, other architects were designing the Kilmer Library, the chemistry building (later Beck Hall), and a combined academic building with a dining hall (Tillett). Anderson, Beckwith and Haible chose modern forms for Livingston, in that there were no references to any historical styles. A less-than-modernist decision was to cover the frame of the buildings. The reinforced concrete frame, poured on site, was veneered with nonstructural dark brick, and the windows were set within precast concrete panels. (In contrast, neighboring Tillett, which contained a dining hall and academic spaces, exposed its concrete and thus shows more influence of the contemporary 1960s style known as "New Brutalism.") The local newspaper reported that the buildings a Livingston would be a "'concrete' expression of a specific educational concept—the small college atmosphere within the large university."[20]

Architectural historian Ricki Sablove has described the way the Quads cannot be comprehended without walking into the outdoor courtyard space and considering the structures from that space, which was the center of each residential unit: "While they were not quadrangles in the traditional sense of the word—but rather crescent-shaped clusters of buildings—the Quads were both a nod to the English collegiate model and an allusion to domestic scale. The Quads invited close inspection: while the River Dorms could be seen from the street—either by motorists or pedestrians—the Quads had to be entered through courtyards, on foot. . . . The idea was to enclose the student in a sort of protective embrace."[21] The three buildings that make up the Quads were not true four-sided rectangles; rather, the shapes were irregular. The breaking down of the long rectangular forms that usually composed traditional quadrangles diminished the formality and regularity of these structures.

This planning strategy was very close to the one used at Cowell College. In both cases, the residential buildings were relatively low (from three to six stories), shaped as informal Cs or Us, and purposely varied. The diverse plans of the dormitories were meant as a reflection of the wide range of students. The smallest social group was between seven and eleven at UC Santa Cruz, and between nine and eleven at Livingston. At both campuses, an academic building and a dining hall were set a short walk from the housing.

The planners designed the residence halls to accommodate increasingly more intimate groups: from fifteen hundred, to five hundred, to fifty, to about ten. All three Quads together housed fifteen hundred students, but that was too big a number to form a coherent group. Quad I, Quad II, and Quad III each provided shelter for five hundred, which was a small enough number so that students could at least recognize each other. A single Quad was then divided into ten "houses" of fifty students each, and within each house there were so-called floors for nine, ten, or eleven students. The floors were originally called "Small Living Groups."[22] While it was not possible to traverse from Quad to Quad without going out-of-doors, a student could move from house to house through underground tunnels. These tunnels provided access to a spacious lounge, laundry rooms, ironing areas, and storage. By placing large congregate rooms underground, the designers could keep the overall height of the residence hall down. And the facilities in the basement were meant to serve the entire Quad, not just one house, so (in theory) the tunnels would act as social glue that would hold

22. Quad III, Livingston Campus, photograph taken from the courtyard.

SOURCE: Photo by Laura Leichtman, 2014.

23. Photograph of model showing the three Quads and Tillett. Photo dated April 20, 1966. The Quads were a reinterpretation of the quadrangular colleges of Oxford and Cambridge. The shape creates an intimate outdoor courtyard.

SOURCE: R-Photo, buildings and grounds, box 33.

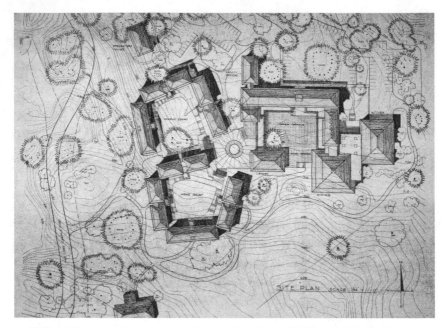

24. William Wurster and Associates, architects, plan of Cowell College, UC Santa Cruz, 1963.
SOURCE: Courtesy of UC Santa Cruz Special Collections.

together the variously sized social groups. Lynton took the problem of size seriously, noting in a *Targum* interview that Livingston would be "small where the dignity of the individual requires it."[23] Regrettably, the idealism behind the tunnels did not work in practice. According to philosopher and longtime Rutgers professor Peter Klein, who lived as a resident adviser in Quad II in 1970, the early residents were susceptible to burglary; if one student propped open a door for a friend, anyone (including a thief) could get inside a house, from there into the tunnels, and then, by finding another unlocked door, move around freely within a Quad.[24] The tunnels turned out to be well suited to other nefarious activities as well.

The interiors of the Quads were extremely complex. On the north side of Quad I, a bar-shaped building included bathrooms, showers, janitors' closets, and a typing room in the middle of the bar, with bedrooms facing north and mechanical rooms facing into the courtyard. Partway around the C-shaped structure, a corridor ran along the inside of the buildings closest to the courtyard, taking many right-angle turns. The bedrooms, mostly doubles, were on the outside of the ring, with windows that looked out toward the remnants of Camp Kilmer and the woods beyond. On the east side, a table tennis room, a seminar room, and the lobby were placed on the courtyard side. On the south side, there was an apartment for a faculty member. There was no clear view down any hallway, and the plan was totally incomprehensible to a first-time visitor. Steps and ramps are scattered throughout the structure. All of these design decisions were made to create community by causing unplanned interactions.

There was no difference between plans for the housing of men or women. Livingston was the first Rutgers coeducational college in New Brunswick/Piscataway, and the dormitories were coed as well. (In comparison, women were not allowed in the River Dorms until 1964, and even then they were permitted in upstairs lounges on weekends only.) The program produced by the Raritan Policy committee back in February 1965 specifically required that the residences be designed to accommodate men or women.

The planners of Livingston College encouraged designers to eliminate the double-loaded corridor, and this the architects certainly achieved. An early programming guide stated, "In the residence unit every effort must be made to avoid the hotel-like atmosphere so common in large universities

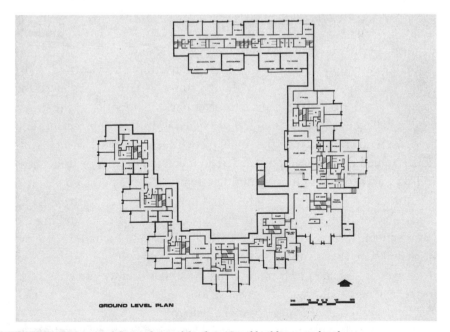

GROUND LEVEL PLAN

25. Plan of the ground floor of one of the three Quad buildings, undated.
SOURCE: Livingston College Papers, box 18.

today."[25] Student life experts considered short, compact halls for ten or twelve people to be desirable for the social development of students, who would form familylike bonds. The preference for such small groups was a direct attack on the fifty-six-man corridors in the River Dorms. The River Dorms were the state-of-the-art back in 1955–1956, but by 1965, the bleak hallways, with exposed masonry block and banging doors, were a magnet for criticism. In fact, the long hallways in dormitories, frequently compared to those found in prisons and psychiatric hospitals, became a flashpoint for student life professionals in the following decades. As one student affairs dean described it in 1963, the "long, windowless and pictureless corridor . . . represents the acme of institutionalization."[26] An expert on college residence halls opined, "If uninterrupted, the typical double-loaded corridor can look like a tunnel and sound like bedlam."[27] The interior arrangements of the Quads reflected this antipathy toward typical institutional forms and practices.

The Livingston College of the late 1960s emerged from a powerful left-leaning youth culture. The college almost came to its end in 1980, when Livingston's distinctive and reputedly "swinging" faculty was disbanded (as was the faculty of Douglass and Rutgers College) and reorganized by department and school. Many of Livingston's radical goals dissipated, but the buildings remain, largely mute in the face of twenty-first-century students who cannot hear their distant message.

By the early 2000s, students on Livingston campus felt isolated. Most of the buildings were forty years old and run-down; many perceived the campus as a lifeless place, especially after dark. Its identity as the urban studies college was lost, although there were (and still are) professors and students who tried to keep the social justice agenda alive. University officials argued that the campus needed an increased density of students as well as spaces for community-building activities. At one point, consultants recommended building fifteen hundred new beds to add to the existing stock—either that, or close the dorms altogether.[28] Instead of taking the latter extreme tack, university officials, led by President Richard L. McCormick and Vice President for Student Affairs Gregory S. Blimling, decided to reinvest in the campus by renovating the student center and constructing several new buildings: a business school and three glitzy, amenity-rich residences called the Livingston Apartments.

Residence life experts prefer to place first- and second-year students in traditional dormitory rooms, with a roommate, because this aids the

26. Design Collective, architects, Livingston Apartments, 2012.
SOURCE: Photo by Laura Leichtman, 2014.

individual student in making friends and creating a peer support network. After a student's second year, he or she is ready for more independence and will likely prefer an apartment over a dorm room. The Livingston campus already had residence halls with lots of double rooms, but no other housing options. The Livingston Apartments, which opened in fall 2012, were aimed at juniors and seniors; they met the best standards of current student affairs practice while also filling a gap in the campus's housing. The complex consists of three buildings, each with its own laundry room and fitness center. The living areas are apartments rather than the traditional rooms and corridors that once signaled dorm life. But building bedrooms was not enough. The campus had to be reconceived as a place that would be lively around the clock, one that would attract (rather than repel) students. The Livingston Apartments now include retail shops, a New Jersey diner, a frozen yogurt shop, a Starbucks, and a cinema. The architects, Design Collective of Baltimore, described their concept this way: "Located on the periphery of the current campus, these new residence halls establish a new urban edge to the campus, creating a sense of place where none previously existed. The design focused on creating a palpable sense of place within each building, as well as forging strong connections with the rest of campus."[29] Each apartment has a full-size refrigerator, an oven, a stovetop, a dishwasher, a microwave, air-conditioning, and Wi-Fi. The apartments are fully furnished, and each houses four students. Students have their own bedrooms, and each unit has a bathroom.

The new Livingston Apartments are part of a national trend to meet the demand for high-quality independent housing for juniors and seniors. Rutgers, like many of its peers, hopes to steer students away from off-campus apartments, because it is economically advantageous for Rutgers to bring students, and their dollars, onto campus. But to compete successfully with market-rate apartments, the university has to provide adult apartments that have living rooms, kitchens, and a lot of bandwidth. Lavish residence halls are now standard at colleges, even state universities. It is a kind of arms race, in which universities cannot attract students without equivalent or better dormitories than their peer institutions. (Needless to say, the bus tour for perspective students shows brand-new residence halls, not the Quads or the River Dorms.) With the burst of construction around 2010, including the Livingston Apartments, Rutgers attained the distinction of managing the largest residence life program in the country—about sixteen thousand beds in 140 separate buildings.[30] In the nineteenth century, Rutgers College lacked the on-campus housing that its peers relied on, but, today, on the eve of its 250th anniversary, the university has embraced residence halls as an essential component of the undergraduate's educational experience.

Another contrast from the past was the amount of student input in the process. The archives do not demonstrate that university officials reached out to students for their opinions when the River Dorms were built. When the Quads were built, Livingston did not yet have students, so there were no current students to consult, but Lynton sought advice from Rutgers and Douglass students. For the Livingston Apartments, students were consulted throughout the process, from the housing master plan (completed in 2004) through the final stages of interior design. Vice President Blimling met weekly with student leaders, and the group regularly discussed residence hall design. The student affairs department arranged a full-size mock-up of a typical apartment in an off-campus warehouse, and students, resident advisers, and other stakeholders toured the model apartment to give advice about everything from furnishings to electronics.

In sum, Demarest represents the old, small Rutgers—a men's college, focused on teaching. The clean lines and boxy silhouettes of the River Dorms suited the fast-growing Rutgers as it became a state university where practicality held sway over sentiment. Modernist towers knowingly rejected the quadrangle and the application of historical styles, which both smacked of privilege in the heady postwar days when state-funded, populist education was on the rise. In the 1960s, public universities had become giant institutions full of disenchanted students who felt anonymous; therefore, smaller, more intimate buildings seemed a way to reverse that trend. Livingston's aspirations for educational revolution could not be met with a mere copying of the buildings of the previous generation, represented by the repetitive and institutional River Dorms. As radical as Livingston's goals were, the designers reinterpreted a historical form, the quad, for their first residence halls. The origins of Livingston College are invisible today on the same campus, where the newest buildings are a business school and massive multiuse residence halls. Today's students live in luxury apartments, as much consumers as students.

And where will future Rutgers students live? That is a difficult question to answer. As more classes are taught online, demand for residence halls might decrease, and certainly living at home will be an inexpensive option for frugal students and their families. But the attraction of living on campus will endure. Students are drawn to move out of their family homes, because that transition traditionally draws a sharp line between high school and college, between adolescence and adulthood. Residing on the physical campus, amid (if not in) stately, ancient, and hallowed halls, will remain a rite of passage, even if the student's home is only a few miles away. Living on campus will remain essential for face-to-face networking, for both friendship and future careers, and that social connection will continue to serve as a major incentive for students to attend college at all. The architecture of dormitories, therefore, is an ever-changing manifestation of the social meaning of higher education.

6

Student Protest

In 1959, Columbia Broadcasting ran a segment on its popular news program, *The Twentieth Century*, titled "Generation without a Cause," which probed the malaise of American college students. Walter Cronkite informed the audience that this generation was called the "most baffling in our history"; after a brief recital by a montage of student voices of the sociological truism of the 1950s about conformity, the scene shifted to a typical American campus—Rutgers. Sitting at a tea table on the Douglass campus, a young woman captured the theme of the evening broadcast precisely: "I think we are too young to be lost, and too old to be forgotten. I think I'd call the generation a waiting generation."[1]

Earlier in the broadcast, viewers heard Richard P. McCormick, introduced as a professor and university historian, explain that the "most striking difference between the students of this generation and the students of my own generation twenty years ago is the lack of radicalism." In the late 1930s, students had been debating fascism, socialism, the New Deal, and, with World War II looming, isolationism; now, they, like their parents, had shed these concerns and seemed most worried about "personal adjustment." John Ciardi, poet, editor, and scholar, followed with a worry that "freshmen come in already acting like bank clerks" and warning that by the time they graduate, "acquire a wife, and a mortgage, and a job, that's going to sober them up fast," so they were better off being a little crazy while they still could.

The highlight of the Rutgers segment—before the show turned to a jazz club, "Five Spot," and the "beats" who congregated there—were two informal, although choreographed, conversations among students, half a dozen or so young men at the Delta Phi fraternity house on College Avenue, and a group of Douglass women in a dormitory lounge. Both groups expressed a sense, Cronkite told the audience, of frustration and futility. One of the fraternity brothers described his fellow students as security-minded, conformist, and naive, getting "very practical training" at Rutgers, "but very little education." Another explained his frustration at trying to get students to sign a petition against nuclear testing, only to have them suggest that the Nobel Prize–winning organization he was supporting might be a communist-front group. A third stated elegantly that he was "not so opposed to the nice gray-flannel [suit] man. He can be happy in his split-level [house] with his vomiting children if you like. But I'm opposed that when a man rebels actively there's no space in which he can [do so]." The Douglass women inflected similar frustrations in a slightly different direction. They accepted the "inevitability of marriage and starting our homes" but worried both about a world on the brink of nuclear annihilation and about the opportunity for personal fulfillment for both themselves and their husbands because of all the pressures to conform.

For the professors, the frame of reference was the 1930s, and 1959 seemed shallow and stale in comparison; for the students themselves, the Cold War, anticommunism, and nuclear destruction were the backdrop, and most interpreted their lives in terms of such college perennials as William H. Whyte's *The Organization Man* or novelist Sloan Wilson's *The Man in the Gray Flannel Suit.* Just around the corner, sit-ins to desegregate southern lunch counters, the election of John F. Kennedy, and the dispatch of military advisers to South Vietnam were to usher in a new era, with Bob Dylan and the Beatles poised to overtake the beat generation.

From the mid-1960s to the mid-1970s, American campuses helped define a new type of politically charged youth culture that radiated out from colleges and universities. The central themes of that culture—antiwar agitation, the black student protest movement, and the women's movement—are well known; their history at Rutgers has been told in other works. Here, I explore student activism through vignettes that capture the range and endurance of student activism at the State University of New Jersey. Most of these stories are rooted in the late 1960s or early 1970s, but some extend beyond that period and illustrate the central theme of this chapter: that at Rutgers, student activism was a persistent aspect of student life, rooted in the experiences that students brought to or confronted on their college campuses.

The Initial Salvo: The *Anthologist* Controversy

In October 1947, the *Rutgers Anthologist*, the student literary magazine at the men's colleges in New Brunswick, published "Pick-Up," by Al Aronowitz. The essay told the story of an attempt by three young men, cruising in a 1929 Ford, to pick up three teenage girls; the banter among the six protagonists was disrupted temporarily by a street cop, who threatened to arrest the men. The men drove off, returning when the cop left, and continued to exchange increasingly sexualized references, until the girls tired of the game and walked off. A sketch of the girls, depicted as young women—not quite the teenagers described by the author—appeared with the story. Under the title, the editors noted that Earl Schenck Miers, the editor of Rutgers University Press, had selected "Pick-Up" as the "most outstanding contribution" to the literary magazine for its "honest writing."[2] Two editors of the *Anthologist* resigned in protest over the printing of the story, and letters poured into the *Targum*, most denouncing the story as rubbish, tasteless, and degrading. The *Anthologist* itself published a selection of student comments, most of which attacked the story as "trite," "lewd," or "dirty."[3] In an *Anthologist* poll asking students to rate recent stories, "Pick-Up" was ranked as both the best and worst publication. The administration stayed out of the fray.

Three years later, the editors of the (briefly) renamed *Antho* would not be so lucky. The October 1950 issue carried a story, "Cumberland Street," depicting an illegal abortion. The story centered on a young, unmarried couple brought to a backstreet abortionist, herself a crass, materialistic woman, by an acquaintance of the couple. It was told from the perspective of the acquaintance, who was compelled, against his own better judgment, to help his friend and his friend's secretary engage in something he compared with "lesbianism, homo-sexuality, gambling, drinking, drugs."[4] The abortion itself was described in some detail, as heard through a closed door by the two men as the abortionist gave the young woman instructions. "Cumberland Street" was well written, had much in common with the *film noir* and pulp fiction of the era, and clearly had involved some background research by its author, Curtis Meanor.

Soon after the October issue of *Antho* appeared, the New Brunswick Knights of Columbus, a Catholic fraternal organization, attacked the story as "utterly blasphemous throughout" and "vile and repulsive."[5] The local press reported the story, other statewide Catholic groups joined the protest, and scores of individuals wrote to the university questioning how a school, especially one receiving public funding, could allow such a publication. The dean of men called in the editor, accused him of being deliberatively provocative, ignoring the faculty adviser's recommended revisions of the story, and withholding the issue from the administration (to avoid its confiscation) while circulating it among the students (none of these charges were, in fact, accurate). President Clothier appointed a special committee, headed by University Librarian Donald Cameron, to review the situation. The *Targum* editors and the Student Council sprang to support of *Antho*. By a 9–6 vote, student leaders supported both the author's realistic treatment of a significant social problem and the right of students to express themselves free of censorship.

The author had originally written the story for an English class. The professor, the Cameron committee reported, had submitted it to the *Antho*. The committee also determined that the faculty adviser, who had authority to require revisions, had edited out the "blasphemous" expressions in the article as well as an objectionable paragraph, but that his editing had been overlooked because of the rush to get the issue out in a timely fashion. Given the import of this editorial failure, the committee concluded that the editor should resign, which he did, and almost immediately thereafter, four associate editors resigned in protest against the committee's decision. The committee report claimed more broadly, in terms that would be echoed in the Cold War cases later in the decade, that "no student and no professor in a university may claim utter freedom since he is a part of a public institution."[6]

To a divinity student at the next-door seminary who protested the censorship policy, the president responded that he agreed that "if there is any place for difference of opinion and freedom of ideas it is in the University."[7] To another letter writer, this one attacking the university for allowing the story to be published, the university responded that "we all completely agree with you that the article in question should never have been published."[8] Squaring the difference between these two university responses may seem impossible, but in an era where *in loco parentis* was assumed, and newspapers and other media presented only what was in good taste, they are not as contradictory as they appeared.

Students lost. Censorship remained, and if anything, was strengthened. A faculty adviser continued to recommend changes, and content now had to have approval of the dean of men. That spring, the *Targum* published a front-page story with excerpts of the galley proofs of two censored articles. In both, the *Targum* noted that the editing had occurred without the author's knowledge, and that the censorship made a fundamental change in the stories. Protest was followed by a more general effort, led by the Student Council, to end censorship of all student publications. Ten years later, however, a faculty adviser still wielded a red pencil over student publications, and a student editor wrote to President Gross in 1963 that he felt he was being asked to turn the *Anthologist* into a "Rutgers' supplement to *The Ladies' Home Journal.*"[9] The outcome is not surprising. Even on the national scene, where a series of Supreme Court cases in the 1950s and early 1960s slowly eroded the power of state censorship boards over movies, First Amendment freedoms were far from absolute.

The *Anthologist* itself survived and even flourished. Cash prizes for outstanding poetry and fiction brought more submissions, and the appointment in 1954 of John Ciardi, beginning a distinguished career as poet and professor of English, as faculty adviser, gave the magazine greater intellectual ballast. In the twenty-first century, the publication, begun in 1927, still circulated on the New Brunswick campus.

Letter from a Sumter County, Georgia, Jail

October 19, 1963

To the Students of Rutgers and Douglass,
I have hesitated to write this letter because I find it extremely difficult to write—not only because I'm in jail and can't feel very much of what is outside—but because I realize at the outset I am incapable of arranging symbols to adequately express my feelings at this time.
    It has been some weeks since I've been in a hot, crowded church and heard the people of Sumter County say,
" . . . and before I'll be a slave, I'll be buried in my grave
and go home to my Lord and be free. . . ." or walk the dusty, red-clay streets of Americus and have a young, black child

call, "Hi, Mr. Freedom Rider," or see a Negro preacher
leaning over the pulpit, trembling with emotion, damp with
perspiration, . . . [and proclaim,] "We are in a dark time,
but stand firm . . . firm in the Lord. Keep Courage!" . . .

Don Harris, Americus, Georgia[10]

Don Harris was in jail. His crime: attempting to incite insurrection against
the State of Georgia. Inciting insurrection was a capital offense in Georgia.
There was no bail in a death penalty case.

Harris had been born in Harlem and grown up in a black neighborhood
in Mount Vernon, New York. Both his parents worked, and their sacrifices,
along with scholarships, helped him attend the Fieldston Ethical Culture
School, where he was one of the few black students. The school sent most
of its graduates to college. In Harris's case, the college was Rutgers.

He entered in 1958, arriving a little early in order to try out for freshmen
football. He was a good student, a member of the Air Force ROTC, and
played lacrosse as well as football at the college. He majored in English and
physical education. He was one of the few black students at Rutgers, and
the only one in his fraternity (Phi Sigma Kappa). He was also a campus
activist. He joined the National Association for the Advancement of Col-
ored People (NAACP) and was a college delegate to the National Student
Association (NSA). He wrote for the *Targum*. In summer 1961, he was one
of some two hundred college students from around the country selected
for Operation Crossroads Africa. He spent most of the summer in northern Rhodesia working with other volunteers at the Mindulo Ecumenical
Center. In summer 1962, he worked with the Northern Student Movement
on tutoring adolescents in Harlem and north Philadelphia. That fall, back
at Rutgers, Harris set up Education in Action, with the support of the New
Brunswick Board of Education, to extend tutoring by college students into
the local community. During one of his college summers, he met Malcolm X
and was instrumental in arranging for him to speak at Rutgers.

Harris had met Student Nonviolent Coordinating Committee (SNCC)
civil rights activists at the NSA convention. In January 1963, with his course
work almost completed, he went south to assist SNCC. Civil rights demonstrations, most involving local high school and college students, had
swept the South after the first lunch counter sit-in in Greensboro, North
Carolina, in 1960. SNCC was one of several organizations that had stepped

in to help local groups of southern blacks organize their efforts to challenge the racial status quo. By 1962, most of these efforts had switched
from desegregation to voter registration and community organizing. Civil
rights workers faced brutal and deadly resistance and received very little
protection from the federal government.

The Albany, Georgia, SNCC headquarters assigned Harris to work in
Americus. Americus was a small, southern town in the center of Sumter
County, about equidistant west from Savannah and south from Atlanta.
About half of the county's twenty-five thousand residents were African
Americans, and perhaps a fifth of the residents were voters, but fewer than
five hundred of these five thousand voters were African Americans. SNCC
organized voter registration drives and attempted unsuccessfully to integrate the town's movie theater. On August 8, 1963, after a meeting of 250
African Americans at the Friendship Baptist Church, protesters moved
into the street and began singing hymns. "The police arrived, bid the
crowd to disperse and when they would not, began firing in the air."[11] They
grabbed Don Harris, who went limp, and was then "beaten in the street
and dragged to a squad car."[12] The county charged Harris and three other
civil rights workers with unlawful assembly, disorderly conduct, resisting
arrest, and other secondary offenses, but also, under a seldom-used and
almost assuredly unconstitutional law that carried a potential death penalty, for attempting to incite insurrection. Over the next three days, protest
demonstrations against the initial arrests led to numerous additional jail-
ings, many of them of students—the foot soldiers of the protests. Among
the stories that would come North and be inserted in the *Congressional
Record* by New Jersey Senator Harrison Williams was one of two hundred
young protesters being held in a temporary jail, in an abandoned building, without bedding or functioning toilets, with their only drinking water
provided by a shower, and their only food a couple of hamburgers a day.

Soon after they returned for fall classes, Rutgers students learned that
their former classmate was in a Georgia jail. The previous spring, they had
read about his imprisonment in Mississippi, where he had been temporarily dispatched to assist in a voter registration drive in Greenwood. In
Mississippi, he was released on bail; this time, however, in Georgia, he was
not. Douglass and Rutgers student leaders sprang into action, and university chaplain, Bradford Abernethy, who had recommended Harris for
"Crossroads Africa," played a major role in organizing support. The *Targum* ran stories almost daily from mid-September detailing Harris's plight,

established a defense fund to channel money to the NAACP (which was representing the SNCC workers), and ran a daily list of contributors. The fund eventually amounted to more than $3,000, with large contributions coming from the student government, the fraternity system, Harris's own fraternity as well as Zeta Beta Tau, Hillel (the Jewish campus group), the Newman Club and the Canterbury Club (campus Catholic and Episcopal groups), WRSU, the *Targum* itself, and literally hundreds of students who added a dollar or two. It also ran a three-part report from John Hanks, a Rutgers student who ventured south to Americus to see in person what was happening, was quickly targeted by the local police, and escaped from his hotel by "fleeing down a water-drain," and then hitching a ride back to Atlanta.[13]

On September 26, Charles Sherrod, the SNCC director of operations in southwest Georgia, spoke at Voorhees Chapel to an overflow crowd about the Georgia campaign. "We've been in Albany [a significantly larger city south of Americus] for over two years. When we got there the fear was so thick you could cut it with a knife. The high school students called it T.T.—Tombstone Terrell County."[14] When Sherrod concluded, the students rose, joined hands, and sang, "Black and white together, we shall not be moved."[15] On October 2, James Farmer, the director of the Congress of Racial Equality, spoke in Scott Hall at Rutgers College and again to an overflow crowd, and on October 8, Bayard Rustin, another prominent national civil rights leader, headlined a rally specifically for Harris at the College Avenue gym. At that rally, Abernethy spoke as well and described his own recent trip to Americus to visit Harris in jail. The *Caellian's* coverage of the rally featured a picture of two Douglass students, one black and one white, rising from their seats along with the rest of the audience to applaud Rustin's condemnation of a do-nothing Kennedy administration.

Harris's ordeal ended with a bit less melodrama. SNCC had gone to Americus without fully preparing for what might happen, but once the arrests occurred, and the NAACP sent in Albany, Georgia, civil rights lawyer C. B. King Jr. to handle the case, momentum changed. Not surprisingly, attempts to bail out the SNCC leaders failed in the local courts, but on November 1, a three-judge federal district court struck down the Georgia unlawful assembly and insurrection statutes as unconstitutional, and the NAACP provided bail money to free the defendants. Don Harris came back to Rutgers two weeks later and spoke at the chapel. He would return to the South and remain active in SNCC through 1965.

Two things stand out about the story of Don Harris. One was the broad support he received on two campuses of the state university from a student population that just a few years earlier had been labeled a "generation without a cause." The frustrations of a 1959 student trying and failing to get other students to sign a petition for nuclear disarmament had given way to unified student effort to support one of their own in the civil rights struggle in the South. More remarkable, of course, was Donald Harris himself. Like many others who would follow him, his activism was rooted in lived experience—a need to negotiate a landscape that few of his white classmates could even imagine, as the only black in an otherwise white fraternity, the only black on an otherwise white football team, the only black in an otherwise white classroom—and then to do something to change that situation. It seemed simple in 1963, as Bayard Rustin had told the students at the gym, "Ask yourself what you want, whatever shape or color you are, what you yourself want is what the Negro wants."[16]

The Puerto Rican Student Movement

On March 4, 1971, during an angry meeting with Provost and Acting President Richard Schlatter, Puerto Rican students from five Rutgers campuses—Camden, Douglass, Livingston, Newark, and Rutgers–New Brunswick—presented the administration with lists of demands. The Puerto Rican student protest came approximately two years after the takeover of Conklin Hall on the Newark campus by black students, and several years after teach-ins had focused the attention of Rutgers students on the Vietnam War. In the late 1960s, few black students and probably even fewer students of Puerto Rican ancestry or birth attended the state university. The black student protest movement gathered local and national attention; the parallel efforts of Puerto Rican students went largely unnoticed outside the university and the Puerto Rican community. In most instances, the students who spoke for Puerto Rican concerns worked closely with black student leaders, attended the same demonstrations, and participated in the same acts of civil disobedience, but they also articulated their own demands and crafted alliances independently of the black student movement.

Puerto Rican immigration to the mainland of the United States shot up dramatically after World War II. The creation of the Commonwealth in 1952, and the Commonwealth's efforts to transform a largely agricul-

tural economy into one based on manufacturing, in part by exporting la-
borers (Operation Bootstrap), pushed rural Puerto Ricans to the United
States. Most came to New York City; many relocated in New Jersey. With
few skills and most without fluency in English, they arrived in New Jersey cities as those same cities were losing the manufacturing jobs that had
one been the hallmark of the urban economy. Another, smaller flow of
migrants came to south Jersey to work seasonally on the truck farms. In
1970, Newark had about twenty-seven thousand residents of Puerto Rican
birth or ancestry, Camden close to seven thousand, and New Brunswick
around fourteen hundred. The summary of the 1970 federal census published by the Puerto Rican Congress of New Jersey concluded that Puerto
Ricans families were "larger, younger," and more likely to be renters living
in overcrowded conditions than was true of any other group in New Jersey.
Family income was "44% less than the family income of Anglo-whites and
17% less than that of black people."[17] The report went on to conclude that
"seven out of every ten [Puerto Rican] families are working poor," and
while college admissions had shot up dramatically between 1969 and 1972,
Puerto Ricans, who constituted 7 percent of the state population, still made
up less than 2 percent of the college students in New Jersey.[18]

The handful of Puerto Rican college students at the state university set
out to change that situation. Approximately two weeks after black students
dramatically brought their ongoing protests on the Newark campus to the
attention of the larger community with the takeover of Conklin Hall, a
"newly formed Puerto Rican student organization" at the college added
its voice to the call for accelerated change.[19] In a letter sent to numerous
university officials, Sigfredo Carrion, the chair of the Puerto Rican Organization (P.R.O.), Pablo Santana, the co-chair, and Jenny Diaz, the executive secretary, acknowledged that the Newark administration had for some
time been cooperating with community groups to improve educational
opportunities for Puerto Ricans. The P.R.O. statement, however, then
went on to accuse the university of tokenism and to list ten demands. The
concerns, in numerous variations, would be expressed on each campus
over the next two years: more personnel devoted to recruitment, better
support programs for those who were admitted, more hiring of Puerto
Ricans, and Puerto Rican student involvement in recruitment and admissions. The P.R.O also asked that work-study opportunities be created for
Puerto Rican students to help the "Spanish-speaking poor" in the local
community and that undergraduates from "disadvantaged environments"

be allowed to register as full-time students yet carry reduced course loads while they completed remedial work.[20] Finally, the P.R.O. voiced its support for the ongoing protests of the black students at Newark.

Four days later, on March 14, 1969, however, the details of the P.R.O. demands probably got lost in the wake of the dramatic, brief announcement by the Board of Governors of the launching of an ambitious new program for the "economically and educationally disadvantaged graduates of secondary schools in those communities where Rutgers has its primary locations and most significant community obligations—Newark, New Brunswick, and Camden."[21] In the next two years, the short-lived Urban University Program (as well as the more resilient New Jersey Equal Opportunity Fund) would dramatically increase the enrollment of disadvantaged students—some white, many black, and very few, initially, Puerto Ricans.

The Newark statement did, however, note the one commitment that the campus had already made to improving opportunities for Puerto Ricans. Rutgers-Newark had a Puerto Rican admissions officer and one dedicated to helping Hispanic students. Maria DeCastro Blake had been born in Puerto Rico in 1911 to working-class parents and moved to New York City at the age of twenty-one. With a high school education but without English language skills, she was closed out of secretarial work and found employment instead in the garment industry. Her wages paid for English classes, a secretarial job followed, and then additional college courses. Shortly after the outbreak of World War II, she married a New Jersey native and moved to East Orange. Until the death of her husband in 1960, she raised three children and did volunteer work at the local Catholic church with Puerto Rican immigrants. In 1960, she went to work in the Alumni Office at Rutgers-Newark but spent a great deal of time assisting the Puerto Rican community and Puerto Rican students at Rutgers. By 1965, she had been promoted to assistant dean of admissions—a post she held into the 1980s. While black students had protested against insensitive admissions officers, in 1969, the Puerto Rican students at Newark asked that Maria DeCastro Blake be given more recognition for the job she was doing (and, of course, more resources as well).

Another indication of personal initiative and institutional commitment came at Livingston College. There were perhaps three dozen students for whom Spanish was the native language admitted in fall 1969 as part of the first class at Livingston. Most were Puerto Rican; one or two were Dominican or Cuban. The students created the United Puerto Rican Student

Organization and staged a cultural festival. By year's end, students had decided to organize the student chamber of the joint faculty-student assembly with proportional representation for black, Puerto Rican, and white students. By the second year, Puerto Ricans had established one section of the three residence halls as largely their own. Against this backdrop, approximately a dozen students, most from Douglass and Rutgers Colleges, successfully argued for a Puerto Rican studies program, which the university placed at Livingston. Livingston Dean Ernest Lynton first asked Hilda Hidalgo, a native of Puerto Rico and a professor of urban studies and community development, to coordinate existing offerings in the field, and then, after an extensive search, brought in María Josefa Canino to organize the new program.

Canino had been born in "El Barrio" in uptown Manhattan, held a master's degree from Columbia in social work, and was engaged in community organization. Her career profile—both academic and activist—was typical of many of the early hires at Livingston. Within a year, the new program was offering courses in Puerto Rican history, migration, art and music, and politics, and students, who were full members of its curriculum committee, helped to plan for the future. Ten Puerto Rican students graduated from Livingston in 1973 (the first official class). Five were majors in Puerto Rican studies, four of whom went on to law or professional school; the fifth went to work for a Puerto Rican educational organization.

At Newark, one of the outcomes of the initial 1969 protest was a stepped-up role of Puerto Rican students themselves to bring additional members of the community to Rutgers. It was this effort that led to Melba Maldonado's enrollment. Maldonado was born in Guayanilla, Puerto Rico, in 1949. Her brother, who had served in the army and been stationed at Fort Dix in New Jersey, brought Maldonado to New Jersey soon after her high school graduation. The English skills she had acquired in school were not good enough to get her a position as a secretary—one of the positions open to Puerto Rican women—so initially she had to accept low-wage work in a production line at a Newark perfume factory and later in a plant in the garment district. Her salvation from the exploitive labor regime was at a community center at the local, largely Puerto Rican Catholic church. She jumped into community organizing in what became "Puerto Rican Youth in Action," helping Puerto Rican tenants negotiate with landlords and the city. It was this activity that brought her to the attention of Rutgers student leader Sigfredo Carrion. Carrion convinced her to apply to Rutgers. At

Newark, she joined the P.R.O., met Maria Blake, who helped her deal with the twists and turns of the college bureaucracy, and by 1970, had become the president of the largely female Newark P.R.O. She and the other women in the P.R.O. orchestrated their own building takeover to claim office space that the university had been reluctant to allocate to them.[22]

At Camden, the spokesperson for Puerto Rican concerns was Gualberto Medina, a junior, history major. Medina was born in Puerto Rico in 1950 in a working-class, Puerto Rican nationalist household where they might be "without bread, but were never without books."[23] They left Puerto Rico for Camden in the early 1950s, drawn by job opportunities associated with Campbell Soup Company. Medina grew up speaking Spanish at home and English in the Camden school system, so when he entered Rutgers-Camden in fall 1968, he was fluent in both. He made friends with some of the leaders of the black student protest movement and antiwar protesters in Students for a Democratic Society, and he participated in protests orchestrated by both groups.

In September 1970, Medina had announced the creation of a new campus group, the Organization of Puerto Rican Students (OPRS) whose goal was, very much like the Young Lords, to work with the Camden Puerto Rican community. (The Young Lords originated in Chicago in efforts by Puerto Rican youths to protect their neighborhoods from gentrification, and by the late 1960s, they had branches in many major cities and were committed to community empowerment.) OPRS also presented Camden dean of Arts and Sciences James Young with a list of demands that called for an accelerated recruitment and admissions programs to bring more Puerto Rican students to Rutgers. Over the next four months, Medina authored a column in the campus newspaper, the *Gleaner*, exploring the efforts of the Puerto Rican people to win their freedom first from Spain and then from the United States. He also submitted a story that urged support for a Young Lords demonstration at the United Nations against American military bases in Puerto Rico. His efforts became part of a broader statewide movement.

That fall, Puerto Rican activists convened in Atlantic City. While the convention approved mostly noncontroversial resolutions about steps that needed to be taken to address the barriers Puerto Ricans faced in New Jersey, the youth movement session, chaired by Walter Martinez, from New Brunswick, erupted in fiery debate over the question of Puerto Rican independence. A Princeton University student ignited the session with a

clenched fist salute calling for self-determination for the island. While established leaders convinced student activists to tone down their demands,
the students brought their energy back to their campuses. The Camden
student declaration of March 4, 1971, referenced the Atlantic City convention and that convention's condemnation of a "racist anti–Puerto Rican
atmosphere which permeates the entire fiber of life in this state" and "especially the conspiracy of educational institutions" that "results in the
cultural genocide of our people."[24] The protest had actually begun three
days earlier. On the first of the month, Camden students took over Dean
Young's office in Armitage Hall. They hung a Puerto Rican flag on the
wall, posted a door sign saying "People's Office," and invited in the press.[25]
When Young arrived, the students received a promise that he would ac-
company them to New Brunswick to present their recommendations to
the central administration.

The March 4 protest, thus, should not have surprised the administration, but the coordinated demands from five campuses probably did. The
students had met on the Douglass campus at some point before the joint
action, probably at the initiative of Douglass Puerto Rican students. When
the students addressed Schlatter, however, it was Medina, not Maldonado
or Zaida Josefina Torres, the Douglass student leader, who spoke publicly
for a group of approximately forty Puerto Ricans. Medina read from a prepared statement that condemned "the discrimination and injustices" per-
petuated by the Rutgers administration and then listed several demands.[26]
The students also gave Schlatter demands drawn up by students at each
campus. The demands paralleled those first made in 1969 at Newark and
those of the black student movement—support for recruitment, admission, and retention of Puerto Rican students; a Puerto Rican Studies program; and more hiring of Puerto Rican faculty and staff—and deplored
the "paternalism" and "insensitive" inaction of the university.[27] Schlatter
responded that he was "unsympathetic to *demands*," but then tempered
his remarks by adding that "if the demands are reasonable, I will see what
can be done."[28] The students, many of whom had been involved in earlier
protests with black student leaders and were fed up with delays, asked for a
response within the week and warned, "if you don't come through, we are
going to move on you."[29]

The next day, Schlatter wrote to the chief administrative officers at the
five colleges. He had not "promised" the students anything, he noted, but
he wanted to make "some sort of response" within a week to "avoid more

serious trouble."[30] One typical response indicates that problem that Puerto Rican students confronted. The students had asked for a recruiter on each campus. Admissions reported they had hired one a year and a half ago, primarily to help at Livingston, but responsible for all the New Brunswick colleges. He had resigned during the fall semester. His replacement was asked to do the same job *and* coordinate with community services at Newark and Camden. He resigned in February. Currently recruiting was being handled by a student, working part-time (again, mostly at Livingston), and the admissions office was attempting to hire a Puerto Rican recruiter.

More generally, campus officials responded either that they did not have the resources to hire new people, or that the changes the Puerto Rican students wanted were dependent on faculty initiatives (for example, the hiring of new professors) or of the governing bodies of the colleges (for example, the appointment of Puerto Ricans to admissions committees). While in 1969 the protests of black (and some Puerto Rican) students had been met with an extraordinary flurry of faculty meetings and proposals, in 1971, Puerto Ricans (and blacks, who were engaged in another round of protest) faced a more difficult negotiating task. The Urban University Program was up and running (however badly); the Educational Opportunity Fund was channeling resources for "educational and economic disadvantaged students" to all New Jersey colleges. Media attention focused more on Vietnam protest than minority concerns. Admissions numbers for black and Hispanic students had, in fact, shot up but so had the numbers for those dropping out before completing their degrees.

That Friday, March 12, 1971, the Board of Governors held its regularly scheduled meeting. They had to consider both a student proposal to establish an Afro-American Studies Department in New Brunswick and a statement drafted by a statewide Puerto Rican education group, ASPIRA, to which both Maria DeCastro Blake and Hilda Hidalgo belonged. ASPIRA representatives had met with President Gross in 1970, and they now returned to address the board, expressing many of the same concerns as the students themselves had. What is particularly impressive here is that the students, while few in number, had mustered support from beyond the campus.

The push from ASPIRA, however, did not produce the substantial change in university policy the students wanted. Schlatter's detailed responses to the specifics of their demands (based on the responses he had received from each campus) set off another wave of protest. On Monday,

April 7, thirty Puerto Rican students blocked the Somerset Street entrance to Old Queens. They then marched to the administration building itself and again met with Schlatter. As the students saw it, the equivocal answers they had been given the week before were "asinine" and "ambiguous."[31] Medina called for a firm and immediate commitment from the university to the Puerto Rican community, and, with what was clearly a street-theater threat, told Schlatter, "By the time we get done with you, you'll be on your knees begging us to stop"—to which Schlatter, according to the *Targum*, had the good sense to respond, "I didn't hear that."[32] As the back-and-forth unfolded, the university was also considering demands from black students in New Brunswick that the Afro-American Studies Program be given departmental status, and in Camden, dealing with an incident in which black students had overturned bookshelves and card catalogs in the library to protest the slow and incomplete response to demands presented to the administration in March. For a university pressed for resources and awaiting the hiring of a new president, crafting a satisfactory response was a challenge.

The semester ended with a bang. Protests by the black student movement, a second Earth Day, antiwar rallies, manifestos from the feminist movement, and the announcement of a new president for the university, Edward J. Bloustein. The Puerto Rican student movement dropped from the headlines of the student newspapers.

That summer, after police dragged a Puerto Rican motorist from his care and beat him in Camden, more than a thousand members of the Puerto Rican community protested at City Hall. The police moved in with dogs and tear gas, and for several days, buildings were burned (including the Puerto Rican community center), and widespread looting occurred. What was both a riot and a rebellion—one of a number staged by Puerto Ricans in an era of urban disturbances—accelerated the flight of middle-class whites to the suburbs from an already battered old industrial city. Student leader Gualberto Medina ran through the streets of Camden urging angry demonstrators to return home and consoling store owners whose shop windows had been smashed and merchandise looted. The Camden disruptions, much like the far larger Newark rebellion in 1967, made it difficult to construct an urban university connected directly to the local community, and fostered, at least for some administrators, a sense of the campuses as "in but not off" the cities in which they were located, sealed off, safe havens for students and faculty.[33]

Within the university, during the two decades of the Bloustein administration, it was two steps forward and one step back. To various degrees the study of Puerto Rican culture and history became possible on all three campuses; enrollment numbers for Puerto Rican students went up, as did employment numbers for faculty and staff. Cultural programming around Puerto Rican and Hispanic themes abounded. Student activism did not disappear, but it became episodic, tied to particular grievances, and much of the prodding of the university to do more came from the outside, particularly ASPIRA and the Puerto Rican Congress of New Jersey. By the mid-1980s, Puerto Ricans, while still the largest group of Spanish speakers at Rutgers, were no longer a majority, as both the Cuban and Dominican populations had grown substantially.

New Brunswick, because of its size, did the best. By the mid-1980s, the campus attracted perhaps 140 Puerto Rican students and 180 other Hispanics each year. The Livingston Puerto Rican Studies Program, founded in 1970, became a department in 1973; beat back challenges to its legitimacy in the late 1970s; and reconfigured itself, as the Puerto Rican and Hispanic Caribbean Studies Department, in 1986, an acknowledgment of the changing demographics of the student population and of the interests of both faculty and students in placing the study of Puerto Rican society and history in a broader context. In 1992, New Brunswick opened a Center for Latino Arts and Culture. At Newark, perhaps two dozen students of Puerto Rican birth or ancestry and three dozen other Hispanic students enrolled each year in the mid-1980s; the comparable figures for Camden were ten or fewer in both categories. In 1974, Newark obtained Board of Governors' approval for a program in Puerto Rican studies, but the state Board of Higher Education rejected the plan, and it took until the end of the decade to launch a revamped interdisciplinary program. Unlike at Livingston, Puerto Rican studies never became a department at Newark, and the major was eventually discontinued and replaced with Latin American studies offerings. Camden, which initiated the 1971 protests, never developed a Puerto Rican studies program, but it offered a Latin American studies minor with several Puerto Rican course options (today, the program is Latin American and Latino studies). The creation in 1992 at Camden of the Center for Strategic Urban Community Leadership was a significant step in repairing the rupture occasioned by the 1971 urban disturbances.

The Puerto Rican and the black student protest movements had tracked each other. Both had drawn from all the university campuses and both had produced remarkable leaders who envisioned a different type of university than the liberal arts colleges they entered. In both cases, the movements led to substantial change in university admissions and retention polices, and the organization of new programs. In both cases, student activists felt that the university response fell far short of what was needed. The movements had occasionally been at odds, separated by language, background, and ethnicity, but numerous participants crossed over to help with a common cause, and members of both movements joined with white activists to protest the war in Vietnam. The Puerto Rican movement differed in its smaller numbers, in drawing less support but occasioning less anger from students of European ancestry, and in the key role played by community organizations in negotiations with the university administration. By the end of the 1980s, the initial efforts of the Puerto Rican students had paved the way for a more diverse Hispanic or Latino/Latina culture at the university. That legacy was symbolized by the student publication *Black Voice/Carta Boricua*, begun in the mid-1970s, and by its eventual renaming as *Black Voice/Carta Latina*.

Fighting for Consumers and the Environment

In fall 1971, just as Edward J. Bloustein became Rutgers's new president, a Rutgers College student, Edward Rosenthal, began agitating for a new type of student group, which would complement the "once-in-the-fall, once-in-the spring outburst followed by a sense of hopelessness" he felt pervaded the campus.[34] He wanted to create an organization at Rutgers that would get students involved in solving "gut-level social problems" that ranged from environmental protection, to consumer fraud, racial and sexual discrimination, and labor conditions.[35] Rosenthal had fertile soil in which to plant his idea. The students of the era had been schooled on Rachel Carson's *Silent Spring* (1962) and Paul Ehrlich's *The Population Bomb* (1968), they had witnessed the first Earth Day (April 22, 1970), and they had seen the federal government establish the Environmental Protection Agency and the National Oceanographic and Atmospheric Administration (1970). Many were inspired by Ralph Nader's efforts to bring public attention to environmental and consumer issues.

Drawing on his knowledge of student activism in Oregon and Minnesota, where the first Public Interest Research Group (PIRG) chapters were founded in 1970, and working with an ad hoc group of activists, Rosenthal launched an effort to establish PIRG at Rutgers. Following the model developed in other states, the organizers created a statewide group, with campus chapters. Students elected campus boards, those in turn elected a state board, and the state board and a professional staff developed projects in which each campus participated. Students worked on the statewide projects and developed their own local projects. Crucially, the organization sought money to support the professional staff through the student fee system—initially, a fee of $1.50 paid by each student in the participating schools.

Selling the idea of PIRG at Rutgers was no easy matter. A small group of activists, with Rosenthal playing a major role, put together petition campaigns (which gathered half the students' signatures at Rutgers, Douglass, and the Newark Law School), fostered discussion in the media, took the idea to the University Senate (which initially turned it down), and in spring 1972, carried the case to the Board of Governors. Political activists on both the left and the right attacked the plan—its coercive nature, its liberal agenda, and its cost. The Board of Governors, however, responded favorably. Its members outlined a new policy for the funding of special student programs. Concept plans had to be approved by the University Senate and the president, and then by a majority vote in which half the student body of a particular college or school participated. Students who did not want to pay the fee could file for a refund.

Student referendums followed. Nader toured the state to help PIRG, lecturing in Camden, Newark, and New Brunswick. The problem, of course, was not "winning" the referendum, but even in the activist 1970s, convincing a majority of students to vote at all. In the first go-round, PIRG won on all the campuses, but fell short of the 50 percent turnout at the School of Agriculture. Then, despite broad student support in the referendum, in fall 1972, almost a quarter of the undergraduates filed for a refund of the new fee. PIRG, however, had been launched, and not only in New Brunswick. Both law schools had chapters, as did the undergraduates at Camden; statewide, PIRG was established at Westminster Choir College, Princeton University, and Seton Hall University and Law School.

In its first half decade, NJPIRG intervened in a broad range of public interest issues. In consumer protection, it created a consumer complaint center at Rutgers, researched gas station pricing policy during the 1973 gasoline crisis and later food store prices in New Brunswick, surveyed unsafe toys sold at local stores, and published a consumer guide (most of its research projects led to low-priced informational pamphlets). It lobbied in Trenton for more open government—fuller public disclosure of regulatory and budgeting information. In some cases, it worked with the state government (for example, in monitoring citizen participation in the federal Community Development and Block Grants program), and in others with Rutgers itself (in advocating for a state income tax).

Even more than consumer protection and government accountability, students associated PIRG with environmental politics. In the 1970s, environmental problems became a worldwide concern. Such incidents as mercury pollution in Japan, strip mining in West Virginia that produced deadly river flooding in that state, tree hugging by Himalayan villagers to stop logging, and the exposure of toxic dumping at Love Canal in New York focused attention throughout the decade on the ecological degradation of the planet. PIRG gave idealistic students a way to fight back locally. Rutgers PIRG volunteers drew public attention to ocean dumping, they fought to improve public transportation rather than build new highways, and they opposed the creation of new nuclear power plants. PIRG, in its most sustained project, joined a coalition working to block the Tocks Island Dam on the Delaware River north of the Delaware Water Gap. The dam and resulting lake, PIRG argued, would produce very little hydroelectric power, be environmentally destructive, and destroy much of the historic Minisink Valley. Occasionally such causes took PIRG to court; far more often, the result was the dissemination of information and working in the legislative corridors in Trenton—within the system rather than against it. Faculty lent their support to PIRG by supervising courses through which PIRG workers received college credit.

Perhaps PIRG's most sustained effort was in fighting against the pollution of New Jersey waterways. The 1972 federal Clean Water Act both set standards that PIRG could help enforce and created new responsibilities for local and state government that they could not initially meet without the assistance of groups such as PIRG. Over the years, sometimes in hip boots, at other times in canoes; sometimes to record pollution levels, at other times to remove trash, student volunteers "streamwalked" repeatedly along New Jersey waterways. In one 1974 project, Rutgers students left College Avenue at 5:30 in the morning headed for the Delaware Water Gap, where they used canoes to assist in the unglamorous work of retrieving the junk left by thoughtless campers along a fourteen-mile stretch of one of "the most beautiful and threatened areas of the country."[36] In another project, PIRG assisted in monitoring streams in four counties, and reporting the results to local officials, who simply did not have the resources to undertake such projects on their own. It was disheartening, one streamwalker reported, to find children swimming in the polluted rivers and parents who did not seem to care when they were told of the danger. Two decades later, PIRG was still at it, pulling tires, beer cans, battered bicycles, and the like from the Raritan River. As one volunteer explained, "I grew up fishing, and realizing so many of our waterways—eighty-five percent in New Jersey—aren't suitable for fishing or swimming."[37] PIRG did not always lead these efforts, but even when it did not, it provided the avenue through which dozens of students, especially at Camden and New Brunswick, became involved in community service projects.

PIRG won most of the student funding referendums. In 1978, for example, at Douglass approximately 40 percent of the students voted (25 percent were needed) and almost 90 percent voted yes; in the 1981 referendum, PIRG won 178 to 24 at the Newark Law School and by 2,318 to 827 at Rutgers College—typical responses. The only setbacks in the early years came in a disputed election at Camden and at Livingston, where in both cases less than a quarter of the student population voted.

But despite widespread support, PIRG faced repeated challenges to its funding through student fees. In 1979, students at Rutgers-Camden initiated a federal suit, arguing that the fee system unconstitutionally compelled them to support an organization whose ideological positions they often opposed. Hundreds of faculty members signed petitions supporting PIRG, most student government associations passed supportive resolutions, and President Bloustein made his support for PIRG's educational mission clear and testified on its behalf. A federal appellate court, however, sided with the plaintiffs, and the Board of Governors had to change the funding procedure to make it simpler for students to opt out of paying.

PIRG had initially collected a $1.50 fee from each student. By 1985, when the federal appellate court resolved the challenge, the fee had risen to $3.50 (in comparison, the intercollegiate athletics fee was $37.50), but payment now was truly optional. When the next challenge occurred, in the early 1990s, the fee had increased to $7.50. PIRG had angered some state legislators by its lobbying efforts and the circulation of PIRG scorecards rating legislators on their voting record on environmental issues. A coalition of business interests and these state legislators sponsored a bill requiring that any group supported by student fees that engaged in lobbying could only be funded through a "positive" check-off on the term bill (that is, a student had to opt-in rather than opt-out of paying the fee). A little more than half of PIRG's half-million-dollar budget in the 1990s came from student fees; two out of five students elected not to support PIRG, and analysis indicated that a voluntary system would cost PIRG much of its quarter-million dollars in student funding. The bill, labeled by the organization's supporters as the "Kill PIRG" bill drew support from the New Brunswick RU Republicans (the student Republican Party organization), but most student leaders and many of the faculty spoke out against it. In 1995, the bill passed, narrowly, and Governor Christine Todd Whitman signed it into law.

Then a second battle began. The administration pointed out that since 1986 PIRG had conducted lobbying through a separately incorporated organization (Citizen Lobby), and initially the administration committed itself to maintaining the opt-out check-off system. PIRG took lobbying out of the concept plan that was submitted to the Board of Governors for approval and stopped contributing money collected through student fees to its lobbying arm, but neither the media nor PIRG volunteers made the distinction clear between the student organization and its professional counterpart. The same legislators who had sponsored the bill pressured Rutgers to adopt a voluntary contribution system (one even suggesting the alternative was "zeroing out" the Rutgers budget), and the administration did an about-face. PIRG took Rutgers to court for breaking the contract established by board approval of its concept plan, and won. Rutgers then stalled on appealing the decision, waiting on the next round of state elections, and PIRG was safe until at least 1998. Nonetheless, both PIRG and the university were hurt in the funding politics of the 1990s. PIRG was forced to adopt an organizational model that was both artificial and highlighted its corporate, rather than its educational, character. The university lost autonomy. Such state regulation of its internal practices was, at this time, virtually unprecedented. More generally, an organization that had begun in the 1970s with the encouragement and support of liberal lawmakers in Trenton had in the 1990s been dealt a serious setback in the more conservative political environment of the 1990s.

In the second decade of the twenty-first century, NJPIRG Student Chapters—the spin-off organization created as a result of the 1980s litigation— was still quite active at Rutgers. In the new century, it ran campaigns to register student voters and educate consumers about recycling and energy use. The Water Watch program continued, and on each of the campuses, campaigns against homelessness and hunger were undertaken. In an effort reminiscent of the Tocks Island Dam fight, PIRG joined with other groups to block a move to allow fracking in the Delaware Water Gap region. PIRG also publicized the high cost of textbooks—now, they stated, more than $1,000 a year for the typical Rutgers student—and lobbied faculty to adopt open access texts for their classes. Critics remained. Some still challenged the refundable student fee, which by the time of the 2013 referendum had risen to $11.20. Others worried about the corporate character of PIRG's fund-raising arm. Internally, PIRG had always dealt with the healthy friction between the enthusiasm of its student volunteers and the legal and technical knowledge of its professional staff. The organization had needed both the bursts of energy of its students, and the continuity and expertise provided by its staff (most of whom, it should be noted, were former students and still in their twenties).

Perhaps NJPIRG's greatest virtue was its staying power. Born of the idealism of the mid-1960s and early 1970s, it outlasted all of the more radical student groups of that era. The notion of civic engagement that NJPIRG championed became at Rutgers an accepted part of college life and the curriculum, fostered in numerous academic and student life programs. The partnerships NJPIRG forged with local and national volunteer organizations, and the internships it sponsored in community service, linked Rutgers students to state residents in creative ways. If the university in the twenty-first century applauded civic engagement, NJPIRG in the 1970s had brought it to campus. Yet university support was not consistent. PIRG initially won over the faculty—who had to oversee the coursework aspect of its internships—and the administration, which approved its concept plans. When the student fee system was challenged in the 1980s, the faculty supported PIRG, and the administration sided with PIRG both in the court case itself and in explaining to the general public and state legislators PIRG's educational role at the university. In the 1990s, facing a more direct challenge from state government, the administration acted more cautiously, and faculty were nowhere as visible in the ensuing controversy, and, in fact, were occasionally critics of particular PIRG initiatives.

Tuition Wars

Hannah Atkins made each year at Rutgers count, and count for something more than her work as a student. She had grown up listening to the music of Pete Seeger and to sermons of her father, an Episcopal priest devoted to social justice. Atkins's childhood had included trips to the Dominican Republic and Costa Rica, where she had seen Latin American poverty close up, and schooling in North Carolina, where her father had battled racial intolerance. When in the early 1980s, the Episcopal Church called her father to its chaplaincy on the Busch campus of Rutgers, Atkins entered high school in East Brunswick, and then in 1986 enrolled at Douglass College. In September of that year, Atkins joined a protest in New Brunswick against the city's delay in opening the Ozanam shelter for homeless men. She was arrested and strip searched (along with several other Rutgers women students) when she could not post bail. Not only would a subsequent municipal court case find the students not guilty, but a suit filed about the strip search in federal court by the New Jersey Public Advocate resulted in a monetary award to the students and an agreement on the city's part that it would change the way it handled such cases in the future.

For Atkins that incident was prelude to three years of activism. Much of her political engagement would involve the plight of people caught up in wars in Central America. Her father had led statewide efforts to challenge the Reagan administration's Central American policies, and he had made Saint Michael's Chapel into a sanctuary for political refugees from the violence in their homelands. Hannah helped organize the campus Committee in Solidarity with the People of El Salvador (and, at a later date, Guatemala). The committee, which included both graduate students and undergraduates, ran film and lecture series to raise awareness and money, but also participated in acts of civil disobedience.

In spring 1989, Atkins was arrested for a protest at the College Avenue career and placement center against Central Intelligence Agency recruitment on campus, and then in the fall, arrested again when she tried to stop the arrest of another student who had been chalking statements on the steps of the New Brunswick train station. Atkins also spoke out on sexual harassment and the pervasive sexism she experienced at Rutgers. At a local tavern packed with fraternity brothers, she and friends challenged the audience who was applauding a song that condoned rape. They stood up to the crowd that they had angered but left depressed that the women in the audience as well as the men had viciously taunted them. "Sexism," Atkins and her friends wrote to the *Targum* in describing the evening, "does not pick out certain women, it oppresses us all."[38] It is not surprising, then, that Atkins joined the most widespread protest at Rutgers during the late 1980s, the fight over tuition increases, and that doing so eventually led to her arrest at a tumultuous meeting of the Board of Governors on May 12, 1989.

One of the dreams of the 1960s was tuition-free education at public universities. That, of course, did not happen in most states, and did not last anywhere. At Rutgers, in the years following World War II, the university kept tuition for more than two decades at $200 a semester, and in the late 1950s, the state actually debated the possibility of a tuition-free public education. Without an income tax, however, New Jersey had a shallow tax base and lagged well behind most other states in support for higher education. In 1971, facing the inflationary spiral set off by the Vietnam War, Governor William Cahill called on the state colleges to pay for a greater percentage of their operating costs by increasing tuition. In spring 1972, the state—with Rutgers following in its footsteps—began a pattern of almost annual tuition increases that continue to this day. The annual cost—tuition, room and board, fees, and books—of attending Rutgers, estimated at $1,628 in 1952, had by 2014 become $26,627.

With increasing tuition came tuition protests. Initially, most of these protests were directed at state officials and conducted in concert with the university administration. Over time, however, the university itself became the target. Where student government leaders played a key role throughout in tuition protests, activists increasingly organized campaigns independent of elected leadership. Demonstrations in Trenton, building takeovers, and disruptions of the meetings of the Board of Governors all challenged the assumption that tuition had to go up year after year and disputed the claim that such increases improved the quality of a Rutgers undergraduate's education. The typical student may have had little part in tuition politics, but they shared the concern, expressed consistently by student government leaders from the 1970s to the present, that the legacy of tuition increases was a burden of debt on each new generation of middle-class college graduates.

In the mid-1980s, the Bloustein administration fashioned an ambitious program to join the ranks of the foremost research universities. Following a report in 1984 from the Future Financing Committee, the administration launched the "Fund for Distinction." It was to be a partnership, the administration proposed, of the university with its students, faculty, and alumni, as well as with the state, the nation, and the corporate community. To help finance the fund, the Board of Governors in its April 1987 meeting approved a $278 (14.75 percent) increase in tuition for the coming year, and a $150 (7 percent) increase for the following year. The administration

"No I don't work for the bank, I'm just paying my tuition."

27. In early 1976, a state commission recommended shifting most aid for higher education to students rather than to institutions. Students could then shop for the best educational choice. The plan would have aided the state colleges but hurt Rutgers. The commission estimated that Rutgers tuition would almost double, to more than $1,400 annually, and students worried that family income caps on financial aid eligibility would make Rutgers unaffordable. President Bloustein called it "a consumerist point of view gone mad" and angrily charged that the report seemed to have been written as if "it were about soybeans rather than higher education" (*New York Times*, February 17, 1977, 83). Rutgers-Camden undergraduate Lee Krystek's cartoon captures the fear of many students at the state university.
SOURCE: *Gleaner*, February 9, 1977, 6.

added that another 15 percent increase would be needed after 1988–1989 to complete the building program planned as part of the fund. At the April meeting, the board stated that a "significantly better education is currently provided at Rutgers per tuition dollar of student cost than ever before," noted that tuition money helped build and renovate classrooms, and pledged that the money would not be used for the "advanced technology centers" that were one hallmark of the drive for academic excellence.[39]

Before voting on the increase, the board heard from elected student leaders and spokespeople for the "Campaign for an Affordable Rutgers Education" (CARE). CARE, a relatively new student group, had been formed to address the issue of accessibility. In their testimony before the board, students argued that increased tuition alongside inadequate federal dollars for grants and loans would create a prohibitive barrier for one in ten students who wanted to attend Rutgers. Those who did attend, the students noted, might graduate with more than $10,000 in debt. A resolution, crafted by CARE to resemble those the board itself used, called on the board to delay any tuition increase for a year, because the building program was primarily to benefit graduate students and faculty research and had never been approved by any university-wide body. As the board was about to vote on the plan, a number of "students dressed in black carried a six-foot Styrofoam 'tombstone' into the BOG meeting. Eight of the students knelt in silence in front of the tombstone as others threw dead roses and daffodils onto the ground," to symbolize, according to their spokesperson Trevor Lewis, the "killing [of] both access and excellence."[40] The tuition plan was approved.

By December, when the Board of Governors had before it the second step in the increase, the rhetoric had become much shriller. Speaker after speaker, including Rutgers College Government Association (RCGA) president Rob Hill, ridiculed the idea that Rutgers students were partners in the Fund for Distinction, or, as Nancy Loughlin, a Douglass student argued, the "partnership with students was a metaphor for wrenching money out of student pockets."[41] Another student referred to the board as "twelve dried-up old capitalists," and doubted the university really cared that it provided such mediocre undergraduate education.[42]

Testimony concluded, the board unanimously approved the 7 percent increase it had scheduled the previous May. The students took over. Angry shouting and chanting halted the proceedings. As the commotion continued, Robert Ochs, in charge of campus safety, read aloud—although it is hard to imagine anyone could hear it—the university disruption policy and then led several students from the room.

Since the days of the Vietnam War protests, late spring had always been a time of political engagement on the Rutgers campus. Spring 1988, however, passed uneventfully, as the board had previously pegged the tuition increase to the inflation rate. In spring 1989, protest resumed. Hit by two state budget reductions, one applied in midyear and the other announced for 1989–1990, the Bloustein administration saw little choice but to raise tuition by 13 percent to maintain the educational commitments it had already made. Given a chance to discuss tuition and the budget crisis at a special forum in April 1989, students explained that the increase would mean that they had to work longer hours, scale back the courses they took, extend their time to degree, and accumulate more debt. As the forum concluded, students marched to Old Queens and wrapped the central administration building in large bands of red tape to protest both the budget cuts and the planned tuition increase.

The students persisted. In early May, they spoke again at a meeting of the Board of Governors' Educational Planning and Policy Committee, then showed up in large numbers at the May 12 board meeting. At least one hundred students occupied the meeting room, stood on the tables meant for the board members, and chanted protest slogans, forcing the Board of Governors to move the meeting location. With the police now controlling access to the meeting, and considerable pushing and shoving occurring as a consequence, the board allowed five students to speak before the vote was taken. Rob Hill, the 1987 protest leader, told the board that the real choice was between empowering students and working with them to pressure the state government, and approving an increase that would "rip apart the university."[43] To the board's and the president's surprise, the vote that followed was not unanimous, as one member concluded that given its "mandate mania," university spending had "exceeded all rational limits."[44] Students then moved to Bishop House—a turreted Victorian structure that served as an administrative hub for student services—locked themselves in, and forced the police to climb through windows and batter down a door. By day's end, campus police had arrested approximately seventy students (including Hill).

The drama was not quite over. University senator Flavio Komuves, one of the five students who had been allowed to speak at the reconvened Board of Governors meeting, filed suit under the Open Public Meeting Act (the sunshine law) arguing that Rutgers had illegally locked out students who had a right to be heard by the board. The university, in turn, began sorting out its recommendations on the fate of the arrested protesters—prosecution, community service, or the dismissal of charges. After the predictable legal maneuverings, Komuves dropped his lawsuit, and the Board of Governors announced a June meeting to hear new testimony and then revote on the tuition hike. After hearing from almost four dozen speakers—several of whom compared the action of the police at the May meeting to the recent crushing of student dissent in Tiananmen Square in China—the board again approved the tuition hike, by an identical 8–1 vote. As the meeting broke up, the *Star-Ledger* reported, "a small band of students set a black, wooden makeshift coffin and plastic foam forms shaped like tombstones in front of the board of governors."[45] They then marched to Bishop House to continue the protest, but were blocked from occupying the building by locked doors and mounted policemen. Later in the summer, all but sixteen students were allowed to avoid prosecution by signing a statement, issued jointly by their lawyers and the university, in which the university acknowledged the "seriousness" of the students' opinions, and the students conceded that the police had had "probable cause" to arrest them.[46] That fall, the trials of the remaining protesters brought the drama to conclusion. In a typical plea bargain reached with these students, a New Brunswick Municipal Court judge accepted Rob Hill's guilty plea to disorderly conduct charges, dismissed the other charges against him, and sentenced him to fifty hours of community service at a men's shelter in New Brunswick and a $265 fine. Hannah Atkins had earlier accepted a similar settlement.

The 1987–1989 tuition protests were dramatic but far from unusual. Protests had begun a decade earlier, and continued over the next two decades. Student government leaders from all the campuses led these protests and testified before the Board of Governors, but ad hoc groups (most of them more short-lived than CARE) also rallied students on campus and for demonstrations at Trenton. In many cases, Rutgers students joined protesters from the state colleges, and some of the protest groups had branches on more than one campus. Students also voiced their concerns as voting members of the University Senate and the Board of Trustees, and through a nonvoting member of the Board of Governors. Trevor Lewis, a spokesperson in the 1987 protests, later served as the student representative on the Board of Governors. Some students, in board testimony or *Targum* letters, countered the protesters, either arguing that the state had primary responsibility for the problem, or pointing to the way research opportunities had improved their education and job prospects.

In the years immediately following the 1987–1989 protests, building takeovers, meeting disruptions, and angry denunciations of the new Lawrence administration became commonplace. Dialogue with CARE, in particular, was difficult and often impossible. In fact, Rutgers had worked successfully, as had the state colleges, to increase financial assistance for needy students. Each increase in tuition costs was matched with increases in the various need-based tuition assistance programs. The administration not only countered the CARE claims, but instituted new policies to control board meetings and stop what it characterized as "censorship [of free speech] by disruption"—the shouting down of board members by "frequently obscene harangues."[47]

At the same time, student protest had raised serious issues: the use of tuition dollars to underwrite the construction and maintenance of buildings designed to make Rutgers a stronger research university, the need to define the goal of excellence in a way that gave greater weight to undergraduate education (which became one of the Lawrence administration's priorities), the concern over accessibility to higher education for lower-income students, and the regressive tax features of using tuition dollars to finance a state university dedicated to benefiting the entire state population (a point made as well and frequently by the Bloustein administration). Edward Hollander, the chancellor of the New Jersey Department of Higher Education and an ex-officio member of the board, speaking at the special June 1989 Board of Governors meeting, captured the larger problem. He sympathized with the students and applauded their activism, knew the dilemma that Rutgers faced too well to counsel rolling back the planned tuition increase, and wondered why undergraduates had not made their case more directly in the legislative offices in Trenton.

Political attention and sympathy, however, seldom translated into concrete victories for the students, for as both Hollander and the university understood, power lay in Trenton. In the last years of the 1980s and the first of the 1990s, and despite strong support of Governors Kean and Florio for higher education, budget cutting trumped spending in the state legislature. Pressure from students certainly contributed to Florio's short-lived tuition stabilization plan (see chapter 2). It is also likely that on one or two occasions, when the university was considering various budget-cut and tuition-increase models in anticipation of a shortfall of state support, that concerns raised by the students led to greater reliance on belt tightening and less on double-digit tuition increases. Student concerns were also responsible for the addition of a second voting student representative on the Board of Trustees. (They failed, however, in their attempt to have three voting members, one from each campus, on the Board of Governors.)

If the tuition debate of the 1987–1989 period had a legacy that distinguished it from those before and after it, it was that it began a concerted effort to make the university's strength as a research university relevant to undergraduate education. Students, despite their primary emphasis on cost, deserve credit for pointing the university in this direction.

The Origins of LGBTQ Politics at Rutgers

James Dale grew up in Middletown, New Jersey, an active member of King of Kings Lutheran Church, for which he had taught Sunday and Bible school classes. He had also been a Scout. Dale joined the Cub Scouts at age eight, went on to the Boy Scouts (BSA), and eventually earned the organization's highest rank, Eagle Scout. In 1989, after he turned eighteen, Dale extended his membership in the organization by becoming an assistant scoutmaster in Matawan. That same year, he matriculated at Cook College. In the summer of 1990, Dale and Sharice Richardson, both nineteen years old and copresidents of the Rutgers University Lesbian/ Gay Alliance, took part in a day-long conference sponsored by the Rutgers School of Social Work on the problems homosexual teens have dealing with adolescence in a society that hardly recognized their existence. Both spoke of their own troubled childhoods, in which they often had to hide their sexual orientation or face silence, hostility, or abuse. The *Star-Ledger* covered the conference, and its story, "Seminar Addresses Needs of Homosexual Youths," published the next day, caught the attention of local Scout leaders.[48] Very shortly thereafter, Dale received a letter revoking his registration with the BSA and ending his service with the Matawan Boy Scout troop to which he had belonged for five years.

In 1992, after New Jersey had amended its law against discrimination to include "sexual orientation," Dale filed suit against the Boy Scouts with the help of the Lambda Legal Defense Fund, which for two decades had fought discrimination against gays. In the interim, Dale had become even more active in campus politics, speaking out against the harassment of gay and lesbian students and challenging the student newspaper to stop accepting advertisements from the ROTC program because of the military ban on homosexuals in the armed services. Dale lost the first round in Superior Court, and the judge could not resist sermonizing that "[t]he criminal law has changed," but "[t]he moral law as to the act of sodomy has not."[49] Dale, however, won on appeal, and when the BSA appealed that ruling to the Supreme Court of New Jersey, Dale won again. The court had to resolve the tension between the right of the BSA to select its own members (freedom of association) and the discriminatory practice of that organization. In the previous applications of the antidiscrimination law, the New Jersey courts had usually struck down such discriminatory practices (for example, in ruling against Little League baseball's unwillingness to let girls play with boys) when a private organization had substantial public features, and here again the court came down against discrimination. In a concurring opinion, Justice Alan B. Handler, responding implicitly to the lower court's sermonizing, renounced the stereotype that "homosexuals are inherently immoral," and seconded the conclusion of the Appellate Division review court that there was no reason to assume a gay scoutmaster lacked "the strength of character necessary to . . . impart BSA humanitarian ideals to . . . young boys."[50]

New Jersey, however, stood alone in its ruling. Other state courts had upheld the right of the BSA to define its own membership and described the organization as a private club, not as a quasi-public organization. With opinion divided in the state courts, the United States Supreme Court accepted an appeal, and at the end of the 2000 term, the nation's highest court ruled against Dale by a 5–4 vote. Dale, whose odyssey had begun as a nineteen-year-old and who was now almost thirty, was saddened by the decision and its implication for young people. In 2012, he voiced the same opinion: "I think if you teach a young gay kid that they're immoral—which is what they say—or unclean, or teach a non-gay kid that they're better than somebody else . . . I think that that's a horribly destructive message."[51]

Dale's three-decade odyssey drew on a history at Rutgers campuses of civil rights struggles and identity politics that stretched back to the late 1960s. As I have noted, the late 1960s produced the black student protest movement, the antiwar teach-ins, and the women's movement. Nationally, the summer of 1969 saw the Stonewall Riots in New York City—gay men and lesbians fighting back against police harassment at the Stonewall Inn in Greenwich Village. The Stonewall Riots did not begin gay protest, but it was a transformative moment, making such protest far more visible and energizing gay men and lesbians in many settings around the country.

There is no way to know how many gay students were at Rutgers College in 1969. One student leader ventured that they constituted less than 1 percent of the undergraduates—the statistical evidence only that most were hidden. As Richard Berkowitz, later the author of a memoir of those years, *Stayin' Alive*, but in the early 1970s a freshman in Hardenbergh Hall, recalled, "Each day was a collection of agonies that left me feeling more hopelessly queer. I made sure no one got close to me."[52] His double bind was common to gay students of that era—harassed if he acknowledged his sexuality and humiliated by the lies he had to tell to conceal his identity. Berkowitz eventually escaped the trap as a writer on the *Targum*, for which he wrote stories and editorials that spoke to gay concerns. For others, the answer came by way of the Student Homophile League (SHL).

In 1969, Rutgers was home to a small, informal group of gay students— the *Targum* reported that approximately four dozen had attended a college

mixer in Manhattan that spring, and in the fall, after Stonewall, some belonged to what the paper called the Gay Liberation Front, and they themselves defined as the Student Homophile League (SHL). The SHL issued a
declaration of principles on November 21, and held its first formal meeting on December 2. It was the second such campus organization in the
country; Columbia University students had already organized a homophile
league before Stonewall, and they assisted Rutgers in creating its organization. One of the campus organizers, Lionel Cuffie, defined the SHL as a
"civil libertarian and educational" organization, not a social group, that did
not "advocate homosexuality," but rather felt that "the homosexual has a
moral right in our pluralistic society to be a homosexual, and that bigotry
and emotional prejudice against homosexuals is unjust."[53] Cuffie, an African American activist, became the group's first chairman and most visible
presence in campus politics over the next two years.

The league drew about fifty men and women to its December 2 meeting and acquired office space in the College Avenue student center. While
Cuffie had emphasized the link of the group to the struggle for civil rights,
the SHL like many other gay and lesbian organizations on and off campuses
nationwide put much of its initial energy into creating meeting spaces and
activities that supported and nurtured those who came out as gay. It began
publishing a newsletter that included poetry, informational articles, political
analysis, and a calendar of events, and that spring, sponsored its first dance.
The dances became one of the organization's most popular activities, and
in many years, aided in fund-raising as well. At the time, gay students at
Rutgers had only a limited number of ways to meet other gay students—at
Manny's Den in downtown New Brunswick (in a "rundown area on Albany
Street," and by one account, "stifling and boring, as well as expensive," with
but a six-foot dance floor) or by evening cruising along "the wall," the stone
fence at the foot of Old Queens along Hamilton Street, where gays were often
targets of antigay violence.[54] The dances provided new options. The league
also brought to the student center an exhibition from the New York Gallery
of Erotic Art. Among the works displayed was one in which a SHL member
stood nude, as a human sculpture ("Silent Soldier"), on a cross and with his
back to viewers. When controversy and confrontation ensued, the university
backed the students' right to free expression, and the league agreed to move
the exhibit to a different site within the center—the exhibit itself and the coverage in the student newspaper assured that the larger student community
now knew of the SHL.

In 1971 at Newark, an invitation to come out elicited only five responses, but led to the formation of the Rutgers Gay Education Committee. By 1974, the group had more than a dozen members. Controversy ensued in 1977 when the organization and the football club had to share office space. The club's adviser commented that "it's past time to get rid of the gays."[55] The football players themselves and the university repudiated the statement, the adviser was dismissed, and the campus held a gay awareness day in April. Several years later, however, finding members to sustain the organization proved difficult. At Camden, in the mid-1970s, the Gay Activists Alliance had a small membership, but no funding, and then disappeared (at least from the pages of the student newspaper).

In New Brunswick, with a membership between fifty and a hundred students during its first few years and funding from the Student Government Association, the SHL took on an ambitious programming schedule. In spring 1970, the league staged the first of a series of annual conferences on gay issues, bringing to Rutgers individuals prominent in the national movement. Cuffie chaired the inaugural conference, which was followed by a barbecue and a dance. Members marched in New York City in the Liberation Day Parade commemorating Stonewall. SHL opened a "Way Out" coffeehouse in the basement of the student center, sent speakers to various religious, educational, and social groups on and off campus, and in 1975, began a broadcast, "So Gay," on the student radio station, WRSU, which later became the programs "Gaybreak" and then "Gay Spirit." It also brought numerous speakers to campus, perhaps most notably poet and activist Allen Ginsberg in 1978.

On April 19, 1974, National Gay Day, and in conjunction with the fourth annual conference, the league advertised and staged the first of what would become an on-again, off-again annual event, Blue Jeans Day. It saturated the campus with posters announcing that on that day, those who "wished to be counted as gay, [should] just wear blue jeans," and one year even promised to have volunteers, clipboards in hand, along the streets to count the turnout.[56] There was no count, of course, as the project was essentially a way to make people think about judging others by external appearances. When Blue Jeans Day was repeated two years later, however, an effigy was hung outside a fraternity house on College Avenue, with a sign that read, "The only good gay is a dead gay—back to your closets homos."[57] The fraternity denied responsibility (as it would when such incidents occurred in future years), and the university, after waiting a few hours and after a group of feminists protested in front of the fraternity, removed the effigy. Blue Jeans Day would be reenacted for several more springs, and then brought back in the 1980s, and in the future, when met with a homophobic reaction on College Avenue, the league itself would protest the outrage.

Most accounts of what became in 1976 the Rutgers Gay Alliance suggest, however, that this was a low point in the organization's history. Student activism had begun to wane more generally on college campuses, and lesbian and gay rights movements became targets of vicious backlash attacks. The political right, never dormant in postwar politics, was energized in reaction to the 1973 *Roe v. Wade* abortion decision. The cultural wars that followed targeted the women's movement as well as gay and lesbian organizations. Anita Bryant's 1977 campaign, "Save Our Children," to repeal a Dade County, Florida, law that protected the civil rights of gays, reinforced stereotypes of gays as sexual predators and fed homophobia nationwide. At Rutgers, the reaction to the second Blue Jeans Day genuinely shocked members of the alliance, as did the failure of the university to respond, and membership in the organization dwindled. The annual conference planned for 1976 was never held. Tension of another sort revolved around the role of women, and later, of bisexuals in the league and alliance.

Campus activism and national rights movements in the 1960s and early 1970s were dominated by men. The SHL formed before women had been admitted to Rutgers College and at the same time that the first class of women and men was admitted to Livingston College. There were undergraduate women as well at Douglass College, of course, but Douglass had its own feminist movement, which provided alternatives to the SHL. Thus, from the outset, the league had more male than female members, men held most of the leadership positions, and male couples outnumbered female couples substantially at the league-sponsored dances. At the very first conference run by the SHL, in spring 1970, female conference participants staged a walkout to protest "chauvinism and male elitism."[58] In the mid-1970s, feminists criticized the league for degrading women with a pornographic poster advertising a Halloween dance, and as late as the mid-1980s, lesbian critics of the alliance tried to dissuade other women from attending the organization's dances. Within the league in the 1980s, bisexual women were rebuked for not "providing proper role models."[59] That said, and in contrast to many other rights movements of that era, the league and alliance made significant efforts at inclusion. In its second year, the league had a female chair (and a male secretary, Cuffie) and a number

28. In spring 1981, Ingrid Wilhite created *Pheminist Phunnies* for the Douglass *Caellian*. Her cartoons attacked the antifeminist backlash of the era. She was an active member of the Gay/Lesbian Alliance based at Rutgers College and an occasional co-host of a radio show on gay issues hosted by the Cook College radio club. Wilhite came to Rutgers from Idaho, attracted by what was one of the oldest gay/lesbian student organizations in the country. In the 1980s, men were in the majority in the Gay/Lesbian Alliance, but Wilhite was comfortable in the organization and became its co-chair as a senior. After graduation she moved to San Francisco and eventually back to her native Idaho.

SOURCE: *Caellian*, April 9, 1981, 3.

of very active female leaders in the years that followed. During the 1980s, perhaps 40 percent of its membership was female, and in 1983, the organization changed its name to the "Rutgers University Lesbian/Gay Alliance" (RULGA). (In the next decade, "bisexual" would officially be added to its title, as would "transgendered" and "queer" in the twenty-first century.)

In 1983, the alliance held its first public discussions of the AIDS crisis. Doctors had first identified AIDS in 1981, and the initial victims were predominantly gay men. Within two decades, almost thirty million people had died worldwide in the HIV/AIDS crisis, and while no region or social class was immune, the epidemic today has taken a horrifying toll of lives in some of the world's poorest communities. In the early 1980s, however, gay activists in United States focused on what was a medical and political crisis in *their* community. Groups such as the Gay Men's Health Crisis in New York led the way, but as the death toll mounted, new, more militant organizations, most notably ACT UP, emerged to pressure an unresponsive government to do more to combat the crisis.

At Rutgers in early 1983, the alliance cosponsored a talk on AIDS with the New Jersey Lesbian and Gay Coalition and sponsored another, before a large audience, in the spring with a speaker from the Gay Men's Health Crisis. By the time HIV/AIDS had become a national issue in the mid-1980s, and a pervasive fear on college campuses, a conference by the alliance on AIDS drew both straights and Rutgers staff members as well as gays, and garnered media coverage beyond the campus. AIDS education became one of the constant themes of the alliance newsletter. In 1990, Rutgers students worked successfully to bring the AIDS memorial quilt to campus. In 1993, students dedicated a panel to Lionel Cuffie of the New Jersey NAMES Project AIDS Memorial Quilt. In 2005, twenty-five panels from the quilt were displayed in the Student Center. Activists had created the quilt in 1985 to memorialize those who had died from the disease, and it had its first public display in 1987 in a gay and lesbian march in Washington, DC. At most displays, the memorialization of individual deaths on distinct panes was augmented by the solemn reading of the names of those who had died. In the 2005 Rutgers display, more than a thousand people visited the Student Center.

The AIDS crisis initially fed the backlash against gays and lesbians that had begun in the 1970s, but the crisis also mobilized the gay community. This mobilization, which of course extended far beyond college boundaries, probably accounts for the new energy on the New Brunswick campus with which the alliance confronted harassment and discrimination. The first sign of a new militancy came with Susan Cavin's Rutgers Sexual Orientation Survey, a summary of which appeared in April 1987 in the *Targum.* Cavin modeled the survey on one done at Yale and had the assistance of students in her women's studies class on "Homosexuality and Society" in distributing the questionnaires, 213 of which were completed and returned by students, staff, professors, and some New Brunswick residents. Unlike other studies, Cavin's documented a higher incidence of unfair treatment of lesbians than of gay men—which signaled a need for more gendered studies of antigay discrimination, harassment, and violence—and, more generally, concluded that "many lesbian, gay, and bisexual members of the Rutgers–New Brunswick community, particularly undergraduates, live in a secret, fearful world where they suffer in silence from a classic double bind: they are damned if they come out (via external discrimination) and damned if they don't (via not being oneself)."[60] Ten years after the first effigy hanging, many lesbian and gay students still doubted that the university was on their side or would take action to prevent harassment.

Cavin's report concluded with a series of recommendations. Initially, they were ignored, but the next fall, after the alliance had written to President Bloustein urging him to take a public stand against discrimination based on "sexual orientation," and had gotten no response, a set of demands, many similar to those in the Cavin report, was sent to the administration. The alliance asked for a full-time coordinator for lesbian, gay, and bisexual concerns, increased funding for the student organization, better library materials in the field, peer counseling services, recognition in university literature, new facilities for the hotline, and a more forceful and public stand against harassment and discrimination. While it took several months of prodding to get the administration to act, when it did, it moved quickly to change Rutgers policy. Most important, Bloustein created the "President's Select Committee for Lesbian and Gay Concerns," chaired by James Anderson, a faculty member, and broadly representative of students, staff, and faculty at the university. In 1989, the committee issued "In Every Classroom," with well over a hundred recommendations that incorporated the student demands and brought to the table new issues affecting the lesbian, gay, and bisexual community. In 1992, the Lawrence administration created the Office of Diverse Community Affairs and Lesbian Gay Affairs and appointed the poet, activist, and former adviser for the alliance, Cheryl Clark, as director of the new office (see chapter 3). That same year, as we have seen, Dale brought suit against the BSA—Rutgers had come a long way from the founding of the SHL in 1969.

Alliance activism did not end in the early 1990s. RULGA continued as both a social group and a rights organization. At the end of the century, what was now BiGLARU was joined on campus by Lesbian and Bisexual Women in Action, the Latina/o and People of Color Lesbian/Gay/Bisexual/Transgender Union of Rutgers University, and the Alliance of Queer Graduate Students, among other organizations. As with the efforts of African American and Puerto Rican students and of various student feminist groups, however, much of what these gay, lesbian, and queer groups sought was incorporated into the work of university committees and the creation of centers and academic programs. That the gay rights movement at Rutgers–New Brunswick had come of age was symbolized by the publication in 1987 of Moe [Morris] Kafka's history of the RULGA in an extended *Targum* essay, by the creation in 1989 of the Rutgers Gay Archives Project by David Nicols, by the convening in 1991 at Rutgers, to a huge turnout, of the fifth annual Lesbian and Gay Studies Conference (previously held at

Ivy League schools), by the establishment of an alumni organization, and by an exhibition in the New Brunswick library, curated by Erika Gorder, chronicling *30 Years of Queer Activism.*

The increasing use of the word "queer," from the early 1990s on, in the cultural and political discourse about the movement reflected a need for an all-encompassing term for an increasingly diverse community. There was a defiant boldness in recapturing a term that in the past had often been one of derision used by homophobes. When in fall 2013, Rutgers-Camden offered the campus's first LGBTQ course, it was titled "Queer America." The term, however, also signaled for some a critique of a movement that had increasingly been mainstreamed on campuses and many communities nationwide. It was hard to imagine the sexual radicals who gathered in Manny's Den embracing marriage equality as their cause, and equally hard to imagine a gay leftist such as Lionel Cuffie protesting against ROTC *because* it would not admit openly gay or lesbian cadets.

The debate about queer politics reverberated in faculty and graduate student circles on campuses but left far less trace in the student movement at Rutgers itself. Among students, homophobia sadly was not dead. Reminders occurred far too often, and the university and queer organizations devoted energy and resources to sustaining a diverse culture on campus. The two most pressing issues were resolved favorably. The university, after a long and dispiriting controversy, began providing spousal benefits for same-sex partners (an issue that mattered to graduate students as well as to faculty and staff). Marriage equality gained the widespread support of the student population, majority support in the state, and finally judicial validation. Looking back from the twenty-first century, alliance alumni could conclude that momentum was now on their side.

Epilogue

"Greeks and Granolas and Steeps and Slackers."[61] Under that title, in fall 1994, *Mother Jones*, a left-wing journalistic voice born in the 1970s, published an essay, adopted from a book on campus radicalism by Paul Loeb. After the article, the magazine announced that "not all activism is created equal" and went on to list its "Top 10 Activist Campuses" of that year.[62] Rutgers came in at number five, behind Oregon, Brown, Wisconsin, and North Carolina at Chapel Hill. The brief summary noted gay, lesbian, and death penalty concerns; women's groups; and tuition protests as signs of political energy. The next year, in what had become an annual poll, Rutgers made the list again, this time at number seven. The African American protest against President Francis Lawrence's comments about genetics, race, and academic achievement and the dramatic disruption of a nationally televised basketball game as part of that protest caught the magazine's attention. In 2004, for a third time, Rutgers made *Mother Jones's* "top ten" because so many students had trekked to Washington, DC, for a pro-choice rally. In a gesture tinged with a little irony, the university newsletter, the *Focus*, celebrated the ranking. By 2004, protest had become civic engagement, a good thing, and for the university, one more way to attract students.

Asked to comment on the 2004 ranking, one undergraduate responded that activism was not primarily about one-time events that registered national attention but rather about day-to-day commitment of particular individuals to particular causes. Her comment helps put in context the gradual shift that occurred in student activism after the mid-1990s. Movements, especially those that sustained protest over more than one cycle of students through the university, were no longer a good way to characterize what became student engagement. Rather, engagement was formalized through several university supported centers and offices—for example, the Paul Robeson Cultural Center and what is now the Center for Social Justice Education and LGBT Communities Resource Center—but also through an ever-changing mix of student organizations, facilitated but not controlled by the university's student life administration. In the middle of the second decade of the twenty-first century, on the New Brunswick campus, there were approximately fifty student organizations devoted to political/social activism and about seventy defined as community service groups. Newark and Camden had their own mix, a somewhat shorter list, but still an impressive range of opportunities for student engagement. Virtually all of the movements explored in this chapter remain in some form on the campuses of the state university today. The environmental, human rights, and social justice problems that today's generation of students face in the larger world are every bit as challenging and devastating as the concerns of student activists as in the past. What has changed most, at least since the 1990s, is the sense of urgency, the confrontational style of politics, and the unity of large groups of students around a small set of key issues.

7

Research at Rutgers

Selman Waksman left the Ukraine, in tsarist Russia, for America shortly before World War I. Just twenty-one, with little English and little money, he pursued the advice of family members and made contact with a fellow Russian immigrant who worked at the New Jersey College of Agriculture. His contact helped Waksman matriculate at the college. Waksman mastered his new country's language and then his coursework to graduate in 1915 with a B.S. in agriculture; he earned his master of science degree at Rutgers as well, and in 1918 completed a Ph.D. in biochemistry at the University of California–Berkeley. At the time Waksman entered Rutgers, most of the university's research was in agriculture, funded directly by the state government, performed at the Agricultural Experiment Station (Ag Station), and enormously beneficial to the Garden State.

Soon after earning his Ph.D., Waksman returned to Rutgers to work as a soil microbiologist at the Ag Station, studying actinomycetes, soil bacteria that share properties with fungi. Almost two decades earlier, Alexander Fleming had observed that certain molds destroyed bacteria, knowledge that would eventually lead to the discovery of penicillin. In this instance, however, although Waksman knew that there was a relationship between actinomycetes and other soil bacteria, his initial interest in that relationship was not in its potential medical value but in the role actinomycetes might play in improving soil fertility.

Two decades later, on the eve of World War II, Waksman had become a world authority on soil microbiology and now headed an ambitious research program at the Ag Station, which had no real parallel at the liberal arts colleges that complemented the College of Agriculture. But he had not yet realized the potential of actinomycetes to attack disease bacteria. Only in the late 1930s, hearing of work being conducted by others, did he begin to experiment with the antibiotic potential of actinomycetes, backed with funding from Merck and Company, a New Jersey pharmaceutical firm. Much of the laboratory work was done, in fact, by his research assistants, and much of it ran into dead-ends. The crucial connection was eventually made by two of his assistants, Elizabeth Bugie and Albert Schatz. In 1943, Schatz established and Bugie verified that a microorganism taken from a particular soil sample produced an antibiotic that killed tuberculosis bacilli. The organism, called streptomycin, gave medicine a weapon against a disease resistant to penicillin and among the world's deadliest killers. All three names appeared as authors of the 1944 article announcing the breakthrough. In 1945, Schatz and Waksman patented the drug, and after rapid testing, streptomycin was first marketed in 1947. Rutgers established a research foundation to handle income from the patent rights, and the foundation, in turn, helped establish an institute to pursue research in microbiology. That institute later was named for Waksman, and it was Waksman who in 1952 won a Nobel Prize for the years of research on soil microbiology that led to the discovery of streptomycin.

Who discovered streptomycin remained disputed. Schatz and Waksman quarreled over recognition and patent rights. Schatz was in the difficult position of a former student who needed his mentor's support to obtain a permanent position, yet who was willing to challenge that same professor legally—"an unprecedented action"—for the recognition and royalties that he believed he deserved.[1] In 1950, Rutgers settled out of court, protecting the newly established institute, acknowledging Schatz as the codiscoverer, and allotting him royalties (less than Waksman had obtained). Schatz eventually found academic employment, but he never had the opportunities that might otherwise have been his. Years later, on the fiftieth anniversary of the discovery of streptomycin, Rutgers presented Schatz with an award in recognition of his pioneering laboratory work. Long before that, streptomycin had ceased to be the antibiotic of choice in the battle with TB, and, in fact, in the twenty-first century, new strains of tuberculosis are again major killers.

During the period immediately following World War II, no name bet-ter embodies research at Rutgers than that of Selman Waksman. There were a few others: Richard P. McCormick, because of his untiring efforts to make New Jersey residents aware of their state's history; John Ciardi, the English Department's poet, translator, and author; and Mason Gross him-self, but in his case more as an academic leader and host of the television shows *Think Fast* and *Two for the Money* than as a philosopher. Beyond them, the ceramics program in the School of Engineering, because of its close association with the Trenton-based ceramics industry, and the Ag Station, heralded for its introduction in the 1930s of the "Rutgers tomato," also shared public visibility. There were, of course, numerous other faculty members writing books, working in laboratories, and publishing articles, and especially through the Experimental Station, a great deal of research occurring that directly benefited the state, but the university was known primarily well into the 1960s for its liberal arts colleges, not for graduate education and faculty research.

Not surprisingly, in the post–World War II attempts to rate graduate programs and faculty strength, Rutgers did not fare well (and often was not even mentioned). Allan Cartter's study, published in 1966 by the Ameri-can Council of Education (ACE), was the first comprehensive attempt to assess liberal arts and engineering graduate programs. The Cartter study, based on a survey of faculty opinions, broke graduate programs into four categories: distinguished, strong, good, and adequate plus. The list was dominated by elite private universities, with California–Berkeley, Wiscon-sin, and Michigan among public universities often in the "distinguished" group. Only one Rutgers program broke into the top twenty: microbiology (the Waksman effect). Many were not even mentioned, and those Rutgers departments that were recognized were generally cited for their faculty, not their graduate programs. English, history, and several of the biological sciences had "good" faculties; physics and psychology, as well as civil and mechanical engineering, were "acceptable plus."

ACE's follow-up study in 1969, published in 1972—the beginning of the Bloustein era at Rutgers—showed significant improvement across the board in graduate education, but the relative rankings of various programs remained about where they had been half a decade before. The study re-placed the descriptive adjectives (such as "distinguished") with numerical categories and warned against pecking-order comparisons, but the results were the same: postwar graduate education continued to be dominated by elite institutions. The survey respondents also indicated, however, that many schools were in the process of playing catch-up. Rutgers was among these schools. A significant number of evaluators left Rutgers graduate programs in English, history, psychology, physics, and mathematics (new to the list) in the third numerical tier but also suggested that they had improved greatly during the past five years.

Early on the Bloustein administration made it a priority to change course. It laid the groundwork for improvement with academic reorganization and physical consolidation of the various New Brunswick college departments. It did so despite the warnings in the 1978 Middle States accreditation report and by outside evaluators in external reviews of individual departments that a federated college system was the best way for Rutgers to preserve its unique blend of undergraduate and graduate education. Cooperation between, for example, the chemistry departments at Douglass and Rutgers Colleges, rather than their consolidation, outsiders argued, preserved the best of both worlds. Nonetheless, relying on a different vision for the future, the Bloustein administration moved ahead, naming a task force to work immediately on a comprehensive ranking and rating of graduate education at Rutgers. It was a small committee, seven members, all accomplished researchers and scholars, and chaired by a mathematician, Daniel Gorenstein. In 1981, after exhaustive study, the Gorenstein committee placed each program in one of five categories: nationally distinguished (Ia); nearly so distinguished (Ib); strong, with great potential (II); adequate (III); or weak (IV). The committee also crafted proposals for each graduate program—whether and to what extent it should be given additional resources. These categories ranged from "substantial increase in support" to "sympathetic support" (maintaining an already strong department by allowing it to replace major faculty losses with the hiring of senior professors but not by expanding the department's size), to "reduction by attrition," to "consolidation" (improving a weak program by adding it to another program), or even to "a candidate for discontinuance."

A typical evaluation, in this case of a program on the cusp of distinction, read as follows:

Medium sized program. Productive and professionally strong faculty who consistently receive grant support. Present external review notes serious split in faculty as well as geographical dispersions which hamper program. Stronger leadership required. Few [graduate] degrees awarded. Despite few applicants, students seem good. Very low percentage of full-time students. Clear service need, particularly in view of New Jersey's special environmental problems. Faculty resources appear to be adequate. Action Recommendation: Maintain present level of faculty allocation. However, needed leadership may require appointment of a senior outside person.[2]

The committee was just as direct about weakness, for example, characterizing one program as a "small, rather weak M.S. program with average to below average students" and "very low scholarly and research activities," and recommending that if the program were to be continued, it be merged with an allied program.[3]

The Gorenstein committee's report had three direct consequences. The report assured that the strong would get stronger; it favored programs with Ph.D. tracks (and thus engineering and the arts and sciences over the professional schools, which primarily awarded master's degrees); and it privileged the larger New Brunswick programs over their smaller counterparts at Newark and Camden (without excluding the possibility that second-tier programs might work their way up). None of this was controversial, and it paralleled the way national funding agencies directed resources to elite educational institutions and to the most promising second-tier schools. Nor were the rankings themselves unexpected. Most Rutgers programs were not yet of national distinction, and those that were had shown up in the national surveys: English, mathematics, physics, and (although hidden by the categories used nationally) ceramic science and engineering. There were more "Ib" programs—which would have to be improved if Rutgers was going to vault into the ranks of major research universities—and they were spread around the academic units in New Brunswick: nutrition, at Cook; mechanics and material science, in engineering; clinical psychology at the Graduate School of Applied and Professional Psychology; and a half dozen programs in the New Brunswick Faculty of Arts and Sciences.

By the end of the Bloustein's presidency, the strength of the Ia programs, along with the improvements in those one or two steps back, had secured the university membership in the American Association of Universities (AAU). One of those "Ia" programs, ceramics, had begun with a special state appropriation in 1902 as the Department of Clay Works and Ceramics, with enthusiastic support from the state's ceramics industry. While its early history was associated primarily with research to improve the production of whiteware, the department joined the School of Engineering, adding an engineering track to its curriculum. The department participated in the postwar research boom by doing work on ceramic high-frequency insulation for the United States Army. In the 1970s, the ceramics faculty led food-safety studies of heavy-metal release from ceramic foodware and contributed to a U.S. Atomic Energy Commission study at Princeton University on nuclear fusion. In the early 1980s, the National Science Foundation (NSF) provided the seed money for the Center for Ceramics Research at Rutgers, the first such center in the nation, and a few years later, with state bond support, the department established a fiber-optics research program.

In the early 1970s, the mathematics and English programs were equally important to Rutgers's modest reputation as a research university. In both, strong postwar leadership was decisive. In the English department, J. Milton French, himself an accomplished scholar of the poet John Milton, guided an expansion of the faculty from ten to thirty-five full-time members by insisting both on research productivity and commitment to undergraduate teaching. During French's twelve years as chair, the faculty produced as many as forty scholarly books and more than three hundred articles. While French remained bound to traditional teaching and scholarly conventions, the department he helped to create gained acclaim in the 1950s owing to the work of literary critic and poet John Ciardi and, subsequently, to Paul Fussell Jr.'s brilliant scholarship on the poetry of World War I. Ciardi introduced a vigorous creative writing program to the curriculum, while Fussell was among those who championed new approaches to literary criticism. A program that had awarded its first Ph.D. in 1947, and no more than one or two a year when Mason Gross became president a little more than a decade later, was now turning out more than a dozen Ph.D.s annually—the most of any graduate program at the university. By the 1970s, the department boasted a dozen faculty members of national acclaim; pointed with pride not only to creative writing but also to its commitment to feminist scholarship and black studies; reminded people that it was home to *Raritan: The Quarterly Review*, edited by Richard Poirier; and took credit for an innovative approach to teaching the college's required basic composition course.

Mathematics, like English a foundational department for the instruction of undergraduates, also profited from the immediate post–World War II boom in enrollment. By 1950, its size had doubled, to fourteen members, but the faculty were not as productive as those in English and did not award a Ph.D. until 1951. That Ph.D. was directed by Malcolm Robertson, the only research-active faculty member of the immediate postwar years, and he single-handedly began and sustained the early graduate program. But Kenneth Wolfson, once he became chair of mathematics in 1961, took the major steps needed to transform the department. Graduate education expanded, the department received major funding from the NSF (see below) to improve salaries and recruit outstanding mathematicians, computer science and statistics programs were spun off, and the department moved from makeshift quarters scattered across the campuses to Hill Center on Busch campus. Wolfson remained the department chair for a decade and a half, then moved to the position of dean of the Graduate School in New Brunswick, where he joined Edward J. Bloustein and T. Alexander Pond in the drive to improve graduate education and research at Rutgers. His successor as chair of mathematics, Daniel Gorenstein, played an equally important role by heading the committee that conducted the first comprehensive review of graduate education at Rutgers.

I proceed now to an overview of five graduate programs and their development as research faculties. The physics department in New Brunswick receives extended treatment because of its early distinction in research. Then follow discussions of the School of Criminal Justice (Newark), the Institute of Marine and Coastal Science (New Brunswick), the history department (New Brunswick), and childhood studies (Camden)—that illustrate distinctive paths in the development of strong academic programs at New Jersey's state university.

The Department of Physics and Astronomy–New Brunswick

Robert Atkinson met Fritz Houtermans while they were both working on their Ph.D. theses under James Franck at Göttingen in Weimar Germany. Houtermans was born near Danzig and grew up in Vienna. In the early 1920s, when he began his college training in physics, neither his Jewish ancestry nor his dabbling in communist politics was a liability. Later, as a well-known scientist then based in the Soviet Union, he was thrown in prison during the era of Stalinist purges, only to be repatriated to Germany after the Nazi-Soviet pact of 1940. He lived out the war precariously, doing nuclear physics secluded in a private laboratory, while the Nazi regime attempted to create an atomic bomb. Atkinson, whose full name was

Robert d'Escourt Atkinson, was born in Wales and trained in physics at Oxford University. Göttingen offered him the chance to use a Rockefeller fellowship for advanced study with a mentor who had recently won the Nobel Prize, and it was in Göttingen, as a Ph.D. student, that he met Houtermans. Houtermans had been exploring the idea that at high temperatures the nuclei of atoms could absorb other (alpha) particles— that is, atomic fusion—while Atkinson had been studying the interior temperatures of stars. At that time, there was no way to test Houtermans's theory in a laboratory, but together they wrote a paper that coupled the two ideas, which they whimsically titled "How Can One Cook Helium Nuclei in a Potential Pot?"[4] Published by the leading German physics journal under a much subdued title insisted upon by the editors, along with some mathematics that turned out to arrive at the right conclusion in the wrong way, the article helped solidify Atkinson's already promising reputation as a physicist and brought him to Rutgers University in 1929.

Atkinson spent a little less than a decade at Rutgers before going to England in 1937 for a post at the Royal Observatory in Greenwich. During his short but productive stay at Rutgers, in a small department of four members, he was the only significant publishing scholar as he pursued his research interest in the creation of energy within stars. Atkinson returned to the United States during World War II to work on various projects related to the war effort, then went back to the Royal Observatory, and concluded his career at Indiana University. Although physics at Rutgers was primarily a teaching field in the prewar era, one could see the future in Atkinson's career. Physicists trained in the 1920s and 1930s who had been called to support the war effort, many of them European-born or educated, would gain both prestige and, in the postwar world, seemingly endless government support for their research. Before the war, research already defined physics departments at the elite universities in the United States, but not at most liberal arts colleges, including the men's and women's colleges in New Brunswick, where physicists were primarily physics teachers. That situation, however, changed, at least at Rutgers, and not by happenstance, but by a decision to pursue a different course.

Atkinson's replacement, Frank Dunnington, would guide the transformation of the Rutgers program. Dunnington earned a B.S. in electrical engineering in 1929 at the University of California at Berkeley and a Ph.D. in physics in 1932 at the same institution, where he worked under Ernest Lawrence. Lawrence, a Yale Ph.D., had been lured to Berkeley with the offer of a tenured position, and by the time Dunnington entered the program, Lawrence was already a full professor, not yet thirty, and at work on what would become the cyclotron, or nuclear particle accelerator (in the popular imagination, an "atom smasher"). After receiving his Ph.D., Dunnington worked at the California Institute of Technology, pursuing questions in nuclear physics that the new technology made it possible to answer with great precision, published an important paper in *Physical Review* (the leading American journal in the field), and in 1937 joined the Rutgers faculty. Physics was still a small department—seven members in the immediate prewar period—and World War II drained it of scientists, Dunnington included, as they enlisted in the war effort. In Dunnington's case, this meant working on radar systems at the Massachusetts Institute of Technology Radiation Laboratory.

Dunnington returned to Rutgers after the war and in 1946 stepped into the role of department chair. He convinced President Clothier to hire a group of researchers who were leaving the radiation laboratory at which he had worked, negotiated contracts for them that reduced their teaching responsibilities, promised to match university support for that research with federal grants, and moved the department into a new building, Van Dyck Hall, with adequate laboratory space. In all, five physicists who had worked at the radiation laboratory, in addition to Dunnington, joined the department, and one of their wives, Ellen Swomley Stewart, joined the physics department at the New Jersey College for Women (NJCW). Three of these hires contributed substantially to the postwar physics department's research reorientation. Henry Torrey and Charles Whitmer both became department chairs, and both did outstanding work on nuclear magnetic resonance. (This was the study of the electromagnetic radiation absorbed and emitted by the nuclei of atoms in a magnetic field, a process from which NMR spectroscopy was developed.) Edward Purcell, who worked with Torrey at Harvard, received a Nobel Prize for their joint work in the discovery of NMR. Peter Weiss, who worked on the theory of ferromagnetism, followed Torrey as chair. A year later, Dunnington hired a New York University postdoctoral physicist, trained at the University of Pennsylvania, Bernard Serin, who would also serve briefly as chair.

At Rutgers, Serin conducted pioneering work on superconductivity. Researchers had known since the early twentieth century that at very low temperatures certain metals (lead, mercury, tin) can carry an electrical current without offering any resistance. Serin discovered that the critical temperature at which a metal became a superconductor (transition temperature) differed for different isotopes of a given element, and that this critical temperature depended on the mass of the atom. This discovery opened the door to a fuller understanding of superconductivity, and superconductivity has made major contributions to modern life (for example, in producing the large magnetic fields needed for MRI scanners). Serin's hiring, then, completed a process that in just two years defined the department for a generation.

Over the next decade and a half, Dunnington's autocratic relationship with his colleagues occasionally unglued personal relationships in the department—a story more fully discussed in Allen B. Robbins's insightful *History of Physics and Astronomy at Rutgers, 1771–2000* (2001)—but these battles did not derail the department's research program. Rather, a seemingly limitless flow of federal research dollars allowed physics in the postwar era, at elite schools first, and more slowly at Rutgers, to enter its golden age.

Support for research in the physical sciences had long come, especially to elite private schools and a handful of great public universities, from state governments, foundations, and benefactors, but World War II brought the federal government into the picture in an unprecedented fashion. The Manhattan Project, which developed the atomic bomb and the MIT Radiation Laboratory, where a British magnetron was the springboard for developing sophisticated radar systems, established the import of physicists and engineers, in particular, to national defense, and the Cold War cemented the relationship between academic scientists and the federal government. In the immediate aftermath of World War II, the question was never if, but rather how, the government was going to support science.

There were two parts to the answer: First, support came from a variety of federal agencies, not one umbrella department. In 1946, Congress approved and President Truman signed a bill creating the Atomic Energy Commission. The commission, with largely civilian leadership, directed and funded both applied and basic research on nuclear defense. Another stream of money came from the various branches of the armed forces, and most important from the newly created Office of Naval Research (ONR), which again was authorized to spend for both military technology and basic science. Yet another source was added in 1950 when, after heated political battles and long delays, the federal government created the National Science Foundation (NSF) to support basic science, but with a much smaller budget than the Department of Defense had for applied research. Each of these, along with support for the health sciences, pumped ever more federal research dollars into the economy.

Second, rather than mount government-housed and -operated research programs, these agencies almost immediately began contracting out projects to industry, and far more often, universities. Outside the AEC, little attention was paid to the applied/basic distinction, and even in nuclear physics, those involved never tired of pointing out that basic science on the atom in the 1920s and 1930s led to the development of a new weapon that ended World War II. Initial fears that research would be unduly controlled by the military soon lessened, and the federal government endorsed funding allotted by peer review—panels of the best scientists selecting the best science to support. This guaranteed that the flow of federal dollars would go primarily to the elite institutions that already dominated the field (a pattern that would persist even as the institutional and geographical dispersal of money broadened over time). Soviet testing of atomic weapons and the subsequent launch in 1957 of *Sputnik*, the first artificial satellite of Earth, only intensified the public and political commitment to the sciences. The funding of medical research excepted, physics was the greatest beneficiary of government largesse, and for many physicists, the 1960s would be a period of accomplishment and prestige.

After an auspicious postwar beginning, the Rutgers physics department just barely held its own in the late 1950s and through the 1960s. Strong physics programs had groups of faculty working in several fields—low-energy nuclear physics, high-energy physics, condensed matter physics—and senior leadership for each field. Nationwide, as a direct result of government support, the number of Ph.D.-granting physics programs was multiplying, and the demand for physicists skyrocketed. Rutgers, where salaries were tied to a state scale, had a difficult time competing. The postwar era had been a period of modest growth. The department had doubled in size, while its graduate program during the 1950s produced two, three, or four new Ph.D.s each year.

Nonetheless, before the mid-1960s, the department made major steps to upgrade its research program, consolidate itself as a faculty, and expand its laboratory space. Allen Robbins's addition to the faculty in 1956 began a commitment to low-energy nuclear physics, which was seconded by President Gross in his 1959 inaugural address, and led to the purchase in 1961 of a 15-million-electron-volt tandem Van de Graaff particle accelerator. The project cost more than $2 million, some obtained from a bequest, some from the state, some from the university's reserves, and some from a partnership with Bell Telephone Laboratories (which worked closely with the physics department for decades). The accelerator allowed Rutgers to attract a distinguished senior scholar, George Temmer, from Florida State, to become director of the nuclear physics laboratory. Among the nuclear physicists who worked on the accelerator was Noémie Koller. Koller, hired in 1960, became in 1965 one of the first two women to receive tenure in the College of Arts and Sciences.

Noémie Benczer-Koller was born in Austria in 1933 to academic parents. Within a year, the family had moved to Paris to escape the growing fascist movement and then moved again to southern France after the Nazi invasion of that country. Escape from Marseille to Casablanca, then to Cuba, where they spent a year, and then to Mexico, followed. The French education Koller had initially received continued at home during the brief sojourn in Cuba and took up again in Mexico at the Lycée Franco-Mexicain, which gave her an outstanding education and a strong background in mathematics, so that when she moved on to Barnard College in 1951, she entered as a third-year student. Skillful advising pointed her to a major in physics. (Can one imagine this happening had she not been at a women's college?) Koller found a position as a research assistant to a Columbia scientist, Chien-Shiung Wu, also a foreign-born woman physicist, who would encourage and mentor Koller as an experimental nuclear physicist.

In 1960, Henry Torrey hired Koller, who now had a Columbia Ph.D., two years of postdoctoral experience, and her name as coauthor on a number of articles written with Wu and other physicists at Columbia. She got a small office in the basement of Van Dyck Hall, $10,000 to purchase equipment and a radiation source, and then NSF support. Her early work, before Rutgers had a particle accelerator, was with Geiger counters and cloud chambers, crude detectors (but less expensive) that allowed her to study atomic nuclei and the properties of solids (what became condensed matter physics). Her first stand-alone article, on the nuclear structure of tin, appeared in 1964. When Rutgers acquired the tandem particle accelerator, Koller became a junior collaborator on research projects and eventually the director of the Nuclear Radiation Laboratory. She continued to receive NSF grants and publish past retirement, well into the twenty-first century. She also won recognition for her commitment to helping women in physics and as an advocate for the academic freedom of scientists.[5]

The other major initiative during this period was in high-energy physics, begun in the mid-1950s, but expanded with NSF support after Robert Plano joined the department in 1960 and began upgrading the program's computer capacity (in the days when vacuum tubes and IBM punch cards defined such machines). Two less dramatic steps during this era also helped the long-term prospects of the program. In 1961, physics departments at the men's and women's colleges consolidated. The Douglass Department of Physics was small and mostly untenured, and had few majors; it taught physics courses primarily for women in other fields of science. A new chair in 1961 convinced a new dean that the program either had to be expanded or moved; it was moved. The department thus accomplished physical consolidation and a unified graduate and research program almost two decades before other programs at the university. Passage of the 1959 bond issue made consolidation easier. In 1963, with bond money and NSF funding, the university completed spacious new office, lecture, and laboratory buildings on Busch campus, and physics left Van Dyck Hall.

Rutgers was thus poised in the early 1960s to join the ranks of the better physics programs in the nation. The university's salary scale, however, set by the state, was inadequate to attract top physicists. In a 1962 letter, supporting a senior hire, Henry Torrey apologized to the dean that "you may be staggered at the total salary of more than $22,000 that [this physicist] would have, but this is an indication of what is now required to attract first-rate people."[6] In this case, the salary problem would have been finessed by splitting the appointment with Bell Labs, Rutgers's frequent partner in physics and engineering, but even the "staggering" sum Torrey wanted to offer was not enough. The solution came when Rutgers applied for a major NSF grant, one of the preconditions for which was an adequate salary scale. The state responded to the pressure, and the NSF gave department the boost it needed to vault into the ranks of the better physics programs in the country.

In 1964, even as other research funding was being cut, Congress authorized an NSF science development program to create new centers of excellence in engineering and the natural sciences. The plan was to help neither the "best nor the worst" but to elevate "the second twenty into the league to which the top twenty belong."[7] Proposals would be judged by scientists from the top-tier schools—MIT, California–Berkeley, Harvard, Chicago, Michigan, Cornell, and the like—and awards would go to programs at schools (not individual researchers) a notch below. Not one of the top twenty, Rutgers submitted a proposal for NSF awards for physics, mathematics, and chemistry. The NSF selected thirty-one universities for the awards, and in 1966, the Rutgers Department of Physics was awarded almost $3 million and mathematics $1 million. In sharing $177 million with science programs at schools such as Arizona, Florida, Maryland, Oregon, Purdue, Rice, Texas, and Washington, physics and mathematics brought Rutgers national recognition as a research university, a step that would eventually lead to membership in the Association of American Universities (AAU). The grant money paid for the initial years of new hires, for graduate support, and for new equipment. When hiring went slowly, the department got a two-year extension and then a renewal and another extension that took the grant through June 1975. A department of around two dozen faculty before the grant grew to a program in the mid-1970s of more than forty physicists, and when a new state funding formula forced the college to consider moving lines to departments that taught more undergraduates, the university switched the NSF physics positions to the graduate school to protect them. Substantively, the hires had added strength to condensed matter (solid state), nuclear, and elementary particle physics, and a number of short-term appointments of visiting professors (also NSF supported) made Rutgers a national leader in theoretical nuclear as well as condensed matter physics, but this left the department, with its added commitments, short of space. For the university as a whole, the initial NSF reluctance to support a program with a salary scale well below that of other physics departments put pressure on the state to improve Rutgers faculty salaries across the board.

In 1976, shortly after the NSF grant had expired, external reviewers from Yale, Cornell, and Penn, using California–Berkeley as the standard to which public universities aspired, concluded that the Rutgers department had a "variety and breadth of research interests which is comparable to the strongest departments" in the country, exceptional quality in several fields, especially nuclear physics, and many imaginative young people who foretold a bright future for the program.[8] The reviewers' most serious concern was that Rutgers had no astrophysicists, and the efforts to address this, to which I will return, would unfold slowly over three decades. In 1982, the university confirmed what the external reviews had said. Physics and mathematics, the two recipients of NSF grants, were designated among the best programs at Rutgers, already ones of national distinction, and a second external review in that year concluded that the program ranked between sixth and tenth in the nation among public universities.

The 1970s, however, were a difficult time for physics and for Rutgers. The "golden age" of higher education was over; and belt tightening was in order. Academic jobs disappeared, and graduate enrollments shrank. Hiring freezes and the elimination of senior appointments were commonplace. Seed money to launch new labs was not readily available. The turnaround came, as has been emphasized before, in the mid-1980s, with the governorship of Thomas Kean; the appointment in 1982 of T. Alexander Pond from SUNY–Stony Brook as the new vice president; the passage of the 1984 jobs, science, and technology bond issue; and the creation of the Fund for Distinction. The Reagan presidency also played a role, as the federal government increased national defense spending, to the benefit of the physical sciences, even as it dismantled other programs.

Hiring accelerated in the 1980s. Some came by way of special programs to attract "world-class" scholars and to enhance the offer packages of junior faculty; other hires came in bundles, and physics made two noteworthy sets of appointments. After a senior high-energy theoretical physicist turned down an offer, the department decided on a package deal that would bring a small group of younger particle theorists to the program together. Daniel Friedan and Steven Shenker, then at the University of Chicago, played the key role in defining the effort, and in 1989, they and two other string theorists, soon known collectively as the "string quartet," joined the department.

String theorists work mathematically with what may turn out to be the smallest building blocks of matter. The discovery of the atom was followed by realization that subatomic particles existed, protons and neutrons in the nucleus of the atom and electrons that orbit the atomic nucleus. Protons and neutrons, in turn, are made up of infinitesimally smaller quarks, particles bound together by such strong forces that they cannot be isolated or pulled apart, but whose existence has been established experimentally with the development of ever-more powerful particle accelerators and detectors. String theory posits that beyond these elemental particles, and the four forces that control them (and all matter and energy)—gravity, electromagnetism, the "strong force" (which grips together particles in the atomic nucleus), and the "weak force" (which, among other things, accounts for the decay of a neutron and its conversion into a proton), there are even smaller, more essential building blocks of the universe, "strings," a "trillion trillionth the size of an atom."[9] Such strings might be thought of as one-dimensional vibrating loops, with certain attributes attached to each string, like little magnets, which determine whether the string is a building block of matter. String theorists work mathematically to understand the properties of these strings, and to use these properties to relate the four fundamental forces of the universe to each other and to the creation of all matter. It is hoped that the study of strings will, some day, explain the nature of the "dark matter" that pervades the universe.

A second such effort brought in a group of condensed-matter theorists, all working on the modern "many-body problem" (broadly speaking, the study of the interaction of many particles, whose behavior has to be interpreted through quantum mechanics and most often with statistical approximations). They joined a program already known for its strength in condensed matter physics. The strategy differed from that in elementary particle physics in that the goal was attracting some of the best young people in the field, not more senior scholars, who would join an already strong faculty (and draw on contacts with Bell Labs and Princeton University). On the experimental side, condensed matter got a boost from the creation of the Rutgers laboratory for surface modification, the attraction of several top scholars to positions at the laboratory, and the recruitment in 1988 from the federal Bureau of Standards of Theodore Madey as a full-time director. High-stakes raids, which became common throughout the academic world in the 1980s, would cost the physics department faculty in the future, but the 1980s established that the department could build from the top down as well as from the bottom up. Senior hires required the commitment of substantial university resources: usually six-figure salaries, generous research support, promises of future appointments to strengthen the field, and reduced teaching responsibilities (to match the teaching requirements in physics at other universities). In the case of the string theorists, each line (faculty position) was split between a research appointment in a new Institute for Theoretical Physics and the Department of Physics (where they thus taught half-time). What the faculty called "differential teaching loads" were uncommon and caused some dissention, but the practice helped the university match offers that came from schools that already had a one-course-a-semester undergraduate teaching requirement.

In 1987, in the midst of this frenetic hiring, physics had yet another external review. The department was obviously aware that external reviews were not so much a challenge as an opportunity, because reviews provided leverage for new resources. The 1987 review, conducted by visitors from Princeton, Bell Labs, Stanford, and California–Santa Cruz, supported the prospective particle theory initiative but also made another recommendation of both cost and consequence: "no major university can afford to be without an astronomy program. The problems addressed—from the origin and evolution of the universe through to compact states of matter, e.g. black holes, neutron stars, white dwarfs, and on through the dynamical influence of the so-called dark-matter whose properties are not yet understood—must now be included in the curriculum at all major centers of learning."[10] And that—a major center of learning—of course, is exactly what Rutgers aspired to be.

The commitment to astrophysics grew slowly. Harold Zapolsky, recruited as chair in 1973, had switched into the field midcareer, and at Rutgers, he tried as chair and failed to appoint a senior astrophysicist to initiate a program. He did, however, manage to make junior appointments in astronomy, and the department began offering the introductory course in astronomy and formally changed its name to the "Department of Physics and Astronomy." The improvement in funding in the 1980s provided the occasion for new hires in astronomy and astrophysics, and by the mid-1990s, there were six members of the department in the field, and in 1996, the first Ph.D. Three years later, Rutgers was invited to join the Association of Universities for Research in Astronomy—a recognition of the program's progress.

From the 1970s onward, Rutgers physicists had increasingly moved their experimental work to national sites (e.g., the Fermi Lab in Illinois, Oak Ridge in Tennessee, and Los Alamos in New Mexico) or international ones (e.g., the CERN accelerator in Switzerland and the TRISTAN accelerator in Japan). For astrophysicists, this meant membership in a telescope consortium. After a failed attempt in 1999 to join a consortium at a telescope site in Chile, Rutgers partnered with the South African government and an international group of universities in a new consortium to build an eleven-meter Southern African Large Telescope (SALT). Construction

29. The Southern African Large Telescope (SALT). Rutgers was a founding partner in the consortium that built and operates SALT. Work began in 2000, and observation began in 2005. The consortium includes South African researchers and American universities such as Dartmouth, North Carolina, and Carnegie Mellon as well as partners in Europe and Australasia. The Rutgers 10 percent share of observational time on this eleven-meter optical telescope has been crucial in the strengthening of the astrophysics program at the university. Since 2006, Rutgers has also been a partner in a six-meter microwave telescope in the Chilean Andes.
PHOTOGRAPHER: Janus Brink. SOURCE: Southern African Large Telescope/SAAO.

was completed in 2005, at a mile-high desert site, a six-hour car trip from Cape Town. Rutgers put in 10 percent of the $20 million cost and received proportional operational time on SALT. SALT membership allowed Rutgers astronomers timely, extended observational access to one of the most powerful telescopes in the world. In 2002, external reviewers noted that the commitment to SALT, the mix of senior faculty and junior hires, and the high level of grant support gave Rutgers one of the most successful new programs in astronomy of the past fifteen years.

There was a side story to this undertaking—in the 1980s, Rutgers had supported the antiapartheid movement by divesting itself of holdings in companies doing business with the racist regime. The future good will this generated helped smooth the negotiations more than a decade later, and part of the SALT agreement committed Rutgers to bringing historically disadvantaged South African students to Rutgers to pursue Ph.D.s in astronomy.

Physics was also representative of departments whose ascending research trajectory was coupled with commitment to undergraduate education, and as a leader in the teaching of physics, the department's work brought in additional grant money. Those teaching efforts dated back to Ira Freeman's design in the late 1940s of a physics course for non-physics majors, to 1950s NSF grants to help update high school physics programs in New Jersey, and to Bernard Serin's introduction of a "self-pacing" method for physics students, which allowed students to determine for themselves how best to prepare (class, tutorials, study on their own), and be tested when they felt they had mastered a particular unit. In the mid-1980s, George Horton established and Brian Holton directed the Physics Learning Centers (later the Math Science Learning Centers), with support from the New Jersey Department of Higher Education. They introduced a Gateway Program to help at-risk students and received grant support (from General Electric, among others) to offer physics courses on the Douglass campus (part of a more general university effort to get more women into physics and engineering programs). Over the years, the department designed distinct paths through the major for students with different career aims: a professional option for those planning on graduate school (with additional options in astrophysics and ocean physics), an applied option, and a general option (which usually led to a career outside physics but where the skills learned in the discipline are useful). Year after year, the program graduated among the largest number of physics majors in the country and also among the highest percentage of women (a statistic that was true as well of the composition of its faculty). In 1998, New Brunswick's Physics Department became the fifth program to win the university award for programmatic excellence in undergraduate education.

For the Physics Department, however, maintaining its research ranking position proved challenging. In 1995, the National Research Council (NRC) ranked the department at number twenty (and in the top ten among public universities). The 2010 NRC ranking, coming soon after the loss of a number of senior faculty, dropped the department substantially. The department, however, was already in the process of regrouping with new hires. In astrophysics, for example, four junior hires and one senior hire expanded the program to ten professors. The senior hire, Rachel Somerville, who had been at Michigan and the Max Planck Institute in Heidelberg, Germany, was appointed to the George and Margaret Downsbrough Chair in Astrophysics. (George Downsbrough was the department's second and Atkinson's first Ph.D., and later a major donor.) In her work, Somerville designed computerized models of galaxy formation and evolution that could make sense of observational data (often collected in partnership with her colleagues)—work that in 2013 brought her the Dannie Heinman Prize, a coveted honor for midcareer astrophysicists. The department also expanded its program in experimental condensed matter physics. It received an endowed chair, opened a nanofabrication facility, developed a low-temperature, high-field scanning, tunneling microscope (the first in the United States), and was ranked among the best in the country. The growth of the field helped adjust the balance overall in the department between theorists and experimentalists (a step strongly urged by external reviewers) and accounted in part for steady growth in external funding (from about $4 million in 1994–1995 to $11 million in 2011–2012).

Taking a longer view, the department has had to hurdle three obstacles in building a distinguished program. First has been the persistent problem, at least since the 1970s, of retaining its best faculty. This, of course, was a problem throughout the academic world, not just in physics and not just at Rutgers. In programs like physics, however, where senior faculty provided direction in a field, this was an acute problem. Second has been the fact that the demand for more space, even as work has moved off-site, has remained one step ahead of physical expansion, and maintenance of what has been acquired has always ranked as a low priority at Rutgers—especially troubling to a laboratory science. Third has been the graduate program. In the early years, external reviews were surprised that the department did not generally attract students worthy of the program's reputation (although it turned out numerous distinguished young physicists). Applications fell off in the 1970s, at Rutgers and elsewhere, but except briefly in the 1980s, Rutgers has had difficulty offering prospective students financial packages that were competitive with those tendered by peer institutions. The growing burden of undergraduate debt, moreover, made financial aid all the more important for those considering graduate school. Thus, while the graduate program has been large (in recent years, about one hundred students) and outstanding (based on placements), it has not kept pace with the overall distinction of the department.

Taking a long view also points to the factors that have defined the program's upward trajectory: the World War II–era national commitment to physics, the international migration of (primarily European) physicists to the United States, support to Frank Dunnington from Robert Clothier and Mason Gross (as provost) for crucial initial hires, the arrival of Bernard Serin and Henry Torrey and their leadership, early physical consolidation of separate college departments, the NSF initiative to diversify the funding of physics research beyond a short-list of elite universities, the partnership with Bell Labs, and the auspicious collaborations of Thomas Kean, Edward Bloustein, and T. Alexander Pond in the 1980s to strengthen Rutgers as a research university. Hidden in these larger factors are the incremental steps by which a program is built. Good and often tough choices about hiring and retention also define a department, and these choices have much to do with the distinction of the Department of Physics. The 1980s also set the stage for major improvements in the life sciences, which put Rutgers in an ideal position to profit from the reacquisition of a medical school in the twenty-first century, but it was physics and mathematics, more than any other programs, whose long, post–World War II history of development vaulted the university into the AAU at the end of the Bloustein era. In 2013, when the National Academy of Sciences added new members, four came from Rutgers, and three of them were physicists.

School of Criminal Justice–Newark

In the 1964 election, Senator Barry Goldwater raised the issue of "crime in the streets" as he challenged Lyndon B. Johnson for the presidency. After Johnson's landslide victory, he appointed a crime commission, chaired by Attorney General Nicholas Katzenbach, that in 1967 issued a sweeping report, "The Challenge of Crime in a Free Society." Congress responded to the report and Johnson's prodding with the 1968 Crime Control and Safe Streets Act. Crime control, thus, became part of Johnson's Great Society, and the approach, with an emphasis on poverty as the root of crime and on rehabilitation rather than retribution, reflected the optimism of American liberals that federal mandates, federally sponsored research, and federal dollars could correct the problems in American society. The optimism quickly waned, but crime had become a national issue; it would remain one.

In the 1960s, many colleges had continuing education programs in police science, but the crime commission report galvanized efforts to develop graduate programs that looked at crime more broadly. The School of Criminal Justice at SUNY–Albany took the lead, but Rutgers was not far behind. Jack Mark, who directed the police science program at University College, played a key role in lobbying for the passage in 1968 of a state act to create a school of criminal justice at Rutgers. An implementation committee, appointed by President Gross, chaired by the dean of the Camden law school, Russell N. Fairbanks, and with Mark as a member, produced a report that embodied the words and the spirit of a "Challenge of Crime in a Free Society" (as well as sections of an equally influential federal report complied in the wake of the Watts rebellion in California). In its response to Gross, the committee, quoting directly from the federal report, stated that "the existence of crime, the talk about crime, the reports of crime, and the fear of crime have eroded the basic quality of life of many Americans."[11] Solutions were possible, the committee optimistically predicted (just as the federal commission had) if one recognized that these solutions had to involve not just the police, courts, and correctional agencies, but the entire society; that a broad range of techniques (beyond more police and more punishment) had to be employed; and that these techniques must be informed by better research and evaluation (which is where a school of criminal justice came in). We have reached, the committee noted, here quoting from the New Jersey governor Richard J. Hughes's 1968 message to the legislature in the aftermath of urban violence in New Jersey, "a day of reckoning."[12] It was time that there was a "revolution in the way Americans think about crime."[13]

Starting such a revolution did not come easily. To create the school, the Gross administration had to negotiate the educational geography of the state system (was the school better situated in New Brunswick alongside stronger sociology and political science programs?), turf questions (might not the law school at Newark or the Graduate School of Social Work take responsibility for many of the committee's suggestions?), political questions (what relation would the school have to the police and city administration in Newark?), and questions about state educational policy (would the school be too heavily oriented toward research and not concerned enough with continuing education for criminal justice personnel?). Fairbanks, in crafting a rationale for the program, argued that the training of criminal justice personnel was best left to the continuing education program and that placing a new institute within an existing program was to hold it hostage to the goals of that program. Instead, he wanted a school that "would be small, aimed at a high level of intellectual endeavor, [and] designed to meet highly visible needs of those involved in criminal justice."[14] The ideal was to train leaders for what by 1972 was being called the "war on crime," and through research, explicate how that war could be won.

In 1973, with the decision made to create a stand-alone school of criminal justice in Newark, the university brought in Don M. Gottfredson, the research director at the National Council on Crime and Delinquency, as the first dean. Gottfredson had earned his Ph.D. in psychology in 1959 at Claremont Graduate School and had done pioneering work systematically classifying and predicting the behavior of California offenders. He came to the position of dean with a strong belief that the school's research and teaching had to be interdisciplinary, analytic, and problem-solving. He also had the attention and support of President Bloustein, especially important to a program potentially out of sight of the central administration in New Brunswick.

Among those Gottfredson persuaded to join the school were Freda Adler and Gerhard O. W. Mueller, who came as a couple (long before the days when spousal/partner hires were a standard recruitment tactic). Adler, a sociologist, was doing pioneering research on women in the criminal justice system (and was soon to publish *Sisters in Crime*), and Mueller, a German-born legal scholar, with degrees from Chicago (J.D.) and Columbia (LL.M.) had a recent appointment as the chief of the United Nations Crime Prevention and Criminal Justice Branch. Richard Sparks, trained at Cambridge in psychology, and coauthor with Roger Hood of *Key Issues in Criminology* (1970), the leading text in the field, came as a visiting professor and stayed on. David Twain had a psychology degree from Pennsylvania State University and had worked at the National Institute of Mental Health. At Rutgers, he began by studying police-community relations in Newark. James Finckenauer's Ph.D. from New York University was in human relations. These and the other hires of the first few years created an academically diverse faculty, ideally situated for an interdisciplinary, problem-solving approach to criminal justice. Outside evaluators would note that the school did not have expertise in police studies, but the real weakness was the failure to hire and retain African American scholars—at a time when New Jersey and the nation were debating issues involving race and crime, and many of the students the school hoped to attract were African Americans.

Gottfredson's energy in pursuing exceptionally talented professors for the school goes a long way to explaining its initial success, but three advantages helped. Criminal justice was a new field, and most of the programs were not on the main campuses of public research universities or at elite private schools. This relative lack of competition made it easier to recruit. Being located near New York City also was a recruitment advantage. In turn, being on the Newark campus, rather than at New Brunswick, made it easier to compete internally for support. (In the 1980s, for example, the school claimed a disproportionate share of the excellence funds allotted to Newark for graduate student recruitment.) This same situation had another, long-term advantage. As an early entry in a newly defined and expanding field, the school was ideally situated to apply for federal and foundation research dollars—this at a time when public concern with crime, stoked by partisan politics, guaranteed that funding would be available. Initially, other than money Gottfredson brought with him to support his own research, the faculty had no direct research support, and until 1976 no Ph.D. program to complement its master's program. From that point on, however, grant funding became crucial, from the federal government (for example, from the National Institute of Justice and the National Science Foundation), from private foundations (for example, the Edna McConnell Clark and Pew Foundations), and from government agencies, such as law enforcement and correctional facilities, which sponsored research about their own concerns. One sign of the health of the school was a continuing string of new hires—Todd Clear, Jeffrey Fagan, Anne Campbell—who spearheaded grant-funded research. By the late 1980s, fifteen years into the school's history, a faculty of a dozen scholars had seven professors who held university chairs or had obtained the rank of professor-II (a rank denoting national or international distinction)—a remarkable concentration of academic strength.

The school designed a graduate curriculum, which like that at SUNY–Albany, reflected the vision of the federal crime commission report—it was designed to meet the needs of actual practitioners in the field and bring together research and outreach to local communities and criminal justice agencies. Initially, however, the effort to recruit good students met with disappointment. As late as the mid-1980s, there were few full-time students at either the Ph.D. or master's levels, morale among the part-timers was not good, and the academic profile of new students entering the school was below what might be expected of a strong program. After the 1986 external review, the Committee on Standards and Priorities in Academic Development (CSPAD) dropped the school's 1982 ranking from "1a" to "1b" at least in part because of the problems the school had shown in recruiting full-time students. Research and graduate teaching developed together, CSPAD knew, and a weakness in one weakened the other.

The new dean, the school's third, Ronald Clarke, made correcting the problem his priority. Aggressively broadcasting the school's distinguished research record and acquiring more fellowship and teaching assistant support from the administration, Clarke quadrupled the number of new Ph.D. students admitted annually from 1987 to 1992 (from five to twenty), and more than doubled the number of full-time Ph.D. students in the school. (The opening of the first graduate housing on the campus in 1988 made this task easier.) Over the same period, the master's program contracted, and the number of full-time students in it increased. After the next external review in 1993, the school again received a "1a" rating.

Along the way, during the 1980s, the school had launched a joint B.S./M.A. program with the liberal arts units of the university, set up scholarly exchange programs or projects with the Soviet Union and China, acquired the editorial responsibility for a second journal (the first was *Criminal Justice and Behavior*), built up what was widely acknowledged as the best criminal justice library in the world, attracted both foreign graduate students and foreign scholars in residence, and begun discussions about the school's relationship to the undergraduate program in criminal justice. At the end of the decade, the school was ranked fourth nationally in terms of the number of Ph.D. students it taught, and external reviewers considered it one of the three best in the country, in competition with programs at Maryland and SUNY–Albany.

The school maintained this strength in the twenty-first century but also branched in new directions. The school moved in 2000 with the Law School into an elegant new building. It acquired its own institute (police) and centers (for the study of terrorism and for crime mapping). It also took over full responsibility for the undergraduate criminal justice program at Newark. If initially the separation from the undergraduate program had reduced teaching responsibilities and provided more time for research, the new arrangement created teaching positions for graduate students and resulted in more financial support from the central administration.

The faculty became more diverse. In one sense, this was an easy task to accomplish. Over a thirty-year period, African Americans had been well represented among the graduates of criminal justice and social science Ph.D. programs, and women made up more than half of the criminal justice Ph.D.s. Good candidates, then, were not lacking. Efforts in the past had often led to hires, but most minorities, once hired, soon left for positions elsewhere. The track record with women was better. Some, like Anne Campbell and Freda Adler, added true distinction over long careers at the school; other, more recent hires, like Bonita Veysey, hired in 1998, and, in the last decade, Jody Miller, added to that distinction and have made girls and women central to their research interests. Ko-lin Chin, who came in the 1990s and did pathbreaking work on human trafficking, also stayed on, but each of these professors was an exception in what was predominantly a male faculty of European ancestry. Todd Clear, appointed dean in 2010, took a hands-on approach to assuring that women and minorities were fully considered for new positions. The initiative led to hires that increased the diversity of the faculty, but left, of course, the question of whether such new faculty members could be retained in the always competitive musical chairs world of academic hiring.

A field born in the politics of the 1960s had fully come of age in the twenty-first century. Nationwide there were about three dozen stand-alone Ph.D. programs in criminal justice, and approximately a hundred programs offering advanced degrees. The Rutgers school ranked fourth in the nation among Ph.D. programs in the *U.S. News and World Report* 2006 rankings; and contributed to the ranking in 2007 of the Newark campus as twelfth best nationwide among small research universities.

In sum, the path to distinction seems clear. Born at a politically opportune time, facing only modest competition internally and externally for resources, and with a dean who recruited skillfully, the School of Criminal Justice had gotten off to a fast start, and then—and the next step was critical—added younger faculty members who thrived in the era of grant-funded research. The recruitment of graduate students improved, and undergraduate teaching, external support, and fund-raising underwrote the development of an academic infrastructure (journals, library, centers) that helped maintain the school's distinction. There were many gems on the Rutgers campuses; the School of Criminal Justice was one of them.

Institute and Department of Marine and Coastal Sciences—New Brunswick

Richard Lutz earned his Ph.D. in 1975 in biological oceanography from the University of Maine, did postgraduate work at Yale University, and joined the Rutgers faculty in 1979. His work centered on marine life in deep-sea environments. In spring 1991, he was part of a three-member crew of *Alvin*, "a red-and-white version of the Beatles' *Yellow Submarine*" operated by the Woods Hole Oceanographic Institution, which traveled to the depths of the East Pacific Rise, five hundred miles off the west coast of Mexico to photograph an opening in an undersea ridge through which gasses and minerals were pouring out from the core of the earth into the ocean.[15] This particular crack in the ocean floor had been discovered several years earlier by a towed camera system sent by the University of California–Santa Barbara, but this was the first chance scientists had to explore the ecosystem directly. What followed was one of those scientific moments for which researchers spend their lives preparing. Recent underwater volcanic eruptions had decimated the marine population at the deep-sea vent that *Alvin* was exploring. Newly formed minerals erupted, water reached temperatures significantly greater than possible on land, and microbial material spewed forth from submarine cracks and crevices, creating the appearance of underwater clouds. Subsequent trips over the next two years uncovered the creation, at a startlingly rapid rate, of a new ecosystem, and provide Lutz with a unique window into the evolution of marine life in the ocean's depths. There were commercial possibilities in the discoveries—if one could harvest the minerals or learn how deep-sea creatures manage to detoxify water filled with otherwise poisonous gasses given off in the volcanic eruptions—but chiefly there was wonder.

Lutz was a Rutgers professor at the Institute of Marine and Coastal Sciences (IMCS). The institute was a product of two sets of historical circumstances, one reaching back to the late-nineteenth-century efforts to manage the state's oyster resources. The New Jersey Agricultural Experiment Station, established in 1880, had an oyster research laboratory that had done crucial work in identifying and combating diseases that threatened the New Jersey shellfish industry, and in the recent past, the service had become home to efforts to study aquaculture. In the early 1970s, Rutgers established centers to deal with marine and environmental problems and in 1976 merged these activities to form the Center for Coastal and Environmental Studies (CCES), directed by Norbert Psuty, a professor of geology and geography. The center drew its researchers from a wide variety of departments in New Brunswick and Camden, and pursued projects funded by state and federal environmental agencies and the National Park Service. Through the 1980s, then, Rutgers had a number of researchers involved in applied, demand-driven, but small-scale projects to understand and improve New Jersey's coastal environment.

The other legacy that brought IMCS into existence grew out of the tangle of state politics. In 1966, the federal government enacted the Sea Grant College and Progress Act, ambitiously conceived as a marine science parallel to the nineteenth-century Land Grant College Act. Despite its obvious economic dependence on marine and coastal resources, New Jersey moved slowly to take advantage of the legislation. When the state finally acted and formed a marine consortium of state colleges (which could apply for sea grant funds), Rutgers dragged its heals before joining. In late 1974, after some testy correspondence that so often characterized Rutgers's relationship with the state in this period, the university finally joined the consortium and became the principal recipient under the Sea Grant Program. Yet as one Rutgers critic of the Sea Grant Program noted, it had fallen far short of making the impact of the Land Grant programs because the consortium pursued research at each "end of the spectrum, i.e., global and oceanic in scope or summer fun in the tidepools, without any deliberate organized major thrust projects of importance to their station and region."[16] The consortium, then, appeared to monopolize a position of leadership in marine research in New Jersey without actually bringing the direction needed to tie scholarship to the needs of the state.

IMCS grew directly out of Dean Stephen J. Kleinschuster's plans for Cook College, Pond's and Bloustein's bold steps to transform research and graduate education at Rutgers, and Governor Kean's support for that strategy. Conceived in the mid-1980s, IMCS built on existing strengths (such as Psuty's CCES, the department of oyster culture, and the state's Fisheries and Aquaculture Technology Center) while incorporating three new, crucial elements: a multimillion-dollar building, a parallel academic program with a graduate component, and the hiring of a director, of "world class accomplishments," who in turn would hire the faculty of the new institute.[17] The institute itself came with a projected price tag of $27 million. Funding came from the Port Authority of New York–New Jersey, the 1988 higher education bond issue, and a university bond issue. State support in leveraging Port Authority financing and voter support on the bond issue were equally crucial in the construction effort, and the new institute building, on the Cook campus, provided researchers with an impressive seawater system designed to model the coastal and estuarine environment of New Jersey.

Just as significant to the successful launch of IMCS was the commitment to the hiring of eleven new faculty members, most to be full-time at the institute (with tenure in the newly created Department of Marine and

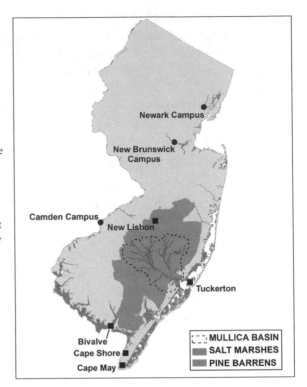

30. The Institute of Marine and Coastal Sciences operates several field stations. The Tuckerton station on the Mullica River is the launch point for research work off the Jersey coast. IMCS also has a pinelands research center in New Lisbon and, at Bivalve and in the Cape May area, centers that have done pioneering work to revitalize the oyster industry and improve aquaculture more generally.

MAP COURTESY OF Richard Lutz and Ken Eng, Institute of Marine and Coastal Sciences.

Coastal Sciences). The hires were expected to be senior research faculty, many with salaries that broke into the six-figure category, and each with large chunks of start-up money and the expectation that they would have funding for graduate students, postdoctoral fellows, and technical support staff. Some of these costs, of course, were picked up as grant money rolled in, but initially the university paid the bills directly. The university also committed itself to improving field station facilities at Bivalve and Tuckerton (Little Egg Harbor Inlet).

Hiring a director for the institute was the first priority. After an extended search and serious discussions with numerous marine scientists of international reputation, the university extended an offer in fall 1988 to J. Frederick Grassle, who accepted contingent on the success of the bond issue and the negotiations with the Port Authority. Grassle had received an undergraduate degree at Yale University in zoology, completed his Ph.D. at Duke University, and done postdoctoral work at the University of Queensland in Australia. In 1969, he took a position at Woods Hole Oceanographic Institute in Massachusetts (perhaps the most renowned center for marine research in the world), stayed for twenty years, and rose to the rank of senior scientist. At Woods Hole, he was one of the pioneers in using submersibles to chart biodiversity in the deep sea. In 1979, Grassle led the first biological expedition to deep-sea hydrothermal vent ecosystems (the same phenomenon that Lutz explored later under less stable conditions), and before arriving at Rutgers, he published key reviews of the literature on the ecology of vent faunas. Part of what made him attractive as a director of the new institute was his commitment at Woods Hole to interdisciplinary teamwork and his deep concern for the marine environment and the life it nourished. In hiring Grassle, the university also secured a position for his wife, Judith, herself an accomplished marine biologist. Traditionally, practice (or public policy) kept schools from hiring spouses, almost always meaning wives, but this began to change in the 1980s as feminists made academics aware of the consequences of the policy. Spousal hiring as a recruiting strategy created controversy, and still does, but Rutgers was among the universities that accepted the idea and used it creatively to build programs.

Among those Grassle hired were Dale Haidvogel, an MIT Ph.D., whom he knew from Woods Hole. In the late 1980s, Haidvogel worked as the principal research scientist at the Johns Hopkins Chesapeake Bay Institute, and he had to be lured away from an opportunity to move to the University of Colorado. Haidvogel's research involved developing mathematically based models that could simulate the complex current flows of both deep-sea and coastal currents. In 1995, with the addition of Oscar Schofield, a phytoplankton ecologist, the string of ten initial hires was completed. Grassle also used joint appointments, most often with the geology department, to shepherd resources and build the IMCS. Among the most prominent hires was Paul G. Falkowski, a biological oceanographer. Falkowski had earned his Ph.D. from the University of British Columbia, and he came to Rutgers in 1998 with more than two decades of experience at the Brookhaven National Laboratory. His early research focused on marine phytoplankton and their role in the chemical cycles that help sustain sea life, and more generally, make the planet habitable. Grassle could also draw on the talents of faculty already at Rutgers, in particular, Lutz, Psuty, and Kenneth Able, all three of whom pursued active research careers at Rutgers into the twenty-first century.

The initial external review of IMCS and the department in 1995 was positive but offered cautions about the future. The program was overly

dependent on Grassle's leadership and on National Oceanic and Atmospheric Administration (NOAA) funding, had to find ways to become
more concerned with traditional areas of research central to New Jersey's
economy (for example, its fisheries), and needed faculty with backgrounds
in chemistry and geology (Falkowski would help there). The reviewers
were taken aback by the complex reporting structures that linked the institute to the rest of the university, found the graduate program too new
to evaluate, and worried whether adequate consideration had been given
to the planned undergraduate major in the field. With all that said, they
concluded that the program ranked in the top twenty of state university
programs in oceanography and marine science and pointed out that IMCS
was among the twenty best externally funded research programs in the
nation (ranked, among public universities, close to Texas, Delaware, and
SUNY–Stony Brook, but well behind Rhode Island, Oregon State, and
Washington). Rutgers's review process similarly ranked the program quite
high, if not quite at the top, with full recognition that making IMCS among
the best in the country would require an enormous commitment of faculty
lines and eventually fulfillment of the initial commitment to construct a
much larger research facility.

In 2003, IMCS had forty faculty members, twenty-four of whom were
on state-funded lines, and it received more than $12.9 million in grant sup-
port; a decade earlier, the institute had had twenty-four faculty members,
twenty of whom were on state-funded lines, and it attracted a little less
than $4 million in grants. This upward thrust of grant-funded research
continued into the second decade of the twenty-first century. The institute
had caught up with Rhode Island and Hawaii in terms of funding, while
still lagging far behind the much larger oceanography centers at Woods
Hole and the Scripps Institute of Oceanography at the University of California–San Diego. The funding base had broadened, although most grants
still came from the federal government (NOAA, NSF, and ONR), rather
than from the state, foundations, or the private sector. The graduate program now enrolled about two dozen students—the target number—and
the department had launched an undergraduate major in marine sciences
in 1999 to complement the already existing minor field. Both public outreach endeavors and cooperative arrangements had multiplied. When the
external review committee reported in 2004, it was enthusiastic about the
progress IMCS and the department had made, and the university ranked
the institute and the graduate program among the best at Rutgers. A more

recent, external ranking that evaluated the impact of papers produced at the top thirty research institutions in oceanography placed Rutgers among the best in the world.

Pulling together in the late 1980s several different groups of researchers in a single center (in much the same way the university had consolidated New Brunswick departments), attracting strong leadership, making a string of good hires, erecting a new facility, and focusing on a research field that was of increasingly significant both to local industry and tourism and to a globalized economy facing the peril of climate change all had helped vault the Institute of Marine and Coastal Sciences to a position of academic prominence.

The Department of History–New Brunswick

In 1919, the then combined Department of History and Political Science at the College of Arts and Sciences in New Brunswick offered the first graduate course and awarded the first graduate degree, a master's to Roy F. Nichols. Nichols became the Pulitzer Prize–winning author of *The Disruption of American Democracy*, the president of the American Historical Association, and, in his teaching career at the University of Pennsylvania, the graduate mentor of Richard P. McCormick. Across town, in the late 1920s, the New Jersey College for Women established its own Department of History and Political Science. Shortly after World War II, the university opened an evening division, University College, and David Cowen, a distinguished historian of pharmacy, joined the faculty. About the same time, the university awarded its first history Ph.D., to Herbert G. Schmidt, who later taught at Rutgers-Newark. These benchmarks defined the early twentieth-century development of what was still primarily an undergraduate teaching program, in a university where most of the research work was undertaken and most of the Ph.D.s were awarded in the agricultural sciences, ceramics, chemistry, and biological sciences.

If we jump ahead fifteen years from the end of World War II, to 1960, we come across a portrait of the history faculty at Rutgers College—a dozen members (and, of course, all were men, and all dressed as conventionally as the students they taught). It is an impressive group. Among them were Ethan Ellis, author of *A Short History of American Diplomacy* (640 pages short); Richard Schlatter, whose *Private Property: The History of an Idea*, was already a classic; Peter Charanis, whose essays on the diplomacy, demography, and politics of the Byzantine empire marked him as the world authority on the topic; Sidney Ratner, a wartime government economist, researcher at the Institute for Advanced Study in Princeton, and author of a history of American taxation and now working on a parallel book on the tariff; John Higham, about to step out the door and go to Michigan, having published *Strangers in the Land*, one of the books that created the field of immigration history; Henry Winkler, a specialist in European diplomatic history, the author of a study on the British response to the League of Nations, and later to become the vice president of Rutgers and then the president of the University of Cincinnati; Ernest McDonnell, whose study of French medieval culture was published by Rutgers University Press in 1948; and Richard P. McCormick, already the author of two studies of New Jersey politics and one of those scholars who was reshaping the way political history was done. The youngster of the group was Traian Stoianovich, a former World War II intelligence officer, trained in France in methodologies that helped remap the terrain of history in America, but with his most ambitious work, *A Study in Balkan Civilization*, still in the future. Under the portrait, which appeared in the *Report from Rutgers*, was a note that three new historians were about to join the faculty—Richard Maxwell Brown, Warren Susman, and Donald Weinstein, two of whom would be long-term members of the faculty and all three of whom would have distinguished careers.

At Douglass, the still combined department(s) of history and political science had eleven full-time faculty members, six identified by "Mr." in the college catalog, and five by "Miss," and seven of whom were historians. Two of the historians were full professors: Margaret Judson, the department chair, and Margaret Hastings, whose study, *The Court of Common Pleas in Fifteenth-Century England*, ranked her among the most important scholars of medieval England. Hastings had earned her B.A. at Mount Holyoke College, and her Ph.D. at Bryn Mawr, and she had served during World War II as a researcher for the army before coming to Douglass as a lecturer. Several other of the female members of the department, like Hastings, had degrees from one or more of the "Seven Sisters"—the northeastern private women's colleges that had trained generations of academics, while two had their Ph.D.s from Cornell. As an assistant professor, Jessie Lutz, a future chair of the department, was beginning work on a book about American missionaries in China, and among the men on the faculty, Emery Battis, a colonial historian, was about to publish a major study of Anne Hutchinson and the seventeenth-century antinomian crisis in the Massachusetts Bay Colony. One of the instructors was Alison Olsen, at work on a pathbreaking study on Anglo-American politics. While Judson believed, as chair, that the department needed both men and women teachers, she was especially sensitive to the plight of the female scholars who were the "trailing spouse" (as Olsen was) of a male academics and for whom temporary employment, until her husband moved on, was the all-too-familiar norm.

Margaret A. Judson gave her life story, *Breaking the Barriers*, the evocative subtitle, "a professional autobiography by a woman educator and historian before the women's movement." Born at the end of the nineteenth century into a family of a Connecticut Congregationalist minister, she attended Mount Holyoke in the era of World War I, fell in love with history and international relations, and then went on to Radcliffe, where she pursued a history Ph.D. at the Harvard Graduate School. Here, all her teachers were men (at Holyoke, virtually all had been women). One, from whom she needed a class to prepare for her qualifying examinations, refused to teach women, but otherwise, she felt respected in the classroom and particularly encouraged by her mentor, Charles McIlwain, an eminent scholar of English and early American constitutional and political history. Her exams complete, she found employment in 1928 as a lecturer at the New Jersey College for Women, where she was one of the first women to teach history. She made a research trip to England in 1931–1932, was awarded a Ph.D. in 1933, and was hired as an assistant professor. The book came later, much later. This was long before the days of "publish or perish" at Rutgers; the emphasis was on teaching, but Judson was able to return to England several times before World War II for additional research—one trip supported by $1,000 from President Robert Clothier, an extraordinary gesture at a time when many of those who ran the men's college thought that NJCW professors were "only inflated high school teachers."[18] Judson's *The Crisis of the Constitution: An Essay in Constitutional and Political Thought in England, 1603–1645* appeared in 1949, published by the newly energized Rutgers University Press. The book remained in print for decades. With support from the Research Council, she returned to England numerous times, continued to publish articles, and produced two more books after her retirement in the mid-1960s. Before that happened she became the first NJCW

historian to teach in the history graduate program, after her colleague
across town, Henry Winkler, agreed to teach an undergraduate course in
English history at NJCW in exchange for the graduate course she taught
at Bishop House on the College Avenue Campus. She and Winkler went
on to train a group of Ph.D. students in English history. She was also one
of the first members of the Berkshire Historical Association, a gathering
of women historians in the northeastern United States begun in the late
1920s to provide a forum where they could share their interests in history. Initially, these interests had little to do with women's history, but
decades later two other Douglass historians, and Judson's friends and
colleagues, Lois Banner and Mary Hartman, convinced the BHA to co-
sponsor a conference on women's history, and in 1973, the first of many
Berkshire Conferences of Women Historians was held on the Douglass
campus.

In history, the "model" was the solitary scholar, alone in the archive,
study, or (in the 1950s) library carrel, working to produce a book. Unlike
in physics, collaborative work was uncommon. Unlike in physics, where
external grants funded the research of a team of faculty and their graduate students, historians competed for fellowships for themselves alone. A
Guggenheim fellowship, not an NSF grant, was a benchmark in a scholarly
career. Historians were often paid less well than scientists but were thus
less costly to recruit. They wrote articles, as do all academics, but promotion generally depended on the publication of a book. These publications
defined a scholar's reputation, in history as well as physics, collectively defined a department, and defined a program's prospects for recruiting others to a department.

In the immediate postwar period, there were few fellowships available
and not yet a sabbatical program to grant research leaves. The establishment
of the Research Council, which underwrote the costs of research and publication in the humanities, and the strengthening of Rutgers University Press
(which published at least one book by most of the history faculty members
during the immediate postwar period) helped departments like history and
made it clear that postwar historians were more than simply history teachers.
Undergraduate teaching remained central to the identity of the faculty, but
the program increasingly measured itself as well by scholarship.

During the next two decades, the Mason Gross presidency and the first
half of the Bloustein presidency, before the self-conscious push to upgrade

graduate education had made Rutgers a member of the AAU, the History Department's path to academic excellence was not smooth. As one faculty member, hired in the late 1960s recalled, "If I were to characterize the six-ties it would be hiring a string of people so good that half of them left for major universities and went on to distinguished careers. I would describe the 1970s as a period when half of them left because they got fired or just not rehired. So there are some good ones, but fifty-fifty is not good enough to be a successful department."[19] While dividing the period by decades does not do full justice to the events of this period, one can note key hires in the 1960s who made their mark at Rutgers, then left—Peter Stearns, the first leader of the federated department of history and the editor of the *Journal of Social History*, and Eugene Genovese, whose work shaped virtually everything written about the history of Atlantic slavery for al-most two decades, were two telling examples. One can also note hires in the 1960s and early 1970s who stayed on much longer or to the end of their careers—Warren Susman, whose focus on the "popular culture" of America in the 1920s and 1930s helped redefine the field of intellectual history; Lloyd Gardner, one of most astute and trenchant critics of twen-tieth-century American foreign policy, and David Oshinsky, whose work on McCarthyism, the development of the polio vaccine (which won him a Pulitzer Prize), and the southern criminal justice system eventually earned him offers, which he accepted, from Texas and NYU.

Fred Harrington announced to his Wisconsin graduate class on its first day, and to Lloyd Gardner, who had just arrived at graduate school in fall 1956, that "your master's thesis is worth an article and your Ph.D. thesis is worth a book, and, if you don't feel that way, you don't belong here at Wisconsin." Gardner had grown up in rural Ohio, the son of a beekeeper, and had been drawn to history at Ohio Wesleyan (his first girlfriend thought this foretold economic ruin and dumped him). A de-bate club scholarship and ROTC helped pay for college, and the air force allowed him to attend graduate school before he was commissioned. At Wisconsin, he studied with Harrington and with intellectual historian Merle Curti, but Gardner was drawn especially to William Appleman Williams, who in the late 1950s was at work on what would become *The Tragedy of American Diplomacy,* a sweeping study that staked out a powerful leftist critique of American foreign policy. Gardner also became one of the graduate student founders of the journal *Studies on the Left,* which got him investigated by the air force, but did not release him from three years of service. In 1963, when he left the air force, the Wisconsin pipeline helped him get a Rutgers job. Warren Susman, still an assistant professor, and a Curti student, suggested Gardner as a replacement for Ethan Ellis, and the department concurred. (Gardner later brought two other Wisconsin Ph.D.s to Rutgers, Michael Adas, in South Asian history and Donald Roden, in Japanese history, helping expand the program's geographic scope.) He got an office on the third floor of Bishop House— the servants' quarters in the building's Victorian past—where on late afternoons he played chess and drank sherry with Gene Genovese—this at a time when the university still had the atmosphere of a liberal arts college at which professors lived nearby, came to work at least four days a week, and lunched together in a faculty dining room.

Gardner's dissertation became a book, as Harrington had said it must, *Economic Aspects of New Deal Diplomacy* (1964), and it was followed by others, on the architects of post–World War II American foreign policy, the Vietnam War, Woodrow Wilson's internationalism, and American involvement in the Middle East, as well as by a study of the Lindbergh kidnapping. He taught to overflow student audiences in the U.S. history survey course (with Susman and McCormick), won numerous teaching awards, helped organize the 1965 teach-in on the Vietnam War, directed numerous Ph.D. students, chaired the department, and served on CSPAD—testimony that service, teaching, and scholarship were not incompatible.[20]

The difficult years of the 1970s actually began earlier and did not fully end until after the department adjusted to academic reorganization in the mid-1980s. Battles within the program were frequent. Some occurred between the senior history faculty of Rutgers and Douglass Colleges; some among the various factions within Rutgers College (the University College and Livingston College history faculties were largely outside the fray). Meetings were punctuated with personal invective; colleagues routinely challenged each other's possession of common sense and academic judgment. Hiring fights were common, and young faculty often did not get the academic "nurturing" (especially in the largest department, at Rutgers College) that would have helped them meet the rigorous tenure standards in the program and university. Young professors were caught between their own and colleagues' enthusiasm for teaching and a vibrant undergraduate culture and clear indications that, during the Bloustein years, promotion and scholarship went hand in hand.

In 1977, and despite the internal troubles in the department, three external reviewers concluded that the history department deserved "to be ranked among the top twenty history departments in the country."[21] On the plus side, it was a large department (fifty-six full-time faculty), with ample research support, and a department in which most members were publishing scholars. Its great strength was American social history, but it also had accomplished scholars in many areas of European history and history of the twentieth-century "third world" (a term then applied to Asia, Africa, and Latin America). The federated college system, the evaluators felt, gave the department the best of both worlds—small, excellent undergraduate programs at the four colleges and a unified graduate faculty. On the minus side, the department had too few senior scholars of international reputation, too many midcareer members who did not publish, too heavy a teaching load for its faculty, too many graduate students who did not find jobs, and too few placements of the students who did at major universities. There was little in the way of scholarly community, and a need for an institute or a seminar and lecture program that made faculty aware they were part of a wider intellectual world. The department shot back, with more ego than evidence, but with a good feel for how the parry and thrust of academic politics worked, that it was clearly in the top ten, better than all but Johns Hopkins, Yale, Harvard, California–Berkeley, and possibly Michigan. When the dust settled, in 1981, CSPAD gave the program its "1b" ranking, noting it needed to "encourage higher standards for promotion and greater selectivity of [graduate] students to bring this program to national distinction." The department might get resources for senior hires, but otherwise, CSPAD recommended "reduction by attrition."[22]

The report captured without fully explicating crucial trends in the development of the program. In less than two decades, the department had tripled in size, and its graduate program had grown exponentially. The evaluators also sensed the import to the department of the resolution of the ongoing campus debate over the federated plan (without fully realizing how split the department itself was over reorganization of the colleges). Most important, it underscored the strength of the field of social history to the department's reputation.

In the immediate post–World War II era, historical scholarship was dominated by political and diplomatic history, secondarily by intellectual, constitutional, and economic history. The "social history revolution" of the 1960s changed this. This new emphasis in scholarship borrowed explanatory models from the social sciences, applied quantitative data to answer precisely formulated hypotheses, paid more attention to everyday life, popular culture, and the lives of ordinary people ("history from the bottom up," as it was often called) than to "great men," adopted methodologies from French and British historians working on similar problems, and offered structural and occasionally Marxist answers to questions of causation. As such work shared a move to the "left" with much of the political and diplomatic history of that era, the differences between the old and the new was not initially all that apparent, but a divide had begun that would ultimately move some of the best work in traditional fields to political science. In exchange, new fields, such as immigration and labor history were invigorated.

The Rutgers program held tight to tradition, but it also had a heady mix of social historians whose interests cut across established chronological and national definitions of historical scholarship. That plus Rutgers's reputation as the "Berkeley of the East" brought graduate students to the program who were politically committed and often somewhat older than traditional students, and many of them came to work with Susman and Gardner (neither of whom were social historians, but both of whom had scholarly reputations that reflected new directions in their fields). One former graduate student recalled that her undergraduate instructors told her to go to Rutgers "because Susman is there." Arriving in the early 1970s, she joined a mix of 1960s radicals who "had been through antiwar and civil rights organizing, consciousness raising groups," and the like. "I actually," she recalled, "sent copies of my agitprop journalism in alternative newspapers from my MIT days along with more traditional evidence of academic writing as part of my graduate application."[23] A social history seminar that drew faculty from all four college departments developed in the wake of the external review, and it became the first such collective collegiate program of the department. The department also initiated a series of visiting professorships that brought the likes of British historians Christopher Hill and E. P. Thompson to Rutgers for extended stays and graduate teaching. Livingston College, opened in 1969, proved particularly receptive to social history, and John Gillis's leadership as chair strengthened that commitment. At Rutgers College, where Samuel Baily, a Latin Americanist, was in 1964 the first "exotic" hire (as colleagues in European and American history called his field), Michael Adas was beginning a career that would shape the emerging field of global (or world) history. Adas's work with Allen Howard, a Livingston College African historian, in establishing a field in world and comparative history helped two generations of graduate students to develop teaching skills outside their major concentration, skills that served them well on the job market.

The next two external reviews, in 1982 and 1987, paid particular attention to undergraduate education (in the wake of reorganization) and were somewhat more positive about the program overall and, in particular, the support given to graduate students. Providing highly competitive five-year funding packages for the best graduate students (who came to be known as the "bonus babies") proved controversial (and would eventually give way to funding all students equally while admitting many fewer) as would the decision, also noted by the reviewers, to reduce the teaching responsibility of faculty from three to two courses a semester (a reduction designed to allow more time for scholarship). The key point, however, stated most clearly in the words of the 1982 report, was that the department could, "with justice, claim to be second to none in the United States in social history, and in women's history."[24] Women's history, not mentioned in the 1977 report, had become in half a decade the department's most visible and greatest strength.

How did this happen? By the time of the second, 1987 review, the consolidation of the four college departments (Douglass, Livingston, Rutgers, and University College) had provided the critical mass of scholars to create fields of inquiry that attracted outstanding graduate students, and under Bloustein and Pond, the university had begun allocating more money for graduate education. From that point on, a series of strong chairs, Richard L. McCormick, Rudolph Bell, and Ziva Galili (the first women to chair the consolidated department), helped the department make its case to the administration for new faculty positions and more adequate graduate funding. It was in women's history, however, more than any other field, that it was easy to substantiate the claim for distinction, and that distinction reached back into the more difficult times of the 1970s noted above.

As was true at most universities in the 1950s and 1960s, there were few women at Rutgers on the history faculty or in the ranks of the graduate students. At Rutgers College, the department had infrequently hired women, and through the time of academic reorganization had not promoted any woman to a tenured position. It had admitted a female graduate student as early as 1953 and awarded a Ph.D. to a woman in 1966, but the graduate program was still largely male through the early 1970s.

The impetus for change came from the departments at Douglass and Livingston. Both hired women with interests in women's history; and somewhat more surprisingly, so did University College. It was a remarkable group—at Douglass, Hartman and Banner, who brought the first Berkshire conference to Douglass and coedited the pathbreaking *Clio's Conscious-ness Raised*; Suzanne Lebsock, whose *Free Women of Petersburg* explored the struggles for autonomy of ordinary white and free black women in a southern town; and Virginia Yans, a historian of immigration who was hired to direct the newly created women's studies program. At University College, these young scholars included Judith Walkowitz, writing about the lives of English prostitutes and the state's effort to control those lives, and Susan Schrepfer, an environmental historian, who later turned her attention to a gendered history of the Sierra Club. At Livingston, Lora (Dee) Garrison studied the history of librarianship, and Phyllis Mack began a career exploring religion and women in early modern Europe. For some of these historians, women's history, with a feminist inflection, defined their scholarship; for others, it was a matter of giving women a voice as they narrated a more traditional topic.

The other parts of the equation were the graduate students. In the late 1970s, a group of female graduate students came together to discuss "the endemic feelings of alienation and marginality" which were affecting women students.[25] They shared with the women faculty—Mary Hartman played a key role—their sense that they were "not taken [as] seriously as their male counterparts, particularly if they evinced any interest in studying women." The initial meetings led in 1979 to a graduate student conference for women that was successful enough that it became an annual event. In the conference's formative years, women organized the gathering and gave most of the papers, many of which dealt with women's history, but almost from the beginning male graduate students participated, as did students from other institutions. The conference, one of the first in the country organized for graduate students by graduate students, remained an annual event, renamed the Warren and Beatrice Susman Graduate Student History Conference. The recognition it brought the program helped alert prospective graduate students to the possibilities for pursuing women's history at Rutgers.

The 1987 reviewers also commended the department's plan to launch "a center for comparative interdisciplinary historical study"—the type of undertaking suggested a decade before by evaluators. The administration had fast-tracked the funding of numerous new centers and institutes in the sciences—part of the push to increase grant funding and join the AAU—and jumped at the opportunity to create some equivalents in the humanities. English got the Center for the Critical Analysis of Contemporary Culture, and history, through the work of Rudolph Bell and John Gillis, both social historians, and newly elected chair, Richard L. McCormick, got the Rutgers Center for Historical Analysis (RCHA). Gillis directed the first of its many two-year projects, a study of the historical construction of personal and collective identity. As a topic that intersected social and cultural history, it drew directly on the strengths of the department, opened the door to collaboration with scholars in other disciplines, and pulled in outstanding applicants for positions as postdoctoral and senior fellows. If RCHA never became *the* center of a departmentwide community, it did bring together groups of faculty and graduate students with shared interests in topics of current scholarship.

Subsequently, in 1994, the Rutgers Class of 1942, with support from Professor John Chambers, established the Rutgers Oral History Archives as an affiliate center of the history department. Initially, the archives were dedicated to collecting the oral histories of Rutgers graduates who served in World War II; it won international recognition for its work and over the years broadened the scope of its mission to include Rutgers military veterans more generally. The archives joined two other major documentary projects linked to the department, the Thomas A. Edison Papers and the Elizabeth Cady Stanton and Susan B. Anthony Papers.

By the late 1980s, then, social and women's history had redefined the program's national recognition; RCHA soon provided an internationally recognized forum for historical inquiry at Rutgers; consolidation had created strong groups of faculty in a number of disciplines; and new leadership was about to embark on a vigorous program of adding to the faculty.

African American history, however, had not caught the attention of the external reviewers, but that situation was changing. The department had enrolled a few African American graduate students in the 1960s, two of whom went on to notable careers: Clement Price, at Rutgers-Newark, as the historian of the city's African American population and the university's ambassador to the city; and Spencer Crew, whose public history work included directing the Smithsonian's Museum of American History. No African American faculty, however, were hired until the early 1970s, and those who were then appointed either failed to get tenure or left soon after they did. That corner was not turned until 1984, when the now consolidated department hired Deborah Gray White. White had written her thesis on black enslaved women, a topic treated with, at best, "benevolent neglect" by those writing about the African American experience, and even the male historians who acknowledged the import of the topic doubted that sources existed to study it. White persevered, and her dissertation became the book *Ar'n't I a Woman? Female Slaves in the Plantation South*, published the year after she arrived at Rutgers. Cutting across the two most important fields of historical inquiry in that era, women's and African American history, *Ar'n't I a Woman?* became a classic and brought more than a generation of graduate students to Rutgers to work with White. A year after White arrived, the university attracted David Levering Lewis, already the author of the first major biography of Martin Luther King Jr. At Rutgers, Lewis wrote a two-volume biography of W.E.B. Du Bois, and both volumes won Pulitzer Prizes. Among the accomplished junior faculty who came to the program and stayed on was Mia Bay, whose first book flipped a traditional question on its head and asked how black intellectuals and public figures imagined white people, and went on to write a major biography of Ida B. Wells. As the new century began, Keith Wailoo moved to Rutgers, with half his line in history and half in the Institute for Health, Health Care Policy, and Aging Research; his work at the intersection of the history of medicine and African American history brought him major grant support. Also at this time, White became the first African American and the second woman to chair the history department. Rankings from that period—which had been fine-tuned to highlight fields as well as disciplines—listed the Rutgers program in African American history as one of the two or three best in the nation.

Strength in African American and women's history created a climate of intellectual excitement in the history department that extended to faculty in more traditional fields, brought good graduate students to the program more generally, and enhanced the program's national reputation. That reputation—it had climbed to a "1a" ranking internally after the 1987 external review—allowed it over the years to rebound with major hires after losses from retirements and raids by other institutions. Following Susman's premature death, the department brought in T. J. Jackson Lears in cultural and intellectual history, and in the 1990s, with the "cultural turn" in historical writing, Lears became the most recognizable presence outside Rutgers, as

Susman had been before, of the U.S. history program. The hiring of Alice Kessler-Harris, a noted historian of women's and labor history, a Rutgers Ph.D., and a future president of the Organization of American Historians, had cemented the initial distinction of the women's history program, and after her departure for Columbia, the department had been able to bounce back with the appointment of Nancy Hewitt, who helped redefine the field as "women's and gender history." Losses of faculty in European history were more than balanced by the hiring of a senior scholar, Bonnie Smith, a noted historian of women and of France, and of such younger historians as Jennifer Jones in eighteenth-century French history and Belinda Davis in modern German history. Just as important was the hiring of Temma Kaplan, whose interests in comparative history opened possibilities for graduate students who wanted to link Latin American or African topics to studies of Europe and the United States. Just as collaboration in the development of women's studies had helped the department earlier, a virtual partnership with Jewish studies helped the department in the late twentieth century and beyond. University support also allowed the department to branch into numerous subfields outside the confines of American and European history—to globalize the curriculum. A group of younger scholars, in South and Southeast Asia and Chinese history, helped the department to mirror in its intellectual pursuits the increasingly diverse population of graduate and undergraduate students it taught.

In history, like physics, nothing mattered as much in building the program as making good choices about hiring and retention. As the 2001 external review noted, virtually every member of the department was a publishing scholar, all of them taught undergraduates, and most of them trained graduate students as well. Careful recruitment to develop specific fields, successful efforts to replace faculty lost to other institutions, and the scholarly accomplishments of individual faculty members, then, probably go a long way to explaining the development of the history department (and most other humanities programs). That said, several key programwide features of that development stand out. The program, like physics, already had a research-oriented faculty in the post–World War II era. Reducing undergraduate teaching responsibilities and improving salary support strengthened the department initially. The early interest in women's history at Douglass, the creation of a new department at Livingston (where social and women's history were both encouraged), and the admission of women graduate students to Rutgers College shook up the mix that became the reorganized, consolidated department of the 1980s. Better funding from the mid-1980s, both because of the Kean-Bloustein partnership, and because of the results of the 1987 external review, allowed top-down recruitment that anchored fields built initially from the bottom up. Consolidation itself was crucial, as was vigorous leadership after the mid-1980s, in maximizing the potential of academic reorganization. Distinction in African American history changed the profile of the department, as did the later efforts to globalize the research and teaching strengths of the program.

Two small, very good departments specializing in American and European history at liberal arts colleges in the late 1950s had become by the second decade of the twenty-first century a very large and still very good department with global expertise at a state university. A snapshot taken of the department's faculty today would picture—if they could all be fit in the frame—more than five dozen historians, about half of them women, with a far greater range of academic interests than the professors in the 1960 photo of Rutgers College historians, and with a national and ethnic diversity not unlike that in the student population of the university.

Department of Childhood Studies–Camden

The flow of resources to strong Ph.D. programs put Camden and Newark campuses in an awkward position. Each campus had good programs that offered master's degrees—in history, English, and the biological sciences, for example—and both had law schools. If Camden or Newark established Ph.D. tracks, however, they risked creating second-rate programs that attracted second-rate students. In the late 1980s, as the drive to improve graduate education during the Bloustein presidency was coming to its successful conclusion with Rutgers's admission to the AAU, Geoffrey Still, the director of the Camden English graduate program, began an assessment of the possibility of creating a Ph.D. program in English, which in 1991, he forwarded to Provost Walter Gordon. Gordon had long championed scholarly excellence as the basic building block for Camden's departments. Still compared the English Department at Camden with those at other medium-size schools that offered Ph.D.s—Rhode Island, SUNY–Albany, California–San Diego—and concluded that a leap into their ranks was essentially impossible. All had larger faculties (ten full professors, for example, rather than one in English at Camden), well-regarded research libraries, generous financial aid for the students, and more established M.A. programs to support their Ph.D. programs. He suggested two alternatives: creating a new interdisciplinary program in American studies that could eventually award Ph.D.s, or formalizing a relationship with the New Brunswick English program that allowed Camden's best students to do Ph.D. work at both schools and get a degree in New Brunswick. In fact, a few Camden graduate students had already gone on for New Brunswick Ph.D.s in English, but nothing came of Still's ideas to introduce Ph.D. options at Camden.

Newark had adopted both approaches. It created Ph.D. programs that defined new fields of graduate study and formed partnerships with New Brunswick and with the New Jersey Institute of Technology in graduate education. Camden took the first approach by fashioning a new interdisciplinary field. Margaret Marsh, a historian and dean of the School of Arts and Sciences, first advanced the idea of a Ph.D. program in childhood studies. Camden had in place three building blocks. One was a center in childhood studies that sponsored grant-supported research. Another was an undergraduate minor in the field, and a third was a cohort of more than a dozen faculty members who were working in areas such as education, psychology, religion, history, sociology, anthropology, and children's literature, and who had an interest in childhood studies. Nationwide, childhood studies was an emerging discipline, with undergraduate programs at places such the City University of New York and Brooklyn College, but there was little graduate work in the field, and there were no Ph.D. programs (except in Scandinavia). The door was open for Rutgers-Camden to launch its first doctoral program.

The program proposed in 2004 had several key features. It was truly interdisciplinary, drawing on faculty from half a dozen departments, but also based in its own, new department with its own faculty. The university committed lines and money for new hires, some in the department, and some of faculty members with a scholarly interest in childhood studies but tenure in affiliated departments. The goal of the program was to "place children themselves at the center of investigation," to give them a voice, to understand their own view of themselves, and to enrich that view by, for example, exploring what historical knowledge can add to sociological insight, and vice versa. The university also committed resources to graduate fellowships, and the relatively new Center for Children and Childhood Studies provided a base for grant-funded research.

The setting—Camden—was crucial. When Jonathan Kozol (whose writings were cited in the program proposals for childhood studies) toured Camden in the late 1980s, he reported on a school system embedded in one of the poorest communities in the United States, where almost 40 percent of the residents were children, virtually all impoverished, and where educators fought against the "demoralizing power" both of structural inequality and the city's reputation for postindustrial urban decay.[26] If in that era Rutgers-Camden had been largely isolated from Camden, by the time the new program in childhood studies was being crafted, many faculty had designed outreach projects addressed to a "city of children."[27] Daniel Hart, for example, a professor of psychology, and Robert Atkins, in nursing, both in the founding faculty of childhood studies, had also developed the STARR program (Sports Teaching Adolescents Responsibility and Resiliency) for African American, Latino, and Southeast Asian adolescents in Camden, while other faculty were involved in the Camden Campaign for Children's Literacy. In addition, the Center for Childhood Studies had provided for professional development of early childhood education staff in Abbott school districts; this program helped hundreds of women from Camden achieve professional credentialing and the salary benefits that went with it in centers throughout the city. Thus there was an outreach component built into the field at Camden that would both serve the community and shape the educational experience of students in the new program.

The department and its graduate programs opened in 2007. By that point, more than two dozen faculty members were affiliated with it, and a full range of graduate courses—historical and religious perspectives on childhood, children's health, children and the justice system, cross-national perspectives on childhood—were in place. In its first years, it ran an innovative set of conferences, some sponsored by the faculty, others by the graduate students, on such subjects as "interpreting normality in childhood" and "children and war"; the program's faculty took on various editorial responsibilities in the expanding list of journals devoted to the field; and Rutgers University Press based its new series on children in the Camden department, with Myra Bluebond-Langner, then the director of the center, as its editor. The university awarded Ph.D. degrees in 2013 to three of the initial group of candidates.

Deborah Valentine was born in Tarrytown, New York, moved around often while growing up as a member of a military family, and attended

Wheaton College in Illinois, where she pursued a program in educational ministry. Her first employment was challenging: working in elementary education in Chicago—as was her subsequent employment after moving to Philadelphia, where she taught early childhood education programs in underserved and diverse communities. Her need to explain to herself the structural and historical factors affecting the lives of the children with whom she worked led her to a Ph.D. program, and while she considered several schools, and several fields, the new childhood studies program at Rutgers-Camden seemed perfect, even though she had to wait a year for it to get off the ground. That year, she was invited to sit-in on interviews as new faculty were hired, and then she began the process of cobbling together a truly interdisciplinary education, which included coursework at Rutgers–New Brunswick as well as Camden. She defended her Ph.D. thesis, "Playing at Learning and Learning at Play: A History of Race, Play, and Early Education in Philadelphia, 1857–1912," completed under the direction of Lynne Vallone, in 2013 and earned one of the first three doctoral degrees (all in childhood studies) awarded at Rutgers-Camden. With degree in hand, she returned to the Philadelphia area to teach at the university level in the field of early childhood education.[28]

The center gradually moved its responsibilities into the new department and the Institute for Effective Education. Grant-funded research diminished in importance, as most of the newly hired faculty were either in the humanities or more qualitative areas of the social sciences. The Ph.D. program stabilized at around two dozen students, with perhaps four or five a year expected to complete a Ph.D. The students themselves continued to come from highly diverse backgrounds—teaching, law enforcement, criminal justice, education, or M.A. programs at other institutions—and looked for employment not just in the academic world but in a broad range of public service agencies associated with children and childhood.

Camden had clearly identified a niche and had fit a new program with exciting possibilities into it. Measuring its academic success will best be done a decade or two down the road.

Epilogue

These individual accounts trace a more general improvement at the university. The administration never again conducted an across-the-board survey as it had in the early 1980s (and dropped the ranking system in the early twenty-first century), but a snapshot of the results of external reviews in 1994 indicated clear progress: "1b" programs that had climbed to "1a" and strong programs ("II") that were now evaluated as nearly distinguished ("1b"). Among these in the School of Arts and Sciences in New Brunswick were art history, computer science, history, and political science; at Cook (later the School of Environmental and Biological Sciences), food science; at Engineering, biomedical engineering, chemical and biochemical engineering, and mechanical and aerospace engineering; at Mason Gross, both the visual and theater arts programs. CSPAD had dropped a number of programs as well, but overall sustained investment in faculty lines and graduate student support had made a difference. At Newark and Camden, however, only one program, that in the School of Criminal Justice in Newark, had, as evaluators saw it, claimed "distinction," but both campuses were about to embark on expansion of their graduate programs. In the twenty-first century, the success of Newark and Camden in launching new master's and Ph.D. programs would be one of the most striking academic accomplishments of the state university. Other success stories were hidden in the rankings. The creation of a unified life science program in New Brunswick during the 1980s, and the development of links between the life sciences and chemistry programs (renamed the Department of Chemistry and Chemical Biology) helped vault chemistry in the second decade of the new century to the top spot nationwide in federal research funding.

The paths to distinction of the five featured programs tell us something about playing catch-up as a public research university. In the postwar period, Rutgers had neither the long tradition of graduate education nor an ongoing partnership with the state that nurtured universities in places such as Wisconsin, Michigan, and North Carolina. Rather, at Rutgers, excellence has been negotiated a few program at a time by focusing resources. In each of the case studies, academic progress depended on exploiting a particular opportunity. For physics, the postwar redeployment of physicists and the continuation of federal support for the sciences; for history, the early identification of social and then women's history as vital and relatively understudied fields of inquiry; for criminal justice and marine and coastal science, the recognition that national attention had focused on these fields and federal funding existed to develop programs at Rutgers; and in childhood studies, the chance to address questions across several disciplines that together defined a previously uncharted field (and a field with the potential to address the needs of the larger Camden community).

A second factor uniting at least four of these stories is senior hiring. Most of the senior hires were midcareer scholars who could potentially provide academic leadership for two decades. In many cases, departments made two or even three such hires in a particular subfield or surrounded a senior hire with several junior hires. Obviously, such hiring cost money, which meant that particularly smart choices had to be made about the programs, the fields, and the individuals involved. Strong leadership, another factor that runs through these stories, was thus crucial in the path to academic distinction. There is little in this that is proscriptive. Nationwide, universities direct uncommitted resources to programs that bring in grant money and funnel tuition revenue toward departments that teach large numbers of undergraduates. There is wisdom in both policies, but they make it harder to duplicate the paths that led in the 1980s and 1990s to research excellence.

It is perhaps best to conclude with a singularly remarkable story of focusing resources to build distinction. In the early 1980s, both the CSPAD review and a national survey of graduate programs had designated Rutgers–New Brunswick's philosophy department as third tier. Its graduate program was only a decade old, and the administration regarded it as primarily a service department that taught undergraduates. Then things began to change. Reorganization gave the program a critical mass of faculty; by the mid-1980s, the department had jumped from third to second tier in the university's evaluations, and outside reviewers placed it just behind the best philosophy departments at public universities. A decade later, when external reviewers returned in 1996, "something dramatic" had occurred.[29] The Bloustein-Pond administration commitment to bring world-class scholarly leaders to the university had primarily targeted the sciences, but philosophy got one as well—Jerry Foder, a luminary in the philosophy of mind, lured from the Massachusetts Institute of Technology to the City University of New York, and from CUNY to Rutgers. Other senior hires followed, as well as the establishment of a Cognitive Science Center (which linked the department to psychology). The 1996 evaluators concluded that the department was now among the eight strongest in the country, but they also cautioned the university that the challenge was to maintain that position for at least a decade—to avoid losing to raids the very professors Rutgers had lured from other universities. It did that and more. In the early twenty-first century, the Rutgers philosophy program was usually ranked as one of the two or three best in the United States—alongside New York University and Princeton—and in the Anglophone world, an equal to Oxford. The department had a small, highly selective graduate program that placed its Ph.D. recipients, despite a bad job market, easily into the best entry-level positions in the academic world.

8

A Place Called Rutgers

Glee Club, Student Newspaper, Libraries,
University Press, Art Galleries

The definition of a university begins with its faculty and students. Not merely a product of the ubiquitous rankings, a school's self-image depends on how well it is teaching its students and how productively its faculty members conduct their research (and, increasingly, how these two components of university life contribute to each other). But universities are often recognized by the public at large as well as by students and the academic community for more than teaching and research. In an effort to capture the broader reach of a place called Rutgers, I will pursue a somewhat serendipitous journey to five distinctive organizations or institutions that, outside the confines of the traditional classroom, have helped define Rutgers in the post–World War II era. All of these are, in the broadest sense, cultural bodies, and all stand in for many other such groups, programs, or organizations that could have been chosen for this purpose. The bookends for this chapter—the glee club (and chorus at Newark) and the art museum (and gallery at Camden)—demonstrate the importance of the arts in a university's stature among peers and the public, while the three central sections (the New Brunswick student newspaper, *The Targum*, the university press, and the library system) explore institutions that have helped define Rutgers in ways parallel to but distinct from its reputation as a public research university with a commitment to both undergraduate and graduate education.

The Glee Club (New Brunswick)
and University Chorus (Newark)

In April 1978, as the glee club prepared for its annual spring concert, Director F. Austin "Soup" Walter (RC '32) was celebrating a Rutgers conducting career that stretched back to the early years of the Great Depression. With the "fraternal warmth and somewhat controlled rowdiness" of its student members, its all-male *a cappella* tradition, and its repertoire of college songs, sacred selections, and classical pieces, the glee club under Walter's guidance evoked a traditional Rutgers in a 1970s world of Billy Joel and Bruce Springsteen concerts.[1] Walter had sung with the glee club in the late 1920s, and by 1978, he had served as the club's director for forty-six years. Under his direction the club had performed nationally and internationally—the 1978 spring concert was followed by a European tour that took the club to Amsterdam, Brussels, Paris, Tours, and Konstanz— and become one of the most visible representations of the college and university. And while club membership produced generations of Rutgers's most committed and enthusiastic alumni, one suspected that, with Walter's upcoming retirement from teaching, yet another Rutgers tradition was winding down. For those who tried to see into the future, the questions were daunting: Did an all-male club belong in a now coeducational school? What would happen to a Rutgers College club with the reorganization of the New Brunswick campus? How would an undergraduate organization fit with plans to strengthen graduate education and with the creation of a new professional arts school? The 1980s would prove a challenging decade for the glee club.

The glee club and the *Targum* are Rutgers's oldest student organizations. Formed in 1872 by the class of 1874, the club was, like the *Targum*, largely independent of faculty or college supervision. In the early 1880s, it acquired faculty leadership—a crucial step in providing continuity as each class of seniors graduated—and began an ambitious concert program that took it up and down the East Coast and to such privileged venues as Carnegie Hall. In the early twentieth century, however, student enthusiasm waned as the repertoire apparently failed to keep up with changing musical tastes. Then, about the time of World War I, music professor and former Rutgers undergraduate Howard McKinney took over as director and reinvigorated the club. An expanded repertoire, marked by more classical music, went hand in hand with expanding membership—up from little more than a dozen to fifty or more undergraduates. In 1932, one of glee club members, F. Austin Walter, a history major, won a competition to select a student conductor for a Carnegie Hall recital, and "Soup" soon became McKinney's assistant, and director of the club in everything but actual title.

The 1932 college yearbook captured Walter at the beginning of his career. He was a member of "Scabbard and Blade," a student leader, and a baseball manager as well as in the glee club, the well-rounded college man of the era, with ambitions to become a "musician pure and simple" and to "lead a great orchestra."[1] After graduating, Walter did advanced coursework at the Julliard School of Music in New York and Columbia University, but the only graduate degrees he ever received were honorary and from Rutgers. At various times he directed the Kirkpatrick chapel choir and the university orchestra, as well as the glee club, and in 1950, he founded the university choir (originally made up of glee club members and New Jersey College for Women students from the Voorhees chapel choir). Rutgers proximity to New York and Philadelphia led, over the years, to many opportunities for the choir to perform with internationally known orchestras. Walter was also a gifted teacher, offering courses in various periods and genres of music history.

Through the 1950s, the club toured exclusively on the East Coast. Each attempt to carry out a more ambitious concert schedule met with failure—beginning with the cancellation of a tour to Bermuda in 1936 because of the death of King George V of England. But in 1960, the club flew to California for a week of concerts, and in 1962, with help from President Mason Gross, they launched their first European tour. Performing with the Yale University wind symphony, they sang at the Bergen International Festival in Norway, and the two organizations then toured and performed in Denmark, West Germany, and the Netherlands. The Bergen concert contained only two European pieces, one by Egil Hovland, commissioned by the tour's sponsor, Carnegie Hall, especially for the tour. Otherwise the highlights were American and modern—in particular, a Randall Thompson composition done as a tribute to Thomas Jefferson, and a set of American folk ballads that included two spirituals, songs from Virginia ("Old Bangum Would a-Hunting Ride") and Vermont ("In the Town of Danville"), and a clipper ship sailor's chantey. A Norwegian review of the initial concert noted the "powerful voices" of the chorus, but also that they were "strangled" on occasion by "too strong an orchestra."[3] During the

1960s, the club appeared overseas several times and in 1971 toured Cold War Czechoslovakia—firmly initiating a tradition that in (better-funded) years assured most club members would have a chance to perform overseas. In 1980, they finally left the confines of Europe and the Americas as a tour to Spain and Portugal included a side trip and several performances in Casablanca, Morocco.

The club thus served as an international ambassador for Rutgers during a transitional era when the university president was traveling overseas with greater frequency but the school itself had not fully defined the international component of its educational mission. Other student groups, of course, did this as well, but the club's visibility was unique, and at least two of the sites it visited, Konstanz and Tours, became outposts for the school's study abroad program. The club also sang and recorded with the university choir (which included Douglass women). In 1960, the choir, with Eugene Ormandy conducting the Philadelphia Orchestra, recorded Carl Orff's *Carmina Burana*. (The recording is still commercially available.) In more recent years, the club has recorded its European tours as well as music drawn from its American concerts.

Walter's retirement in 1982 brought the glee club to a crossroads. The odds against the club were formidable. The 1982 European tour, the last Walter directed, was a financial disaster, and funding through student activities fees became problematic. In the 1950s, the glee club was one of about a dozen organizations to receive student support; by the 1980s, it had to compete with many dozens of others for the money. Even more crucially, academic reorganization in the early 1980s resulted in the consolidation of the arts programs on the Douglass campus. Neither the university nor the Mason Gross School of the Arts (MGSA) saw much purpose in continuing, under the umbrella of a professional school and on a women's campus, an all-male glee club. The club's rowdy parties had given it a reputation among many as a "fraternity that sang" rather than a fraternity of singers, and the time devoted in recent years to executing the touring schedule had drained energy from establishing a repertoire of equal quality to those of the past.[4] Under a series of part-time directors, membership dropped to no more than thirty men. Joint appearances with the Harvard glee club in the early 1980s, in the memories of some former members, were an embarrassment for Rutgers.

At many other schools, glee clubs were being demoted in just this way or completely abandoned. But not at Rutgers. Club leaders galvanized alumni support and persuaded officials at Mason Gross, very much against their will, to continue the club. They threw their efforts into fund-raising and established an endowment in Walter's honor. An advisory committee for the club was organized, thus giving both faculty and alumni a stake in its future. The club and most of the other musical performance groups remained affiliated with MGSA, and students received course credit, whether majors or not, for participation. More crucial for the glee club, the arts school defined a new faculty position of director of choral music to lead both the glee club and the concert choirs. In 1993, it hired Patrick Gardner.

Gardner had been director of choral music at the University of Michigan, which had one of the oldest and most distinguished glee clubs in the nation. He had taken the university's club on national and international tours, and it had sung the national anthem at Tiger Stadium before the start of the seventh game of the 1984 World Series. He moved to the University of Texas in 1987, and then to the New York City area in 1990, attracted by the opportunity to direct the internationally acclaimed Riverside Choral Society as well as by a position at Wagner College. In 1993, Rutgers hired Gardner. Over the next twenty years, he provided the club the continuity it had lacked during the preceding decade and remolded the club into one of the most prestigious in the nation. He also continued as the director of the Riverside Choral Society.

The November 1994 celebration of the 125th anniversary of the famous Rutgers-Princeton football game of 1869 highlighted as well the energy that Gardner brought to the club. The performance, which included the Voorhees Choir, the cheerleaders, and the marching band in addition to the glee club, opened with "On the Banks of the Old Raritan," the alma mater, while glee club members, dressed in traditional football garb, reenacted Rutgers's six-goal (touchdown) to four-goal victory over Princeton. Walter returned to conduct "Nobody Ever Died for Dear Old Rutgers," and as the *Targum* reported, Gardner paid tribute to his predecessor by "donning a Rutgers sweatshirt" and cartwheeling across the stage for him (a feat "Soup" had added to performances many times in the past).[5] The women of the Voorhees Chapel Choir supplied a note of reciprocity to the occasion by singing "Princeton, Forward March."

Gardner rebuilt the glee club. He improved recruitment by developing relationships with New Jersey schools and then using the newly computerized admissions records to seek likely singers. He unified the auditions for the schools' three choral music clubs, recruited from more campuses, and broadened the musical repertoire to reflect the rapidly changing musical tastes of the era. Membership rose from around forty students when Gardner arrived to eighty or more by the twenty-first century, and the quality of the applicants improved (some of whom, after their glee club work, would go on to professional careers in music). Foreign trips became an every-four-year event, and, continuing a tradition that Walter had encouraged, trips to women's colleges, such as Wellesley and Mount Holyoke, become common (and were often returned by a visit of those schools' choral groups). The traditional Christmas and spring concerts continued, but both now helped raise money to fund the choral music programs. The success of fund-raising was most dramatically evident on Douglass campus in the new Robert E. Mortensen Hall, designed for the five vocal ensembles of the Mason Gross School of the Arts, and the Richard H. Shindell Choral Hall within it. Both are named for benefactors and former members of the glee club.

At Newark, the male glee club's counterpart was the men's and women's Rutgers university chorus, founded in 1947 by Alfred Mann, the first chair of the Rutgers-Newark music department. Mann, German-born and trained in Europe, came to the United States in the late 1930s and obtained advanced degrees from Columbia University in musicology. He directed the chorus—at that time perhaps three dozen students—for its first twenty years. Lacking a performance space on the Newark campus, the chorus performed in community halls and churches, and occasionally at the Newark Museum (where one year, the repertoire included Handel's *Messiah* and Gluck's opera *Orfeo*).[6]

Mann stepped down as chorus director in 1967, retired from Rutgers in 1980, but returned for the fiftieth-anniversary concert in 1997. At that point, the chorus was under the direction of John Floreen and was about to change course dramatically. The story begins with Mann's departure. He was followed by a series of interim directors before Louie L. White took over in 1970. A distinguished composer, bass singer, and choral director, White nonetheless struggled with declining student interest in choral performance during his tenure. After White's death in 1979, Floreen was hired as an instructor in the music program and put in charge of the chorus. He faced the immediate task of building the chorus back to a point where it had enough accomplished sopranos, altos, tenors, and basses to perform a broad if traditional American and European repertoire. Floreen brought to the task a D.M.A. in orchestral conducting from Iowa and great enthusiasm. The chorus, even more so than in the past, became a Rutgers ambassador to the communities of northeastern New Jersey, while it worked into its repertoire pieces by the Viennese classical composer Johann Nepomuk Hummel (whose works were one of Floreen's research interests) and American premiers of sacred works by Antonio Vivaldi.

In 1997, at the time of the chorus's fiftieth anniversary, its ambassadorial role took on new meaning. That year, the chorus went on the first of many European tours. The initial trip to Germany and the Czech Republic was followed by tours in the Netherlands, France, England, Scotland, Wales, Italy, and Spain. The tours helped recruit students, gained the attention of university administrators, improved fund-raising, and allowed Floreen to set higher performance standards (a goal secured by partnership with Susan McAdoo, hired in 1998 as assistant conductor). Floreen worked more African American and Hispanic folk music into the repertoire to reflect the diversity of the Newark campus and to alert foreign audiences to the breadth of the American choral tradition. After teaching at Sichuan State Conservatory of Music in China, he also began arranging Chinese songs for the Newark chorus. None of this distracted the chorus from its primary focus on bringing music to the local and Rutgers communities—which included a concert in 2000 at the Dutch Reformed Church in Belleville, where chorus members helped repair the cemetery in which they had reason to believe (incorrectly, it turned out) that the Revolutionary War hero Colonel Henry Rutgers was buried, and an equally well publicized concert at the Greystone Park Psychiatric Hospital in Parsippany. As with the New Brunswick glee club, a student organization in Newark became one of the most recognized symbols in New Jersey of support for the arts at the state university.

The Student Newspaper: *Rutgers Daily Targum*

Michael Perlin entered Rutgers in 1962 and began working as a *Targum* reporter the following spring. As a new reporter, he was handed a weekly assignment each Monday but was also allowed to branch out on his own and do a little investigative reporting as well. As he recalled, "We covered student council as if it was Congress . . . as if this was really serious stuff. I also used to do the music reviews as well, too, both jazz and classical, because I knew it, and enjoyed it."[7] He was elected editor in chief after submitting a column, modeled on a piece he read in the *Saturday Review*, about how you find out about a college by looking at bulletin boards: those with "a million notices all posted up on top of each other, going every which way," like Rutgers, were a great place to be.[8] Perlin may also have been the choice of the editorial board because, like so many editors, he was active in numerous campus activities. He chaired "Young Citizens for Johnson," served on committees for the soph hop and junior prom, and was a member of the Rutgers bicentennial committee and the class of 1966 council. As editor in chief, he made the decision to pull all the advertising and the sports from the issue that covered the first teach-in over the Vietnam War. The editorial he and his follow editors ran on the teach-in proclaimed "The Dawn of a New Era."[9] It was a frenetic year: they would work every night until midnight "making sure the paper got to bed."[10] The *Targum* seemed central to everything that was happening on campus and in America: "I loved being the editor of *Targum*. It was in every way the best experience. My teachers were great."[11] Peter Charanis (Byzantine history), Gerald Pomper (political science), Lloyd Gardner (American foreign policy), and Richard Heffner (journalism) were among those he remembered. "I had so many interesting, thoughtful, intelligent friends to talk [to]. . . . We used to talk all night long about politics, and about music, and about the world."[12] The world of print journalism not only attracted and inspired many of the best students at the state university but also chronicled and interpreted the school's history for generations of students and alumni.

Of the many university and student news publications, only two, the Rutgers-Newark *Observer* and the Rutgers–New Brunswick *Targum*, have published print editions continuously from 1945 through the second decade of the twenty-first century. The *Targum*, more than any other newspaper, has been the publication of record for the university.

In 1867, students first published an issue of the *Targum*. It began as an annual, but by 1869 was a monthly paper. Originally largely a literary journal as much as a newspaper, it gravitated toward coverage of campus events in the late nineteenth century, with its staff increasingly drawn from the fraternity system. In the first half of the twentieth century, the *Targum* appeared as both a weekly and semiweekly, concerned with college and New Brunswick events. It was as a weekly that it resumed publication in October 1945 after a nineteen-month suspension at the end of World War II; and by 1946–1947, the editors were publishing semiweekly editions.

In a 1954 feature story, the director of the School of Journalism described the *Targum* as "a faithful recorder of routine campus news," which deserved "commendation for [the] vitality of its editorial page." He went on, however, to note that while the paper could analyze fully "the sudden departure of a baseball pitcher to withdraw from college," when it had the opportunity to scrutinize a new plan to "deal with excessive class cutting" it had "ducked it with sloppy coverage."[13] In fact, during the late 1940s and throughout the 1950s, the *Targum* routinely featured sports events and beauty contests as front-page news, chronicled campus dances, poked fun at the "Coopies" across town, and highlighted college government in-fighting. The editors also introduced an annual "Mugrat" ("Targum" spelled backward) issue with sensational stories that just might have been true—a tradition that continues to the present. Yet they also ran stories critical of the fraternity system, leading to a notorious incident in spring 1949 when a group of fraternity brothers marched on the Targum House, "unzipped their pants, and urinated in unison on the walls of" the building.[14] During the 1950s, the *Targum* took the lead in trying to end discriminatory practices in the fraternity system, protested McCarthy-era firings of three professors, and defended the *Antho*, a campus literary magazine under attack for a publication about abortion.

In the 1960s, with the growth in enrollments and in readership came more issues, more pages, more staff, and more investigative reporting. The Targum in 1960 was a four-page daily, with a staff of about sixty students. It printed the WRSU schedule, ran the comic strip *Peanuts*, reprinted nationally syndicated columns and sponsored homegrown columnists as well, and included an exhaustive list of official university notices. Cigarette companies and potential employers provided much of the advertising revenue. A cultural editor was added to the staff, coverage of Douglass events became common (as well as distribution to the Douglass campus), and Douglass students became staff members. The paper's alignment with student protesters—on Vietnam, civil rights, and campus government—was evident each year, regardless of the editor.

By 1970, the *Targum* had grown to eight pages. It had a staff of almost a hundred students (some paid for production or advertising work). The editors now always allocated at least an entire page to sports and ran student classified as well as commercial advertising. Editorial cartoons by national (usually Herb Block) and collegiate artists appeared on the editorial page, and the paper carried regular opinion columns, each with a catchy byline,

alongside the traditional letters to the editor. "Critiques," a four-page literary supplement, appeared weekly. While the advocacy of the 1960s had
waned, editorial policy still focused on national and campus politics, and
with a decidedly liberal bent.

During the 1970s, the paper grew to a standard sixteen-to-twenty
page daily, with most of the extra space devoted to campus stories. National news, generally from the Associated Press, appeared on the second page. (The teletype machine made so much noise that it had to be
kept in a wooden crate.) New features included weather reports, cross-
word puzzles, police reports of campus crime, and announcements of
campus events. Oliphant became the political cartoonist of choice; *Peanuts* remained (it outpolled *Doonesbury* 3–1 when students were asked
in 1975 which they wanted). Reporters and editors worked at a hectic
pace—usually at the paper or in the field after classes each day until late
in the evening. While the switch from "hot lead" to "cold type" printing made things a bit easier, the final product still had to be finished at
midnight, driven to Princeton, run off, and then gotten back to campus for distribution by six in the morning. The "Critiques" supplement
gave way to "Weekend" in the early 1980s, and then, a few years later, to
"Inside Beat." Each supplement reflected the changing student interest
in music, movies, reading, and fashion, and the best work presented
edgy reviews that challenged readers to look beyond the mainstreams
of popular culture.[15]

In the 1980s, *Doonesbury, Bloom County, Calvin and Hobbes*, and *Dil-
bert* supplemented *Peanuts*, and sports received increasing coverage. The
editorial feature, "Laurels and Darts," which handed out awards for the
best and the worst around campus, first appeared in the mid-1980s, and
"Campus Profiles" (stories about individual members of the Rutgers community) became a regular feature. The editors worked to make the paper
the equivalent of a good regional newspaper, with extended coverage of
national news and of events at other universities, and with modest coverage of Douglass, Livingston, Cook, Newark, and Camden (identifying the
Targum as *the* university student newspaper). The Royal typewriters the
staff had used through 1984 were replaced that year with video display
terminals, the first step into the electronic age. By the mid-1990s, the paper
had begun to shrink (to sixteen pages or less), an online edition appeared,
and sports took up even more of the paper. Print and online versions sponsored polls on student opinions (the equivalent of the more political refer-

enda run by the student government in the 1960s). The editors added more comics, a horoscope column, and Sudoku puzzles.

The 1979–1980 academic year marked a crossroads in the arc of *Targum's* history. For almost half a decade, the paper's leadership (Targum Council) had considered making the paper independent of university control, and in 1979, a detailed report by an alumni committee argued that such a move was feasible and desirable. As a student newspaper, *Targum* had been censored by the dean of students, it had lost funding when it displeased student government, and even after winning a battle to provide the primary editors with honorariums, it had no authority to pay other staff members. A student referendum approved the change, and in early 1980, the University Senate did as well. In October 1980, the university finalized a new arrangement that made the *Targum* the nation's twenty-eighth independent college newspaper. The student government allocation was replaced by a $2.50 student fee that had to be supported periodically in referendum on each campus, and a new oversight board, with significant alumni representation, was created to allow long-range planning.

Targum's hallmark, as both a Rutgers College and an independent newspaper, has been its investigative and its national political reporting. Stories such as the 1971 "winter soldier" feature on a Vietnam veteran and member of "Veterans for Peace" and its 1976 "witch hunt" investigation on firings at Livingston College made the paper required reading for a politically active student body.

These stories had their counterparts in the decades that followed. Investigative reports ranged broadly across campus, local, and national issues, and sought out multiple sources of information. Equally creative were many of the columnists whom the *Targum* attracted. A few were former students or members of the larger university community: the ubiquitous Gene Robinson in the 1970s, a student leader who for more than a decade contributed opinion pieces about the black experience at Rutgers; Arthur Kamin, a former *Targum* editor and member of the Board of Trustees; and William Dowling, an English professor, whose frequent letters in the 1990s and early 2000s subjected the university to searing criticism. But far more typical were the students whose bylines appeared regularly, and from the 1990s onward provided, along with the contributions to "Inside Beat," the most creative aspect of the modern *Targum*.

How critical did this contribution remain to the typical student, whose media world now originated in the Internet? A failed effort in the

University Senate in 2008–2009, by a very close vote, to make student fees for the *Targum* (then at \$9.75) completely optional, suggests the problem that the student newspaper faced, especially as advertising revenue diminished. The advertising that remained, in turn, made *Targum* dependent on the university athletic program for revenue, just as sports reporting became the area that best sustained student interest in journalism (and the topic that filled multiple back pages of every issue).

Libraries

All the Glory of the World Would Be Buried in Oblivion Unless God
Had Provided Mortals with the Remedy of Books.
    —Richard de Bury, 1345 (from a tribute to Donald Cameron, head of the
    Rutgers Library, upon his retirement in 1966)[16]

[A] fundamental principle . . . needs to undergird Rutgers' aspirations:
great universities equal great libraries equal great dollars.
    —"To Join the First Rank of America's Public Research Universities," A
    Report of the Library System of Rutgers, 1985[17]

The traditional definition of a research library is a comprehensive repository of materials for both current use and future, anticipated need.
No research library has been able to realize this model for some time.
    —"Strategic Directions—An Outline of the Issues," *RUL Report*, Spring 1997[18]

In the early 1950s at the New Jersey College for Women, the librarian estimated that "the average young lady . . . use[d] thirty-five library books per year," but almost half of them borrowed additional books from the Voorhees Library across town at the men's colleges.[19] About nine out of every ten students at the men's colleges took out books during the school year. Borrowing was so heavy that Donald Cameron, the library's director, had to admonish the staff not to check out for their personal use more than two popular books at a time. Fifty years later, at the dawn of a new century, the librarian would report that while circulation figures were continuing a steady decline from a peak in the early 1990s, the library website had grown to almost three thousand pages and that patrons had conducted almost two and a half million database searches, most from computer terminals outside the library system. These statistics capture the obvious: the nature and role of university libraries had changed fundamentally.

Change, of course, was driven by technology. Traditionally, librarians focused on the collection and circulation of books and periodicals, and their success was measured in the number of volumes they had and lent.

The larger the collection, the more students and faculty could accomplish, and thus "great libraries" helped define "great universities." College libraries, to be sure, did other things as well. They provided study hall space for students and instructional classes; served as museums, acquiring and exhibiting historical artifacts; collected manuscripts and rare books; and archived the university's own records. All of these, however, reinforced the primary goal of building strong collections of use in teaching and research. Then, in the 1990s, and rather abruptly, the library world changed. The emphasis on physical collections of books and the circulation of materials to patrons gave way to a new focus on information and access. Librarians had to become specialists in locating and evaluating new forms and sources of information, and in providing guidance to a much broader online public. If technologically driven change is the storyline, however, it also obscures a significant point: librarianship itself has always been about information and access, about identifying and evaluating informational resources, and teaching others how to use these resources.

At Rutgers, this story had an added twist. In the 1980s, strengthening the library system had helped Rutgers reached its goal of membership in the American Association of Universities—the academic elite of American institutions of higher education. Almost immediately, however, for the university's library system, the rules of the game began to change. The success at building a print collection had defined the library's strength; in the 1990s, traditional print collections did not disappear, but maintaining these collections—adding to them at an ever decreasing rate—while also providing users with the online resources they needed, created unparalleled budgetary challenges and ever greater uncertainty about exactly what defined a great library. What follows is not a general history of the Rutgers library system, but a brief overview of some of the features that have defined its place in the university and the public imagination.

Mortar and Bricks

In about a decade, from the middle of the 1950s to the middle of the 1960s, Rutgers transformed its sleepy little liberal arts reading libraries into modern structures with the capacity equivalent to that at other state universities to serve the baby boom generation of students and the growing research needs of the faculty. Most of that growth came with generous support from the state legislature and from bond issues that testified to the singular importance of higher education to the voters during this era. Most of that growth was directed by Donald Cameron, who spent twenty-one years as head of the library system. Born in Scotland, Cameron arrived in the United States at age eleven, was educated at Union College, received a master's at Princeton, and started at Rutgers as an English instructor in 1929. In 1945, he became Rutgers librarian, and during his tenure "may well have had a hand in planning more college libraries than any man who ever lived."[20]

Several examples will flesh this picture out: In the immediate postwar period, the College of South Jersey's library was a small room, containing about three thousand volumes and a table that seated eight students. It had one librarian and a budget of $3,600. Rutgers converted the two-year liberal arts junior college into a four-year branch of the state university in 1950, and by 1957, a $400,000 library had become the first new building on campus. The librarian reported that she now had almost fourteen thousand books in her collection (and space for one hundred thousand), which served not only the liberal arts but also business, education, and law students, and an acquisitions budget of more than $10,000. There were seats for more than three hundred students—that is, for virtually every undergraduate—and the library was defined precisely in those terms, as an undergraduate, not a research, library.

In New Brunswick, venerable Voorhees Library, a charming but inadequate library built in 1903–1904, was replaced by a six-story building, a "librarian's paradise," that had the capacity to shelve a million and a half volumes, seat more than a thousand students, and provide study carrels for thirty faculty members.[21] In summer 1956, books and unbound periodicals were carried down spiral staircases from the second floor of Voorhees by "brawny undergraduates," most of them from the football, wrestling, and basketball teams (students tall enough to get to every nook and cranny) to Lend-Lease wooden boxes supplied by the United States Army, then shipped down College Avenue to the new building.[22] Many of the books probably made the trip by a different route, as for a number of years the faculty had been encouraged to keep their checkouts at home because the Voorhees library had no shelving for them. For the dedication of the new library in October 1956, the university held a convocation, and Governor Robert Meyner addressed the assembled crowd—a tangible recognition of the centrality of a library to a university's aspirations.

Across town in 1961, Douglass College got its first building specifically designated as a library. The existing library, built in 1926 and never intended to be more than a temporary home, had floors that were buckling and more than 125,000 books, many piled on the floor, with shelf space for only 75,000. The new million-dollar, three-story structure, dubbed "The Teahouse of the August Moon" by students because of its roof design, was built on a site that sloped down into a wooded ravine, so that it appeared only two stories high, and thus dramatized the height of the nearby chapel.[23] Large plate glass windows provided elegant views. (The same windows were invisible walls into which unwary patrons and one of the designing architects stumbled.) The new library had shelving for 150,000 books (once again, budget constraints shortchanged the future) and enough seating for the current Douglass student body.

This early burst of building was rounded off with new libraries in the Newark Law Center and the Institute of Management and Labor Relations, the erection of a new home for the Graduate School of Library Service, and two stand-alone libraries—Science and Medicine (completed just as Rutgers lost its medical school) and the Kilmer area library for Livingston College. In the decades that followed, buildings were renovated, additions added, libraries moved—whenever the need for more space coincided with state funding.

During the last phase of building under the 1988 state bond act, the main libraries at Camden (Robeson), Newark (Dana), and New Brunswick (Alexander) all acquired additions. The Art Library was completely redone. In 1966 the Art Library had been transferred from the Central Library (i.e., Alexander Library) to Voorhees Hall—not coincidentally the past home of the college library, and now the home of the Art History Department and the newly conceived Rutgers Art Gallery. In fifteen years, the collection tripled in size, and matching the art history program, the holdings broadened to encompass scholarship on art from around the world. The architects—the same firm that had designed the Zimmerli and the Library of Science and Medicine—ran at least three design possibilities by a deeply engaged committee drawn from the library and teaching faculty in art. Each of the designs—known colloquially as "Historic Williamsburg" (brick facade), "Bridgewater Mall" ("art deco with a lot of glass"), and "Sea Captain's Berth" (large round window)—found its way into the final building, as did numerous carrels for the growing number of art history students, oversized shelving for the "elephant folio" volumes (thirty inches or more) that are common in the art world, and a semicircular information desk and spacious reading room filled with the electronic

31. John Cotton Dana Library, Rutgers-Newark, in the 1950s. The library was located at 40
Rector Street in the former Ballantine Brewery building. In 1927, during Prohibition, the New
Jersey Law School purchased the brewery building. The law school became Dana College,
and the college evolved into the University of Newark (which included a college of arts and
sciences as well as a business school). In 1927, Rutgers acquired the Newark-based College
of Pharmacy, and in the early 1930s, began negotiating a merger with Dana College. Those
negotiations failed, but in 1945, the merger with what was by then the University of Newark
was completed. The library was named for the philanthropist and long-time librarian of the
Newark Public Library. The reading room had a depression in the center of the floor from
when it had been a malt room and used to store hops, and there were stains on the ceilings
above the stacks where various liquids had dripped down. In the immediate postwar era,
with returning GIs on campus, the library served the needs of the three thousand students
enrolled at Rutgers-Newark, and during the 1950s, student enrollments hovered a little above
two thousand.
SOURCE: R-Photo, buildings and grounds.

technology that led one commentator to compare it to the cockpit of the
starship *Enterprise*.[24]

While the tweaking of existing structures continued, the university built
one completely new library, the Stephen and Lucy Chang Science Library,
in 1995, at what was then Cook College. The library housed collections
previously at the Library of Science and Medicine in fields such as agriculture, food science, oceanography, and plant and animal science. Three
features distinguished the building: a technological infrastructure that was
part of the design rather than added after-the-fact; the location within an
academic building, the Walter F. Foran Hall (a plant science and biotech-

nology complex); and the role of fund-raising, as opposed to state support, in building the library. The library's benefactors, the Changs, had been born in China and come to the United States after World War II, where they both had earned advanced degrees. Stephen Chang had joined the Rutgers faculty in 1960, and for almost three decades published, taught, and patented in the area of food technology.

Libraries never have enough space—for their collections, or, more recently, for the students who crowd the computer terminals in their reading rooms. Yet in comparison to the underfunding of library collections and staff, two constants in the university dialogue about libraries, buildings have done relatively well. Aware of the import of libraries to the teaching and research of a university and to the public perception of the stature of a university, the Rutgers administration built a foundation of mortar and brick in the postwar era.

People

When World War II ended, librarians at Rutgers were members of the staff, like but not the same as the faculty. Their professionalization played a key role in defining the place of the library system at the university. Were they faculty? Would they be paid equally with faculty members? Would they receive tenure, which protected their academic freedom and their jobs, but also meant they risked being fired if they did not meet the standards for tenure? Would those tenure standards be the same as for other faculty?

In the immediate postwar period, there were approximately sixty librarians at Rutgers, handling half a million books, distributed among six libraries. (In the early twenty-first century, ninety professional librarians and more than two hundred staff members handled over three and half million books in eighteen libraries.) Cameron began his campaign to improve salaries by asking that the university librarians get the salaries suggested by the American Library Association of "professional employees" who perform "real professional service."[25] Very soon thereafter, the university committed itself to parity between the salaries of professional librarians and the teaching faculty. (Librarians, of course, taught as well, but the term "teaching faculty" was often used to distinguish librarians from other faculty members.) For staff members who were not professional librarians, salaries remained so low, the Douglass librarian reported, that she could not attract "today's high school graduate" to do the clerical and cataloging work that the library needed.[26]

Parity did not solve the problem for the professional librarians. Teaching faculty moved through the ranks based on research and teaching accomplishments; librarians, in contrast, were virtually trapped in positions defined by administrative responsibilities. In response, librarians recommended that both administrative responsibility and subject area specialization be pathways to promotion, that new hires have not only professional library degrees but also advanced degrees in their subject area, and that those promoted beyond the equivalent of assistant professors hold tenure. By the late 1960s, these issues had come to a head. Librarians in the state colleges raised the same professionalization issues, and the American Association of University Professors did so as well in Rutgers contract negotiations. University Librarian Roy Kidman called on his colleagues to help define the standards for promotion, and in so doing, "demonstrate there is a profession called librarianship."[27]

In 1970, the librarians won the war, but lost the battle. Their faculty status was recognized, but pay parity came about more slowly, and Kidman resigned and moved to the University of Southern California. He was replaced by Virginia P. Whitney, the first woman to serve as university librarian and one of the only two in America at that time to head a library system. By 1972, there was general agreement that librarians had equivalence in rank, salary, tenure, academic rights and responsibilities, and academic freedom with the teaching faculty. Unlike the teaching faculty, however, who were evaluated on research, teaching, and service (with the former two weighted more strongly than the latter), librarians were evaluated in a broader range of categories that took into consideration their professional effectiveness and general usefulness as well as scholarly activities and research accomplishments.

Librarians at Rutgers, thus, won two crucial victories in defining their place within the university. They acquired the status, pay, and academic rights of the teaching faculty, and they helped craft a set of promotion standards that recognized the unique role they played in the life of the institution—as teachers and researchers with specific service responsibilities. These accomplishments would be challenged during the crisis of the mid-1980s, but it should not pass unnoticed that this initial success at professionalization came at a time when the library system was one of the very few units in the university were a majority of the faculty were women.

Interlude—A Dysfunctional Library?

In the mid-1980s, external reviewers of the library concluded that a road map that would lead Rutgers to join the first rank of America's public research universities seemed "so fraught with difficulties that the team was often tempted to dismay."[28] They pointed to an unwieldy administrative structure, confusion about the appropriate domains of faculty governance and administration, lack of planning for the technological future, hopelessly inadequate resources for collection development, and the unique challenges of geographical decentralization. In the two years before their arrival, the university had set in motion a planning process (specific to the library but also part of the general effort in the 1980s to strengthen Rutgers as a public research university) that had bubbled over into a nasty academic brawl. At issue between University Librarian Hendrik Edelman and many of the faculty were questions about library organization and the faculty status of librarians. In an "environment of growing distrust," Edelman resigned as the university paused to consider how to address the problems outlined in the report.[29]

Librarians retained their faculty status. A year of calm and consultation under an acting university librarian, Ralph E. McCoy, and the appointment of Joanne R. Euster to the post helped point toward other long-term solutions. Some of the resulting plans, such as one for collection development, would never receive the funding they needed; but two interrelated trends stand out—one was a serious effort to define the missions of the twenty-one Rutgers libraries (fifteen of which were part of the library system). The second was the growing emphasis on using technology to deliver library services more effectively. In the long run, technology allowed the creation of a unified system. Libraries specialized, avoided duplication of holdings, and served local students and faculty by shared electronic access or rapid transfer of materials. To grapple with the technologically induced change, the library defined new positions and brought in people with new sets of skills, for example, a copyright librarian to deal with the intricacies of intellectual property in the digital age and digital data curators for the Scholarly Communication Center (SCC). The university librarian, as technology changed what the library did, became as well the vice president for information services. The story of how technology and librarianship evolved, however, has roots that dig well into the twentieth-century past.

Technology

Just as librarians did not become informational specialists in the 1980s, technology did not suddenly overtake university libraries in that decade either. Technological improvements, some offering illusive solutions to problems of buckling shelving and diminishing resources, were already available throughout the postwar era. Early on, microfilm held out a promise that it almost fulfilled. The technology to produce reduced photographic images of printed material dates to the nineteenth century, but significantly scholarly use of the technique did not begin until the 1930s, when thirty-five-millimeter microfilm copies were made of the *New York Times* and a number of academically backed projects began. World War II saw great improvements in the technology, and in the immediate postwar period, Rutgers acquired its first microfilm—a comprehensive collection of pre-1800 American periodicals. In 1948, the library bought a microfilm reader, began substituting microfilm for back files of the *New York Times*, purchased the New Brunswick *Daily Home News* on microfilm, and started doing its own microfilming of materials in a laboratory that was already handling another new technology, photographic copying for the faculty. There was every expectation, Cameron noted, that such services would be expanded and continued. In the second decade of the twenty-first century, in fact, the library would own some four and a half times more microforms than books.

Technology also intervened to improve the circulation of library materials. By the late 1960s, no area of the library was more poorly funded than staffing, and no staffing problem greater—as borrowing grew along with the student body—than the managing of circulation. Before the 1970s, the main bottleneck was cataloging. In 1950, a typical year, the library acquired about thirteen thousand new books but had to type more than ninety thousand cards (which in human terms, meant about a thousand hours of typing by student assistants). While numerous improvements were made in the cataloging system in the next three decades, it was not until the mid-1980s that the process of converting the catalog to machine readable form began (with the installation of terminals in each library that allowed patrons to search the computerized catalog). By 1987, no new cards were being added to the system, and within three years, the library had a computerized catalog. The new system, dubbed IRIS—after a naming contest among librarians came up with "Integrated Rutgers Information System"—

allowed a student or faculty member to search the catalog by dialing in from home to the campus network as well as from an in-library terminal.[30]

On the circulation side, in 1968, the Board of Governors funded the development of a computer-controlled system, and soon thereafter, faculty and students could present a machine-readable library card, rather than fill out forms by hand, to check out a book at the main library. (No longer could someone find a library slip in the back of a book with the signature of Paul Robeson or Milton Friedman indicating he had taken out the book!) This innovation did not last long. In the early 1970s, the library began keypunching IBM cards for each book that went through circulation; the master card would be left in the book but duplicated when the book was circulated, and information about the borrower added to the duplicated cards. Shortly thereafter "tattle-tape" strips were fitted into the binding of high-risk books (the library targeted political science and history but initially skipped religion and music) that set-off an electronic warning if the book was carried out of the library without being checked out.[31] In 1983, in three days, the staff at the central library, now called the Archibald Stevens Alexander Library, bar-coded 125,000 books to launch a new circulation system, and with two electronic swipes, one of the patron's library card and one of the barcode, a book could circulate.

Online information access offered the library system a way of catching up with libraries at other state systems—AAU peers that often had collections twice the size of Rutgers's. The electronic library, imagined in the late 1980s, would be judged "not by what it *has*, but by what it can *provide*."[32] The first intimations of a "new age" in information access came about 1980 with the Rutgers Online Automated Retrieval Service.[33] To use ROARS, as it was labeled, a faculty member (or brave student) first made an appointment with a librarian to design a search strategy; they then signed on to the system through a library terminal, paid for the "connect time" personally, and initiated a search in a set of indexes and abstracts (for example, in the National Newspaper Index). About a week later, the faculty member received a printout of the results, again getting billed. As unbelievably ponderous as this may seem to a twenty-first-century reader (particularly one who never used a dial-up system), library patrons, who conducted only about a thousand searches a year initially were annually requesting three thousand to four thousand by the early 1990s. The late 1980s and early 1990s also saw many printed databases, mostly indexes to periodical literature, become available as CD-ROMs (Compact Disk and Read-Only

Memory). In 1987, for example, Medline, produced by the National Library of Medicine, became available in this new format.

It is amazing how quickly these first steps, of dial-up connecting and CD-ROMs, gave way to a revolution in information access in the mid-1990s. Overseeing the change was Marianne Gaunt, who in 1996 took over direction of the library system. Gaunt had worked in a public library, received an M.L.S. from Drexel, served as serials librarian at Brown University, and come to Rutgers in 1979 as a reference librarian. She had become head of circulation when that system went online in the mid-1980s. The breadth of her background made her an ideal person to step into the role of university librarian.

A typical acquisition in the 1990s was UnCover, which allowed the user to search the table of contents of more than ten thousand journals. By the late 1990s, the UnCover database had grown to seventeen thousand journals, and the university subscription now allowed a faculty member to designate specific journals and subjects, and receive e-mail updates of new citations. What was increasingly offered online, however, was not merely citations and abstracts, but full-text versions of what a researcher had found in an index. By the middle of the first decade of the new century, when a source had been located in an online index, a simple click on a link would bring the user to the article itself. By the end of the 1990s, librarians reported fewer than fifty mediated database searches a year (recall that the figure was greater than four thousand earlier in the decade), while there were more than 365,000 "hits" on the Proquest database, which gave full-text access to many academic journal articles (at a cost to the library of about nine cents a search). When Internet searching and access were welded to accelerated electronic book and article retrieval—almost completely freeing users from concern about the location of particular books or journals in particular collections—and to the online "Ask a Librarian" service, the era of information access had triumphed.

Technology also created new paths for collaboration. Rutgers-Camden had pioneered such collaboration by providing library support for Rowan University and Camden Community College. In 1996, such partnerships went a step further with planning for a Virtual Academic Library Environment (VALE) for all of the state higher education system. VALE launched its website in 1998, with half a million dollars of state support and databases that users at participating schools could access, but its broader significance was in creating an ongoing effort by academic libraries to cooperate in the ever-more expensive development of services and collections. One ironic but useful footnote to this effort was the "last copy program" to assure that at least one library retained a print copy of books published before 1900. VALE was symbolic of Rutgers libraries' involvement in numerous state and national consortia for digitalization, faster sharing of materials, and collaborative purchasing.[34]

Technology changed the way the libraries looked. In 1997, Alexander got the fourth-floor SCC. The center combined a teleconference lecture hall, high-tech classrooms that could be used for distance-learning courses, and a resource center to help scholars create and utilize digital texts. Among its first projects was a collaborative effort to launch a "New Jersey Women's History" website. Another was to help the authors, Rudolph Bell of Rutgers and Martha Howell of Columbia, launch the "Medieval and Early Modern Database" website. The original database had been sponsored by the Research Libraries Group (RLG) and was initially available only on a CD-ROM. The website greatly facilitated the process of tracking prices across time in medieval Europe and converting the currencies of one jurisdiction into those of another. With each renovation or addition to the library's mortar-and-brick infrastructure, niches were carved out for technological upgrades in traditional services. In 2001, the John Cotton Dana Library at Newark, for example, began planning for a new center for instructional technologies, while Mabel Smith Douglass Library began an upgrade of its multimedia facility that would enhance support for both the arts and women's studies.

Building a Collection

As technology advanced, the traditional hallmarks of library rankings— collection size, books purchased, and the like—stagnated. Collecting, however, remained central to the teaching and research functions of the university system and to the roles of professional librarians. Developing the libraries' collections occupied the attention of a high percentage of the library's professional staff, but one way to explore this process is to look at Special Collections and other units within the library where "collecting" played a special role.

Donald Sinclair shaped the postwar development of Special Collections in New Brunswick. Sinclair had been a Rutgers student during the Great Depression and done graduate work at Columbia University before serving

in Army Military Intelligence during World War II. After the war, he returned to Rutgers, and Cameron appointed him curator of New Jerseyana,
and soon thereafter, curator of Special Collections.

In a typical year, Sinclair reported that he spent much of his time brows-
ing catalogs, talking to dealers, attending sales, visiting bookshops, and
writing letters (160 in 1947–1948) in search of New Jersey material the library lacked. Of particular import were New Jersey maps, newspapers, and
almanacs (by the mid-1950s, the library had acquired three thousand in a
quarter-century of collecting). Special Collections had newspapers microfilmed, and maps and books restored or preserved. Rare books and manuscripts often came in one gift at a time—in the late 1940s, for example,
two colonial New York property deeds, one in English and one in Dutch,
that contained the first-known use of the patronymic "Rutgers." That
same year, a rare edition of the first compilation of New Jersey laws from
1717 to 1722 had to be rebound, while the complete run (from 1813) of the
Elizabeth Journal, donated to the library by its current publisher, became
a candidate for microfilming. Each month the Voorhees Library would
feature an exhibit drawn from Special Collections. One, worthy of a *New
York Times* story, was of "ad cards" from the 1880s. These were commercial
trade cards, given away with purchases, and often issued in sequences that
told a story. Thus, cards distributed by the Great Atlantic and Pacific Tea
Company depicted the journey from saloon to jail of a drinker who would
clearly have been better off substituting tea for alcohol.

Special Collections, as a place, grew as the library did. The new 1956
library featured a New Jersey Room with a window looking out on a brick
replica of the state and a garden of native plants, shrubs, and vines. The
much-needed addition of 1993 to Alexander Library obliterated brick map
and garden, and put SC in the basement without the same commanding
window views. Similarly, SC marched to the technological beat of the recent past—perhaps, however, a half-step slower; it launched its first web-
page in 1995 (and now has most of its detailed finding aids available online), and mounted its first digital exhibit in 2011. None of this, to be sure,
detracted from its focus on collecting.

The appointment of the first university archivist in 1964 announced
the import of one form of collecting. By the mid-1990s, archivists were
collecting everything from the personal papers of the faculty, to student
yearbooks and newspapers, to official university correspondence (some
eight thousand cubic feet of material). They were also beginning to puzzle

about the best way to retrieve and preserve the digital records of the institution. This massive collection, in turn, served as the basis for graduate and undergraduate theses, scholarly articles on subjects such as student protest and coeducation at the men's college, and books that include archivist Thomas Frusciano's *Rutgers University Football Vault: The History of the Scarlet Knights* (2008) and university historian Richard P. McCormick's 1966 bicentennial history of the university and *The Black Student Protest Movement at Rutgers* (1990).

Special Collections also holds the Donald Sinclair New Jersey book collection, and Sinclair, working his entire career and well past his official retirement, crafted more than a dozen published guides to the holdings in the collection. One of those guides, *A Bibliography: The Civil War and New Jersey* (1968), superseded by a second Sinclair volume in 2003, cataloged a half-century of collecting Civil War journals, maps, letters from the battlefields, and reminiscences—in 2003, the description of these sources came to 696 pages. The Civil War manuscripts were, of course, only one part of a much larger manuscript collection, much of it concerning New Jersey, but also accessions, acquired through innumerable fortuitous channels, not related to state history. The manuscripts shared space with a rare book collection, with roots well before World War II but built up (to more than fifty thousand titles) far more systematically since that date.

In Camden, the library was initially designed to support undergraduate teaching, but as it developed collections to support graduate and professional education, it also built a distinctive set of research materials focused on the city itself. In the postwar era, Camden had changed from a midsize, thriving industrial city to one of the poorer communities in America, and Camden librarians set about collecting materials that would allow scholars to trace and explain the change. Librarians acquired materials with persistent enthusiasm and make-do methods—borrowing, photocopying, microfilming. Central to this collecting was the work of Tim Schiller, the business librarian. In the early 1970s, he began a clipping file from local newspapers about events in Camden. The clippings went into scrapbooks, and as the size and complexity of the collection grew, Schiller developed a citation index, later turned into a true database by the humanities librarian. That database, in turn, through collaboration with the Scholarly Communication Center, became the online CamdenBase. CamdenBase contained abstracts from several thousand stories in the *Camden Courier Post*; Rutgers users could get full-text articles from a separate newspaper database, while the general public could use the citations to find the articles in microfilmed copies of the paper. Alongside the database, the Robeson Library's special collections still held the scrapbooks themselves, as well as a wealth of other materials on Camden that librarians have tracked and scavenged over the years.

At Rutgers-Newark, the spotlight fell on the Institute of Jazz Studies, founded in the 1950s by Marshall Stearns (a jazz enthusiast and professor of medieval literature at Hunter College) and transferred to Rutgers in the mid-1960s. The institute built up an unrivaled collection of recordings—literally thousands of seventy-eight-rpm records—and manuscripts of the early jazz performers. Initially the institute made its home at Dana Library and sponsored concerts, which during its first year included performances at Carnegie Hall, the Newark Student Center, and Kirkpatrick Chapel in New Brunswick. The chapel concerts drew, stated its first annual report, "perhaps the most racially integrated student audiences ever seen at Rutgers."[35]

The institute moved to Bradley Hall, then in 1994, back to a renovated Dana Library as part of a new jazz/media complex. During much of this time, critic, author, editor of *Down Beat*, and annotator of record albums Dan Morganstern guided the institute's development and helped it build its collection. One of the great additions to the collection, in the male-dominated world of jazz performance, were Mary Lou Williams's personal papers, music scores, tapes, and videos. Williams, who began her career in the 1920s and died in 1981, had contributed not only to jazz but also to swing, blues, bebop, and boogie-woogie and composed religious work as well as secular music. Another addition was the Jazz Oral History Project, first compiled in the 1970s, maintained thereafter by the Smithsonian, and transferred to Rutgers in 1979. In 2002, the National Endowment for the Humanities awarded the institute more than a quarter of a million dollars to help preserve and extend the collection. An institute that served scholars and enthusiasts would also create the teaching foundation for a new master's program in jazz research. Even if most students, and most people more generally, accessed information in the twenty-first century through the Internet, the traditional art of collecting still mattered.

Epilogue

A story arc from circulation to access, a story of progress driven by technology—through it all, the role of librarians in locating, evaluating, and disseminating information has remained a constant. The Internet age, however, has posed new challenges: among them so much easily accessible information, much of it of uncertain provenance, and a good deal of it likely to vanish completely, as well as open-access policies to digitalized materials that frighten those associated with traditional print culture and raise challenging copyright problems. Librarians will have much to do educating and assisting patrons in the future.

For Prestige and Not for Profit: Rutgers University Press

While the commercial publisher is looking for a book that will sell, the institutional publisher seeks first of all a book that will endure and which may, in the long run, influence the course of human affairs.
—Earl Schenck Miers, director of Rutgers University Press, 1941[36]

In 1953, approaching its twentieth anniversary, Rutgers University Press ranked in terms of quality and the range of its publications in the top third of forty-five university presses. The presses of elite private schools—Yale, Harvard, Princeton—and the American wings of British publishers—Oxford and Cambridge—dominated the list, but among public schools (Rutgers was adapting to its new role as a public university in 1953), Rutgers's fledgling press stood alongside those at North Carolina, Oklahoma, Minnesota, and California. This was good company as universities entered an era when presses were seen as benchmarks of a school's academic prestige. At Rutgers, however, the foundation of academic publishing was anything but secure. The press was known widely for the Book-of-the-Month Club's adoption of *The Lincoln Reader* (1947), and the subsequent publication of the multivolume edition of Lincoln's collected works. Beyond that, neither its financial nor its scholarly direction was clear.

Rutgers founded its press in 1936. The original purpose was quite modest and specific—to publish faculty research and to contribute to knowledge of the state of New Jersey. The initial accomplishments were equally modest. The first imprint did not appear until 1938, virtually nothing was published during World War II, and through 1946, the press had issued only fifty-nine titles. Not until 1944 did it have a full-time director. Over the first postwar decade, in contrast, the press brought out about twenty titles a year, but except for its association with Lincoln, what the press published remained "random and haphazard."[37] Its best sellers, aside from its Lincoln books, were the *Artificial Insemination of Farm Animals* (which, of course, highlighted the research of Rutgers agricultural specialists), and *You Can Talk Well*, another practical how-to manual. Harold Munger Jr., the second full-time director of the press, told the *Sunday Times* in 1950, "We don't try to make money," and that the press's purpose was to publish "useful scholarly books," primarily, in Rutgers's case, on American history, American biography, and New Jerseyana.[38] A few years later, however, an outside evaluator criticized the lack of attention at the press to accepted accounting practices, as well as its publishing list that "seems to lack unity" and "gives the impression of a 'miscellany' without distinguishing characteristics."[39]

Typical of press publications in the early 1950s were four books authored by members of the Rutgers faculty who went on to distinguished careers: Henry Winkler's *The League of Nations Movement in Great Britain*; Moses Finley's *Studies in Land and Credit in Ancient Athens*; Richard Schlatter's *Private Property*; and Richard P. McCormick's *Experiment in Independence: New Jersey in the Critical Period, 1781–1789*. Winkler and Schlatter were scholars who were appointed to high-level administrative posts at Rutgers; Finley was fired during the McCarthy era, obtained a better position in Britain, and years later returned to Rutgers as an honored guest lecturer; while McCormick became a leading political historian, and, of course, the historian of the university itself. Each book was supported by a Rutgers Research Council grant to the author. Each cost more to produce than was returned in sales revenue during the first two years in print. *Experiment in Independence*, published in 1950 and with 532 copies sold by the summer of 1953, was the best seller of the group. By way of comparison, the nine-volume collected works of Lincoln, priced at $115, sold almost fourteen hundred copies in its first year in print, and generated revenue beyond costs for the press.

Three steps taken during the postwar period had long-term consequences for the press. In 1949, a committee recommended the establishment of what became the Rutgers University Press Council to review and approve all publications. The council was initially chaired by the provost, Mason W. Gross, and composed of faculty members, alumni, and figures from the publishing world. Second, in the mid-1950s, the university assumed the responsibility for the salaries of the professional staff of the press and agreed to a "permissible annual deficit" of $20,000 in the production of its publications. As helpful as having this assurance was to the press, the "permissible deficit" also embodied an enduring contradiction.

Most other units of the university dedicated to the production of knowledge were simply funded to that end; the press, in contrast, did not have a "university appropriation in aid of publication," but rather a "permissible deficit." The press was a business, yet something more than a business—and so it would remain.[40]

Third, in 1954, Gross convinced William Sloane to leave the publisher Funk & Wagnalls to direct the press. Sloane was a thin, urbane, pipe-smoking intellectual, a wonderful counterpart for Gross, with whom he exchanged letters frequently pondering not just publishing but the state of the humanities more generally. He had worked at Henry Holt (where he published the wartime reports of Ernie Pyle), run his own publishing enterprise (and published Theodore White's first book, *Thunder out of China),* and written two science fiction novels. For almost three decades, including his time at Rutgers, he taught in the summer at the Breadloaf Writers Conference in Middlebury College in Vermont. Sloane provided the press stability, remaining in the post for two decades, and his friendship with Gross (who even as president occasionally reviewed manuscripts for Sloane) cemented the press as central to the university's identity. Twice during his tenure as director, Sloane served as president of the Association of American University Presses—an indication of the status that Rutgers University Press had obtained.

Sloane died in 1974. Under his direction the press had published some exceptionally good scholarship, but each book had been coddled along through production with excessive attention from a large editorial staff. When Herbert F. Mann Jr. became the new director, the provost, Henry Winkler, told him to reduce costs (this was the early 1970s, and the Bloustein administration was dealing for the first time with serious budget problems) and speed up the production process. Mann reorganized the press. Senior editors were fired, copyediting contracted out, and the publication list expanded. As Mann told university officials, the press needed "editors who edit ten books a year, nor two or three; [and] sales and advertising people who will persuade institutions and individuals to buy our books, and [who have] a knowledge of the size of the relatively inelastic but easily identified market we are dealing with."[41]

Mann inherited two other significant changes in press policy. One was the beginning of paperback editions of hardcover books. This was considered a risky proposition in the 1970s for all but trade books because of the effect it might have on the sales of the hardcover edition. Second, the press gradually abandoned Linotype composition. (Initially, there were some dispiriting adventures with magnetic tape composition, then better results with offset lithography, and eventually computer typesetting.) With other university presses cutting back, Mann wanted to see Rutgers undertake a prudent expansion, especially in the fields of history, American and English literature, philosophy, and comparative literature, and become a nationally and even internationally more recognized publisher. Yet, at the same time, Mann acknowledged, the press had a responsibility, with help from the Research Council, to publish Rutgers authors, and a commitment to the state, as long as it could be done without significant losses, to publish books of local interest. The long-standing commitment to Rutgers authors, one of the original rationales for expanding the press, meant that the press continued to publish a somewhat eclectic list and face budgetary pressures.

The 1970s were difficult years for the university financially and for the press. Net sales—one benchmark of publishing—went down, and the annual list, which had been twenty to thirty books under Sloane, stayed about the same. In 1982, after Mann's resignation, serious thought was given to closing down the press, but instead, the university committed more money to it, and brought in a new director, Kenneth Arnold. Arnold, like Sloane, had a literary and publishing background. He was a playwright and poet, and had extensive experience at university presses, having last served as editor in chief at Temple University Press.

Unlike the 1970s, the 1980s would prove to be prosperous for both the university and the press. The book list expanded to about sixty titles (and approached seventy by the decade's end); in 1987, sales for the first time passed the symbolic million-dollar benchmark, thanks in part to three best sellers, *Wordsworth and the Age of English Romanticism, Black Athena*, and *The Lindbergh Case*. Film, anthropology, health and medicine, and the sciences more generally were added to the publications, while trade books—those designed for a general audience—took precedence over academic titles.

The press continued to acquire a broad range of manuscripts, but not because the press did not try to launch more tightly focused publishing ventures. Excursions into the hard sciences, launched with *Vertebrate Fetal Membranes*, did not find the anticipated market, and five years of trying to market fiction and poetry titles also resulted in disappointment. One very successful humor book, *Einstein Simplified: Cartoons on Science*, did not lead to others. An ambitious project to create a family life kit of a flipbook, teacher's manual, and workbooks for New Jersey schools ended up with few sold and most of the materials stored in a warehouse. Prosperity, then, allowed for failed experiments, but did not deflect the primary emphasis of the press on a (shrinking) list of scholarly titles, Jerseyana, and trade books. Books by Rutgers faculty became the exception—perhaps one in fifteen publications—rather than one of the key purposes of the press. And by the end of the 1980s, prosperity was over.

The early 1990s were a period of adversity, uncertainty, and austerity not only for Rutgers but for university presses more generally. As Arnold explained, in better days, he would have published six thousand copies of *Prime*

Representative and Distinctive Titles from More Than Four Thousand Books Published by Rutgers University Press since 1938

1938 *James Madison: Philosopher of the Constitution*, by Edward McNeil Burns

1946 *The Lincoln Reader*, edited by Paul Angle

1953 *The Collected Works of Abraham Lincoln*, edited by Roy P. Basler

1959 *Camus*, by Germaine Brée

1967 *William Troy: Selected Essays*, edited by Stanley Edgar Hyman

1974 *The Ramapo Mountain People*, by David Steven Cohen

1986 *Quicksand* and *Passing*, by Nella Larson; edited and with an introduction by Deborah McDowell, inaugurating the American Women Writers series

1987 *New Jersey, A Guide to the State*, by Barbara Westergaard

1987 *Black Athena: The Afroasiatic Roots of Classical Civilization*, vol. 1: *The Fabrication of Ancient Greece, 1785–1985*, by Martin Bernal

1988 *Strangers in the Land: Patterns of American Nativism, 1860–1925*, by John Higham

1990 *The Black Student Protest Movement at Rutgers*, by Richard P. McCormick

1993 *Gender Play: Girls and Boys in School*, by Barrie Thorne

1996 *Jersey Diners*, by Peter Genovese

1996 *A Naturalist along the Jersey Shore*, by Joanna Burger

1999 *Twin Towers: The Life of New York City's World Trade Center*, by Angus K. Gillespie

2004 *Encyclopedia of New Jersey*, edited by Maxine N. Lurie and Marc Mappen

2009 *500 Years of Chicana Women's History / 500 Años de la Mujer Chicana*, by Elizabeth "Betita" Martínez

2009 *Mapping New Jersey: An Evolving Landscape*, edited by Maxine N. Lurie and Peter Wacker, cartography by Michael Siegel

Time and Misdemeanors, a scholarly book with good prospects in the trade market on the game-show scandals of the 1950s, but with demand down, he had to cut the print run to four thousand, and, he speculated, he should have cut it to three thousand (by the end of the 1990s, even three thousand would be optimistic). An initial effort at electronic publishing, "floppybacks," went nowhere, and efforts to become the distributor of scholarly journals failed.

In 1995, Marlie Wasserman took over as director of the press. She was the eighth person to hold the position and the first woman. She had been at the press since 1978, except for a short period when she worked in New York with a commercial academic publisher. During her tenure, she served, as had Sloane, as president of the Association of American University Presses. She took charge as net sales climbed to more than $2 million a year, but also at a time when the Internet and electronic publishing were radically challenging traditional print culture, when library purchases and individual buying were evaporating, and when the press was still orphaned in facilities so shabby that it embarrassed staff to meet prospective authors on site. She tackled these problems with enthusiasm. She believed strongly in the "enduring value of the book." "Everybody thought radio would be dead," she stated. "But radio is alive and has taken on all kinds of new life. I believe we live in a world of parallel media."[42] Survival, however, required the press, even more than in the past, to publish books that had appeal to a general reading audience. "Our mission is to disseminate knowledge in the broadest sense, and that doesn't just mean knowledge from one chaired professor to another chaired professor."[43]

The press launched its "Rivergate" series to improve the marketing of books about New Jersey, while at the same time defining its regional works to encompass New York and Pennsylvania as well as New Jersey. It switched from standard first-runs of fifteen hundred to two thousand copies of new books to reduced runs coupled with "print on demand" publishing, with corresponding savings in cost. Wasserman coauthored a successful grant effort to the Andrew W. Mellon Foundation to begin a collaborative e-book project, and e-books became the companion of traditional publications. Finally, in 2012, the university provided the press with handsome new offices above the university Barnes & Noble bookstore in the Gateway building, connected by a walkway to the New Brunswick train station. Along with these changes came the success of perhaps the most ambitious project at least since the days of *The Collected Works of Abraham Lincoln*.

The *Encyclopedia of New Jersey*, published in 2004, found its way onto coffee tables, onto the shelves of scholastic libraries, and into the hands of scholars. The initial printing sold out. After reprinting, a total of eighteen thousand copies were sold. A massive project—almost a thousand pages, weighing about seven pounds—it included three thousand entries written by eight hundred scholars. The press raised more than a million dollars to finance the project, and a team of thirty experts on New Jersey sifted through potential topics and authors. Its editors, Maxine Lurie and Marc Mappen, were both scholars of New Jersey history, and the volume, as well as its 2009 companion, *Mapping New Jersey*, benefited from high-quality cartography by Michael Siegel. Entries ranged from lengthy ones, such as the essay on the economy by James W. Hughes and Joseph Seneca of the Rutgers Edward J. Bloustein School of Public Planning and Policy; to a three-paragraph entry on Bruce Springsteen (a living person had to be *truly* well-known to warrant an entry) by Joseph V. Hamburger, a writer on popular music; to Peter Genovese's succinct discussion of cloverleafs, New Jersey's contribution to "solving" the problems of highway congestion. While perhaps a third of the authors were drawn from the Rutgers faculty, many others had a Rutgers affiliation, marking the volume as a unique contribution by the university community to the state. The two projects, however, also pointed to the twenty-first-century problems besetting university presses. Both would have benefited from online versions, with more color illustrations and updated entries, but without funding support, such ventures were simply not commercially viable.

When Wasserman became director, the press was publishing about sixty-five books a year and had net sales of about $2.5 million; nationwide, there were about a hundred university presses that collectively published perhaps eight thousand books annually. Two decades later, Rutgers University Press remained in approximately the same position—in the middle of the university publishing ranks, but one of the leaders among public universities. The largest presses were at elite private universities, and the recognition that they were integral to the reputation of their institutions was backed by significant endowments. Smaller, successful presses made their mark by exploiting specific markets. Kansas, with a list of perhaps fifty books a year, for example, ran highly successful, specialized series in military and constitutional history, in addition to featuring regional publications. The University of North Carolina Press was at the other end of the spectrum among public university presses. It had a list of some hundred books a year, and with a direct state subsidy; the press could specialize in multiple fields and publish more monographs than smaller presses could afford to gamble on.[44]

For each of these presses, however, the changing world of book publication poses problems that go well beyond the presses themselves: university presses have long been "gatekeepers" for the evaluation and dissemination of knowledge, especially in the humanities and social sciences. As this role changes, the very nature of the university itself will have to change.

Art at Rutgers: Museums and Galleries

In 1959, Mason Gross addressed New Jersey political leaders who had, more than a decade previously, met at Rutgers to draft a new state constitution. That task accomplished, he told them bluntly, greater challenges lay ahead: "Let's face it—if New Jersey is educationally impoverished and in debt, she is culturally almost bankrupt. . . . [T]here is no legitimate theater, and even very little popular theater except for summer re-runs; there is absolutely no opera and no ballet; most of the efforts at symphonic music fall far short of professional standards, and there is no effort at publicly supported chamber music. Exhibitions of first quality painting or sculpture are at a minimum, and even local shows designed to encourage genuine developing talent are few and far between."[45]

The situation at Rutgers was not much better. Rutgers had a symphony series featuring outstanding touring orchestras; the events calendar listed numerous chamber music and vocal recitals each semester; and student organizations on each campus offered a variety of theatrical productions. The glee club in New Brunswick attracted student participants and large audiences. The university had solid programs in music, theater, and the visual arts, but there was, however, no art museum at the university and no opera, and much of the attention of the fine arts programs was directed toward training undergraduates for high school teaching. This would change in the mid-1970s with the creation of a new school for the arts in New Brunswick—what became the Mason Gross School of the Arts. The existing programs in dance, theater, music, and the visual arts were not only brought together and their professional aspirations raised, but the university created new art centers and theaters on each of the three campuses to enhance the cultural life of the entire university and the surrounding communities.

One of the most crucial steps taken to meet Gross's challenge to the state and university to erase the "cultural desert" in New Jersey was taken by Gross himself and then furthered by Edward Bloustein: the establishment of art museums, the most prominent of which would be the Rutgers Art Gallery (renamed the Zimmerli Art Museum). It is to that story that I now turn.

The lineage of the university art museum reaches back to the creation of the Ashmolean at Oxford University in 1683, built from Elias Ashmole's gift of his "Cabinet of Curiosities." The Ashmolean and the American college museums that followed in the nineteenth century mixed art works with objects of natural history and created collections dependent on gifts but geared to the teaching interests of the faculty. In 1831, Yale established the first true American university art museum; Vassar in 1863 is usually credited with being the second. In the late nineteenth century, wealthy industrial leaders helped erect the first great public art museums in America, including the Metropolitan Museum in New York and the Fine Arts Museum in Boston. In the wake of this museum movement, many colleges and universities built their own (Princeton in 1882, was typical). Not, however, Rutgers College. The college neither had a gallery to display the artworks it collected from benefactors and alumni, nor did it teach art history on a regular basis. That situation would not change until the 1960s with the presidency of Mason Gross and with new commitments to the fine arts by both the state of New Jersey and the federal government.

In 1966, William Sloane, the director of Rutgers University Press, wrote to university officials that "Rutgers, the State University, in regard to the arts . . . is so deficient as to constitute a nearly fatal weakness in our position as an institution of higher learning." There were no plans for catching up, no faculty committed to the goal, no hope of matching the money pouring into the sciences. "Rutgers is not now, and never will be in our lifetime," Sloane continued pessimistically, "in a position to duplicate or imitate present art structures of other institutions of higher learning."[46] Yet, more optimistically, he continued, with imagination and dedication, even in advance of money, it could set out to do something new and innovative. Mason Gross, of course, had said much the same thing about New Jersey. A very modest beginning at correcting that situation had, in fact, begun several years earlier when the Board of Governors approved the remodeling of what had been the ivy-covered Voorhees Library for an art gallery on the New Brunswick campus.

Completed in 1966, the University Art Gallery opened officially at a ceremony January 10, 1967. The building had been thoroughly renovated at a cost of more than $600,000, with a two-story exhibition space, faculty offices (for the art [history] department), classrooms, a new lecture hall, stone facing where windows had once been, and a facade shorn of foliage. The first curator was a graduate student, Richard J. Wattenmaker, completing a dissertation on the American painter, William Glackens, and Glackens's works borrowed from art museums in Princeton, Newark, and New York as well as private collectors, were the subject of the first exhibition at the new gallery. Wattenmaker called it "the most important show in Rutgers history," and he pointed to a future of "modest, quality exhibits."[47] The second curator, Marian Burleigh Motley, hired in 1969, also a graduate student, quit half a year later, explaining that it was impossible to run the gallery without additional curatorial staff, more space for a growing collection, better facilities for the graduate students and faculty studying the holdings, and ultimately, a new building.

At that point, Rutgers turned to Phillip Dennis Cate. Cate had graduated from Rutgers in 1967 with a fine arts degree. He had been a Henry Rutgers Scholar, and as an undergraduate intern he had helped catalog the university's collection of paintings and sculpture. In June 1970, he completed a master's in art history at Arizona State University and then moved to Philadelphia, where he taught art history on a part-time basis. When he submitted his *vitae* for a position at Rutgers, it listed, among his relevant experience, a bicycle trip across Europe that he had made after college graduation. At that point the art gallery faced a crisis. It had only two rooms to showcase its holdings, no storage space for new works, and no way to mount "those frequently varied small exhibitions which could [draw in] the general public as well as students and faculty."[48] Starting almost from scratch, Cate would spend the next thirty years giving the gallery the artistic direction and finding the financial support to turn it into one of the better university art museums in the nation.

Cate had arrived at the right place at the right time. A century after the initial museum movement, the arts were again a center of public attention and public policy. Concerns expressed in the 1960s about the miserable state of arts education at Rutgers had brought positive responses. Rutgers was constructing a new performing and fine arts building at Douglass College and applying to the state to become a center for the arts. At the federal level, the creation of the National Endowment for the Arts and the National Endowment for the Humanities opened new funding possibilities.

Cate's immediate predecessors had tried to extend the breadth of the holdings, filling in gaps in what had been a haphazard history of collection, to better serve Rutgers art students as well as to help with outreach and public education. Cate pointed the gallery in a different direction. Cate (and the gallery) were little fishes in a big pond, but therein lay the opportunity for the gallery to define its own niche and create a distinctive identity. It began with an emphasis on nineteenth-century French prints (Cate's field as a student), other areas being added over the years as fundraising made it possible. Donors not only helped expand the collection, but also enlarge and modernize the gallery itself. A museum that had two full-time staff members and a $35,000 budget in 1970, when Cate arrived, had at the time of its first external review, in 1987, a dozen full-time employees, a three-quarters-of-a-million-dollar budget, some thirty thousand paintings and other art objects, and its exhibition spaced had increased sixfold.

In 1973, Cate held his first major exhibition, *The Ruckus World of Red Grooms*. The exhibit drew more than twenty thousand people to the gallery in a two-week period and resulted in the publication of the first of many exhibition catalogs. Grooms, a thirty-six-year-old New York–based pop artist (but as the *New York Times* said, in "a school by himself"), and Cate put together an exhibition of two dozen multimedia works—"the most diverting art exhibition . . . very possibly in the entire metropolitan area."[49] It was an exhibition, another critic noted, that the Museum of Modern Art or the Whitney would have held "if the curators at those institutions had the first idea of what art is all about."[50] Visitors were greeted by a fifteen-foot figure of an astronaut, "realistically rendered but with delightfully whimsical exaggerated and fanciful detail." One gallery was filled by Grooms's tribute to the city of Chicago: "The visitor enters it through a 'historical arch,' which is decorated by cut-out figures of famous Chicagoans. Among them are Lincoln and Douglas debating, Cyrus McCormick, the reaper manufacturer, Al Capone, Sally Rand, the fan dancer, and Mrs. O'Leary with her cow. A 12-minute sound track blares appropriate music and sound effects—burlesque music for Sally, gun fire for Capone."[51]

The exhibition had made a splash and caught the attention of the New York art world. It also caught the attention of other art galleries. In 1975, Cate received an unsolicited offer for a better-paid position as curator at a San Francisco museum. After a meeting with Vice President Henry R.

Winkler, Cate got a salary increase, the assignment of a new full-time assistant curator, and, most important, President Bloustein's commitment to make fund-raising for an expansion of the gallery a priority of the Rutgers Foundation. Bloustein and Winkler both made it clear, however, that if expansion were to occur, the money would have to be raised from donors. Two other steps taken by Cate thus mattered a great deal. In 1973, he established Friends of the Art Gallery, to raise money for the acquisition of new works. Initially the friends' contributions were modest, but over time they raised substantial amounts. In 1975, a faculty advisory committee for the gallery was established, and, more significant, in 1979, a committee consisting of art collectors, major donors to the university, and artists was created to advise Cate on collection development. In fact, the committee was designed to give those most likely to contribute to the gallery a vested interest in its future. (Today, these have become a board of overseers and a membership program.) Cate also negotiated with more than a dozen print-making studios in New York an arrangement under which each print shop donated to the gallery a copy of each print to become part of the "Rutgers archives of printmaking studios"—a major addition to the print collection at little cost.

Meanwhile, alongside a regular exhibition program, the gallery hosted another pathbreaking exhibit. In 1975, it cosponsored with the Cleveland Museum of Art and the Walter Art Gallery in Baltimore the first major exhibit in the United States of *japonisme* (works illustrating the influence of Japan on Western art), and Cate would contribute the essay in the exhibition catalog on the incorporation of Japanese themes in late-nineteenth-century French prints. Cate's father had been "born in Japan, his grandfather had served as a missionary, and his grandmother helped introduce Shakespeare's works" to Japan—so Cate drew on both his scholarly interest in French art and his personal relationship to Japan in defining one of the initial forays into collecting and exhibitions.[52] Cate, however, had help. Not only did three museums combine their collections, but the curators were drawn from the Rutgers Art History Department as well. Collaboration between the staffs of university art museums and the faculty of art history programs did not always go smoothly, at Rutgers and elsewhere. Curators often complained that they were undervalued and underutilized by their tenured colleagues, but while that was occasionally a problem at Rutgers, on the whole the strong reputation and high quality of the exhibition program was built around a partnership to which both contributed.

These features—traveling exhibits built using loaned pieces and drawing on the talents of multiple curators—had by the 1970s become very much a part of the art world. "Blockbuster exhibitions"—as shows at major museums were now routinely labeled—replaced the emphasis on permanent exhibits and unique holdings of particular museums. For university galleries, this trend also meant an increasing emphasis on the museum as a public space, as opposed to a primary focus on research and teaching. Subsequent exhibits, such as *Circa 1800: The Beginning of Modern Printmaking* in 1980 and *The Circle of Toulouse-Lautrec* in 1985, helped solidify the gallery's reputation as a center for print collections. Equally important was Cate's ability to attract National Endowment for the Humanities funding, which, for example, in 1979 underwrote *Vanguard American Sculpture, 1913–1919*, an exhibit that incorporated works from the famous 1913 New York Armory show.

The ambitious exhibition program and greater attention to donors and fund-raising went hand in hand with capital construction. In 1979, with a gift of $1.5 million, the university launched a $3 million expansion of the gallery and in 1981 renamed the building the Jane Voorhees Zimmerli Art Museum. The museum, no longer merely an art gallery, reopened at a gala celebration in February 1983. The celebration coincided with a new exhibit, *Haarlem: The Seventeenth Century*, organized by a recent Rutgers art history Ph.D., and meant to memorialize the university's long relationship with the Netherlands and to be a tribute to the Voorhees family. John Russell, writing in the *New York Times*, praised both the "distinctive and unpretentious" new galleries and extolled the way the exhibit recaptured a golden age of art and culture in the Netherlands, where, for "anyone who liked to read, to hear good talk and to look at beautiful pictures Haarlem between the 1620s and the 1670s was one of the best places to be."[53]

A second gift in 1986 allowed the renovation of Ballantine Hall and the addition of the Carl W. and Nettie C. Holstrom Gallery—both gifts came from families long associated with Rutgers. (The swimming pool, dating to the days when Ballantine Hall had been the college gymnasium, remained in the basement of the new art museum, used now for storage.) The next year, Cate announced the opening of a new center devoted to the study of the Japanese influence on the West from the Meiji period (1868–1912) forward. The center built on the existing print collection (as Japanese culture had particularly shaped French printmaking). It also strengthened a focus of the collection that dated back to the 1975 exhibition, and reinforced Rutgers's long-standing relationship with Japanese educational institutions. Subsequently, in a 1997 exhibit curated by Jeffrey Wechsler, the museum displayed works that blended Asian styles and European abstract expression by American artists of Chinese, Japanese, and Korean descent.

If the Zimmerli built its reputation initially on its collection of nine-teenth- and twentieth-century British and French prints, modern American prints, and children's books, its greatest achievement was Cate's acquisition of unique collections of Russian and Soviet art. In 1989, Cate met George Riabov, a Russian-born, Polish émigré and Rutgers graduate (RC '51). Riabov owned an unparalleled collection of "icons, nineteenth-century paintings, posters from the Russian Revolution, and costume and stage designs," objects dating from the sixteenth to the twentieth centu-ries.[54] Not only did Riabov donate his collection to the Zimmerli, but he also put Cate in touch with Norton Dodge. Dodge, a retired economics professor from St. Mary's College in Annapolis, had first gone to the Soviet Union in 1956, just as its new leader, Nikita Khrushchev, was announc-ing the lifting of some of the artistic restrictions of the previous Stalinist era. During the thaw that followed and then the return of more repres-sive policies in the Soviet Union, Dodge collected representative pieces of underground Soviet art, some subtly, some overtly critical of the Soviet re-gime. When in the late 1970s, Dodge's activities closed the door on return visits, he continued to collect through a network of contacts. Dodge stored his collection—by the 1990s, ten thousand objects, ranging from posters to photographs, paintings, and sculpture—in barns on his Maryland farm, and Cate convinced him to transfer the collection to the Zimmerli.

The Zimmerli thus established itself in the fields of Russian and dis-sident Soviet art at just the moment the Soviet Union was disintegrating and communism was losing its political grip on Russian society. Cate used the occasion of the twentieth-fifth-anniversary celebration in 1991 of the Zimmerli to display works from the Riabov and Dodge collections, and two years later, the Zimmerli opened a permanent gallery for works from its George Riabov collection. Riabov's holdings of children's books comple-mented the American collection the Zimmerli had been building for more than a decade, and these were the basis for a separate exhibit. Two years later, in 1995, Cate organized the first of many exhibits from the Dodge collection. The 1995 show, *From Gulag to Glasnost: Non-Conformist Art from the Soviet Union*, introduced the public to a sampling of about three hundred pieces from the massive collection. One striking example was a

32. Viacheslav Sysoev (Russian, 1937–2006), *Human Rights*, 1978. Gouache and ink on paper, 21.5 × 30.2 cm. Sysoev began using art in the mid-1970s to criticize the Soviet Union. He was driven underground and eventually arrested and jailed. Albums of his work first appeared in print in France in the early 1980s; later work on the Chernobyl nuclear disaster was published in the Soviet Union. In 1989, Sysoev moved to Germany. This work was among the many examples of Soviet dissident art collected by Norton Dodge and donated to the Zimmerli Art Museum.

PHOTOGRAPH BY Jack Abraham. SOURCE: Zimmerli Art Museum at Rutgers University, the Norton and Nancy Dodge Collection of Nonconformist Art from the Soviet Union. 1991.0870/06904.

recreated Soviet-era apartment hung with small artworks—a representation of an art world where dissidents gathered in apartments to view each other's work, and pictures could be quickly and easily hidden. With these two exhibits, and the collections they represented, Rutgers and the Zimmerli had become, almost overnight, a worldwide center for the study of Russian and Soviet art and culture. What followed was yet another expansion and remodeling of the museum, completed in 2000 at a cost of $5 million, for a collection that now numbered sixty thousand works of art.

The expansion allowed both permanent (upstairs) and temporary exhibits (downstairs) to be drawn from the Dodge collection, but the remodeled building was ushered in as well with a retrospective exhibit of the work of Michael Mazur, a pioneer in printmaking—thus reinforcing one of the traditional collecting fields of the museum. A decade later, the museum added an additional element to its print collection. In the 1970s, Judith Brodsky, then a professor in the Art Department at Douglass, had interviewed June Wayne, a California printmaker, for an article she planned on women printmakers. Wayne's Tamarind Lithography Workshop, established in 1959, had "reinvigorated American printmaking in the 1960s."[55] Her documentary on printmaking, *Four Stones for Kanemitsu*, had been nominated in 1974 for an Academy Award. Wayne had spoken out in the 1950s against McCarthyism, she had long championed government support for the arts, and she was a leader in the women's movement in the arts. Brodsky's interview led to a lifetime friendship, while Brodsky's own work in printmaking led to the establishment in 1986 of the Rutgers Center for Innovative Print and Paper (in the Mason Gross School of the Arts). In 2002, Wayne donated more than three thousand works of art (by herself and more than a hundred other artists) to the Mason Gross School of the Arts.

Cate spent part of 2001–2002 on a sabbatical research leave and purchasing expedition in France. On his return, and after thirty-two years as director, he abruptly stepped down, to be replaced by Gregory J. Perry, the associate director, who had come to the museum from the Art Institute of Chicago. The museum that Cate left behind ran more than a dozen exhibitions a year, acquired several million dollars' worth of new works through purchases and donations annually, competed successfully for state and federal grants, and lent works internationally to other museums. It was also a museum hit by the same state funding cuts as other branches of the university and thus one that had to eliminate staff positions to minimize operating losses; and while it received generous private support, much of that money was restricted to use for the Dodge Collection.

Under Perry, the exhibition program was somewhat more restricted but still highlighted the major strengths of the Zimmerli. Typical was the exhibit of Soviet nonconformist photography, curated by Diane Neumaier, a professor of photography at the Mason Gross School. Neumaier had begun visiting Russia as a graduate student in 1991 and returned numerous times. She worked for seven years with Dodge and Alla Rosenfeld, the Dodge collection curator, to mount an exhibit juxtaposing photographs of everyday life and official Soviet photography. If the photography exhibit linked the Zimmerli with its past, specifically the premier 1995 Dodge exhibit, then the 2012 exhibit, *"Le Mur" at the Cabaret des Quat'z'Arts*, reprised, as the museum had done in 1985, 1996, and in 2006, works from Montmartre. This time the focus was on a group of young artists who frequented the cabaret and posted their drawings and writings, satirical and comical, on "Le Mur" (the Wall).

Suzanne Delahanty, the founding director of the Miami Art Museum, became director in 2008–2009. She came to the Zimmerli well prepared. In 1978, she had served as an outside consultant for an evaluation of the Rutgers museums. The museum she inherited was regularly mounting ten new exhibitions a year, employing three dozen staff members, and training two dozen volunteers to lead visitors on tours. It faced the challenge, as did the fine arts more generally, of balancing its budget, as both state and private funding became more problematic. Where the art gallery had been one of the few high-quality small museums in New Jersey in the 1970s, over time, because of generous funding for the arts in the 1970s and much of the 1980s, the competition for the attention of the museum-going public had intensified. Cutbacks in print journalism posed new challenges in converting reputation into attention from patrons and visitors. With a collection almost too large for storage, the primary challenge was not to acquire new works, but to modernize the building, conserve the works already in the collection, and sell some works not central to plans for exhibitions. For most museums, including the Zimmerli, the future also meant attracting new audiences by strengthening their "digital footprints." More generally, the future would involve returning to the museum's roots as a teaching and outreach institution—a mission central to the university's smaller galleries as well.

And what about these other galleries? In 1980, Judith Brodsky, then a professor at Rutgers-Newark, wrote to President Bloustein about the plight of the newly opened Robeson Center Gallery. The gallery, located in the Robeson Campus Center, had just run its first major exhibit—*New Deal Art: New Jersey*—and had won glowing reviews in the local press and the *New York Times*. Financially, however, the gallery was entirely dependent on campus center funding (and the vicissitudes of the student politics that allocated the funds). If the curator's part-time salary of $2,800, Brodsky wrote, could be picked up by the university, then at least there would be a little money to build a collection. Over the past decade, the university had frequently assisted the New Brunswick gallery with matching funds for external grants and with new staff positions, but the administration had no extra money for the fine arts at Newark. Newark eventually got permanent gallery space, and in the twenty-first century, imaginatively rotated art-works between its gallery, the library, and the molecular and behavioral neuroscience center.

At the time of the Brodsky-Bloustein exchange, the university had just completed its first external review of its diverse museums and galleries. One was the Geology Museum—"a gem of traditional museum architecture"—and another a massive collection of historical farm implements (which never found a permanent home).[56] The remainder, however, were art galleries: two at Douglass, one in Walters Hall, used by the art department, the other at the Douglass Library; an "unattractive" downtown New Brunswick gallery that served as a venue for the work of Mason Gross students and faculty; the newly conceived Robeson Gallery at Newark; and the Stedman Art Gallery in Camden.[57] The university supplied the Stedman, the largest of these galleries, with an operating budget of just over $3,000 (endowments and fund-raising increased the budget to about $14,000); in comparison, the art gallery in New Brunswick had an operating budget of about $80,000. The New Brunswick art gallery was large enough to attract the attention of significant donors and small enough that a donor's contribution brought the donor and the gallery recognition. Smaller venues did not have these advantages, and with tight university budgets, their development depended in large measure on competitive public funding.

All these museums developed as teaching museums, tied to art, art history, or museum studies programs, and all placed major emphasis on community outreach. The Mason Gross School of the Arts acquired a new gallery in a new building in 1996, and while it remained primarily a teaching gallery, its curators also staged exhibits that attracted critical reviews and broad audiences. The gallery was renovated yet again in 2003 for the opening of the *Critical Mass* exhibit, on Fluxus—an art movement "that everyone's heard of, but nobody really understands."[58] Fluxus combined "humorous, iconoclastic performances, happenings and public spectacles," and many of its practitioners were associated with Rutgers (most prominently Geoffrey Hendricks). The exhibit recaptured a period in American art when, as *New York Times* said, "New Brunswick Was Where It Was Happening."[59]

In 1971, the small art gallery in the Mable Smith Douglass Library began a series of exhibits of the work of women artists. Lynn F. Miller, a newly hired reference librarian, concerned with "the struggle women artists" had gaining recognition in the "male-dominated art world," initiated the effort.[60] In its first decade, the series featured works of some 150 artists and remains today, under the auspices of the library and the Institute of Women and Art (in which, once again, Judith Brodsky played a key role), the longest running series in the nation devoted specifically to women artists.

Outside New Brunswick, however, it was the Stedman Gallery in Camden that stood out. An initial bequest in 1968 from A. Weir Stedman, a south Jersey businessman, in honor of his mother, an artist, led to the gallery's opening in 1975 as part of the new fine arts building on the Camden campus. More than three decades of continuous leadership from Virginia Oberlin Steel as curator gave the Stedman focus, and a relatively large exhibition space (about 2,400 square feet) made a trip to the campus worthwhile for an off-campus audience.

The Stedman hosted many small-scale exhibits of nationally known artists, including, for example, in 1980, an exhibition of Dorothea Lange photography. The distinctive qualities of the Stedman, however, lay elsewhere. Over the initial decades, it ran two sets of juried exhibitions, one in conjunction with Camden County featuring local artists and a biennial "Works on/of Paper." By the 1990s, "Works" attracted several thousand submissions from virtually every state and had the support of distinguished jurors who had to whittle down the submissions to a couple of dozens chosen for display. Many of the half-dozen exhibitions the gallery staged annually featured local artists or the works of the Camden faculty and students. The 1996 exhibition, for example, *Moving through Memory: Caribbean Folk Arts in New Jersey*, re-created the culture and art of south Jersey residents from the Caribbean. Other exhibits, such as the 2013, *Visions of Camden*, highlighted local themes in the work of national artists.

Equally crucial, especially in attracting funding, was the extensive outreach the gallery undertook with local schools and the Camden community. In 1987, the gallery began an ongoing museum enrichment program that served several thousand students annually. "Mathematical Visions," which went through several iterations over the years, helped students link visual arts with mathematical reasoning. One of the most innovative undertakings was the CLICK! project (Camden Life Interpreted by Camden Kids). During a summer in the late 1990s, some eight hundred children from summer camps and community organizations were given twelve-exposure cameras and guided around the city to picture their neighborhoods, looking, as one ten-year-old recounted, for "trash on the floor, so everyone knows this has to stop" but also for "kids having fun." [61] Another venture was the development of a museum studies curriculum that by the 1980s had become an undergraduate major taught by the museum staff, and which placed student interns in many local museums.

Much of what the Stedman initially accomplished was made possible during the 1980s by generous state funding from the New Jersey Council for the Arts. Belt tightening, thereafter, became the rule of the day. The 1994 external reviewers were shocked by "the extraordinarily low percentage" (one-third) of support the Stedman received directly from the university, and in the wake of the report, money was allocated to much-needed renovation of the gallery. University art museums, the external reviewers reflected, emphasize either scholarship or community service, and the Stedman, with its small permanent collection (about four hundred objects), limited budget, and deeply committed staff, had made the correct choice in creating a gallery that was a unique resource for both the university and the city of Camden. In the new century, the gallery, along with the six-hundred-seat Gordon Theater, became part of a better-funded center for the arts, which along with the Walt Whitman Arts Center, led a *Philadelphia Inquirer* writer to conclude that a quiet "cultural revolution" had taken place in south Jersey.[62]

Epilogue

In 2014, on the last Saturday of April, the university held "Rutgers Day" on its New Brunswick/Piscataway campuses. More than eighty thousand people attended the event, described as a celebration of the university and the state. They were treated to parades with floats and marching bands, games, a puppet show, jujitsu demonstrations, a greenhouse exhibit of poisonous plants, an egg toss at Passion Puddle on the Douglass campus, examples of outreach activity by many campus organizations, free health screenings from Rutgers's new medical school, and an enormous variety of food from vendors. The event was billed the "sixth annual" Rutgers Day, but it incorporated two far more venerable spring traditions: Ag Field Day and the New Jersey Folk Festival. Ag Field Day, begun in 1906 as a way to bring farmers to campus, became a celebration of New Jersey agriculture for the state's increasingly urban and suburban population; today, visitors can still view farm animals, but the event focuses primarily on agricultural research and outreach on the Cook campus. Angus Gillespie, a professor in the Douglass American Studies Department, launched the folk festival in 1974. Initially, he thought of the festival as a one-time event, part of a "year of the arts" on the campus to celebrate the construction of a new complex of theaters and performance spaces. Financed with $1,300 of seed money and the sale of hot dogs, T-shirts, and beer, the festival was so successful that Gillespie made it an annual, and largely student-run, event. Along with athletics and the arts, Rutgers Day has helped attract people to the university campuses and made Rutgers a significant place in the lives of the state's residents.

9

Women's Basketball

In 1974, Rutgers hired Rita Kay Thomas to oversee women's athletics in New Brunswick. Born in the Midwest and encouraged by her parents to pursue her athletic interests, she played three different styles of basketball, with three different set of rules during her college years (women's, men's, and international), and graduated with a degree in physical education. Soon after the passage of Title IX (1972), Thomas applied for the newly created position at Rutgers of director of women's athletics. (At that time, there was no parallel position of director of men's athletics, but rather an overall athletic director to whom Thomas reported.) One of Thomas's first responsibilities—in a story that captures the situation in mid-1970s—was to assure that the hand-me-down locker room women athletes were assigned in the College Avenue gymnasium was painted and refurbished. She got the money but found that even more was then given to refurbish the much larger men's locker room area, and that while the men got new benches, the women had to sit on the floor while changing. There was, however, a passageway below the gymnasium pool that connected the two locker rooms; thanks to a little ingenuity, some of the new men's benches made their way to the women's locker room.

For Thomas and for women student athletes at Rutgers, recognition and support have been a long struggle, but success on the field and court has matched that of their male counterparts. Of the women's sports programs, none has caught the public imagination more than basketball, and no

33. Newark cheerleaders, 1953–1954. At various times cheerleading was listed as a sport for women, and in New Brunswick, occasionally became a matter of controversy when Douglass women joined the male squad at the men's colleges for football games. The Newark cheerleaders, who in some years included men, attended the men's basketball games. Newark was the first Rutgers school to have an African American cheerleader, a year before this picture was taken. SOURCE: R-Photo, athletics, and *Encore 1954*, 128.

other better exemplifies the expanding athletic opportunities for women as student athletes and as coaches at New Jersey's state university. In the immediate postwar era, however, little of the story of women's basketball at Rutgers could have been predicted. Initially there were very few opportunities for women in competitive sports, and the door that was first opened in the late 1950s is now largely forgotten. This chapter recaptures that early history and then brings the story up to date.

In the 1950s, women and men at Rutgers shared campuses and classrooms in Newark and Camden, but not common athletic programs. Newark provided little in the way of physical education for women, and the College of South Jersey ran its small program for women in a rented YMCA building. There were no opportunities for women's intercollegiate play and even by the mid-1960s, no place for women in Camden intramurals except for bowling. (A few women were also cheerleaders for the basketball team; at season's end, the men received school "letters" and the women "charms.") At Newark, the women's recreational association staged "play days" with women from other New Jersey colleges. Women traveled to a neighboring campus, chose up teams in a sport (archery, tennis, ice skating, swimming, and badminton were popular as well as basketball) without regard to school affiliation, played, then celebrated at a social event. At both schools, small budgets and inadequate facilities limited the required physical education programs for both women and men.

The New Jersey College for Women (NJCW) was different. In the 1950s, the college had adequate gym facilities, a two-year required program in physical education, a full staff of female physical educators, a course of study to prepare women for teaching in the field, and a budget of greater than $70,000 (more than twice that of the Newark program for both men and women). There were no intercollegiate sports, not even basketball. The women had play days (like those at Newark), intramural clubs, and recreational sports. Women took a required first-year course in hygiene (including lectures on courtship and marriage) and signed up in large numbers for swimming and folk dancing, but the club program in sports like basketball, softball, and field hockey languished because, as the department chair saw it, students spent too much time earning money, going home, and engaging in "social dating" and "aimless visiting with friends."[1]

In 1958, when Marjorie Myers Howes arrived, the Douglass (no longer NJCW) Health and Physical Education Department was best known among students for its outstanding synchronized swimming and extensive dance programs. Howes was hired while still a senior at the University of Cincinnati, where she was completing a degree in physical education and coursework in biology and health. Her brothers had taught her basketball and baseball, and she had played several varsity sports in high school and college. Nothing seemed more natural to her than to post signs encouraging students to sign up for varsity basketball. The department told her to change it to "extramural" basketball but reluctantly allowed her to proceed. Physical education majors enrolled first; they then recruited other young women. By the second year there was a field hockey team as well, and, by Howes's third year, softball.[2]

The basketball game that Howes coached was strikingly different from today's contest, but every bit as much hard work and fun. It was played six-on-six. Three of the six players on each team had to stay on one side or the other of center court, and the players' movements were constrained by the restriction on dribbling. Frontcourt players (those near the opponent's basket) such as Judith Pease and Mary Ann Poggi were five-foot-three to

34. Charlene Cato (*left*) and Joyce Countiss in March 1964 were Douglass College juniors, in their third year of playing basketball, field hockey, and softball for coach Marjorie Howes. In those three years, the women had won thirty-three basketball games and lost four playing for Howes, and had a similarly accomplished record in softball, but that success worried some the college's physical education faculty, who felt that the women had become too competitive. In 1997, Howes was inducted into the Rutgers basketball hall of fame.

SOURCE: Photo provided by Marjorie Howes; published previously in the *Home News*, March 15, 1964, 30.

five-foot-five and did most of the scoring. The taller women played defense in the backcourt.[3]

Home games were in the old "packing-crate" Douglass gym (named for its past as an airplane hanger and assembly facility). The gym had wooden backboards, walls that left little room for spectators (or even players from the opposing team), and a floor that had registers in it that blew air up at the players. Steel beams hung down from the ceiling. Nancy Newmark, one of Pease and Poggi's teammates on Howes's first teams, became adept at arching her high set shots to avoid the beams. Her teammate Joyce Countiss, one of the few women to shoot a jump shot rather than a two-hand set, led the team in scoring. The women played in their gym outfits (green plaid tunics). After each game, they shared oranges, cookies, and soft drinks with opposing players, but one mother who watched her daughter play told her that if she had known how rough the game was, "I would never have let you play."[4]

The basketball schedule in 1961–1962 included games with Hofstra, Bridgeport, Monmouth, Panzer, and Misericordia, and Coach (Myers) Howes assured that at least one game involved an overnight stay, usually in New York City. In spring 1963, they moved across town and played a game in the Barn before eight hundred spectators, mostly Rutgers College males, and more fans than the mediocre men's team generally drew. Howes's background as a basketball official as well as a player and coach, gave her a leadership role in introducing the "rover" to New Jersey girls and women's basketball—a player allowed to dribble the ball from one side of center court to the other. Douglass had a rover for the 1963 season, and with help from a coach from the men's junior varsity, developed a "fast-break" offense.

Most of the basketball players played three sports—field hockey in the fall, basketball in the winter, and softball in the spring. Sarah Noddings, another of Howes's basketball players, for example, hit third in the lineup on the softball team, in front of another basketball player, Charlene Cato, the clean-up hitter on the team. In an era when student athletes practiced only three or four times a week and never worked out with weights, and when "fast-pitch" softball meant the pitcher threw the ball "as fast as she could pitch," the Douglass team won virtually all its games.[5] Most of the Douglass student athletes were also physical education majors who went on to coach, officiate, and teach in the field or to careers in physical therapy. A major in physical education included grounding in biology and physiology, and academic work took some women, such as Susan Ann Laubach, across town for courses offered only at Rutgers College. (Pease also traveled across town as one of the first Douglass cheerleaders at a Rutgers football game.)

For coaching all three sports and teaching skills in a dozen others, Howes made $4,000 when she began. Six years later when she left, she made $4,200. She was ready to leave, but she would not have been asked back by the physical education program. The dean applauded and the local press extensively covered the Douglass women's teams, but her supervisors in physical education told her that she had won too many games and took competitive sports too seriously. Nonetheless, in the years after her departure, Douglass enlarged its extramural sports program to include lacrosse and swimming, and many years later, Rutgers recognized Howes's pioneering efforts by inducting her into the university's basketball hall of fame.

Within a decade after Howes left Douglass, the outlook for women's sports at the university changed dramatically. Part of the change was internal. The opening of Livingston College (1969) and the admission of women to Rutgers College (1972) meant that the university had to confront questions about women and education in New Brunswick that had previously pertained only to the NJCW/Douglass. Even more important, changing attitudes in the 1960s about women's roles created aspirations among schoolgirls and their parents to which colleges and universities in the 1970s increasingly responded, and when high schools dragged their heels on varsity sports for girls, lawsuits filed under the federal equal protection clause of the Fourteenth Amendment of the Constitution opened doors. In 1972, Congress passed Title IX, barring sex discrimination in education at colleges and universities that received federal funds, and while enforcement followed slowly, federal law now also supported greater opportunity for female student athletes.

Rutgers women student athletes first excelled in the new intercollegiate context not in basketball, but in track and field. One of the physical education instructors, Sandra Petway, launched the first track and field program for women. Petway had enjoyed an outstanding high school and college career as a runner, graduated with a degree in health and physical education from Trenton State College, and then earned her master's degree. Before she resigned after the 1980 season, Petway had made her indoor and outdoor teams among the best in the East, and routinely sent hurdlers, sprinters, and javelin throwers to national competition.[6]

Women's basketball got off to a slower start. The program was launched in 1974. For the first two years, the team played a limited schedule and had two coaches, Ellen Johns (hired at Douglass) and Karen Loupassakis. The second coaching change, in 1976, brought Theresa Grentz to Rutgers. Grentz had played college ball with the "Mighty Macs" of Immaculata College in Pennsylvania, helping lead her team to victory in 1972 in the first Association for Intercollegiate Athletics for Women (AIAW) national championship game. In 1974, she played in the first nationally televised women's basketball game, and after graduating, coached at Saint Joseph's before being hired at Rutgers.

When Grentz arrived at Rutgers, the women's basketball budget was less than $15,000 (the men's almost $75,000), there were no scholarships for women, and they had been playing in the Barn on College Avenue (the men played at the new athletic center). She was the first full-time coach for a women's sport at Rutgers (and among the first in the nation), but she and her entire coaching staff made less in total than the least-well-paid men's assistant.

Grentz made her team, the "Lady Knights," a national power. She got them moved to the Rutgers Athletic Center, and when they played Yale

35. Theresa Shenk (Grentz), on the left, celebrating the 1972 AIAW national championship victory of Immaculata College. Her coach, Cathy Rush (*center*), took Immaculata to six consecutive national championship finals and won three of them.
SOURCE: Philadelphia Archdiocesan Historical Research Center: Robert and Theresa Halvey Photographic Collection.

in their first game on the new court, one of the officials was Susan Ann Laubach, who had been on Marjorie Howes's first teams. In an era before the high-stakes recruiting of contemporary women's basketball, Grentz's knowledge of local teams and coaches brought her outstanding athletes, and she had guided the Lady Knights into the AIAW tournament by 1979 (with twelve of them on scholarship). She went to the next three AIAW tournaments and won the national championship with a 1982 victory against Texas. Every year between 1983–1984 and 1993–1994, her teams went to the NCAA tournament. Kris Kirchner and June Olkowski won All-American honors on her early teams, and Sue Wicks, Regina Howard ("Wicks" and "Sticks"), and Telicher Austin propelled the team's NCAA tournament runs. Howard and Austin were the first African American women's basketball players at Rutgers to win national recognition (at a time when most African Americans played at historically black colleges, such as rival Cheyney State in Pennsylvania).

The AIAW collapsed shortly after Rutgers's victory in the 1982 tournament, a victim of a struggle with the NCAA. The NCAA had been until that time an organization for men's collegiate sports, and at least initially had accepted the AIAW. Rutgers joined the AIAW in 1973. Throughout the 1970s, the NCAA led the attack on Title IX, and in fact, when the major football powers were polled at the end of the decade about revenue policy, about the only thing they could agree on was that women's athletics should not get more funding. Despite such attitudes, in the mid-1970s, the NCAA leadership began thinking about sponsoring national women's collegiate sports tournaments, parallel to those for men. At that point, the AIAW had almost a thousand member schools and sponsored thirty-nine national championships; it had worked to develop standards for recruiting and scholarships that would avoid the abuses and excesses it saw in men's sports; and it put women in charge of the administration of women's athletics. The NCAA, however, had the revenue from the men's national

36. Terry Dorner, All-American June Olkowski, and co-captain Chris Dailey holding up the 1982 trophy for Coach Theresa Shenk Grentz's Rutgers Lady Knights' victory in what turned out to be the last AIAW national basketball championship game. On the same day, future Rutgers coach C. Vivian Stringer's Cheyney State Lady Wolves played in the first NCAA women's basketball championship game. The controversial NCAA decision to stage its own national championship tournament led to the almost immediate demise of the AIAW.
PHOTOGRAPHER: George O'Gorman. SOURCE: R-Photo, athletics, published in the *Trentonian*, March 29, 1982, 44.

37. Assistant coach Jolette Law (*left*) and head women's basketball coach C. Vivian Stringer. While at Cheyney State, Iowa, and Rutgers, Stringer took teams to the "Final Four" of the national championship tournament. In 2009, she was inducted into the Naismith Memorial Basketball Hall of Fame. Law played on Stringer-coached teams at Iowa and soon thereafter joined Stringer at Rutgers as an assistant coach.
PHOTOGRAPHER: Larry Levanti.
SOURCE: R-Photo, athletics.

basketball tournament that it could use to lure schools into the organization with the promise of underwriting women's competition.

Rutgers resisted. Virtually all the female campus leaders, members of the Women's Organizational Network, led by Jewel Plummer Cobb, the dean of Douglass College, urged President Bloustein to fight any motion at the NCAA convention for the creation of women's tournaments. Bloustein shared their concerns. Rutgers opposed the motion to introduce postseason championships for the 1981–1982 season, and when that motion passed, fought to have it rescinded and lost. So the year that Rutgers won the AIAW title, the NCAA awarded its first national championship in women's basketball, and when an AIAW lawsuit against the NCAA failed, the AIAW folded, and an alternative path for developing women's college athletics closed. Yet it should also be noted that many of the women who had entered the basketball coaching profession in the 1970s and struggled with inadequate funding and facilities supported the decision, however reluctantly, as a necessary step in a process begun by Title IX.

Grentz was among those pioneers. She had complained to the director of athletics, Fred Gruninger, about her salary, and he had admonished her for not attracting enough fans to the women's basketball games. (In football and men's basketball, the athletic department held coaches accountable for winning, not for attendance.) In the mid-1990s, in fact, a coach, speaking on behalf of herself and several others, voiced concerns about the inequitable compensation for Rutgers women coaches. Grentz had not signed the complaint, but shortly thereafter, she announced her departure to accept the head coaching position at Illinois.

The Lawrence administration not only responded by improving the salaries of women's coaches but also by hiring C. Vivian Stringer as the new women's basketball coach. Stringer had led teams to the "Final Four" of the NCAA tournaments while at Cheyney State and Iowa. Her starting salary at Rutgers was an unprecedented $150,000 (more than any Rutgers men's coach at the time), and other clauses in the contract gave her the potential of earning $300,000 a year.

After Stringer replaced Grentz, the women's basketball team went to the NCAA tournament every year except 2002 during the first decade of the twenty-first century; in 2000, reached the "Final Four"; and in 2007, played for the national championship. Cappie Pondexter, Matee Ajavon, and Epiphanny Prince won All-American honors for Stringer, and like many others on teams from the decade, each went on to play in the women's professional league, the WNBA. Stringer was inducted into the Women's Basketball Hall of Fame in 2001, and the Naismith Memorial Basketball Hall of Fame in 2009. In 2014, denied an NCAA tournament bid, Stringer took Rutgers to the sixty-four-team Women's National Invitational Tournament and won the WNIT crown.

10

Athletic Policy

After World War II, Rutgers ran its physical education program, including intercollegiate athletics, on a budget of approximately $100,000 year, mostly supplied by football revenues. Students at both Rutgers College and the New Jersey College for Women took a required physical education course. Men could try out for approximately a dozen intercollegiate athletic teams; women for none. College football, not professional football, was the passionate fan's fall sport, and that was as true at Rutgers as at most other universities. Rutgers, an independent, played a round-robin with Lafayette and Lehigh, scheduled Princeton and Columbia from the Ivy League, and took the field against one or more of the service academies (most often Army), filling out its schedule with northeastern teams like Holy Cross and Colgate. In those glory days of amateurism, Rutgers tasted success often enough to keep its alumni happy and its students involved both as athletes and spectators.

By the early 1970s, the postwar athletic regime at Rutgers and many other schools had been shattered. Increasing costs, greater competitive pressures in virtually every aspect of athletics, and the temptation of television revenues led to athletic soul-searching and a debate at Rutgers about going bigger-time, if not big-time, in athletics (meaning, above all else, football). Students' complaints ended required physical education, and pressure generated by federal legislation would increase exponentially sports opportunities for women (and the costs of supporting athletic programs). The struggle to maintain academic standards and contain the cost of athletics while remaining competitive produced a long history of half-steps and missteps on the way to big-time athletics. The university embarked on a building program to upgrade intercollegiate athletic facilities, as well as enhance the quality and availability of student recreational facilities, not just in New Brunswick and Piscataway, but also at Camden and Newark. The undergraduate of the twenty-first century was more likely to be a spectator than a participant, and still more likely to be neither, but if that student followed or engaged in athletics, the university had become a much more welcoming place.

While the story of Rutgers athletics from the end of World War II through the early twenty-first century parallels national trends in intercollegiate sports, Rutgers's version is unique. Not many other colleges made the same hesitant climb as did Rutgers from third-level athletics at a liberal arts college to big-time athletics at a research university. In this chapter, I pursue a chronological account that presents two arguments. First, factors external to the university or at least to the athletic program itself exerted enormous pressure to create a bigger, more expensive, more competitive sports program, led by intercollegiate football. The growth in the size of the university, the loss of autonomy over sports to the federal government and to the National Collegiate Athletic Association (NCAA), the increasing importance of conference participation for the scheduling of games and for television revenue, and, more recently, the watchdog activity of the media over college athletics have all shaped the expansion of intercollegiate sports. Second, despite these pressures and constraints, the university made choices that changed the trajectory of athletic policy.

The analysis that follows is of athletic policy, not of athletics itself. The story of Rutgers football has already been told, and several other university sports have found chroniclers as well. This chapter, then, pays particular attention to the budgetary and academic issues that have defined athletic policy, and to the way in which that policy was framed by the collegiate sports culture in America more generally.

The Post–World War II Athletic Regime

Athletics, in the immediate post–World War II era, was a valued part of the mission of liberal arts colleges to educate the whole person. At Rutgers, the athletic component of the liberal arts enterprise was defined by three factors. First, the athletic regime was broadly participatory. Students took physical education and competed in intramurals, and at the men's colleges, perhaps a quarter of them played intercollegiate sports. Second, intercollegiate sports were local contests with nearby opponents and without the distraction of postseason play. Third, intercollegiate athletics were supposed to pay for themselves. The administration expected football revenues to cover the direct costs of other intercollegiate sports (with many costs hidden in the way the sports were run at that time). Throughout the immediate postwar period, Rutgers remained an independent, flirting periodically with the notion of joining the Ivy League, the ideal home for a historic, northeastern liberal arts college.

For presidents Robert Clothier and Lewis Webster Jones, intercollegiate athletics was primarily an extension of an educational program that provided all students the opportunity to train themselves physically as well as mentally. In New Brunswick, at the men's colleges, the physical education department oversaw required courses for first- and second-year students, a robust intramural program cemented by rivalries among the fraternities, and intercollegiate sports that recruited perhaps a fourth of the students in any given year. Newark and Camden also had physical education courses and modest intramural programs, but both lacked the facilities to offer students many options. Throughout the system, athletics were primarily for young men. At the College for Women, students had gym classes and some very loosely organized opportunities to participate in sports through an athletic association, but no intercollegiate teams; and at Camden and Newark, lack of facilities for women limited athletic endeavor even more than for men.

Intercollegiate athletics were local. Rutgers played a football schedule of nine games that included at least one Ivy League team (Princeton), the twin opponents Lehigh and Lafayette, and then a random collection of regional opponents, ranging from William & Mary and George Washington to the south, Penn State to the west, and Syracuse and Colgate in upstate New York. The basketball schedule of about twenty games was even more local (and included a game against Rutgers-Newark in 1947). Wrestling and swimming rounded out the higher-profile sports of that era, although there was competition in fourteen varsity sports.

Intercollegiate athletics were not only local, but also subordinate to academics. Clothier ordered review of scholarship policy to determine if any money was going to students primarily because they were athletes. He

38. Rutgers football stadium, 1950. During the Great Depression, federal grants, administered through the Works Progress Administration, underwrote the building of a new football stadium. The dedication of the new stadium on November 5, 1938, was also the occasion for the renewal of the Rutgers-Princeton rivalry. This postcard of the stadium was produced twelve years later to promote the "Hall of Fame" game between Rutgers and Brown. Rutgers was a prospective site for a college football hall of fame, and many of the greats of the sport were in attendance. On the left is Amos Alonzo Stagg, football's oldest and best-known coach; on the right is the son of the president of the New Brunswick Touchdown Club.
SOURCE: R-Photo: buildings and grounds.

responded to talk about postseason bowl appearances by stating publicly that the "men of the Rutgers [football] team have done their full duty, and more, in playing through a nine-game schedule. Important as athletics are, they are secondary in importance to scholarship and to the educational purposes for which the men came to college," and thus Rutgers would not extend its playing season by accepting a bowl offer.[1] Clothier also balked at allowing freshman to play on the varsity and scheduling spring football practices, even though it gave other schools, which had adopted such policies, a competitive advantage.

The one step that Clothier and Jones contemplated for upgrading Rutgers athletically was membership in the Ivy League. The Ivy League was not only one of the birthplaces of college football; it fielded teams that were nationally competitive, produced All-American players, garnered enormous alumni loyalty (and with it financial support), and had high academic standards. The formation of the Ivy League, however, came with an explicit commitment among the eight member schools to deemphasize athletics, and, in particular, football. Clothier felt Rutgers was a natural for the Ivy League as one of the eight pre-Revolutionary colleges, a northeastern school, and one, with its recent growth, that was now more comparable in size to those in the Ivy League than before. Rutgers, of course, was never asked, and during the presidencies of Clothier and Jones never seriously considered joining any other conference for intercollegiate sports.

The most intriguing alternative, one that defined a path not taken, came in a 1954 letter from Richard P. McCormick, at that time a young member of the History Department, to Jones. McCormick asked Jones to envision a conference made up of the state universities in the northeastern states. None of these schools, Penn State excepted, were football powerhouses, but many had made "amazing forward strides" academically and a conference of such schools might well help solidify public support for higher education.[2] One is struck by three aspects of the proposal. First, McCormick recognized that Rutgers, even if admitted to the Ivy League, would never be considered an equal by schools like Columbia or Harvard. Second, he looked to the future of public education, rather than to the school's past as an elite liberal arts college, and suggested a way Rutgers could shape that future by taking the lead in developing a northeastern conference of state universities. Third, McCormick was virtually alone as a faculty member until the 1990s in concerning himself enough with athletics to write a letter about it to the university administration.

In addition to being participatory and local, athletics were expected to be self-supporting financially. Some costs were covered externally. The coaching staff, for example, were generally faculty members, that is, professors, who had other teaching and administrative duties, and were paid on state lines, nor were the costs of building gymnasiums and stadiums a part of the athletic budget. For other costs, there were football gate receipts. Typically, home football games drew ten thousand to fifteen thousand fans, but that often was not enough to fund the varsity sports program fully. When financial problems became severe, teams (except for football) were not allowed to schedule games more than 125 miles away, and coaches and parents often drove players to games in their own cars.

If intercollegiate athletics contributed to the "physical, social, and character development of participants," as athletic director Harry Rockafeller stated, and if Rutgers urged its students to take part in intramurals and intercollegiate athletics "according to their ability," then intercollegiate athletics (as well as intramurals) ought to have been funded out of the regular budget rather than limited by football revenues.[3] That, in fact, was exactly the conclusion the university reached in presenting its 1954–1955 budget request to the New Jersey Board of Education. In the early 1950s, physical education was costing Rutgers a little more than $160,000 a year, and intercollegiate athletics added more than $100,000 to the cost, while revenues, chiefly from football, amounted to about $80,000. The days of financing athletics from football gate receipts were over.

Mason Gross: Athletics at a Public University

Thus, when Mason Gross became the president of Rutgers in 1959, budgetary problems alone meant that the university would have to consider the role and scope of athletics at the school. In 1960, Gross spoke directly to this issue in a speech he delivered at a meeting of the Eastern Collegiate Athletic Conference (ECAC). Gross had been an undergraduate at Jesus College in Cambridge, England, where athletics were truly amateur (as well as very much a part of the system of class and privilege in English society) and he had rowed crew. As much as he had loved the English experience, he knew it did not suit American public universities. He believed, as did Clothier and Jones, that Rutgers assumed responsibility for the physical as well as the intellectual development of its students. If both were important, then athletics, like other aspects of education, should be funded from general university funds, not from gate receipts or alumni giving (both of which could create vested interests that distorted university policy). Acknowledging, moreover, the educational value of athletics meant that financial aid could be given to students because of their involvement in athletics, and that coaches should be professionals, not volunteers (put differently, if students were to be educated in athletics, they deserved to be educated well). That said, Gross argued that a university could avoid the pitfalls of professional athletics at the college level by making clear to coaches that a school's goals were educational, and not financial; by making public the aid given to athletes and their academic accomplishments; and by scheduling contests primarily with schools with similar profiles of student athletics.

Was it possible? Could a state university steer a course between professional athletics and the abandonment of intercollegiate competition? The 1960s placed new pressures and imposed new constraints on how Rutgers thought about and managed athletics. Rutgers's growth, the success of school's athletic programs, the greater involvement of the NCAA in governing college sports, the benefits of conference participation, and new concerns about women and minorities in sports all pushed Rutgers, and many other schools, in new, more competitive directions.

One factor was size. Rutgers's total enrollment grew from 16,250 in fall 1959 to 35,435 in fall 1970. On the physical education side, the staffing problems and requests for equal facilities for a geographically scattered set of colleges applied one set of pressures; on the intercollegiate side, the growth of the New Brunswick/Piscataway population of men created inequalities between Rutgers and the smaller liberal arts colleges with which it competed.

A second factor was athletic success, with the resulting rise in expectations. The basketball team, coached by Bill Foster, went 22–7 in 1966–1967, usually playing before home crowds of about two thousand in the gymnasium on College Avenue. In football, after John Bateman took over as head coach in 1960, came two of Rutgers's best seasons—an 8–1 record in 1960, followed by a "perfect season" in 1961. When Rutgers rejected feelers about postseason bowl game competition, the students were angry, but All-American center Alex Kroll, speaking for the team, said that Rutgers had nothing to prove playing "Western agriculture schools or Eastern [football] factories" in a bowl game. Rutgers was not about, he concluded, "so-called 'big-time football.'"[4] There was, however, a hidden logic at work, which Gross and his athletic director, Albert Twitchell, understood. Rutgers had never successfully competed with the Ivy League schools for scholar-athletes, and as it grew in size and redefined itself as a state university, it became ever harder to do so.

A third factor defining the choices the university could make was the growing import of the NCAA in defining eligibility of students as athletes, determining the rules of competition, and directing the flow of revenue for televised football and basketball games. The NCAA had been around since the first decade of the twentieth century but until the 1950s had not been a dominant factor in athletic policy. In the 1950s, pressure built to "reform" basketball and football programs that recruited star players with slush funds and kept them in school with what amounted to salaries. Simultaneously, almost paranoid anxieties about the impact of television and professional football on college game attendance and fierce struggles about revenue allocation from the broadcast of college games threatened to set schools and conferences against each other in a Darwinian struggle to survive. As the NCAA worked to regulate competition, it imposed new restrictions on college athletics.

Conference participation, especially in football, was another factor affecting Rutgers athletics. Twitchell and Gross had given up on "out Ivy-ing the Ivy League" but struggled to define an alternative.[5] In the mid-1960s, Gross brought together an ad hoc committee of board members, administrators, and faculty (the first such body at Rutgers) to help him with intercollegiate athletics. The fundamental question was not whether to join a football conference, but at what level Rutgers should compete. His athletic council affirmed that Rutgers was now involved in a second-level football world. Given the growing size of the university, schools like Lehigh and Lafayette would soon no longer be suitable opponents, but the costs of first-level play (with schools such as Penn State) seemed prohibitive to most. Moreover, the council added, "we can't fight internal faculty non-acceptance."[6]

Not everyone agreed. At least two members of the Board of Trustees wanted to see Rutgers adopt first-level football. The most insistent was David "Sonny" Werblin. Werblin graduated from Rutgers in 1931, went to work for Music Corporation of America (and by the 1950s was director of its television division), and subsequently became involved with professional football when he and partners purchased the New York Titans, which he renamed the Jets. Werblin signed Alabama quarterback Joe Namath (who in 1969 engineered the victory of the Jets from the upstart American Football League over the Baltimore Colts of the rival, more established National Football League), and he also directed the building of the Meadowlands Sports Complex in East Rutherford, New Jersey. In 1965, Werblin was elected to the Rutgers Board of Trustees and, in 1971, appointed to the Board of Governors.

Werblin responded to the rejection of first-level football by sending Gross and Twitchell a detailed "Projection for Rutgers University Football." He argued that if the university financed the transition to this higher level of competition, the program would ultimately pay for itself. Twitchell found the proposal "tremendously exciting." but cautioned Werblin that questions about admissions, financial aid, and eligibility were not under control of the athletic director, and that the building of a larger football stadium would be costly.[7] Moreover, some of the institutions Werblin thought Rutgers should compete against had quite different academic profiles.

In subsequent discussions, Werblin angered Gross and annoyed Twitchell, but did not immediately provoke a drastic policy change. Twitchell put the disagreement bluntly in a letter to Gross: "Sonny and [Trustee] Bill [Sahloff] want us to be a college professional team, and this we cannot be."[8] The modest transition to second-level football, to be eased in by the mid-1970s, and in response to the growth in enrollments, was as close as the president came to defining Rutgers's intercollegiate athletic future, but before Gross left office, Werblin had seized the initiative.

Even such a limited transition as Gross envisioned, however, had its costs, and one such expense was scholarship support for athletes. In the early 1960s, all financial aid was distributed by a single faculty committee, which in any given year might decide to parcel some of it out to prospective student athletes. If the "philosophy [of favoring other students over scholar athletes] is continued," Twitchell feared, "our [intercollegiate athletic] program is dead."[9] Into this crisis stepped Thomas Turner Barr, or, more accurately, his will. Barr had played a year of subvarsity football at Rutgers before World War I, then, after graduating, made his fortune on Wall Street. When he died in 1949, he left his widow a trust fund, which at her death (in January 1966) went to the Rutgers football program to provide scholarships. The will stipulated that the awards were to be $1,000 to $2,000 and to go to football athletes. The decision to accept the Barr endowment had a hidden price—as college costs rose above Barr's $2,000 limit, as players without financial need were recruited, and as other sports programs clamored for scholarships, new costs would be added to intercollegiate sports at Rutgers.

Rising costs (and spiraling inflation in the Vietnam War era) could not be so easily met in other areas. Ice hockey was a popular club sport, and the team played against junior varsities and other club teams throughout the Northeast. The team used local rinks, and efforts to finance a rink on the campus collapsed. Keeping the lightweight crew team in the water was equally problematic. The team lacked money for oars and travel, and it needed a full-time coach. The program struggled on, but the threat to Rutgers's non-revenue-producing intercollegiate sports remained.

The cost factor was directly related to Rutgers's role as the state university. More students required more facilities, gymnasiums as well as chemistry labs, seats in the football stadium as well as seats in lecture halls, playing fields alongside parking lots. Athletic facilities at Newark and Camden were particularly bad. At Camden, outdoor sports were played in public parks, and many indoor activities conducted at the YMCA and YWCA. Newark had a gym and pool, but both were completely inadequate. The intercollegiate fencing team—which won national recognition—had to practice in a local church and was only able to do so after Mason Gross stepped in and gave the team the rental fee. Just as critical was the need for a gymnasium for Livingston College, which expected its first students by the end of the decade. Two of these problems were addressed by the 1971 passage of the higher education construction bond. Of the $53 million allocated, $4.5 went to gyms at Camden and Livingston. Newark would have to wait, as did the men's colleges for a replacement on "the Heights" for the 1931 College Avenue gymnasium.

Costs played a major role in one very popular change. In 1968, the student council of the men's colleges published a damning indictment of the physical education requirement and pushed hard to end the policy. As a *Targum* editorial put it, "Gym classes at present are poorly organized and conducted. They offer a limited range of activity and little opportunity for team development or skills instruction. Supervision is poor, playing conditions worse, and enthusiasm absent."[10] Twitchell recommended that voluntary physical education replace the current program, and his suggestion was incorporated into the more general plan of curricular reform being considered at the time by Rutgers College. The speedy demise of the physical education requirement, of course, mirrored what was happening at campuses across the country in the late 1960s, and surely some of its appeal to Twitchell was because it saved the athletic department money.

Through much of discussion of athletics in the 1960s, Rutgers remained outside of the scrutiny of the NCAA, but in 1967 that situation changed dramatically. Several years earlier, the NCAA had made its first serious attempt to create minimum scholastic standards for athletes. Under the new rule, a student could not be admitted with financial aid as an athlete or play in intercollegiate competition in his first year if his predicted first-year grade-point average was less than 1.6 (C-/D+); thereafter he had to maintain a 1.6 GPA to receive aid or be eligible to play. Schools not in compliance were banned for two years from NCAA-sponsored events.

The reform was supported, in part, because some schools already had such rules and wanted to "level the playing field" with institutions that did not have similar academic standards. The new rule was vigorously protested by many of the schools in the ECAC because it threatened their autonomy and used measures of achievement that they felt could not be applied to either admission or eligibility at their schools.

In March 1967, Mark Singley, who chaired Gross's faculty advisers on athletics, informed the president that a football player admitted with a Barr scholarship had a predicted 1.542 average. Twitchell had already certified to the NCAA that Rutgers was "functioning within the spirit of the 1.6 rule," and when Gross wrote to inform the national body of this apparent violation, he pleaded for flexibility in the application of the rule.[11] Gross argued that the NCAA formula did not measure accurately the likelihood of a student's success in college if that student came from a small, highly competitive high school, but his primary concern was that NCAA policy undermined efforts to achieve equality in 1960s America. "Times have changed," Gross stated, and it is the university's responsibility, he continued, to admit students from "culturally disadvantaged backgrounds" and then devise a program that allows them to meet the same standards for graduation as other students.[12] Gross's stand won sympathetic recognition from the local and national press, but it did not change the mind of the NCAA, which, as a penalty, barred Rutgers track members from an NCAA event.

How did it end? Rutgers tried to get the rule repealed or amended at the January 1968 NCAA convention but failed. Then Gross himself attended a spring meeting of the NCAA in Denver to plead Rutgers's case. Shortly thereafter, the NCAA informed Rutgers that the decision to admit the student, provide him financial aid, and allow him to play football did not constitute an "institutional policy of nonconformity," and Rutgers agreed not to admit student athletes who did not have at least a predicted 1.6 average.[13] Phone calls between the university and the NCAA had resulted in a face-saving retreat by both sides.

Mason Gross announced his retirement in June 1970 but remained in office until September 1971 when Edward J. Bloustein became president. During the last year and a half of Gross's tenure as president, athletic policy moved much more rapidly toward "first-level" football. Past decisions about scholarship policy, capital improvements, recruiting, and scheduling helped push the program in this direction, and by the late 1960s, Twitchell was convinced that such a course was desirable, but the key element was vigorous leadership from David Werblin on the Board of Trustees.

In March 1970, the Board of Trustees, at the request of the Rutgers College alumni, constituted an ad hoc committee to look into intercollegiate athletics and appointed Werblin as its chair. That spring, Twitchell outlined a scheduling plan for the 1980s defined by first-level opponents such as Penn State and Georgia Tech, urged an increase in stadium capacity to forty-five thousand seats, and supported an expanded grant-in-aid program for football recruiting (non-need-based scholarships). He also recommended that Rutgers follow the lead of most of its opponents and allow freshmen to compete on the varsity teams in sports other than football, basketball, ice hockey, and crew. Twitchell and Werblin both recommended to Gross that the admission process for athletes be expedited by placing an athletic liaison officer in the admission's office. In June, Werblin's committee endorsed these recommendations, with the tacit approval of the president's faculty advisory committee, and the Rubicon had been crossed.[14]

In December, Werblin presented the trustees with a multipart motion to assure that the "proper emphasis be given to the development of athletic teams which will truly be representative of the State University of New Jersey and that such athletic teams be of a caliber which can meet competitively with athletic teams of other state and private universities whose educational values and standards are comparable with Rutgers."[15] The proposal, which endorsed the construction of a new multipurpose field house seating fifteen thousand people, more scholarships in all sports, and an athletic budget financed by state support as well as gate receipts and student fees, was approved by the trustees in March 1971. In December 1972, having been asked by the new president for advice about establishing an advisory committee to study athletic policy, Werblin wrote back that it was not necessary, as the Board of Trustees and the Board of Governors had already done that, and now all that was needed was "implementation." That was an audacious assessment of a motion that had never been considered by the University Senate or the Board of Governors, the ultimate decision-making bodies of the school. Exactly how Bloustein would handle the endorsement of major-league athletics, however, remained to be seen.

Mason Gross brought a coherent approach to the place of athletics in university life, devoted more time to athletics and sought advice about football more widely than any previous president, and helped Rutgers adjust to the realities of its status as the state university. Yet on the crucial question of athletic policy he left Rutgers about where it has been before, apparently accepting policy changes only after he had announced his resignation from office and with the prompting of both his athletic director and a strong-willed member of the Board of Trustees. Those changes, however much the product of individual influence, were also, as Twitchell in particular realized, the product of challenges brought on by factors over which Rutgers had little control: growing enrollments, scheduling with schools of like size, and the need to finance athletics.

Edward J. Bloustein and Bigger-Time Athletics

Edward J. Bloustein (1971–1989) is remembered as the president who steered Rutgers toward "bigger-time" athletics. He did this in considered steps. Rather than endorse outright the Board of Trustees' resolution of 1971, he convened a committee in 1973 to study athletics. He informed Werblin that while they both wanted better varsity athletics for Rutgers, there were differences in their views of "degree and detail."[16] As he did this, he also cleaned house in the program, asking for the resignation of John Bateman, the football coach, and Albert Twitchell. Frederick Gruninger became the new athletic director (1973–1998). Like his predecessors, Gruninger was a former Rutgers student, athlete (baseball), and coach, and he had served as Twitchell's assistant. Frank Burns took over as football coach.

The 1973 athletic report, called for by Bloustein, was pioneering and puzzling. The committee, chaired by Vice President Henry Winkler, gave the faculty greater voice over athletic policy than ever before and produced the first serious review of sports financing. Yet the committee wrote a report that failed to map out a concrete path for either more or less emphasis on intercollegiate athletics. The brief section on intercollegiate athletics, based on the work of two faculty members who had served on Gross's advisory committee, tentatively supported higher-profile football, if athletics could be financed by state support, the alumni, and gate receipts, but rejected the quasi-professional, big-time athletics found at some other institutions. The remainder of the report emphasized the overwhelming needs of the larger student population on all three campuses for opportunities to participate in sports. It deplored the appalling state of athletic facilities at Newark and Camden, asked that student fees no longer be used to finance intercollegiate sports, and recommended that scholarship money be earmarked for academic achievement. The report called for proportional support for women's athletics, suggested renewed emphasis on club sports and intramurals, and hinted that some of the more costly, non-revenue-producing intercollegiate sports ought to be discontinued. If a field house were to be built, it should be a multiuse facility that served university-wide needs, not just intercollegiate athletics. In an ambiguous coda, the committee reported the concerns voiced by black athletes about their alienation and frustrations, but took no position on their statements and made no recommendations on the matter.

What should have been much more clearly confronted was that Rutgers was already in a transition period to higher-profile athletics, with its football schedule set into the 1980s and its fund-raising reorganized under the newly formed Scarlet R club. During this transition, and until revenues caught up with costs, the university would have to pay the annual deficits out of its own reserves and student fees. If, as the committee suggested, women's athletics were to receive equal emphasis, these costs would be significantly higher. At a deeper level, the report revealed a divide between faculty perceptions of athletics and the university's sports programs. The committee took little note that for student athletes involvement in sport was a vital part of their educational experience. Mason Gross understood this, but for most members of the committee, intercollegiate sports had little to do with the values they cherished in higher education.

The Winkler report was thus a protest at the drift in athletic policy, but one that provided an inconclusive resolution. Rutgers, under Bloustein and Gruninger, would pursue higher-profile athletics, as actively as circumstances permitted, while initially drawing the line at big-time sports. The path, as had been true in the 1960s, was significantly shaped by the growth in the university's size, by the increasingly intrusive federal and NCAA policies, and by budgetary considerations.

First, Bloustein and Gruninger had to deal with the implications for athletics of the university's growth. When Gruninger stepped down in 1998, the total enrollment at the campuses had reached 48,000 students, with approximately 9,000 of those students at Newark and 4,500 at Camden. Multiple intercollegiate programs, periodic upgrading of recreational and athletic facilities, and scheduling at the New Brunswick/Piscataway campus of football and basketball games with schools of equivalent size and stature were consequences of this growth.

Second, NCAA influence over policy grew in the 1970s and 1980s. In 1972, the organization permitted freshmen to play varsity football and basketball (Rutgers, as did virtually every other program, immediately adopted the policy). Then, in 1973, as a cost-cutting measure, the NCAA limited the number of football scholarships and coaches teams could have and allowed schools to replace four-year grants with one-year grants (and rid themselves of a financial obligation to players who were "weeded out" or quit). Rutgers, however, continued to make four-year awards (which protected student athletes but put the university at a competitive disadvantage). That same year, the NCAA also repealed the 1.6 rule, primarily because of protests about its discriminatory effects, and not until 1986 would new academic recruitment standards take its place.

NCAA leverage over college sports came from its control of television revenue. Initially, schools feared that broadcasting football games would kill gate revenues, and NCAA policy evolved as a way to limit television exposure. But as lucrative deals were struck with the highest-bidding network for monopoly rights, a fierce power struggle occurred within the NCAA between the major football powers and the smaller schools about how to share the wealth. The growing popularity of the NCAA men's basketball tournament added even more television revenue to what was at stake. The major football conferences initially banded together to control television revenue, but after a setback in 1984 in the courts, a decade of free-market telecasting chaos followed. For eastern independents such as Rutgers, these changes pressured them to join basketball conferences to increase the probability of getting the exposure and revenue the NCAA tournament provided, and a little less strongly, to join (or form) a football conference that could leverage a network television package. Finding competitive equals was now not simply a matter of enrollments (and academic equivalence) but also of the size and variety of revenue streams the athletic program could tap.

Rutgers athletic success fueled the dreams and allayed some of the financial fears of those charting a course for intercollegiate athletics. In 1975, Frank Burns's football team compiled a 9–2 record, and a year later, they were perfect, 11–0, ending the season ranked seventeenth nationally (but shunned by the major postseason bowls). On the basketball court, Tom Young's 1975–1976 team compiled a perfect 31–0 regular season record and make it to the Final Four of the NCAA tournament, and in 1981–1982, Theresa Grentz's Lady Knights won the Association for Intercollegiate

Athletics for Women (AIAW) national championship, solidifying women's basketball as the third revenue sport at the university. In 1977, Gruninger took pride in a program that operated "at the fringe of the circle of universities that make up the intercollegiate power elite," as well as in the fact that approximately 1,500 of the 19,000 students in New Brunswick competed in intercollegiate athletics."[17] At Newark in 1971, however, when the intercollegiate men's volleyball team, coached by a volunteer from the History Department faculty, went 37–1, and was invited to the NCAA tournament, a student wrote plaintively to Bloustein to ask why there was no money for "the neglected, forgotten fourth rate campus" to send fans and cheerleaders to California to support the squad.[18] Bloustein had, in fact, made additional money available to help out a non-revenue sport, but it was not and would never be these sports that directed athletic policy or captured the imagination of New Jersey journalists or ordinary citizens.

As bigger-time sports came to Rutgers in the late 1970s and the 1980s, two concerns directed athletic policy—women's sports and the budget—and in both, football played a key role. The dramatic increase in the late 1960s and throughout the 1970s in the participation of girls in scholastic sports, equal-protection lawsuits challenging the lack of athletic opportunities for girls in the secondary school system, and in 1972 the federal enactment of Title IX, barring sex discrimination in education at schools receiving congressional funding all helped make possible a more inclusive sports culture in America.

Many universities dragged their heels on Title IX. Rutgers did not. At Rutgers Title IX was thought of more as an opportunity than a disaster. This was in part because intercollegiate athletics was not a virtually autonomous empire, as it was at some schools, and did not hold the administration hostage with the threat of diminished sports revenue. It was also a reflection of the fact that for two decades Bloustein was consistently committed to expanding opportunity for historically disadvantaged groups, and it was Bloustein more than anyone who shaped athletic policy. Expanding opportunity meant spending money. Title IX did not require a dollar-for-dollar match of men's and women's sports, but court cases pushed universities toward that goal while leaving some wiggle room for programs. What was clear was that as football and men's basketball budgets spiraled upward, so had to the budgets for women's sports.

Funding women's sports was, thus, part of the second major concern facing Bloustein and Gruninger, the budget. In the early 1950s, the direct costs of running the intercollegiate sports programs was about $80,000. By the early 1970s, before Title IX, those costs had risen in New Brunswick to about $600,000, and when student aid was added to the total, the figure approached $1 million. By the end of the decade, the cost of the athletic program was $2.3 million, and scholarships added another half a million to that total. The most crucial fact was the deficit: from fiscal year 1972–1973 to fiscal year 1978–1979, the deficit in men's sports rose from $152,000 to $234,000, while the overall deficit rose to $653,000 (from the same base), most of that added deficit occasioned by the addition of women's sports programs. The offset from gate receipts for football and basketball was variable, meaning that deficits could never be predicted accurately and short-term financial planning was difficult.

By the late 1970s, the Board of Governors had set in place a three-part strategy for dealing with these costs, an approach that would govern intercollegiate athletics into the twenty-first century. First, student fees for intercollegiate athletics, which had first been established in the late 1950s, and capped in the early 1970s, were allotted to the non-revenue sports, and allowed to increase with the rate of inflation. Second, the funding for non-revenue sports and basketball were equalized for men and women (including scholarship support). Third, deficits for the three revenue sports were to be met from university reserves. The Division of Intercollegiate Athletics, for its part, instituted a tier system in the mid-1980s for assigning financial aid—providing full funding for the three revenue sports and different levels of support for the Olympic sports, depending on the tier into which each was placed (from first-tier programs like men's and women's soccer to fourth-tier programs such as crew, men's fencing, and women's golf). The rationale for continuing down the path of bigger-time athletics as deficits mounted was framed in terms of the interests and expectations of New Jersey's high school students (and made more persuasive by Title IX), the relationship of the university to state government, and the identification athletics created among students at Rutgers and between students and the university. There remained the hope, as well, that success on the gridiron and the court would erase the deficits and that the state would back its admiration for a winning football team with budgetary appropriations.

The other conclusion reached in the budget considerations of the late 1970s was to delay most of the capital improvement projects that both intercollegiate and recreational sports needed—a decision that reverberated at Newark and Camden. The administration doubted if urban universities with commuter populations and little land could do more than run indoor sports programs. Camden would have to wait to improve its 1973 gymnasium and purchase new playing fields adjacent to the campus. Newark, which finally opened a new gymnasium in 1978, would have to wait on an auxiliary gym, and New Brunswick/Piscataway, where in 1977 a new athletic center had been completed (an intercollegiate basketball facility, not the multiuse field house first envisioned for the campus) would have to wait for better recreational facilities and more seating at the football stadium. Little of this was possible, the administration concluded, unless private donors or the state stepped in.

While Title IX and budget concerns shaped athletics in dramatic ways, the Bloustein-Gruninger era also saw concerns surface about academic standards for student athletes. In part this was occasioned, once again, by nationwide trends, as scandals exposed programs where academic records were doctored to assure the eligibility of athletes and schools that allowed athletes to graduate without acquiring basic literacy. No such problems surfaced at Rutgers, but in 1980, Bloustein asked for a report on the procedures used to admit and provide aid for athletes and for information about their academic achievement and graduation rates. The report confirmed that while the athletics program made recommendations on recruited athletes, it had no decision-making authority on matters of admissions and aid. Unlike many other schools, Rutgers did not recruit a significant number of student athletes from two-year colleges and did not cut off financial aid if a student stopped participating in sports. The graduation rate in football, the report noted, was good. The report also explained that the Division of Intercollegiate Athletics maintained an extensive academic support system in which first-year student athletes had to participate (and others could). In 1979–1980, that program had employed forty graduate students to work with seventy-nine student athletes in twelve different varsity sports.

One particularly poignant story from the 1980s captures some of the tensions emerging over the recruitment of student athletes. The applicant came from a small, rural community in the South. He was black, male, and a football player. In his small high school, his work was well below average, and because his school was poor, there were no programs to provide him the help he needed in the classroom—so on his own, he enrolled in special education classes to get remedial help. Then he applied to Rutgers.

Should he be admitted? To many of the faculty, who made the admissions decisions at the individual colleges, such cases were challenges to be approached on an individual basis and without placing undue weight on standardized test scores—an approach implicit in Mason Gross's fight over the 1.6 rule. To others, including the professional staff that coordinated admissions, even considering such cases indicated slippage in academic standards at the university. What is clear is that as Rutgers moved into the world of bigger-time athletics, the graduation rate for recruited athletes fell (but then so did the rate for the student population in general) and that if that pattern was going to be changed, Rutgers would have to develop a more comprehensive academic counseling program for athletes.

The Era of Big-Time Football

Edward Bloustein's death in 1989 brought Francis Lawrence to the presidency. More a fan than Bloustein had been and a college athlete himself, he devoted more time to the athletic program than had his predecessors. The program had grown enormously during the Bloustein years, and Gruninger, as athletic director, had years of experience to bring to the tasks he faced. Until his resignation in 1998, Gruninger made the key recommendations, and Lawrence provided support (to the board) for decisions that moved Rutgers further down the path to big-time football.

During Gruninger's tenure as athletic director there was little question that the president (and increasingly the Board of Trustees) kept close watch on the athletic program. At the same time, however, the role of the athletic director expanded, and decisions that might have been made in an earlier era by Mason Gross were now a matter of routine and at the discretion of the athletic director. This trend made the selection of Gruninger's replacement all the more important. The man hired by Lawrence for that position in winter 1998 was Robert E. Mulcahy, the president of the New Jersey Sports and Exposition Authority (which had helped Rutgers finance athletic capital improvement projects). For the first time since World War II, the athletic director was not a former Rutgers student and athlete, but an "outsider" brought in to change course in a sports program that one local political leader described as a "dinosaur" that was not "competitive with the real world."[19]

After an overview of the changing culture and economics of big-time college sports in America, I will discuss the challenges that Gruninger,

Mulcahy, and two subsequent athletic directors, Tim Pernetti and Julie Hermann, faced in guiding Rutgers intercollegiate sports programs. Rather than present a chronological account, I will look at three central themes that run through the big-time era, spanning the tenure of three athletic directors and the initial years of a fourth, and two presidents (Francis L. Lawrence, Richard L. McCormick) and the initial years of a third (Robert Barchi). This introduction is followed by consideration of (1) conference participation; (2) compliance (with NCAA rules and federal regulations), scandals, and reform; and (3) academic integrity. Threaded through all three discussions are references to costs. Big-time sports, especially big-time football, have big-time costs.

Big-time football had always been commercial, but by the 1990s it was aggressively so. In what critics called the arms race of college sports, universities dueled with each other by building bigger stadiums, filling them with luxury boxes, and insisting that fans purchase "seat licenses" to obtain the season tickets. Stadiums were named for sponsors, specific soft drink companies given exclusive rights to sell in the stadium (or on the campus), and undergraduates prompted to wear the school colors on clothing marketed by the school. Lavish academic study facilities were constructed for student athletes and staffed by an ever-increasing number of academic advisers and tutors. Universities, once their conferences had secured television contracts, rearranged scheduling to maximize exposure, even when it meant holding football games on weeknights and basketball games at midnight (and moving the games of non-revenue sports to less desirable times). Most strikingly, the salaries paid head football and basketball coaches and their staffs increased exponentially. In 1995, the first million-dollar coach led a college team; two years later there was a two-million-dollar coach, and by the early twentieth-first century there would be two dozen football coaches making more than a million dollars a year (most at universities whose presidents were making half that much or less).

Big-time took on new meaning in 1992 with the creation of the bowl coalition in college football, and in 1998, with the initiation of the Bowl Championship Series (BCS). These linked major football conferences to major postseason bowls and matched up two teams from the coalition for a national championship game. The television networks entered into a bidding war to broadcast the BCS bowls, with huge payouts promised to the participants and their conferences. While there was a half-open backdoor by which a nonconference school could make it to a BCS game, the BCS funneled revenue and recognition toward several dozen schools to the exclusion of everyone else. For every school except Notre Dame, playing big-time football meant belonging to a major conference. Such schools could promise recruits more national exposure and fans greater likelihood of year-end bowl games, and if that paid off, begin to tap into greater television and gate revenues. The demise of the BCS system after the 2013–2014 season and its replacement by a four-team national championship series promised a "fairer" annual determination of the best team in college football but had little chance of helping the wannabe big-time schools overcome the advantages of schools that had dominated the BCS era.

Reform and the quest for profits within the NCAA went hand in hand. Some of this reform, as in the past, was aimed at leveling the playing field (assuring that particular schools did not have unfair advantages); some at assuring that student athletes belonged in college, could handle college-level work, and graduated; and some at quieting critics. In 1983, the NCAA had established a new standard (a variation on the 1.6 rule) for admitting and providing scholarship support for student athletes. In 1992, it refined the system (after mounting criticism, similar to that leveled at the 1.6 rule, that the rules unduly affected African American student athletes) and began collecting and publishing data on graduation rates, and in 2005, it began to use the Academic Progress Rate (APR) to evaluate whether athletes were completing their college careers in a timely fashion (and backed it with the loss of scholarships for sports and programs that could not meet certain standards). Compliance became complicated, its practitioners professionals, its implementation expensive, and its outcomes often unexpected. In the competitive world of big-time college sports, most of the losers were the smaller schools that could not afford to meet the costs of the new rules (and, of course, the student athletes at these schools).

Federal oversight also affected Rutgers athletics. Two federal court cases changed the ways universities thought about federal regulations. In 1992, the Supreme Court allowed monetary damages in Title IX litigation, increasing the danger of noncompliance. Next, in a highly publicized case, lower-level courts blocked Brown University's attempt to cut women's volleyball and gymnastics, and the Supreme Court declined to review the decision. Brown, like most other Ivy League schools, and like Rutgers, supported a very large number of sports for women and men, and like many schools faced severe financial problems in the early 1990s. In a budgetary move, it cut two women's and two men's sports. The courts, however, noted that after the sports were dropped, women constituted little more than a third of the varsity athletes but almost half of the students at the university, and given women's demonstrated interest in volleyball and gymnastics, the school could not deny them the opportunity (unless, of course, it cut men's sports even more drastically than it had). As the costs of intercollegiate athletics spiraled upward over the next two decades, *Cohen v. Brown* set the parameters within which universities had to maneuver as they looked for ways to balance their sports budgets. When Congress followed up with the Equity in Athletics Disclosure Act in 1994, it meant that those budgets—at least in broad brushstrokes, and as they reflected the proportional commitment to women and men—became public documents. A new era of transparency lay ahead.

Transparency had to occur in a more critical and rapidly evolving media regime than the one that Twitchell and Gruninger had faced. As newspapers nationwide lost their readership to online publications, they compensated with more investigative reporting and exposés to attract the public back. What had been a close and comfortable relationship between local papers and college athletics became quite often an adversarial one in the late twentieth century. The major media outlets for Rutgers sports information in New Jersey, the New Brunswick *Home News Tribune*, the Newark *Star-Ledger*, and the northern New Jersey *Record*—all of which had bemoaned the university's dismal athletic record in the 1980s and early 1990s and encouraged its efforts to change course—each turned far more critical eyes on the athletic program, and especially football, in the twenty-first century. When this dialogue was joined by online critics and supporters of intercollegiate athletics and became a topic of conversation on the region's two all-sports talk radio stations, WFAN and ESPN, it became more challenging for the university to manage the way the public perceived the athletic program.

Big-Time: Conference Participation

In 1991, Rutgers finally joined a football conference. In 1975, the school had been among the founding members of the Eastern Collegiate Basketball League, which soon became an all-sports conference, football excepted, and throughout the 1980s was known as the Atlantic 10. In 1989, one of the founding members, Pennsylvania State University, jumped to the Big Ten, setting off more than two decades of conference realignments and an even greater scramble for television revenues. Conference membership, then, became more crucial to a school's financial future and, at the same time, inherently unstable.

Rutgers repositioned itself. The Big East had formed in 1979, with Rutgers turning down an invitation to join, but in 1991, it accepted an offer to join as a football-only participant, and in 1995, left the Atlantic 10 for full sports participation in the Big East. Creation of the football conference put Rutgers on the schedule of the only true regional football power, Syracuse, as well as with prominent eastern programs such as the University of Miami and the University of Pittsburgh. In basketball, after 1995, it meant that Rutgers played in what was one of the most competitive leagues in the nation. The potential revenue payoff was alluring, but there was also the possibility of wallowing in mediocrity if the university's sports programs could not match their competitors in terms of recruiting, facilities, and coaching.

Under Bloustein, Rutgers had taken initial steps to upgrade its football facilities, adding an artificial surface practice field, an indoor training facility (the Bubble), and the Hale Center, all on the Busch Campus and near the football stadium. The Werblin Center, with an aquatic center for intercollegiate competition and extensive new spaces for recreational sports, was completed in 1991. In 1992, the state authorized a bond issue that provided for the rebuilding of the Rutgers stadium and increased seating capacity to more than forty thousand by 1994. In that same year, the university opened Yurcak Field for soccer and lacrosse (projects that year totaled about $30 million), and in 1996 it added the Bauer Track and Field Complex. By the time Gruninger resigned, Rutgers had adequate sports facilities to match its Big East aspirations.

Rutgers joined the Big East at a low point in its athletic fortunes. Of the three primary revenue sports, only Theresa Grentz's Lady Knights did well during the Gruninger years. Men's basketball and football had a few good seasons, but too few to generate sustained fan enthusiasm and the revenue needed to balance rising costs.

The Olympic sports programs paid the cost. In the late 1980s, Gruninger made the decision to drop lightweight football and demote women's lacrosse to a club sport, although a Title IX challenge reversed the lacrosse decision. In the mid-1990s, similar budget problems at Newark led to the elimination of wrestling as a varsity sport, at the same time that men's and women's cross-country was being introduced (thus, presumably, bringing the campus more fully into accord with Title IX). A "Campaign to Restore Rutgers Newark Wrestling" fought a protracted and losing battle to restore the sport.

When Gruninger retired as athletic director, Lawrence turned to Bob Mulcahy to establish Rutgers as a legitimate competitor in the Big East. Mulcahy's background in business and marketing suggested how he would try to turn Rutgers's sports fortunes around. Making money on athletics required putting fans in the seats, and that required winning. Winning, in turn, meant hiring and keeping good coaches, and providing them with the facilities that would attract blue-chip recruits. This presented an enormous challenge. Coaches, like college professors, no longer thought of themselves as lifetime employees of a cherished institution. To move two, three, or more times in a career, and if lucky to work in the professional leagues as well, was the norm for a successful coach. Mulcahy met this challenge by hiring younger coaches with New Jersey connections—those who initially could be paid less and who could recruit effectively in New Jersey.

Mulcahy's first major decision came in 2000, when he fired the football coach, Terry Shea, and hired Greg Schiano. Schiano had professional experience with the Chicago Bears, had been an assistant at the University of Miami (a national power), came originally from New Jersey, and had the energy of "youth" (at age thirty-four, he was the youngest Division 1-A coach in the nation). Despite the continued struggles of the football team in Schiano's first two seasons, Mulcahy gave him a two-year contract extension in December 2002. Three years later, after Rutgers's first bowl appearance, Schiano received a seven-year extension and a salary increase. Other raises would follow to keep Schiano at Rutgers, as would salary hikes for the women's basketball coach, C. Vivian Stringer, whom Gruninger had hired at the then unprecedented salary of $150,000 after Grentz left. Schiano took Rutgers to a string of bowl games; Stringer took the women's basketball team in 2000 to the "Final Four" of the NCAA tournament and in 2007 to the national championship game. Bowl bids and tournament play fueled dreams of even greater success (and created a willingness to accept the costs of further expanding the programs).

Dreams have costs in the world of college athletics, and at Rutgers they had a price beyond mere dollars. In 2006, Mulcahy and Richard L. McCormick decided to cut six intercollegiate varsity sports: men's heavyweight and lightweight crew, men's and women's fencing, men's swimming and diving, and men's tennis. Rutgers fielded more varsity sports programs than most of its Big East rivals, and the cost savings were substantial. Criticism, however, poured into McCormick's office, filled the local newspapers, and animated discussion on the Internet. The university had to resist a move by state legislators to provide additional funding for the programs (even as they were cutting the overall Rutgers budget). The loss of the men's rowing program, one of the traditional sports most associated with Rutgers's past and its Ivy League longings, was particularly disheartening to many of those who took exception to the move. What the university did do, however, was provide a year of additional life to each of the programs, and then allocate funding that would allow for the reestablishment of the sports in the club program.

While Rutgers was cutting back on the number of intercollegiate sports it offered, Mulcahy pushed to expand the football stadium. The original upgrade in 1994 had cost about $30 million and increased seating capacity to 40,500, still below that of other Big East schools. In 2007, Rutgers drew up plans for a $116 million expansion of the stadium to include luxury boxes (with higher ticket prices) and a recruitment lounge but had to scale back the proposal when the state failed to provide bond money and the governor, Jon S. Corzine, was unable to raise funds privately for the project. Nonetheless, more than fifty-three thousand fans saw the team open on Labor Day 2009 in the renovated stadium. The recruiting lounge was added later when private donors supplied additional funding.

Nationwide, the athletic arms race led to faculty protests. At Rutgers, protests were led by the "Rutgers 1,000." William C. Dowling, a widely respected scholar in the English Department, some of Dowling's students, and alumni put together a petition campaign to the Board of Governors. The petitioners wanted to abolish athletic scholarships and to move Rutgers from the Big East to the less competitive Patriot League. As at most universities, this faculty-led athletic reform effort lost energy and led to little change. What the Rutgers 1,000 campaign did do was to work at cross-purposes with what were increasingly the primary justifications given for big-time athletics—enhancing the recognition and reputation of the university with students, elected officials, other state residents, and the national public.

Mulcahy hoped the renovated stadium would keep Schiano at Rutgers and help attract to the school athletes who would allow it to win Big East football titles and major bowl bids. The Big East itself, however, was not a stable conference. As the weakest football entity in the BCS, the Big East was particularly vulnerable to raids. Other conferences, angling for marketing advantages in the Northeast, targeted Big East schools. In 2003, the conference lost three members to the Atlantic Coast Conference (including football powerhouse Miami), and during the next decade, four more schools (including Pittsburgh and Syracuse, whose academic profiles most closely matched that of Rutgers) left. After the first raid, the conference rebounded by adding new schools; after the second, the conference collapsed. The Catholic basketball schools went their own way and retained the name "Big East," while the remaining schools, including Rutgers, formed the American Athletic Conference (and looked for chances to jump to financially more viable conferences themselves). Both realignments exposed the weakness of northeastern football relative to the commercial power of conferences elsewhere in the country, and the continuing tensions between the football schools (which contemplated breaking away to form their own conference) and basketball schools (which resented demands placed on them by the football schools).

By the time of the second realignment, Tim Pernetti had become Rutgers's athletic director. McCormick had appointed Pernetti after a national search in 2009, when Bob Mulcahy had been asked to step down (see below). Pernetti had been a Rutgers undergraduate and football player, had a master's degree in communications, and had worked at ABC and CBS sports. He was young (thirty-nine), enthusiastic, and shared McCormick's commitment to accountability and transparency in the athletic program. Early in 2012, he dealt with the loss of Greg Schiano, lured to the NFL, and later that year, in what was his most striking accomplishment, negotiated an invitation for Rutgers to join the Big Ten in 2014. Soon thereafter came an invitation from the Committee on Institutional Cooperation (CIC), the academic consortium of the University of Chicago and the Big Ten schools.

If the move to the Big Ten seemed like the attainment of the holy grail to some, it did not silence the critics. The athletic "subsidy"—money from Rutgers's reserves used to cover the amount by which expenses exceeded revenues and student fees—had come down slightly in McCormick's last year (from $19.4 million in FY11 to $18.5 million in FY12). The next year, however, as the media reported and concerned faculty members pointed out, the subsidy skyrocketed (to $37 million) as Rutgers bought itself out of both the Big East and its marketing contract. The hope, as new president Barchi explained, was that as the new marketing partnership matured and payouts from the Big Ten pumped more money into the program over the next half decade, athletics would finally become self-supporting.

Big-Time: Compliance, Scandal, Reform

Since the 1980s, most college athletic programs have had problems with federal regulations or NCAA rules. At Rutgers, these problems have been relatively minor, and far overshadowed by attention-grabbing missteps in the administration and running of athletics.

Under Francis L. Lawrence, the primary concerns were with Title IX. As noted above, women's lacrosse was cut in a budget-saving move, and then the decision was reversed without a season being missed. Even without an official complaint, Rutgers was vulnerable to a Title IX challenge. Women's lacrosse was the only "Olympic" sport to share a coach with another team (field hockey), and she had only part-time status. The fact that Rutgers already had a team indicated there was interest in the sport at a university where women continued to be underrepresented in intercollegiate athletics. Strikingly, soon after the reinstatement, President Lawrence set in motion a comprehensive Title IX review, which led to two additional changes in New Brunswick. First, enough money was added to the allotment for women's athletic grants-in-aid (albeit slowly because of the budget problems) to equalize average awards for men and women. Women's soccer, among the newest sports offered in New Brunswick, was upgraded to the revenue sport category in terms of tier funding to accomplish this. Second, the university undertook a new Title IX compliance strategy that focused on ascertaining annually the demand in the secondary school system and among entering students for opportunities to play particular sports at the college level. Not surprisingly, with fifteen sports already in place for both women and men, the university concluded it had met student demand. When in 1995, some women coaches voiced complaints about salary inequities, the university initiated efforts to improve the salaries of the coaches in women's Olympic sports.

Jumping ahead briefly, let me note what Title IX compliance has meant. In 2014, on the eve of joining the Big Ten athletic conference, Rutgers fielded twelve intercollegiate women's sports in New Brunswick/Piscataway, as well as six in Newark and eight in Camden. Almost half of the more than six hundred varsity athletics in New Brunswick were women, and they received almost half of the $10 million in student aid that Rutgers

39. Chelsea Intrabartola playing defense on the women's 2013 lacrosse team. That year
the players wore patches on their jerseys monogrammed with "RKT" in honor of Rita K.
Thomas, the long-serving assistant athletic director in charge of women's intercollegiate
sports. Women's lacrosse was for budgetary reasons at one point in jeopardy of being
dropped as a varsity sport, but when the university understood the Title IX implications,
the decision was reversed. Intrabartola, a history major, did her history research paper on
Thomas's career.
SOURCE: Rutgers University Athletics.

awards student athletes in New Brunswick/Piscataway. (Newark has one
Division I team, in men's volleyball, and provides modest student aid for
the team; Camden has no Division I teams and provides no student aid.)
Only in head coaching, where there are no women coaching men's teams,
and more men coaching women's teams than women, has Title IX yet to
work a revolution, and Rutgers has, of course, helped pioneer another
change in intercollegiate sports with the appointment of athletic director
Julie Hermann.

At Rutgers, Title IX compliance proved relatively easy in comparison
with general oversight of athletic matters. When Richard L. McCormick
became president, he inherited both an energetic athletic director and a
Board of Governors committed to big-time athletics. He asked the board
to consider a comprehensive review of Rutgers athletics—something that
had not been attempted since the 1970s—but could not muster the support
he needed to carry it out. Publically, he announced four goals for Rutgers
athletics: the academic success of Rutgers student athletes, a program of

unquestioned integrity, movement toward budgetary self-sufficiency, and success on the field.

McCormick soon had a chance to carry through on the promise of integrity. In 2003, Mulcahy informed him that the athletic department had made a large number of inadvertent mistakes, dating back to the 1980s, in determining the eligibility of student athletes. After a systematic audit of the mistakes, the university reported the problem to the NCAA and accepted the scholarship penalty it was given. Mulcahy, meanwhile, carried out a complete overhaul of the antiquated procedures for determining eligibility. This was, as McCormick noted, Rutgers's only serious brush with NCAA rules.

In 2008, McCormick faced a more serious crisis. As stadium work went forward, the Newark *Star-Ledger* ran two stories about Greg Schiano's most recent contract—one that questioned an indirect annual payment in lieu of salary of $250,000 to the coach from Nelligan Sports Marketing (the company that handled Rutgers's athletic publicity) and the other that described an agreement that released Schiano from the money he would have to pay Rutgers if he left the university before the expiration of his contract and if stadium construction had not gone forward in a timely fashion. While much of this had been known previously, the new story, coming amid doubts about the stadium financing, raised serious questions about the transparency and oversight of the athletic program.

McCormick responded with a full investigation, carried out by a committee he appointed of both outsiders and insiders. The Koeppe-Gamper report found no illegality. It criticized numerous aspects of the contract negotiations and provided specific recommendations to ensure greater oversight and transparency in the future. It allocated blame to Mulcahy, McCormick, and the board. Beyond that, it made three more general points about intercollegiate athletics, especially at schools such as Rutgers that were trying to catch-up with national football powers: (1) that the public recognition that football can bring to a school and that is used to justify increasing budgetary allocations can easily turn against a school when things go bad (as they had here); (2) that support from boosters, alumni, and legislators for athletics create external constituencies that may work against internal university controls; and (3) that the frenzy of building a program rapidly and renegotiating coaching contracts in response to outside offers and escalating salaries tends to invest athletic directors with unique authority to operate autonomously. McCormick accepted responsibility for the shortcomings under his watch, made the report public, and took the lead in making transparency and accountability goals of athletic administration at the university.

Less than a month after he received the report, McCormick fired Mulcahy. The firing brought calls for explanations from state political leaders. McCormick's public statement balanced praise for Mulcahy's accomplishments with a need for new leadership in Rutgers athletics. From almost any perspective, Mulcahy had done what President Lawrence had wanted, and his decade-long tenure as athletic director was among the most consequential in the modern history of Rutgers athletics. At enormous cost, he had laid the foundation for a competitive, Division I football program. He had made difficult cost-cutting decisions in Olympic sports and maintained academic standards throughout the university's intercollegiate programs. The missteps that cost him his job were in no way essential to what he achieved, even if they pointed to larger structural problems in the way athletic policy was made at the university.

In April 2013, shortly after the announcement of Rutgers's opportune move to the Big Ten, a new crisis in the athletic program shocked the university. Tim Pernetti, McCormick's choice for athletic director, and President Robert Barchi were now at the helm. ESPN televised a video clip, supplied to the network by a former Rutgers basketball staff member, showing the Rutgers men's basketball coach, Mike Rice, berating his players with homophobic slurs (deleted in the telecast) and throwing basketballs at them during practices. Pernetti had seen the video the previous winter, brought in an independent investigator to review Rice's conduct, informed the president and the board about the issue, and then, with their approval, suspended and fined Rice. When that spring the story "went viral" and protest mounted nationwide, Pernetti and Barchi fired Rice, and Barchi, a few days later, accepted Pernetti's resignation. Various state politicians called on Barchi himself to resign, and one suggested that a member of the board who had seen the tape before the story broke should resign as well, but the governor, Chris Christie, made it clear that however much he deplored the coach's conduct, Rutgers's president still had his support.

The subsequent appointment of Julie Hermann—"a historic pick to right the ship," the *Star-Ledger* said—created another crisis.[20] Hermann's résumé included coaching at the University of Tennessee and serving as assistant athletic director at the University of Louisville during a period when the school climbed to national athletic prominence. After her appointment at Rutgers, some of her former volleyball players at Tennessee alleged that sixteen years earlier, she had emotionally and verbally abused them. Having conducted its own background investigation before the hire, Rutgers and its president stood by its appointment, and the controversy died.

The athletic missteps and crises of the past two and a half decades at Rutgers were not necessarily related to the decision to pursue big-time athletics. They were, however, a product of the pressure to compete and win that dominates sports more generally. They also made clear that however much university administrations may wish to think of athletics as a distraction from the more substantive policies a school pursues, no president can afford to take that position. And under the microscope of media investigative journalism and faculty criticism, these crises challenged Rutgers to respond with greater transparency, as McCormick had called for in the wake of the 2008 investigation.

Big-Time: Academic Integrity

As big-time athletics has become increasingly commercial, concerns about and scrutiny of the academic aspects of college sports also increased. Pressure from the NCAA, but also genuine concern within the university itself, made academic integrity a central concern of athletic policy during the Lawrence and McCormick presidencies.

In the early 1990s, after the NCAA, responding to federal pressure, began publishing graduation rates for student athletes, Lawrence asked the newly appointed chair of the Athletic Academic Oversight Committee (AAOC), Richard Budd, the dean of the School of Communications, Information, and Library Sciences, to carry out a comprehensive review of academics and athletics. The committee had been established in 1983, primarily to recommend each year whether specific recruited athletes, who did not meet the regular academic standards at the colleges, could nonetheless be admitted with a reasonable chance of academic success at Rutgers. Lawrence wanted the AAOC to take on much broader responsibilities for monitoring the ongoing academic success of student athletes. Paralleling this initiative, an idea was briefly floated, investigated, and then quickly dropped (probably as a result of faculty anger) to create a general studies major that might add more academic options for athletes, and additional resources were directed to developing the athletic support program. An outside consultant review of the Rutgers athletic program in 1997, which focused almost exclusively on academics and marketing (a clear indication of the drift in sports that Big East membership occasioned), urged the university to increase the number and expand the role of tutors, and to target at-risk players, especially those in football and basketball.

How well were student athletes doing at Rutgers academically? In 1995, for example, the NCAA reported that 70 percent of the student athletes who had enrolled at Rutgers between 1983 and 1988 had graduated within six years, compared to 75 percent of all students at Rutgers, while the rate was 67 percent for football players and 60 percent for male basketball players. These rates were better than those at most other Big East universities and roughly the same at those at other AAU institutions with Division I football programs. Student athletes were spread across the disciplines, and while many majored outside the liberal arts—in criminal justice, communications, and education—many also pursued degrees in the social sciences and humanities. Perhaps fifty or so student athletes made the dean's list each semester, including three or four players each term from Theresa Grentz's women's basketball program. The worries that remained concerned the two primary revenue sports, football and men's basketball (as was true at most universities).

During McCormick's presidency, in 2004, the NCAA adopted a new standard to monitor the academic success of student athletes, the Academic Progress Rate (APR). The APR was calculated by allotting points for academic eligibility and retention (the two factors that best correlated with graduation) for each student athlete and then summing them up to create team rates. Schools that did not have a high enough APR were penalized with the loss of athletic grants-in-aid. The NCAA also rolled out a new, and it hoped more accurate, system for calculating graduation rates. The initial reports from the NCAA indicated that Rutgers was doing fairly well, with only wrestling and fencing in jeopardy of losing resources when the penalties began; fencing, however, was dropped as a varsity sport, and a new wrestling coach turned the program around not only competitively but academically as well. Over this same period, the grade point average of student athletes inched ever-closer to that of the student body as a whole (roughly a "B" or 3.0 on a 4.0 point scale). These results, of course, at Rutgers, as at other schools, reflected a significant commitment of resources to the academic success of student athletes approximately a dozen full-time advisers, graduate student assistants, and tutors, as well as study halls and computer labs, and monitoring programs that tracked attendance and classroom performance throughout the academic year.

Nationwide critics of the NCAA wondered whether the focus on graduation rates was distorting the choices student athletes made about pursuing rigorous academic programs and selecting majors. At Rutgers, at least, that had not been the case in the 1990s and did not appear to be the case in the new century. The typical Rutgers student athlete was in a professional school more often than the School of Arts and Sciences and was most likely to major in exercise sciences, criminal justice, business, or communications and information sciences, but approximately 40 percent pursued more traditional majors in subjects such as English, political science, economics, history, sociology, and psychology. More than sixty distinct majors were listed among the student athletes nominated in 2010–2011 for Big East academic honors. That list, however, and earlier ones as well, had very few names from the three major revenue sports—highlighting the ongoing concern that graduation rates only reflect one aspect of the academic profile of an athletic program.

Conclusion

By the second decade of the twenty-first century, Rutgers had a competitive intercollegiate sports program and participated in a premier athletic conference. It would only have been surprising if this were not true, as most of the AAU public universities could make the same claim. Moreover, the factors that led it to this position were much the same as those that affected its peer institutions (increasing enrollments, scheduling dilemmas, and tapping revenue streams from conference television exposure, while staying within NCAA rules and Title IX requirements). Unlike many state universities, however, Rutgers had emerged from World War II with an athletic regime of a liberal arts college and then had needed to plot an expensive catch-up strategy. At several key moments, that strategy involved choices that reoriented policy profoundly, and each had something to do with football.

Two of those choices were almost afterthoughts, steps forward that hardly seemed like choices at the time, and whose consequences were scarcely anticipated. The first was the acceptance of the Barr scholarships for football athletes with financial need. What was at first free came with time to be quite expensive, as tuition rose and the initial awards had to be supplemented with other funds, and then as Title IX compliance added additional costs. As aid packages enlarged and their numbers multiplied, Rutgers gained a competitive advantage over many of its traditional football opponents, and upgrading the schedule became inevitable. Equally consequential was the commitment of successive university leaders to expanding opportunities for African American and women student athletes. Much of what followed would have happened eventually, but Rutgers's commitment to social justice accelerated these trends and made athletic policy about much more than merely athletics. The size of the football program established the framework in which opportunities would be made available to African American and women athletes.

Two other decisions were of even greater consequence and more self-consciously choices. When Edward Bloustein became president, David Werblin, then a member of the Board of Trustees, pushed hard for a more competitive intercollegiate athletic program. Bloustein, however, not Werblin, appointed the Winkler committee to inquire into the state of the athletic program, while announcing even before it completed its work that he was committed personally to bigger-time athletics—which meant football and men's basketball. The committee, with broader faculty representation than any subsequent body that would review athletics, wrote a report that expressed doubt that athletics could ever become self-supporting and recommended that unless it did, that there should be no steps taken to expand what currently existed. Bloustein disagreed, and his personal report at the end of the process committed the university to moving forward cautiously toward bigger-time sports. In retrospect, both the caution and the commitment can be second-guessed, as a more definitive choice in the 1970s (or earlier, under Gross) might well have resulted in a more sustainable program half a century later.

The other crucial decision was President Lawrence's choice of Robert Mulcahy as athletic director. The appointment launched Rutgers on a short-term, extremely costly path of catching up with other collegiate athletic football powerhouses. Upgraded facilities and academic support, new marketing initiatives, high-salaried coaches, and better recruits dramatically changed the profile of the programs, the expectations of fans, the grumbling of the faculty, and the scrutiny of the media.

Within this framework of constraints and choices, there are several conclusions worth noting. One overarching theme of athletic policy has been the quest for adequate revenues to make the program self-sustaining.

Every president has made that goal a matter of policy. Yet it is arguable that athletics at Rutgers has never been self-sustaining and that the relative cost of the program to the university has almost tripled since World War II. In the immediate postwar era, the direct costs of intercollegiate athletics constituted about 1 percent of the university budget. The program broke even almost every year, as football revenues were expected to cover the costs of other men's intercollegiate sports, but there were no scholarships during those years, and some of the program expenses were in the state-supported budget for the general physical education program, while most of the coaches held appointments on state lines as faculty members. In the Mason Gross years, as the university's overall budget grew enormously, intercollegiate athletics usually accounted for less than 1 percent of the university's expenses. Some costs were still absorbed by the physical education division, but coaches were now being paid, and paid more, to coach (as well as teach in physical education), and despite the use of student fees to support the program (a practice that began in the mid-1950s), deficits were common in the athletic budget (and dependent on the success or failure of the football team).

After intercollegiate athletics became a stand-alone division of the university, and after the opening of Livingston College, the establishment of Cook College, the admission of women to Rutgers college, and Title IX led to the addition of new intercollegiate programs for women, balancing the athletic budget became virtually impossible (even when one accepts that student fees are part of the revenue for athletics and that fellowships are not an expense, but a form of student aid—propositions debated by those who analyze college athletics). Bloustein's overview of the budget, using FY1983 figures, indicated expenses for intercollegiate athletics had now risen to approximately $4.6 million, or about 1.5 percent of the university budget.

A decade later, when Lawrence became president, the athletic budget had grown to $9.9 million, still about 1.5 percent of university expenses. Inflation pumped these costs up over the decade, but their relative importance in the university budget remained much the same throughout the 1990s. A decade and a half later, after the Mulcahy era, and as Rutgers was experiencing unprecedented success in football, the athletic budget had climbed to more than $40 million, roughly 2.5 percent of university expenditures. Direct university support generally ran between $13 million and $18 million a year (actually, a very small percentage of the school's overall budget) but ballooned when Rutgers bought out its existing marketing and conference commitments. By 2012, athletic spending accounted for 3 percent of the university budget—a testimony to the changing import since World War II of intercollegiate sports at Rutgers.

How one thinks about the costs of the athletic program depends on how the purpose of that program is defined. Initially, much greater emphasis was placed on its value to student athletes, and in the days when Rutgers was emerging from its past as a liberal arts college into its new stature as the state university, these student athletes often made up a fourth of the entire undergraduate population. The proportion of student athletes in the general student population has shrunk almost continuously, and arguments in support of intercollegiate athletics have shifted as this has occurred. While the academic success of student athletes remained a primary concern, the program was now more often justified for the publicity it brought the university, the support it engendered among state residents and the legislature, and the boost it gave to enrollments. This last was crucial, as state aid has increasingly gone to students rather than institutions, and the larger university budget has come to depend far more than before on tuition and enrollment increases.

Camden and Newark have had a different experience. With local schedules, modest transportation expenses, little or no money spent on athletic scholarships, and more modest coaching salaries, the cost of running programs is not inordinate. The students who come to Newark and Camden to play intercollegiate sports actually bring tuition dollars into the university and help the campuses attract out-of-state students.

The history of athletic policy also has something to say about decision making and governance at the university. Four groups have been involved—the administration, especially the president; the athletic department, especially the athletic director; the Board of Governors and the Board of Trustees (and through it, the alumni); and the faculty. Initially, the administration paid little attention to intercollegiate athletics, except when it came time to draw up the budget, and intercollegiate athletics existed as part of the physical education program (or, hardly at all in Newark and Camden). As the costs of intercollegiate athletics rose, and questions about conference participation were raised, Mason Gross brought the faculty (although only a select few) into the discussion, and by the end of his time as president, the Board of Trustees had begun to take a more active interest in sports and established a committee to deal with athletics.

Edward Bloustein exercised decisive leadership in athletics, but the mounting costs and public awareness of the program engaged the attention of the Board of Governors, while the faculty, after the Winkler Committee report, dropped out of the picture, except for a few individuals in specialized roles (NCAA representatives and members of the academic oversight committee). The formation in 2002 of a standing committee of the Board of Governors to oversee intercollegiate athletics reflected the sea change that had occurred in intercollegiate athletics at the university since the Bloustein years, just as did the unwillingness of the board when McCormick became president to pursue a comprehensive review of the program. In the wake of the review in 2008 of financial oversight of the program, the role of the Board of Governors in defining the future direction of the program has become even more crucial.

How might Mason Gross respond if he could comment on the changing relationship of intercollegiate athletics to the university? He would certainly continue to deplore the boorish behavior of fans that occasionally accompanies athletic competition, and in the same vein, would probably dislike the branding and other aspects of commercialization that have become the necessary norm in collegiate sports. More seriously, he would warn again about a program that became overly dependent on outside constituencies for financial support. He would also, however, applaud both the opportunities that intercollegiate athletics have given to disadvantaged students, and be surprised and delighted that these opportunities had been extended to women (but saddened that men's crew was no longer an intercollegiate sport). Having served in an era when the program simply could not afford to operate beyond its means, but when it was also subsidized through state support for physical education, he would be shocked by the deficits and angered that the state now did so little to help out a program that its political leaders had long encouraged. And while he might repeat some of the criticisms that faculty have made of intercollegiate athletics, he would emphasize anew that the university's mission as a public school and state university meant it had to embrace in a meaningful way the place of athletics in American culture and education.

Perhaps it is best to give the penultimate word to two professors who knew Mason Gross. Both commented in 1998 on big-time athletics, soon after Gruninger's resignation and just as Robert Mulcahy was about to embark on a sustained effort to make Rutgers a major football and basketball power. Both McCormick and Gardner were historians, both were sports fans, and both were loyal to Rutgers over decades of teaching in New Brunswick. Richard P. McCormick, the preeminent historian of the university, asked to comment on Rutgers's efforts in the late 1990s to turn the sports program around, doubted it could be done at a northeastern school. For him, the priorities were wrong: "There is more to be achieved in terms of academic programs, and public service," he stated. "We have aside from athletic prowess, a lot of good messages for the people of New Jersey but many are not being heard."[21] Lloyd Gardner, McCormick's friend and colleague for almost three decades, saw the matter differently. "We are not the University of Chicago. It is a state institution. If you want to critique something in terms of big-time athletics, then critique all of American culture. Rutgers has so few things to bring the community together, and athletics is another way of doing it. There is no necessary division between big-time athletics and being a scholarly institution. Just look at schools like Michigan, Wisconsin, Stanford, and Northwestern."[22]

Today, there are ironies in these comments. Rutgers's move to the Big Ten has finally placed it in a football conference whose schools match Rutgers's academic aspirations—exactly what McCormick advocated decades earlier in a different context. Gardner's point still rings true, and universities always defend athletics in terms of the creation of community and the benefits to student athletes, but in the high-stakes world of commercialized intercollegiate sports, the trump cards have become branding, marketing, and revenue flows. These, too, are part of American culture.

11

Epilogue

In the halls of Old Queens, people recall vividly the arrival of Robert Barchi. He spotted a nineteenth-century tall-case clock. Decorative, but it had not worked for decades. Barchi loved clocks; he built them himself. He set to work on the Old Queens clock and soon had it doing what it was intended to do: keep time. As he told Bob Braun of the *Star-Ledger*, "It's not a great clock, but if it's going to be here, it should work properly."[1]

When Richard L. McCormick left office on July 1, 2012, Richard L. Edwards, who had come to the university as a new dean for the School of Social Work and had stepped into the position of executive vice president when Philip Furmanski resigned, became the Rutgers interim president. By September 1, Rutgers had a new president, its twentieth, Robert Barchi. Barchi was born in Pennsylvania but grew up in New Jersey. He did undergraduate work at Georgetown University and then earned both a Ph.D. and an M.D. from the University of Pennsylvania. With a background of distinguished research in neuroscience, and administrative experience as provost of the University of Pennsylvania and as president of Thomas Jefferson University (a school with an outstanding reputation in the health sciences), Barchi had the experience Rutgers needed to guide it through the difficult process of integrating its newly acquired medical schools with the university's existing colleges and schools.

On July 1, 2013, after a year of planning, Rutgers launched an entirely new unit, Rutgers Biomedical and Health Sciences (RBHS), and became a truly comprehensive research university. A university of more than fifty thousand students now had almost sixty thousand. A budget that had topped $2 billion would now top $3 billion. Chancellors had overseen Camden and Newark for more than a decade; the Board of Governors established a chancellor's position for RBHS (and one for New Brunswick as well). In December, Brian L. Strom, a professor of biostatistics and epidemiology, attracted to Rutgers from the University of Pennsylvania, became the first chancellor of RBHS, overseeing more than a dozen schools, centers, and institutes, and taking responsibility for the exciting opportunities and the messy details involved in the venture.

For any new president, the first years pose three challenges. The president has to carry forward inherited initiatives, deal with unanticipated (most often budgetary) crises, and chart a new course. For the Barchi administration, launching RBHS was both an inherited challenge and a new undertaking. Another initiative, carried forward from the McCormick years, but of considerably smaller dimension, was the partnership with Devco to build a new academic complex on land formerly occupied by the New Brunswick Theological Seminary—the first such undertaking on the College Avenue campus in decades. The seminary itself acquired a new building at the College Avenue end of the block where it had always been; in spring 2014, Rutgers students could see that the structure, adjacent to the venerable Sage Library, was nearing completion. On the rest of the block, cranes and bulldozers toppled older edifices, making way for two new buildings. One, atop the hill, bookending the view from Old Queens down the Voorhees campus, was an academic building that would house several arts and sciences departments and provide upward of two thousand classroom seats. The other was an honors residential building, meant to create a living-learning community that would attract the best students in New Jersey to the campus (an effort dating back to the founding of the Rutgers College honors program in the late 1970s). For the president, the goal was to have the complex built properly, like a well-constructed clock, and he weighed in personally on the aesthetics of the planned buildings.

The ongoing building program was not limited to the College Avenue campus. In Camden there would be a new nursing and science building, in Newark a life science center and graduate housing in the historic but refurbished 15 Washington Street location, and on Busch campus, a new chemistry and chemical biology building and a gateway engineering building.

The other particularly notable initiative begun during the previous administration was in athletics (see chapter 10). Planning for Big Ten membership was largely a matter for the athletic department—and a marketing opportunity for the university—but the administration's public announcements also stressed repeatedly the positive academic consequences of association with the midwestern universities of the Big Ten. Barchi, whose college years at Georgetown had included participation in both football and lacrosse, recognized the value of intercollegiate athletics both to the students involved and to the university's public image; at the same time, he committed the university to making intercollegiate athletics eventually self-supporting (with the exception of money for athletic scholarships).

Athletics also occasioned one of the unanticipated crises for the new administration when the behavior of the men's basketball coach became a matter of public record. That story has been told above and need not be repeated here, but it is important to note that the Barchi administration learned early on that big-time athletics was a two-edged sword—a marketing tool that could cut both ways.

Hurricane Sandy, which struck soon after President Barchi's arrival, was a less predictable and far more widely experienced crisis. With a radius of almost a thousand miles, winds that gusted up to one hundred miles per hour, and an ocean surge topping twelve feet, Sandy was the worst storm ever to hit the Mid-Atlantic coastline. None of Rutgers's three main campuses were as hard hit as many shore communities in Monmouth and Ocean Counties, but all three, especially New Brunswick/Piscataway, sustained significant damage. When Sandy struck, "residence halls and laboratories lost power; trees and downed power lines blocked streets," computer network capabilities were compromised, "and the New Brunswick water supply was threatened."[2] With electrical and water problems in the residence halls, more than six thousand students on the south side of the Raritan were evacuated to the Livingston and Busch campuses. The university cancelled classes for the week in New Brunswick and Newark; fortunately, no lives were lost at Rutgers during the storm. For many students, there was a journey home to deal with the effect of Sandy on families and friends, and there was volunteer work in neighboring communities, helping with relief and cleanup efforts.

The university had been prepared. Since the 1980s, Rutgers had long had plans in place for emergencies, but the nature and scope of what became the Office of Emergency Management changed dramatically after the terrorism of September 11, 2001, and the shootings in 2007 on the campus of Virginia Tech. In general, a posthurricane review found, through a combination of planning, good luck, and commitment and teamwork of the professional personnel and, in many cases, student volunteers, the university came through the crisis successfully. On the other side of the ledger were communications failures and the inadequacy of backup power sources. Given global climate change, there was every reason to believe that such disasters were no longer "unprecedented," and the university set to work to improve its response system.[3]

During the Francis L. Lawrence administration, Rutgers had engaged in strategic planning. With the addition of RBHS, President Barchi and the Board of Governors embarked on a new round of planning. The strategic planning process engaged a broad cross-section of the Rutgers community, in committee work, at forums, or through survey research. It began with the premise that "Rutgers is already counted among the nation's great research-intensive universities."[4] Even so, the planning process changed yet again the way the university defined itself. Rather than being a traditional research university, Rutgers now had a medical school, and bolder aspirations. The standard of comparison was now Rutgers's "aspirational peers"—the elite of elite public universities.[5] Against that standard, Rutgers–New Brunswick was not doing well (although both Camden and Newark, compared to similarly sized schools, were).

The central academic problem identified in the strategic planning report was that Rutgers lagged behind its aspirational peers in the rankings of programs that were among those in greatest demand by contemporary students. Education, business, law, engineering, and medicine and public health were all such areas. In other areas, long recognized as programs of excellence—English, mathematics, physics, history, the fine arts, public affairs (the Bloustein School)—Rutgers ranked with the best public universities in the nation. The report pointed to additional strengths—student diversity and good graduation rates—but reiterated concerns that had been raised for at least two decades: inadequate state financial support for higher education, the failure to attract out-of-state students, modest alumni giving, and the overly complex bureaucratic world that undergraduates had to endure.

In the broadest terms, the report argued that Rutgers needed to be governed less by its past and more by the changing academic universe of the twenty-first century. Traditional models of education were inadequate.

How students learned, what students wanted to learn, and how faculty members communicated across established disciplinary boundaries had changed. The report argued for maintaining Rutgers's traditional strength in the humanities and core sciences. But in looking toward the future, one shaped by technology and the career aspirations of college students, the report recommended strengthening engineering, medicine, the life sciences, and business.

Stepping back from the report, but looking forward, one should note that Rutgers shares many of the problems that beset higher education: inadequate state funding, the uncertainties in federal funding, competition from for-profit schools, adjusting to online education, controlling the costs of big-time athletics, revitalizing faculty governance, protecting the humanities as students' interests turn to more vocationally oriented disciplines, and managing the increasingly corporate, bureaucratic structure of the university. The university also has many of the same exciting challenges that engage other schools: improving public health, providing ways to cope with climate change, creating technologies that drive economic growth, educating leaders for the twenty-first century, and addressing the inequalities in American life.

One unique challenge stands out—Rutgers's relationship to the State of New Jersey. Richard P. McCormick made that the central theme of the second half of his *Bicentennial History.* As the university approaches its 250th anniversary, being the *state* university remains a challenge and an opportunity. McCormick dealt primarily with the political aspects of the relationship and recognized that in New Jersey educational politics was as often regional as partisan. That is still true. Today, however, the opportunities for and commitment to local outreach are greater, particularly at Newark and Camden. The growth of these campuses is one of the distinctive features of the university's early-twenty-first-century history. Maintaining the research distinction of the New Brunswick/Piscataway campuses is one of the university's great challenges. Both growth and distinction will help Rutgers serve as New Jersey's state university.

NOTES

Only quotations, student work, and interviews conducted by the authors are cited. Full citations are included in a draft of this manuscript deposited in Special Collections and University Archives (SC/UA), Archibald S. Alexander Library (ASAL), Rutgers University Libraries (RUL). Copies of cited student work are also in SC/UA.

Abbreviations

Abernethy Papers. Records of the Rutgers University Chaplain (Bradford S. Abernethy) 1928–1974 (RG 23/H3), SC/UA.

AWN. Access World News, RUL. Newspaper database. Database source is noted when the page number of an article is not available.

Bloustein Papers. Records of the Edward J. Bloustein Administration, uncataloged (RG 04/A17), SC/UA. Titles cited are of current folders.

BOG Minutes. Board of Governors Minutes, SC/UA.

Buildings and Grounds Papers. Board of Trustees, Committee on Buildings and Grounds, Committee Meetings Minutes, October 1952–December 1956 (RG 03/C6), SC/UA.

Caellian. Douglass College student newspaper. Microfilm, ASAL.

Cameron Papers. Records of the Rutgers University Office of University Librarian (Donald F. Cameron), 1925–1971 (RG 40/A1/03), SC/UA.

Clothier Papers. Records of the Robert C. Clothier Administration, 1925–1952 (RG 04/A14), SC/UA.

Douglass College Papers I. Records of the Dean of Douglass College (Group I), 1887–1973 (RG 19/A0/01), SC/UA.

Focus. Rutgers Focus. Copies, SC/UA through 2006; thereafter online.

Gleaner. Rutgers-Camden student newspaper. Copies and microfilm, Special Collections, Paul Robeson Library, Rutgers-Camden.

Gross Papers. Records of the Mason Welch Gross Administration, 1936, 1945–1971 (RG 04/A16), SC/UA.

Home News. Central New Jersey newspaper called at various times *Home News & Tribune, Home News Tribune,* and the *Home News.* Microfilm, ASAL.

Jones Papers. Records of the Lewis Webster Jones Administration, Group I: Administrative Records, 1951–1958 (RG 04/A15/01), SC/UA.

Lawrence Papers. Records of the Francis L. Lawrence Administration, uncataloged (RG 04/A18), SC/UA. Titles cited are of current folders.

Livingston College Papers. Records of the Office of the Dean of Livingston College (Ernest A. Lynton), 1943–1974 (RG 21/A0/04), SC/UA.

McCormick Papers. Records of the Richard L. McCormick Administration, uncataloged (RG 04/A19), SC/UA. Titles cited are of current folders.

Observer. Rutgers-Newark student newspaper. Copies in John Cotton Dana Library, Rutgers-Newark; and microfilm, ASAL.

OIRAP. Office of Institutional Research and Academic Planning.

Record. Hackensack newspaper called the *Bergen Evening Record* and the *Record.* Online (AWN).

RfR. Report from Rutgers, Library reports, SC/UA.

Richard P. McCormick Papers. Richard P. McCormick Papers, 1929–2003 (R-MC 050), SC/UA. Not fully cataloged. When materials as yet uncataloged are cited, this fact and the current folder name are indicated.

ROHA. Rutgers Oral History Archives.

R-Photo, Rutgers photographic collection, SC/UA. Citations include the general location within the collection where an image is found (for example, "buildings and grounds"). Fuller citations are given in the library draft copy of this book.

Rutgers Library Records. Records of the Rutgers University Library, R-Vertical Files (RG 40), SC/UA. Not yet cataloged.

Scarlet Letter, [year], Rutgers College yearbook, SC/UA.

Schlatter Papers. Records of the Rutgers University Provost and Vice President (Richard Schlatter), 1945–1972 (RG 15/A2), SC/UA.

Star-Ledger. Newark newspaper called at various times *Newark Star Ledger, Sunday Star Ledger,* and the *Star-Ledger.* Online (AWN); microfilm, RUL; and personal clippings file.

Targum. New Brunswick campus newspaper called at various times the *Daily Targum, Rutgers Daily Targum, Rutgers Targum,* and the *Targum.* Microfilm, RUL, through 1988–1989; thereafter, print copies, ASAL.

Vietnam Teach-Ins. Inventory to the Records on the Vietnam War Teach-Ins at Rutgers University, 1965–1966 (RG 07/A2/01), SC/UA.

1. Becoming a State University

For the background of higher education, see David R. Thelin, *A History of American Higher Education,* 2nd ed. (Baltimore, MD: Johns Hopkins University Press, 2011). On Rutgers during the Clothier and Jones presidencies, see Richard P. McCormick, *Rutgers: A Bicentennial History* (New Brunswick, NJ: Rutgers University Press, 1966). On the Cold War on campus, see Ellen Schrecker, *Many Are the Crimes: McCarthyism in America* (Princeton, NJ: Princeton University Press, 1998), and for Rutgers's involvement with Cold War issues, see Thomas F. Richards, *The Cold War within American Higher Education: Rutgers University as a Case Study* (Raleigh, NC: Pentland Press, 1999). For protest at Rutgers, see Richard P. McCormick, *The Black Student Protest Movement at Rutgers* (New Brunswick, NJ: Rutgers University Press, 1990).

1 Thelin, *History of American Higher Education,* 260.

2   McCormick, *Rutgers*, 226.

3   Ibid., 247.

4   Ibid., 258.

5   Ibid., 264.

6   Ibid., 283.

7   *Faculty News-Letter* 7 (January–February 1951): 349.

8   Jones, "Let Us Hold a Standard," Rutgers press release of inaugural address, May 8, 1952, 2, 3, 10, R-Vertical, RG 4a/15, SC/UA.

9   Jones, *The Spirit of '76 and the Barbarian Culture: Phi Beta Kappa Anniversary Address* (New Brunswick, NJ: Rutgers University, 1951), 10.

10 Jones, "Let Us Hold a Standard," 11, 13.

11 Jones, Presidential Address to the Annual Convention of the Association of Land Grant Colleges and Universities, November 15, 1955, *Faculty News-Letter* 11 (December 1955): 550.

12 *Targum*, December 17, 1948, 2, 4.

13 Lewis Webster Jones, *Academic Freedom and Civic Responsibility: Statement of President Lewis Webster Jones of Rutgers University on the Heimlich-Finley Cases, January 24, 1953* (New Brunswick, NJ: Rutgers University, 1953), n.p.

14 Jones, "Let Us Hold a Standard," 10–11.

15 *Targum*, September 16, 1958, 1.

16 McCormick, *Rutgers*, 314.

17 *Targum*, May 7, 1959, 7.

18 Richard P. McCormick and Richard Schlatter, eds., *The Selected Speeches of Mason Welch Gross* (New Brunswick, NJ: Rutgers University Publications, 1980), 74, 78.

19 Ibid., 79.

20 Ibid., 18.

21 *Rutgers Newsletter*, October 20, 1967, 1.

22 *Rutgers Newsletter*, May 22, 1970, 6.

23 *Targum*, April 26, 1965.

24 Ibid.

25 Board of Governors, "A Report on the Genovese Case," Vietnam Teach-Ins, 1/4. For *Targum* wording, April 26, 1965, 3.

26 Ibid. The description of the university regulations in the text is a paraphrase of a slightly different statement in the original record.

27 *Targum*, December 14, 1967, 1.

28 "A Letter to the Rutgers Community," September 16, 1969, Gross Papers, 115/10.

29 Daniel Kleinman, "Rutgers in Vietnam: The State University's Position in a Tumultuous Time," History Department seminar paper, April 2013.

30 McCormick, *Black Student Protest*, 7.

31 Ibid., 21.

32 McCormick's interview of Predow-James, November 11, 1988 (personal copy).

33 Gilbert Cohen interview of Donaldson, November 12, 1991, available at Rutgers University Community Repository, https://rucore.libraries.rutgers.edu/rutgers-lib/40843/.

34 McCormick, *Black Student Protest*, 46, 69.
35 Gross's response to the twenty-one questions is attached to a letter to state legislators William T. Hiering and Thomas H. Kean, May 1, 1969, Gross Papers, 35/3. Quotes from his answers to questions 1, 7, and 11.
36 Transcript of National Broadcasting Company, "Frank McGhee Sunday Report," May 11, 1969, attached to George H. Holsten Jr. to Gross, May 16, 1969, Gross Papers, 33/7.
37 *Rutgers Newsletter*, May 10, 1971, 1.

2. Rutgers Becomes a Research University

For background, see David R. Thelin, *A History of American Higher Education*, 2nd ed. (Baltimore, MD: Johns Hopkins University Press, 2011); and Roger L. Geiger, *Research and Relevant Knowledge: American Research Universities since World War II* (New York: Oxford University Press, 1993); for a comparable story, Robert C. Alberts, *Pitt: The Story of the University of Pittsburgh, 1787–1987* (Pittsburgh: University of Pittsburgh Press, 1987). On Rutgers, Edward J. Bloustein, *The University and the Counterculture: Inaugural and Other Addresses* (New Brunswick, NJ: Rutgers University Press, 1972); Susan L. Poulson, "'A Quiet Revolution': The Transition to Coeducation at Georgetown and Rutgers College, 1960–1975" (Ph.D. diss., Georgetown University, 1989); and Richard P. McCormick, *Academic Reorganization in New Brunswick, 1962–1978: The Federated College Plan* (New Brunswick, NJ: Rutgers University, November 1978). On New Brunswick, Eric Schkrutz, "Urban Development in the City of the Traveler: The Story of New Brunswick and Why It May Never Resolve Its Identity Crisis" (honors thesis, Rutgers Department of History, 2011); and Christopher Rasmussen, "'A Web of Tension': The 1967 Protests in New Brunswick, New Jersey," *Journal of Urban History* 40, no. 1 (2014).

1 *Faculty Newsletter*, September 24, 1971, 2.
2 Bloustein, *University and the Counterculture*, 3.
3 Ibid., 57.
4 Ibid., 18.
5 Ibid., 27.
6 Caitlin Foley, "Religion at Rutgers University," History Department seminar paper, December 2013, 19.
7 *Targum*, September 21, 1970, 1, cited in Matthew D. Knoblauch, "Scarlet Beat: The Evolution of Law Enforcement at Rutgers, 1963–1988," History Department seminar paper, April 2013, 33.
8 *Focus*, February 26, 1982, 1.
9 *Targum*, February 16, 1982, 4.
10 *Focus*, February 26, 1982, 3.
11 Bloustein, "The Academy, Political Activism, and Civil Disorders," March 27, 1974, BOG Minutes, April 5, 1974 (appended material).
12 Richard P. McCormick, Academic *Reorganization*, 62–63.
13 Ibid., 77.
14 *Rutgers Newsletter*, September 13, 1974, 2.

15 *Rutgers Newsletter*, January 24, 1972, 1.
16 Minutes of the Meeting of the Administrative Council, Bloustein Papers, no-confidence folder.
17 *Rutgers Newsletter*, April 28, 1978, 1.
18 *Rutgers Newsletter*, March 30, 1979, 1.
19 Ibid., 3.
20 *Rutgers Newsletter*, April 9, 1976, 3.
21 *Rutgers Newsletter*, September 14, 1979.
22 *Targum*, October 16, 1990, 1.
23 Sarah Stuby, "The Johnson & Johnson World Headquarters: Revitalization and the International Style," Art History Department seminar paper, December 2013.
24 *Rutgers Newsletter*, November 11, 1977, 1.

3. Negotiating Excellence

For background, see David R. Thelin, *A History of American Higher Education*, 2nd ed. (Baltimore, MD: Johns Hopkins University Press, 2011); Hugh Davis Graham and Nancy Diamond, *The Rise of American Research Universities: Elites and Challengers in the Postwar Era* (Baltimore, MD: Johns Hopkins University Press, 1997); and Roger L. Geiger, *Knowledge and Money: Research Universities and the Paradox of the Marketplace* (Stanford, CA: Stanford University Press, 2004). For Rutgers, see Richard L. McCormick, *Raised at Rutgers: A President's Story* (New Brunswick, NJ: Rutgers University Press, 2014); and Gloria Bonilla-Santiago, *Miracle on Cooper Street: Lessons from an Inner City* (Bloomington, IN: Archway Publishing, 2014).
1 Thelin, *History of American Higher Education*, 381.
2 *Rutgers Magazine*, Fall 1990, 2.
3 Lawrence, "Undergraduate Education at Rutgers: An Agenda for the Nineties" (November 12, 1991), 2.
4 Ibid., 28.
5 *Focus*, September 11, 1992, 1.
6 "In Every Classroom: The Report of the President's Select Committee for Lesbian and Gay Concerns" (1989), 76.
7 *Star-Ledger*, January 31, 1995 (AWN).
8 *Focus*, February 3, 1995, 1.
9 *Focus*, February 6, 1998, 1.
10 *Targum*, February 22, 2002, 9.
11 Thelin, *History of American Higher Education*, 360.
12 "A Bold Idea: Transforming Undergraduate Education on Our Largest Campus" (Fall 2005), http://richardlmccormick.rutgers.edu/writings/speeches/bold-idea.
13 Paraphrase of Margaret Marsh to Reverend William Howard et al., August 5, 2008, McCormick Papers, Camden, 2008 folder.
14 University of Medicine and Dentistry of New Jersey Advisory Committee, "Final Report" (January 25, 2012), iv.
15 Daniel Hart, Board of Trustees Minutes, February 23, 2012, attachments, 18.
16 *Star-Ledger*, May 29, 2011, 1.

4. Student Life

For background, see Helen Lefkowitz Horowitz, *Campus Life: Undergraduate Cultures from the End of the Eighteenth Century to the Present* (New York: Alfred A. Knopf, 1987); and Nicholas L. Syrett, *The Company He Keeps: A History of White College Fraternities* (Chapel Hill: University of North Carolina Press, 2009). For college life at Rutgers, see Michael Moffatt, *Coming of Age in New Jersey: College and American Culture* (New Brunswick, NJ: Rutgers University Press, 1989); and George P. Schmidt, *Douglass College: A History* (New Brunswick, NJ: Rutgers University Press, 1968).

1 Philip Roth, "Joe College: Memories of a Fifties Education," *Atlantic Monthly*, December 1987, 45.

2 S. Mitra Kalita, *Suburban Sahibs: Three Immigrant Families and Their Passage from India to America* (New Brunswick, NJ: Rutgers University Press, 2003), 2.

3 *Targum*, February 21, 1997, 1.

4 *Targum*, October 1, 1946, 1. On veterans at Rutgers, Marc Snitzer, "Bring the Boys Back Home," Department of History seminar paper, fall 2013.

5 "Report of President's Committee on Fraternities," November 5, 1963, 10, Gross Papers, 47/4.

6 Clothier to H. Maurice Darling, December 22, 1943,1, Clothier Papers, 21/10.

7 "Memorandum Regarding Fraternities," April 18, 1945, 2, Clothier Papers, 21/11.

8 "Report of President's Committee on Fraternities," 1.

9 "Report of the Commission on the Study of Fraternities and Sororities in New Brunswick, 1979," January 15, 1980, 25, 33, New Brunswick Provost's Office Papers (uncataloged).

10 "Student Council Recommendations," March 21, 1949, Clothier Papers, 21/9.

11 *Targum*, May 8, 1956, 1.

12 *Scarlet Letter*, 1956, 186.

13 *Targum*, March 21, 1956, 1.

14 *Targum*, October 4, 1955, 1.

15 New Jersey College for Women, *Handbook of the Government Association* [*Red Book*], *1948*, 1. For the relationship between college architecture and ideas about women's education, see Chelsie Y. Güner, "The First Ten Years; Architectural Development at the New Jersey College for Women from 1918–1928," Art History Department seminar paper, December 2013.

16 The term "quiet revolution" comes from Susan L. Poulson, "'A Quiet Revolution': The Transition to Coeducation at Georgetown and Rutgers Colleges, 1960–1975" (Ph.D. diss., Georgetown University, 1980).

17 *Red Book*, 1948, 5.

18 *Red Book*, 1960, 65.

19 *Red Book*, 1960, 23.

20 *Caellian*, February 23, 1968, 1.

21 *Targum*, February 26, 1968, 1.

22 *Caellian*, February 5, 1971, 1.

23 *Douglass Red Book*, 1972–1973, 4.

24 *Rutgers Newsletter*, September 13, 1972, 1.

25 *Targum*, February 26, 1973, 4.

26 *Targum*, November 8, 1972, 12.

27 *Targum*, February 19, 1971, 7.

28 *Targum*, April 6, 2009, 1.

29 *Encore, 1973*, 131.

30 Ibid., 44.

31 Moffatt, *Coming of Age*, 1.

32 Ibid., 48.

33 Ibid., 182.

34 Ibid., 47.

35 Lauren Caruana, "Sororities at Rutgers University," History Department seminar paper, December 2013.

36 *Targum*, February 15, 1990, "Inside Beat," 5.

37 *Targum*, August 28, 1998, 34.

38 Kyle Madison interview, November 2, 2011.

39 Horowitz, *Campus Life*, 11.

40 Ibid., 12.

5. Residence Hall Architecture at Rutgers

For background, see Alex Duke, *Importing Oxbridge: English Residential Colleges and American Universities* (New Haven, CT: Yale University Press, 1997); and Helen Lefkowitz Horowitz, *Campus Life: Undergraduate Cultures from the End of the Eighteenth Century to the Present* (New York: Alfred A. Knopf, 1987).

1 *Scarlet Letter*, 1957, 84.

2 The author wishes to thank Rutgers students Cristina Toma and Eric Kaplan for their research papers on the River Dorms.

3 Boocock to Jones, June 10, 1953, Jones Papers, 10/9.

4 Minutes of Joint Committee Meeting on Buildings and Grounds, Finance and School of Law, March 25, 1954, Building and Grounds Papers, box 1, folder "Buildings and Grounds, Committee Meeting minutes, October 1952–December 1957," SC/UA.

5 Clothier to Lansing, February 5, 1954, Jones Papers, 10/9.

6 Ibid.

7 Ibid.

8 Boocock to Jones, June 3, 1954, Jones Papers, 10/9.

9 Boocock to Jones, August 31, 1954, Jones Papers, 10/9.

10 Ibid.

11 Ibid.

12 BOG Minutes, November 12, 1956, 9.

13 Horowitz, *Campus Life*, 220.

14 Richard P. McCormick, *The Black Student Protest Movement at Rutgers* (New Brunswick, NJ: Rutgers University Press, 1990), 30.

15 *New York Times*, June 8, 1969, 50.

16 McHenry to Lynton, January 21, 1965, Livingston College Papers, 17/12.

17 Annual Report, Livingston College, 1965–66, Livingston College Papers, box 1.

18 "Summary of Progress on New College" (ca. 1965), Gross Papers, 62/2.

19 *New York Times*, June 8, 1969, 50.

20 *Home News*, March 16, 1966.

21 Ricki Sablove, "Building for the 1960s Generation: Livingston College at Rutgers University" (master's thesis, Rutgers University, 2007).

22 "Program for the Raritan Campus," February 19, 1965, Buildings and Grounds Papers, box 2, SC/UA.

23 *Targum*, April 20, 1965, 3.

24 ROHA, Peter Klein interview, June 6, 2011.

25 "Program for the Raritan Campus," February 19, 1965, Buildings and Ground Papers, box 2.

26 Office of Student Affairs, Executive Dean, RG 9/A, box 10; "Report to the Board of Trustees: River Residence Halls," November 15, 1963, Ohio State University, Special Collections. In this report, the authors, all student life deans, paraphrased a document put together by the National Association of Student Personnel Administrators.

27 Harold C. Riker, *College Students Live Here* (New York: Educational Facilities Laboratories, 1961), 44.

28 Gregory Blimling, interview with author, June 5, 2014.

29 DesignCollective, "Living-Learning Community, Rutgers University," http://www.designcollective.com/portfolio/project/rutgers-university—living-learning-community/.

30 Blimling interview.

6. Student Protest

Useful works include Richard P. McCormick, *The Black Student Protest Movement at Rutgers* (New Brunswick, NJ: Rutgers University Press, 1990); Van Gosse and Richard Moser, eds., *The World the Sixties Made: Political Culture in Recent America* (Philadelphia: Temple University Press, 2003); and Marc Stein, *Rethinking the Gay and Lesbian Movement* (New York: Routledge, 2012).

1 "Generation without a Cause," 1963, SC/UA. The show was broadcast March 1, 1959. All quotes in the text are taken from the author's transcription of the broadcast.

2 *Rutgers Anthologist* 19 (October 1947): 9.

3 *Rutgers Anthologist* 19 (December 1947): 4.

4 *Antho* 22 (October 1950): 16.

5 "Associated Press Dispatch," December 12, 1950, Gross Papers, 17/3.

6 "Statement by Special Committee of Trustees Re 'Antho,'" 2, Gross Papers, 17/3.

7 Clothier to Stanley Albanesius, November 28, 1950, Gross Papers, 17/3.

8 Gross to Erico T. Palomba, November 30, 1950, Gross Papers, 17/3.

9 Ivan J. Silverman to Gross, April 11, 1963, Gross Papers, 17/4. *Anthologist* was again the formal name of the magazine.

10 Abernethy Papers, 6/1.

11 Senator Harrison Williams's account, Abernethy Papers, 6/1.

12 Ibid.

13 *Targum*, October 8, 1963, 1.

14 *Targum*, September 27, 1963, 1.

15 Ibid.

16 *Caellian*, October 11, 1963, 1.

17 Alfonso Roman, *Educational Opportunities and the Hispanic College Student: Final Report on Needs Assessment of the Processes, Programs, and Services Used to Enroll Spanish-Speaking Students in Higher Education in New Jersey* (Trenton: Puerto Rican Congress of New Jersey, 1974), 6.

18 Ibid., 38.

19 Diaz, Santana, and Carrion to Malcolm D. Talbot, March 10, 1969, Schlatter Papers, 34/13.

20 Ibid.

21 BOG Minutes, March 14, 1969, 10.

22 Maldonado interviews, January 23, 29, 2014.

23 Medina interview, January 29, 2014.

24 "Declaration against the Discrimination by Rutgers University Camden Campus Administration against the Puerto Rican Students," March 4, 1971, Schlatter Papers, 34/13.

25 *Gleaner*, March 10, 1971, 1.

26 Statement undated and untitled in Schlatter Papers, 34/13.

27 "Declaration against Discrimination."

28 *Targum*, March 5, 1971, 6.

29 Ibid.

30 Provost to Dean Henry Blumenthal et al., March 5, 1971, Schlatter Papers, 34/13.

31 *Targum*, April 8, 1971, 6.

32 Ibid.

33 This phrase was used by several interviewees at the Camden and Newark campuses to describe the way their campuses were two or three decades ago.

34 *Targum*, December 8, 1971, 1 (misdated November 15, 1971).

35 Marcia Carlisle Michaely, "NJPIRG: The First Five Years" (1977), 2.

36 *Targum*, October 15, 1974, 3.

37 Ibid., 6.

38 *Targum*, November 29, 1988, 10.

39 BOG Minutes, April 10, 1987, 8.

40 *Targum*, April 13, 1987, 1.

41 BOG Minutes, December 11, 1987, 4.

42 Ibid., 5.

43 BOG Minutes, May 12, 1989, 7.

44 Ibid., 5.

45 *Star-Ledger*, June 10, 1989 (AWN).

46 *Star-Ledger*, September 13, 1989 (AWN).

47 "Notes for Interviews with Cook College Students," February 9, 1993, 8–9, Lawrence Papers, CARE, 1991–1993 folder.

48 *Star-Ledger*, July 8, 1990, Accent/Health section, 11.

49 *Record*, November 29, 1995, "Religion and Values," 1.

50 *Dale v. Boy Scouts of America*, 160 N.J. 562 (1999), at 647–648.

51 *Star-Ledger*, August 5, 2012, Perspective, 1.
52 Berkowitz, *Stayin' Alive: The Invention of Safe Sex; A Personal History* (Boulder, CO: Westview Press, 2001), 22.
53 *Targum*, November 25, 1969, 1.
54 Moe [Morris] Kafka, "The History of the RULGA," *Targum*, April 16, 1987, "Inside Beat," 8.
55 *Observer*, February 11, 1977, 15.
56 David Nicholas and Morris J. Kafka-Hozschlag, "The Rutgers University Lesbian/ Gay Alliance, 1969–1989: The First Twenty Years," *Journal of the Rutgers University Archives* 51 (December 1989): 66.
57 *Targum*, April 26, 1976, 1.
58 Nicholas and Kafka-Hozschlag, "Rutgers University Lesbian/Gay Alliance," 62.
59 Ibid., 85.
60 *Targum*, April 16, 1987, "Inside Beat," 3.
61 *Mother Jones* 19 (September/October 1994): 56.
62 Ibid.

7. Research at Rutgers

For background, see Morton A. Meyers, *Prize Fight and the Rivalry to Be the First in Science* (New York: Palgrave Macmillan, 2012); Roger L. Geiger, *Research and Relevant Knowledge: American Research Universities since World War II* (New York: Oxford University Press, 1993); Allen B. Robbins, *History of Physics and Astronomy at Rutgers, 1771–2000* (Baltimore, MD: Gateway Press, 2001); and Richard P. McCormick, "Jottings on the History of History at Rutgers," 1988, McCormick Papers, 45/9. Two useful sources for first-person accounts are Margaret A. Judson, *Breaking the Barrier: A Professional Autobiography by a Woman Educator and Historian before the Women's Movement* (New Brunswick, NJ: Rutgers University Press, 1984); and Deborah Gray White, ed., *Telling Histories: Black Women Historians in the Ivory Tower* (Chapel Hill: University of North Carolina Press, 2008).

1 Meyers, *Prize Fight*, 103.
2 "Program Evaluations and Proposed Action Recommendations," August 6, 1981, unpublished supplement to the "Report of the Task Force on University Policy and Future Directions in Graduate and Graduate-Professional Education at Rutgers," September 1981, Bloustein Papers, graduate education folders.
3 Ibid.
4 Iosif B. Khriplovich, "The Eventful Life of Fritz Houtermans," *Physics Today* (July 1992): 30.
5 Interview with Noémie Benczer-Koller, August 6, 2013.
6 Torrey to Harry Owen, October 5, 1962, Schlatter Papers, 31/10.
7 "Centers of Excellence: New NSF Science Development Program Aims at 'Second 20' Universities," *Science* (18 December 1964): 1564.
8 "Report on the Rutgers University Physics Department," June 29, 1976, 2, OIRAP.
9 Mary B. Jones, "The Smallest Frontier," *Rutgers Magazine* 70 (Fall 1991): 19.

10 "Report of the Rutgers External Review Committee" (1987), 4, OIRAP.
11 "Report of the Committee on the School of Criminal Justice," November 24, 1969, 2, Schlatter Papers, 13/4.
12 Ibid., 1.
13 Ibid., 4.
14 Fairbanks to Richard Schlatter, May 4, 1971, 2, Schlatter Papers, 13/4.
15 John Carpi, "Deep Secrets: The Undersea World of Richard Lutz," *Rutgers Magazine* 73 (Winter 1994): 28.
16 Stephen J. Kleinschuster to Pond, February 6, 1986, Bloustein Papers, marine science consortium folders.
17 Kleinschuster to Pond, February 6, 1986, Bloustein Papers, Institute of Marine and Coastal Sciences (1985–1989) folder.
18 Judson, *Breaking the Barrier,* 44.
19 ROHA, Rudolph Bell interview, August 26, 2010.
20 ROHA, Lloyd Gardner interviews, March 27, April 17, 2008.
21 Robert Forster, Gordon S. Wood, and Richard S. Kirkendall to Edward J. Bloustein, June 30, 1977, 1, OIRAP.
22 CSPAD Evaluation, July 1981, OIRAP.
23 Margo Anderson, "Learning to Count," *Department of History Newsletter,* March 1995, 1.
24 "Report of the Visiting Committee to the Department of History," July 30, 1982, 13, OIRAP.
25 Margaret Darrow, "The Early History of Women's History at Rutgers," *Department of History Newsletter,* March 1991, 1–3.
26 Jonathan Kozol, *Savage Inequalities: Children in America's Schools* (New York: Crown, 1991), 182.
27 "Expanded Concept Paper for M.A. and Ph.D. Programs in Childhood Studies," personal copy, June 25, 2004, 4 (citing Kozol).
28 Deborah Valentine interview, September 16, 2013.
29 External Review Exit Interview Notes, Department of Philosophy (New Brunswick), February 9, 1996, 1, OIRAP.

8. A Place Called Rutgers

For background, see Blake Gumprecht, *The American College Town* (Amherst: University of Massachusetts Press, 2008); Dee Garrison, *Apostles of Culture: The Public Librarian and American Society, 1876–1920* (New York: Free Press, 1979); and James Axtell, *The Making of Princeton University: From Woodrow Wilson to the Present* (Princeton, NJ: Princeton University Press, 2006).

1 *Targum,* April 28, 1978, 4.
2 *Targum,* May 2, 1962, 5 (reprinted from *Scarlet Letter,* 1932).
3 *Scrapbook, 1961–62, European Tour,* Glee Club Collection, RG 48/C1, SC/UA.
4 Matt Weismantel, "[Notes on] Rutgers University Glee Club 1970's–1980's History," 2013 (personal copy).
5 *Targum,* November 8, 1994, 3.
6 John Floreen interview, May 16, 2013.

7 ROHA, Michael Perlin interview transcript, February 18, 2010, 40.

8 Ibid., 40–41.

9 *Targum*, April 26, 1965, 1.

10 Perlin interview, 64–65.

11 Ibid., 65.

12 Ibid., 65.

13 *Targum*, March 10, 1954, 2.

14 *Targum*, November 27, 1979, 3, on April 24, 1949, incident.

15 Interview with Ann Kiernan, reporter and news editor, 1973–1977, January 15, 2013.

16 *RfR*, June 1966, 1.

17 Edward G. Holley [chair of the external review committee] to T. Alexander Pond, September 9, 1985, R-Vertical Files, RG 39G12-40, box 39, SC/UA.

18 *RUL Report*, Spring 1997, 3.

19 "Annual Report of the Librarian of the University 1950–1951," 4, Cameron Papers, I, 1/6.

20 *RfR*, June 1966, 1.

21 *Newark Sunday News*, November 11, 1956, 22.

22 *New York Times*, August 18, 1956, 15.

23 *RfR*, March 1961, 1.

24 Halina R. Rusak, "The Art Library: A New Art Landmark at Rutgers Mall," *Journal of the Rutgers University Libraries* 54, no. 2 (1992): 29, 32.

25 Donald F. Cameron to Dean A. E. Meder Jr., May 16, 1947, Cameron Papers, II, 1/16.

26 New Jersey College for Women Annual Report, 1951–1952, Cameron Papers, I, 1/7.

27 Kidman to "All [Library] Academic Staff," December 8, 1969, 2, Rutgers Library Records.

28 "To Join the First Ranks of America's Public Research Universities," September 1985, 1, Rutgers Library Records.

29 [Hendrik Edelman], Progress Report 1984/85, July 1985, 6, Library Annual Reports, box 3, SC/UA.

30 Natalie Borisovets, May 22, 2013, recalled the IRIS naming contest.

31 *New Brunswick Home News*, September 12, 1973, 12.

32 "Rutgers Advantage: A Long Range Plan for the Library," November 1988, 4, Library Annual Reports, box 4, SC/UA.

33 *Rutgers Focus*, February 11, 1994, 3.

34 VALE New Jersey, *Triennial Report, 2009–2011* (2012), 4, at http://www.valenj.org/pressroom/vale-news/vale-triennial-report-2009-2011.

35 William M. Weinberg to Dean Harry S. Layton, Annual Report: Institute of Jazz Studies, June 4, 1968, 1, Rutgers Library Records.

36 *Print* 2 (1941): 5; as reprinted in Chester Kerr, *A Report on American University Presses* (Washington, DC: Association of American University Presses, 1949), 13.

37 William Sloane, "History of Rutgers University Press," August 1, 1958, 2, Gross Papers, 98/12.

38 The *Sunday Times* interview was published November 5, 1950, and is in Gross Papers, 96/6.

39 Dudley Meeks, "A Survey of Rutgers University Press," April 1954, 1, Gross Papers, 96/9.

40 Sloane to Gross, August 13, 1956, Gross Papers, 96/6.

41 Mann to Winkler, April 12, May 5, 1976, Bloustein Papers, Rutgers University Press folder.

42 *Focus*, October 17, 1997, 4.

43 Ibid.

44 Discussions with John Sherer, director of the University of North Carolina Press, and Fred M. Woodward, director of the University Press of Kansas.

45 Mason Gross, "The Cultural Dependence of New Jersey," September 12, 1959, n.p., Gross Papers, 120/47.

46 Sloane to Schlatter, May 20, 1966, Schlatter Papers, 6/3.

47 *Rutgers Newsletter*, January 1967, 3.

48 Jack Spector, Marian Burleigh Motley, and Roger Tarman to Mason W. Gross, December 13, 1969, Gross Papers, 17/14.

49 *New York Times*, September 30, 1973, 78.

50 *New York Times*, December 16, 1973, 177.

51 *New York Times*, September 30, 1973, 78.

52 *Focus*, July 12, 1994, 2.

53 *New York Times*, March 13, 1983, H35.

54 *Focus*, April 28, 1995, 5.

55 *Focus*, November 4, 2002, 4

56 "Rutgers University's Museums and Galleries: A Committee Report," May 30, 1979, 10, Bloustein Papers, art gallery folder.

57 Ibid., 7.

58 *New York Times*, October 12, 2003, NJ12.

59 Ibid.

60 *Rutgers Newsletter*, March 6, 1981, 2.

61 On the CLICK! project, *Philadelphia Inquirer*, July 30, 1997, D01.

62 *Philadelphia Inquirer*, April 21, 2004, G13.

9. Women's Basketball

For background, see Pamela Grundy and Susan Shackelford, *Shattering the Glass: The Remarkable History of Women's Basketball* (Chapel Hill: University of North Carolina Press, 2005). A personal account is C. Vivien Stringer and Laura Tucker, *Standing Tall: A Memoir of Tragedy and Triumph* (New York: Crown Archetype, 2007).

1 NJCW Physical Education Department, Annual Report, 1952–1953, 2, Douglass College Papers I, 3/1.

2 Interview with Marjorie (Myers) Howes, November 16, 2012.

3 Interviews with Susan Ann Laubach, December 4, 2011; Mary Ann Poggi McRae, December 9, 2011; Sarah Noddings, March 3, 2012; Nancy Newmark Kaplan, January 20, 2012; and Judy Pease Smith,. February 3, 2012.

4 McRae interview, December 15, 2011.

5 Noddings interview.

6 Sandra Petway interview, March 2, 2012.

10. Athletic Policy

On Rutgers sports, see Thomas Frusciano, *Rutgers University Football Vault: The History of the Scarlet Knights* (Atlanta: Whitman Publishing, 2008); and Richard P. McCormick, "Going Big-Time: The Rutgers Experience" (unpublished essay, 2003). Background on college sports came from Ronald A. Smith, *Pay for Play: A History of Big-Time College Athletic Reform* (Urbana: University of Illinois Press, 2011); Michael Oriard, *Bowled Over: Big-Time College Football from the Sixties to the BCS Era* (Chapel Hill: University of North Carolina Press, 2009); Andrew Zimbalist, *Unpaid Professionals: Commercialism and Conflict in Big-Time College Sports* (Princeton, NJ: Princeton University Press, 1999); and Susan Ware, *Title IX: A Brief History with Documents* (New York: Bedford/St. Martin, 2007). For a different view, see William C. Dowling, *Confessions of a Spoilsport: My Life and Hard Times Fighting Sports Corruption at an Old Eastern University* (University Park: Penn State University Press, 2007).

1 "Summary of Statement by Dr. Robert C. Clothier concerning Rutgers University's Policy in respect to Post-season "Bowl" Football Games," Fall 1947, Clothier Papers, 6/2.

2 McCormick to Jones, April 7, 1954, Jones Papers, 13/14.

3 Rockafeller to Kenneth Fairmen (athletic director, Princeton University), July 19, 1956, Jones Papers, 13/14.

4 *Targum*, November 20, 1961, 1.

5 Twitchell to Gross, March 6, 1964, Richard P. McCormick Papers (uncataloged), athletic folders.

6 Twitchell to Gross, January 24, 1966, ibid.

7 Twitchell to Werblin, April 18, 1966, Gross Papers, 19/5.

8 Twitchell to Gross, January 1, 1968, Gross Papers, 19/7.

9 Twitchell to Gross, March 6, 1964, Richard P. McCormick Papers (uncataloged).

10 *Targum*, April 5, 1967, 2.

11 Twitchell to Walter Byers, March 1, 1967, Gross Papers, 71/9.

12 Gross to Twitchell, January 5, 1968, Gross Papers, 71/9.

13 Walter Byers to Gross, May 13, 1968, Gross Papers, 71/9.

14 "Crossing the Rubicon!" is a handwritten comment by Richard P. McCormick on Twitchell to Gross, June 5, 1970, Richard P. McCormick Papers (uncataloged).

15 Board of Trustees minutes, December 18, 1970.

16 Bloustein to Werblin, February 14, 1973, Richard P. McCormick Papers (uncataloged).

17 *Rutgers Alumni Magazine*, April 1977, 2.

18 Newark student to Bloustein, April 25, 1977, Bloustein Papers, athletics folder.

19 State Senator John A. Lynch, *New York Times*, January 10, 1998, B5.

20 *Star-Ledger*, May 16, 2013, 1.

21 *New York Times*, January 10, 1998, B5.

22 *Record*, April 15, 1998, s1.

Epilogue

1 *Star-Ledger*, September 4, 2012, 1.

2 *Emergency Preparedness Task Force Report, Hurricane Sandy 2012* (March 2013), i, at http://emergencymanagement.rutgers.edu/OEM_files/TF_Report.pdf.

3 Ibid.

4 *In a 250-Year History, A Singular Moment in Time . . . Our Moment: A Strategic Plan for the New Rutgers* (February 2014), 17, at http://rci.rutgers.edu/~presiden/strategicplan/UniversityStrategicPlan.pdf.

5 Ibid., 11.

INDEX

ABOUT THE AUTHORS

Paul G. E. Clemens teaches history at Rutgers University in New Brunswick. He received his Ph.D. at the University of Wisconsin–Madison. He has published *The Atlantic Economy and Colonial Maryland's Eastern Shore: From Tobacco to Grain* (1980) and *The Uses of Abundance: A History of New Jersey's Economy* (1993), which is on the 101 Great New Jersey Books list.

Carla Yanni is a professor of art history at Rutgers University. She is the author of *Nature's Museums: Victorian Science and the Architecture of Display* (2000) and *The Architecture of Madness: Insane Asylums in the United States* (2007).